Landscape and Subjectivity in the Work of Patrick Keiller, W.G. Sebald, and Iain Sinclair

Landscape and Subjectivity in the Work of Patrick Keiller, W.G. Sebald, and Iain Sinclair

DAVID ANDERSON

OXFORD
UNIVERSITY PRESS

OXFORD
UNIVERSITY PRESS

Great Clarendon Street, Oxford, OX2 6DP,
United Kingdom

Oxford University Press is a department of the University of Oxford.
It furthers the University's objective of excellence in research, scholarship,
and education by publishing worldwide. Oxford is a registered trade mark of
Oxford University Press in the UK and in certain other countries

© David Anderson 2020

The moral rights of the author have been asserted

First Edition published in 2020

Impression: 1

All rights reserved. No part of this publication may be reproduced, stored in
a retrieval system, or transmitted, in any form or by any means, without the
prior permission in writing of Oxford University Press, or as expressly permitted
by law, by licence or under terms agreed with the appropriate reprographics
rights organization. Enquiries concerning reproduction outside the scope of the
above should be sent to the Rights Department, Oxford University Press, at the
address above

You must not circulate this work in any other form
and you must impose this same condition on any acquirer

Published in the United States of America by Oxford University Press
198 Madison Avenue, New York, NY 10016, United States of America

British Library Cataloguing in Publication Data

Data available

Library of Congress Control Number: 2020933789

ISBN 978-0-19-884719-9

Printed and bound by
CPI Group (UK) Ltd, Croydon, CR0 4YY

Links to third party websites are provided by Oxford in good faith and
for information only. Oxford disclaims any responsibility for the materials
contained in any third party website referenced in this work.

I dedicate this book to Alice, Marie, and the city of Rotterdam.

Acknowledgements

There are many people whose assistance and support have been, in various ways, invaluable to the completion of this project. I owe a particular debt of gratitude to Matthew Beaumont; Patrick Keiller; Gregory Dart and Rod Mengham; Neil Rennie and Helen Hackett; Zoltán Biedermann and Mererid Puw Davies; Simon Hammond, Charlotte Jones, Elizabeth Mills, and Alexandra Parsons; the staff of the Deutsches Literaturarchiv Marbach, the British Artists' Film and Video Study Collection at Central St Martins, UCL Special Collections, Museum Boijmans Van Beuningen, Nederlands Fotomuseum, Het Nieuwe Instituut, and Rotterdamsch Leeskabinet; Stephen Watts; Uwe Schütte; and Owen Pratt, Jan Piasecki, Nathaniel Lee Jones, Tom Hastings, Bella Marrin, Mary Hannity, Sriwhana Spong, and Philip Ewe.

The research on which this book is based was generously supported by a Doctoral Research Grant from the UK Arts and Humanities Research Council.

Copyright Notices

World (excluding US and Canada):

Quotations from *After Nature* are reproduced from *After Nature* by W.G. Sebald, translated by Michael Hamburger, published by Penguin Books. With permission from Penguin Books Ltd. Copyright © The Estate of W.G. Sebald, 2002. Translation copyright © Michael Hamburger, 2002.

Quotations from 'Bleston: A Mancunian Cantical' are reproduced from *Across the Land and the Water* by W.G. Sebald, translated by Ian Galbraith, published by Penguin Books. With permission from Penguin Books Ltd. Copyright © The Estate of W.G. Sebald, 2011. Translation copyright © Iain Galbraith, 2011.

US:

Excerpt(s) from *After Nature* by W.G. Sebald, translated by Michael Hamburger, copyright © 2002 by W.G. Sebald. Translation copyright © 2002 by Michael Hamburger. Used by permission of Random House, an imprint and division of Penguin Random House LLC. All rights reserved.

'Bleston: A Mancunian Cantical' from *Across the Land and the Water: Selected Poems, 1964–2001* by W.G. Sebald, translated by Iain Galbraith, translation copyright © 2011 by Iain Galbraith. Copyright © 2008 by The Estate of W.G. Sebald. Used by permission of Random House, an imprint and division of Penguin Random House LLC. All rights reserved.

Canada:

'Dark Night Sallies Forth, II', 'Dark Night Sallies Forth, I', 'Dark Night Sallies Forth, IV', '... As the Snow on the Alps, VI', '... As the Snow on the Alps, VIII', and 'And If I Remained by the Outermost Sea, XIII' from *After Nature* by W.G. Sebald and translated by Michael Hamburger, copyright © 2002 W.G. Sebald. Translation copyright © 2002 Michael Hamburger. Reprinted by permission of Vintage Canada, a division of Penguin Random House Canada Limited. All rights reserved. Any third party use of this material, outside of this publication, is prohibited. Interested parties must apply directly to Penguin Random House Canada Limited for permission.

Excerpts from AFTER NATURE and ACROSS THE LAND AND THE WATER by W. G. Sebald. 'After Nature' by W.G. Sebald, Copyright © 2002 W. G. Sebald; "Across the Land and Water" by W. G. Sebald. Copyright © 2008 by the Estate of W. G. Sebald., used by permission of The Wylie Agency LLC.

Contents

List of Figures   xv

    Introduction: Landscape and Subjectivity—Imagining England at the End of the Twentieth Century   1

1. The Camera-I: Patrick Keiller's Early Short Films and Essays   19
       Surrealism, the Situationists, and the Creative 'Acquisition' of Space   20
       The Royal College of Art and the London Film-Makers' Co-operative   26
       'Tape-Slide Assemblies' and 'Subjective Camera'   30
       A Bridge between Imagination and Reality: *Stonebridge Park*   33
       'Unemployed Reverie': *Norwood*   40
       The 'Subjective Townscape' and Spatial Critique   45

2. A Vagrant Sensibility: Patrick Keiller's *Robinson* Films   50
       'A Fictional Journal about the Year 1992': *London*   51
       The 'Problem' of Cities   53
       The Enigma of Robinson   56
       'Shipwreck and Protestant Isolation'   59
       The Redevelopment of Docklands   64
       An Outmoded City: 'Reflective Nostalgia'   67
       A Dissatisfying Success Story: *Robinson in Space*   70
       'Space' and Spatial Theory   71
       Deregulation and the 'Derangement of the Senses'   74
       Appearance and Reality: 'Material Flows'   77
       Heritage and Stately Homes   81
       The Transformation of Space and the Fragments of an Imagined Future   85
       The *Ur-Past* as the Image of Hope   89
       Domesticity and Decay in *Robinson in Ruins*   91
       The 'Problem of Nature'   94
       'Dwelling' and Heidegger's 'Simple Oneness'   99
       'Picturesque Views', Estrangement, and Expropriation   103

3. W.G. Sebald's Early Writing: 'A European at the End of European Civilization'   109
       Genre, Form, and Motion: Sebald's Transgressive Essayism   114
       'An Elementary Poem': *After Nature*   116
       Sebald's 'Original Journey' from Germany to England   118
       'A Steady Production of Dust': Memory and Place in 'Max Ferber'   124
       'Bleston' and Michel Butor's *Passing Time*   128
       Abyss to Abyss: Writing and 'Translation' after Auschwitz   132

xii CONTENTS

4. An English Pilgrim: Sebald's *The Rings of Saturn* and *Austerlitz*   137
   A 'Prose Book of an Indeterminate Sort': *The Rings of Saturn*   137
   The Structure of Space: Threads, Mazes, and Elective Affinities   139
   Literacy, Topography, and Destruction   143
   The Religion of a Doctor: Thomas Browne   144
   East Anglia, Rambling Tours, and the Idea of Englishness   147
   Social Documentaries: *Akenfield* and Lowestoft   153
   Illumination, Enlightenment, and Combustion   157
   The Contrasting Perspectives of Pedestrianism   161
   The Fifth Emigrant: *Austerlitz*   165
   The Uncanny Experiences of Belgium: Antwerp, Brussels, and Breendonk   166
   Sites of Memory and Myth: England and Wales   170
   'I am a Kind': Liverpool Street Station and East London   175
   Austerlitz's 'Research' in Paris   181
   Theresienstadt and Marienbad: the Dissimulation of Memory and Identity   184

5. Iain Sinclair's Early Writing: The Arcane Scholarship of Place   191
   'The Spiral We Are Pacing Out': Low Experience and Occult Speculation   192
   Semiological Enthusiasm in *Prehistoric London* and *Lud Heat*   197
   Suicide Bridge, Buried History, and the Mythology of Jack the Ripper in *White Chappell, Scarlet Tracings*   204
   Downriver and Sinclair's Representation of the Thames Estuary   214
   Exclusivity, Negativity, and the Narrator's Fantasy of Self-Effacement   219

6. Crosses, Circles, and Madness: Iain Sinclair's *Lights Out for the Territory*, *London Orbital*, and *Edge of the Orison*   225
   Walking as Chaos and Curation in Sinclair's Later Work   225
   Essayistic Alchemy: The Paranoiac Curation of London in *Lights Out for the Territory*   228
   'Spraying', the Appropriation of Urban Space, and the City as a Frontier   232
   The London Psychogeographical Association   237
   The Contentious Spaces of Image-Making   239
   The Unofficial Countryside and *London Orbital*: Absence, Fecundity, and Madness   243
   The Millennium Dome as a Sublime Object   247
   Spaces of Consumption and Crime: Bluewater and Carfax   250
   The Eleanor Crosses and Freud's 'Unpractical Londoners'   254
   The 'Idea of Landscape' and John Clare's Journey Out of Essex in *Edge of the Orison*   258
   Sinclair's Elective Affinities: A Landscape of Duplicates   262

The Torpid Landscape of the Fens: Walt Disney and Walter Benjamin	265
Opening and Closing the Loop: Sinclair's Later Work	268
Conclusion	273
List of Works Cited	277
Index	287

List of Figures

Introduction

0.1 The territory covered by Keiller, Sebald, and Sinclair.   16

Chapter 1

1.1 Coal Hopper, Nine Elms Lane, London, 1979, photograph, Patrick Keiller. Courtesy of Patrick Keiller.   24

1.2 Footbridge above junction of Harrow Road and North Circular Road, London, 1981, frame from *Stonebridge Park* (1981), Patrick Keiller. Courtesy of Patrick Keiller.   35

1.3 Footbridge above railway near Lyon Park Avenue, London, 1981, frame from *Stonebridge Park* (1981), Patrick Keiller. Courtesy of Patrick Keiller.   38

1.4 Bloom Grove, West Norwood, London, 1982, frame from *Norwood* (1983), Patrick Keiller. Courtesy of Patrick Keiller.   42

1.5 Peabody Hill, London SE21, view through matte box, 1982, frame from *Norwood* (1983), Patrick Keiller. Courtesy of Patrick Keiller.   43

Chapter 2

2.1 People 'sleeping out' in Lincoln's Inn Fields, frame from *London* (1994), Patrick Keiller. Courtesy of BFI National Archive and Patrick Keiller.   54

2.2 The 'London Stone', Cannon Street, frame from *London* (1994), Patrick Keiller. Courtesy of BFI National Archive and Patrick Keiller.   59

2.3 The view of the Thames from Monet's hotel room, frame from *London* (1994), Patrick Keiller; the same scene as depicted in Monet's 'Charing Cross Bridge' (1903), one of a large series. Courtesy of BFI National Archive, Patrick Keiller, and the Saint Louis Art Museum.   62

2.4 1 Canada Square emerging from a shrubbery, frame from *London* (1994), Patrick Keiller. Courtesy of BFI National Archive and Patrick Keiller.   66

2.5 Brunel's bridge over the Thames at Maidenhead, frame from *Robinson in Space* (1997), Patrick Keiller; the same scene as depicted by Turner in *Rain, Steam and Speed—The Great Western Railway* (1844). Courtesy of BFI National Archive, Patrick Keiller and the National Gallery Picture Library.   78

xvi LIST OF FIGURES

2.6   The 'spectacular dereliction' of the Liverpool docks, frame from *Robinson in Space* (1997), Patrick Keiller. Courtesy of BFI National Archive and Patrick Keiller. 82

2.7   The NSA's 'listening station' at Menwith Hill, frame from *Robinson in Space* (1997), Patrick Keiller. Courtesy of BFI National Archive and Patrick Keiller. 87

2.8   T.H. Mawson's 'dream' of Blackpool, in *The Life and Work of an English Landscape Architect* (1927). Courtesy of British Library. 88

2.9   Rock art, Northumberland, frame from *Robinson in Space* (1997), Patrick Keiller. Courtesy of BFI National Archive and Patrick Keiller. 90

2.10 Details of road sign, Oxford, 2008, frame from *Robinson in Ruins* (2010), Patrick Keiller. Courtesy of Patrick Keiller. 98

2.11 USAF fire hydrant, Greenham Common, 2008, frame from *Robinson in Ruins* (2010), Patrick Keiller. Courtesy of Patrick Keiller. 105

2.12 Satellite earth station, Enslow, Oxfordshire, 2008, frame from *Robinson in Ruins* (2010), Patrick Keiller. Courtesy of Patrick Keiller. 106

Chapter 3

3.1   The apparition of Sebald's face in Jeremy Millar's 'A Firework for W.G. Sebald' (2005), frames from *Patience: After Sebald* (2012), Grant Gee. Courtesy of Grant Gee. 111

Chapter 4

4.1   Photograph of All Saints Church, Dunwich, c.1880 by H.H. Lanman, reproduced in Jean and Stuart Bacon's *Dunwich Suffolk* (1988). Courtesy of Stuart Bacon. 149

Chapter 5

5.1   Photograph of Sinclair with his lawnmower, standing in front of Hawksmoor's church of St George-in-the-East in *Lud Heat* (1975). Courtesy of Iain Sinclair. 193

5.2   Map of 'Albion Village' printed on the inside covers of *Back Garden Poems* (1970), drawn by Renchi Bicknell. Courtesy of Iain Sinclair and UCL Special Collections. 195

5.3   'Plan of the London Mounds' in Elizabeth Oke Gordon's *Prehistoric London: Its Mounds and Circles* (1914). Courtesy of British Library. 199

5.4   'Plan of the Inter-relation of Mounds' as depicted in Gordon's *Prehistoric London: Its Mounds and Circles*. Courtesy of British Library. 200

LIST OF FIGURES xvii

5.5 'Map of the 8 Great Churches, the Lines of Influence, the Invisible Rods of Force Active in this City', drawn by Brian Catling and included with Iain Sinclair's *Lud Heat* (1975). Courtesy of Iain Sinclair. 201

5.6 William Gull looking up at Tower 42 (formerly known as the NatWest Tower) in Alan Moore and Eddie Campbell's *From Hell* (1989–98). Copyright Alan Moore and Eddie Campbell. *From Hell* is published by Knockabout. 213

Chapter 6

6.1 The route of the 'V' in *Lights Out for the Territory* (1997), as drawn by Marc Atkins. Courtesy of Marc Atkins. 229

6.2 Sinclair 'doubled' in the reflective glass of Jeffrey Archer's penthouse in *Liquid City* (1999), by Marc Atkins. Courtesy of Marc Atkins. 241

6.3 A motorist gestures at Sinclair and Petit in the film of *London Orbital* (2002). Courtesy of Iain Sinclair. *London Orbital* directed by Chris Petit and Iain Sinclair, produced by Illuminations. 246

6.4 CCTV footage in the film of *London Orbital* (2002). Courtesy of Iain Sinclair. *London Orbital* directed by Chris Petit and Iain Sinclair, produced by Illuminations. 253

Introduction

Landscape and Subjectivity—Imagining England at the End of the Twentieth Century

'The landscape garden', Rebecca Solnit observed in her 2001 cultural history of walking, *Wanderlust*, 'is one of the great English contributions to Western culture.'[1] A brief detour into the history of this contribution would be an apt starting point for the following study, which makes no such claim for itself but does aim to suggest that the work of two writers and one film-maker, by thinking about landscape and subjectivity in original and critical ways, marked a moment of special cultural interest at the end of the twentieth century.

This detour begins with Christopher Hussey's seminal 1927 study of the 'picturesque', in which the long-time architectural editor at *Country Life* magazine discovered the English landscape garden to be the site of an unexpectedly *modern* clash of 'nature' and artifice. Hussey's interest in the history of picturesque landscape began, in fact, precisely with an experience of alienation. Gazing out upon the beautiful scenery visible from his grandfather's window, which he and other family members had spent many happy hours blithely sketching and painting, Hussey suddenly realised that what he saw was not, as he had formerly assumed, the result of chance or 'happy coincidence', but rather 'must have been planned on picturesque principles'. Far from being 'nature' in the raw, this was a site that his grandfather had 'evolved' into existence based on the teachings of Uvedale Price, a volume of whose work Hussey had chanced to discover 'on the mellow shelves beside me'.[2] In this moment of recognition, what Hussey had originally thought to be a natural scene turned out to be a stylized, artificial one; the act of painting or drawing it was not, in the end, an organic response to nature's bounty but rather part of a strange and even unnerving feedback-loop of creation and perception. Looking at it through the window was like standing at a touristic 'photo point' facing a confected backdrop.

Hussey's critique of the picturesque—which he himself modestly described as 'a pioneering venture in the field of visual romanticism'—emphasized the twofold sense in which a taste for landscape emerged in the late eighteenth century through

---

[1] Rebecca Solnit, *Wanderlust: A History of Walking* (London: Verso, 2001), p.89.
[2] Christopher Hussey, *The Picturesque: Studies in a Point of View* (London: Cass, 1967), pp.3–4.

Landscape and Subjectivity in the Work of Patrick Keiller, W.G. Sebald, and Iain Sinclair. David Anderson,
Oxford University Press (2020). © David Anderson.
DOI: 10.1093/oso/9780198847199.001.0001

the cultivation of both space and sensibility. On the one hand, humanity's dominance of nature changed the 'natural world' from something mysterious and threatening into an object of aesthetic contemplation and consumption. On the other, it became the focus of the escapist urges that were fuelled by a sense of the 'restrictions and systems' of cities and the institutions of state.[3] On reflection it might seem that, if this second part of Hussey's analysis were correct, the imposition of 'picturesque' restrictions and systems of proportion and composition onto nature would have been counter-intuitive. In fact, it was part of a confidence trick: as 'nature' became a stylized version of itself, the detached, urbanized observer—like Hussey peering from his window—increasingly became its dupe.

In Hussey's experience we find, in kernel form, issues that preoccupied writing about space, place, and subjectivity from the late eighteenth century on. The formulae set out in works like William Gilpin's *Observations on the River Wye* (1782) and Price's own *Essay on the Picturesque* (1794) both provoked and problematized the relationship that Romantic artists and thinkers had with their environment. Two decades after Gilpin's *Observations*, Wordsworth was denouncing the 'comparison of scene with scene' and calling for a more vital link or 'ennobling interchange' between 'the object seen, and the eye that sees' in *The Prelude* (1805).[4] Yet the Romantic longing for both nature and 'natural man', as depicted in the work of Jean-Jacques Rousseau, for instance, was issued in the same breath as the desire to lend 'the familiar a mysterious appearance', as Novalis put it.[5] By transferring onto (and into) nature the 'contradictoriness, dissonance and inner conflict of the Romantic mind', Romantic artists arguably contributed to its construction as a mysterious and impenetrable ideal.[6]

Perhaps it is no surprise that the evolution of landscape art, concomitant with the unfurling Industrial Revolution, produced an *idea* of nature that was not, itself, inherently 'natural'—idealizing and 'enchanting' nature just as the '*disenchantment of the world*', as Max Weber later put it, was setting in. As Gilpin himself observed of a particular scene at Goodrich Castle in Herefordshire, attesting in passing to the widening gulf between actual and idealized nature: 'this view, which is one of the grandest on the river, I should not scruple to call *correctly picturesque*, which is seldom the character of a purely natural scene.'[7] The demands of an emerging aesthetic sensibility are clearly detectable here. In fact, the subtitle of Hussey's work, 'Studies in a Point of View', neatly characterizes the

---

[3] Ibid., pp.5–6.
[4] William Wordsworth, *The Prelude* (1805), in *The Prelude: 1799, 1805, 1850*, eds. Jonathan Wordsworth, M.H. Abrams, and Stephen Gill (New York: Norton, 1979), XII.376–9.
[5] Novalis, cited in Herbert Uerlings (ed.), *Theorie der Romantik* (Stuttgart: Reclam, 2013), p.14 (my trans.).
[6] Hans Georg Schenk, *The Mind of the European Romantics* (Oxford: Oxford University Press, 1979), p.xxii.
[7] William Gilpin, *Observations on the River Wye and Several Parts of South Wales* (London: R. Blamire, 1792), p.31.

way that any study of 'landscape' has to maintain a bifocal perspective on both the scenery itself and the privileged position of the individual seer. After all, as the critic John Barrell pointed out in his 1972 study *The Idea of Landscape and the Sense of Place 1730–1840: An Approach to the Poetry of John Clare*, the English word 'landscape' is problematic in the sense that it refers not so much to space or 'nature' in itself as to the depiction of it from a particular perspective. As Barrell points out, English has no clear way to refer to a tract of land in an abstract sense without implying its being *seen*. Landscape, properly speaking, requires the presence of an observer in order to come into being: an observer who takes up a position as both the point at which the scene resolves and, ultimately, as a figure removed from it, at liberty to gaze disinterestedly on the spectacle.[8]

The cultural ferment surrounding the ideas of 'landscape' and 'nature' at the turn of the eighteenth century bears an intriguing similarity to recent thinking about 'space and place' and the set of ideas referred to collectively as the 'spatial turn', which have had the effect of complicating perceptions of landscape, space, and environment. Thinkers such as Henri Lefebvre, Edward Soja, Michel Foucault, and David Harvey, emerging from Geography and Philosophy departments, have all made significant contributions to this inter- or pan-disciplinary movement, as have literary critics such as John Barrell and Raymond Williams. Facing up to the twentieth century's experience of globalization and the apparently seamless flow of people, information, and commodities around the world, this shift has seen a reassertion of the significance of space in the complexity of actual lived experience. In fact, as Barney Warf and Santa Arias have stylishly observed in their account of how the 'spatial turn' has transformed human geography from 'a net importer of ideas from other fields into an exporter', 'far from annihilating the importance of space, globalisation has increased it'.[9]

The French anthropologist Marc Augé has produced some of the most stimulating work of this context. His short 1995 study *Non-Places: An Introduction to Supermodernity* examined global capitalism's perceived destruction of 'anthropological place' by anaesthetic, banal, and homogenized 'space'. *Non-Places* outlined a contemporary tendency towards the 'high-up' viewpoint (suggested by his coinage '*sur*-modernité'): 'Seen on the individual scale and from the inner city,' Augé wrote,

> the global world is a world of discontinuities and interdict. By contrast, the dominant aesthetic is that of the cinematic long shot, which tends to make us forget the effects of this rupture.[10]

---

[8] John Barrell, *The Idea of Landscape and the Sense of Place, 1730–1840: An Approach to the Poetry of John Clare* (Cambridge: Cambridge University Press, 1980).
[9] Barney Warf and Santa Arias (eds.), *The Spatial Turn: Interdisciplinary Perspectives* (London: Routledge, 2009), p.5; p.1.
[10] Marc Augé, *Non-Places: An Introduction to Supermodernity*, trans. John Howe (London: Verso, 1995), p.xiii.

Elaborating on this idea, Augé diagnosed the traveller's space as the archetypal 'non-place': 'travel' he continued, 'constructs a fictional relationship between the gaze and the landscape.'[11] The emphasis on motion is significant, since this world, or this perception of it, has much in common with what Manuel Castells referred to in his seminal study *The Rise of The Network Society* (1996) as the preponderant 'space of flows'.[12] Existing within this 'traveller's space' launches the experiencing subject into the role of the landscape-connoisseur, soothed by the banal if reliable perspective of the 'cinematic long shot'. Map and territory seem to elide here in a manner that recalls Jorge Luis Borges's 1946 story 'On Exactitude in Science', which describes the production of a useless 1:1 scale map. In a new and highly contemporary way, reality and representation threaten to become as blurred as they were for Hussey at his grandfather's window.

It is Augé's insistence on the 'discontinuities and interdict' that continue to be found on a more local scale that makes his work so compelling. Anatomizing the various dispiriting ways in which the freedoms afforded by modern technologies of transport and communication can be illusory impressions—as artificial as that in which the connoisseur of the 'picturesque' indulged two centuries before—his work nevertheless suggests the lingering, tantalizing presence of some glittering, authentic fragment of 'place' that might yet be discoverable under the creeping corporate monoculture of 'space'. In this respect, his work bears similarities with the more invigorating approach of the geographer Doreen Massey, whose 2005 monograph *For Space* insisted that in fact 'space' itself should be considered not as a smooth whole so much as something that is always 'under construction': our world, Massey maintained, is not 'a coherent, closed system [...] in which everywhere is already linked with everything else'.[13] Disrupting straightforward historical narratives of 'progress', Massey advocated a perception of space as relational, multiple, and provisional, full of 'loose ends and missing links' and not merely an empty 'container' in which history unfolds.[14] Her analysis reminds us that, even if modern technologies have seemed to collapse distance, abolishing space in a way that complements the 'end of history' declared by Francis Fukuyama in 1992, then it is not the case that everything and everybody participates equally in the free-flowing 'network society'.[15] Indeed, like the capitalist modernity that produced it, globalization's uneven spread means that points of friction and stasis are arguably still the rule rather than exception and that the diffusion of centres into networks has had the effect not so much of abolishing peripheries as simply of relocating them out of view.

---

[11] Ibid., pp.69–70.
[12] See Manuel Castells, *The Rise of the Network Society* (Oxford: Wiley-Blackwell, 2010).
[13] Doreen Massey, *For Space* (London: Sage, 2005), pp.11–2.   [14] Ibid.
[15] See Francis Fukuyama, *The End of History and the Last Man* (London: Penguin, 1992).

This book examines three figures whose work, produced at the end of the twentieth century and in the early years of the twenty-first, is pre-eminently a product of this context. Patrick Keiller's *London* (1994), W.G. Sebald's *The Rings of Saturn* (De. 1995, Eng. 1998), and Iain Sinclair's *Lights Out For The Territory* (1997), it argues, are some of the most significant contributions to writing and thinking about space and place in England to have emerged from this fraught period. By working both within and against the experience of the 'non-place' and 'the space of flows', such contributions take the form of 'travel' documents that interrogate and agitate the perspective of Augé's 'cinematic long shot' by means of foregrounding immediate, subjective experience of space and place and staging this in relation to an increasingly globalized imagination. Occupying the space of tension *between* interdict and flow—the territory, that is, of lived experience—they offer a distinctive vision of landscape and culture for the end of a century and a millennium.

Whether or not the work of Keiller, Sebald, and Sinclair can be considered to offer a consistent, or even coherent, critical theory of contemporary space and place is one question that will remain a guiding principle in what follows. What can be noted to begin with is the relation their work bears, whether consciously or not, to two broad lineages. On the one hand, there is the domestic tradition of the 'English journey', within which works like Daniel Defoe's *Tour Through The Whole Island of Great Britain* (1724), William Cobbett's *Rural Rides* (1830), J.B. Priestley's *English Journey* (1934), George Orwell's *Road to Wigan Pier* (1937), and Beryl Bainbridge's own *English Journey* (1984) might all be included, complemented by a particular strand of English naturalism that includes topographical studies such as W.G. Hoskins's *The Making of the English Landscape* (1955) and Richard Mabey's *The Unofficial Countryside* (1973). On the other, there is a continental tradition clustered around the ideas produced by Surrealist and Situationist artists and theorists in twentieth-century France. Significantly, this includes the practice of 'psychogeography' and the 'dérive' (commonly translated as 'drift'), theorized in 1955 by the thinker and agitator Guy Debord as 'playfully constructive behaviour and awareness of psychological effects' and 'the study of the precise laws and specific effects of the geographical environment, consciously organised or not, on the emotions and behaviour of individuals'.[16] In this latter tradition, the notion that subjective exploration of landscape can, or indeed should, function as social and political critique is axiomatic. The analysis in this book places greater focus on the second, continental tradition while at the same time suggesting that, by their association with it, Keiller, Sebald, and Sinclair all occupy a significant place within the first, domestic one. It further suggests that, if such a thing as 'English psychogeography' existed as a coherent *topos* in the late

---

[16] Guy Debord, 'Theory of the Dérive' (1958), trans. Ken Knabb (http://www.bopsecrets.org/SI/2.derive.htm).

twentieth century, as writers like Merlin Coverley have claimed or implied, then it is within this creative nexus that it has been produced, with these three figures as its most important actors.

One apt way of considering the commonality between the work of Keiller, Sebald, and Sinclair is by means of the idea of the 'affective topography', a coinage of the photography theorist Ian Walker in his 2002 study of Parisian Surrealism, *City Gorged With Dreams*. This term is useful not only because of the way it implies a strong emotive connection with environments, where a *feeling for* places pushes aside the anaesthesia of the 'non-place', but also because of its suggestion of a certain 'affection' for space and place. In fact, it is precisely in this 'loving' aspect that the trajectories of the English and continental traditions can be seen to meet: if the Surrealists and Situationists proposed a romancing of space—with areas of Paris even imagined as mapping onto the human (female) anatomy—then figures like Keiller, Sebald, and Sinclair are certainly *amants* after the manner of the medieval *Romance of the Rose*, with its thinly allegorized landscape. But if Surrealism posited an amatory relationship between self and environment, as in texts like Louis Aragon's *Paris Peasant* (1926) and André Breton's *Nadja* (1928), then this also finds a parallel in W.G. Hoskins's reference to the 'patient and minute topographical research—of the sort that is wrongly despised by most historians' and its suggestion of affectionate *amateur* enquiry.[17] In Keiller, Sebald, and Sinclair's work, it is this meeting of *amant* and *amateur* that is often highly distinctive: emotive responses to space and place are routinely couched in a spirit of non-professional activity, a garden-shed atmosphere that blurs work with leisure and pays little heed to formal boundaries.

Other family resemblances between Keiller, Sebald, and Sinclair's work are manifold and frequently play to this *amateur* sensibility. They centre principally on the way that each cultivates a highly stylized form of reportage, enmeshing 'objective documentary' with fictional tropes in the ordering and depiction of space. The result is a form that might be termed 'documentary fiction' or 'essayism': investigations of space and place and the subjectivity of the self that passes through it. The act of foregrounding a narrator figure who is either the author himself or a variously stylized version, and who moves principally on foot, partly facilitates this process, permitting a certain parity between the formal and disciplinary vagrancy of the artist and the spatial vagrancy of the errant explorer. The mixture of visual and verbal material is another manifestation of this transgressiveness, anticipating what has more been recently described as a 'new nature writing' that is 'an experiment in forms: the field report, the essay, the memoir, the travelogue'.[18] Essayism is also legible in terms of what, in an unpublished PhD thesis, Christopher

---

[17] W.G. Hoskins, *The Making of the English Landscape* (Toller Fratrum: Little Toller, 2013) p.32.
[18] Jason Cowley, 'The New Nature Writing', *Granta* No.102 (Summer 2008), p.10.

Gregory-Guilder has termed 'autobiogeography': 'works of life-writing in which self and other are mediated and put into productive dialogue through the representation of space and its traversal' resulting in an 'entwining of self, other and place into inextricable patterns'.[19]

If there is a kind of 'essayism' here, then it is important to note its focus on the idea of exploratory trials or attempts, and open-ended, formally transgressive work—entirely reversing the terms of, say, Rebecca Solnit's description of the essay form as 'a kind of literary birdcage capable of containing only small chirping subjects, as distinct from the lion's den of the novel and the open range of the poem'.[20] The form and style adopted by Keiller, Sebald, and Sinclair have more in common with Brian Dillon's recent manifesto for 'essayism' as 'a form that would instruct, seduce and mystify in equal measure'; it is closer to the 'errare' or 'straying' theorized by Giuliana Bruno in her 2002 study *Atlas of Emotion*: a methodology (conceived within the field of film studies) organized around 'tours and detours, turns and re-turns, opening up on different vistas of the production of space', where the act of wandering off course generates accidental or unexpected connections between themes and ideas.[21]

As part of this 'errancy', an *amateur* quality reasserts itself: the French 'bricoleur' is re-imagined as the English 'tinkerer' or hobbyist, 'pottering about', as Sebald has it, engaging in the 'patient and minute' study advocated by Hoskins.[22] And if there is both an anorakish and a gentlemanly aspect to this amateurishness, then it is apt that one motif referred to by all three figures, in their imagining of landscape and townscape as vast compendia of ideas and narratives, is that of the invented or actual cabinet of curiosities: respectively those of John Evelyn (in *London*), Thomas Browne (in *The Rings of Saturn*), and Elias Ashmole (in *Lights Out For The Territory*). Paralleling the way in which 'English Journeys' have often been undertaken by figures better known for their work in fields other than travel writing, these models also suggest a certain degree of self-consciousness to Keiller, Sebald, and Sinclair's disorderly variation on the 'museum art' that Foucault saw

---

[19] Christopher Gregory-Guilder, *Autobiogeography and the Art of Peripatetic Memorialization in Works by W.G. Sebald, Patrick Modiano, Iain Sinclair, Jonathan Raban and William Least Heat-Moon* (unpublished PhD thesis) (University of Sussex, 2005).

[20] Solnit, *Wanderlust*, p.124.

[21] Brian Dillon, *Essayism* (London: Fitzcarraldo Editions, 2017), p.15; Giuliana Bruno, *Atlas of Emotion: Journeys in Art, Architecture and Film* (New York: Verso, 2002), p.15.

[22] For this comparison I am indebted to an interview between film-maker Chris Marker and critic Chris Darke in *Chris Marker: A Grin Without A Cat*, ed. Darke and Hadba Rashid (London: Whitechapel Gallery, 2014): 'He was a "bricoleur", he explained. Nothing more. The technology he'd assembled simply enabled him to pursue this humble activity in the most up-to-date manner possible. It was the means that were sophisticated, not the method. I suggested that in French bricolage sounded like an elevated calling, bringing to mind Roland Barthes and Claude Lévi-Strauss, whereas "tinkering", its English equivalent, made me think of a bloke in a garden shed. Marker observed drily that he didn't have a garden.'

in modernism.²³ The interest in the cabinet of curiosities, as a forerunner to the modern museum, also places Keiller, Sebald, and Sinclair in step with the way that the 'network society' and correspondent 'information economy' produced an emergent awareness of the way that the organization of data—*curation* of one kind or another—has become an increasingly prominent feature of the lives not only of artists but also of many 'ordinary people'.

If cabinets of curiosities seem like an inefficient way to store objects and information, and if the interest in them might be read as responsive to an emergent anxiety about the increasingly tidy organization of all things, then the way that Keiller, Sebald, and Sinclair depict movement through this 'archival' landscape—principally on foot—should also be read as a deliberate attempt to disrupt the imperatives of capitalist modernity's 'rhetoric of efficiency', as Solnit put it in *Wanderlust*, rubbing up against the idea that 'the vast array of pleasures which fall into the category of doing nothing in particular, of woolgathering, cloud-gazing, wandering, window-shopping, are nothing but voids to be filled by something more definite, more productive, or faster paced'.²⁴ Indeed, the idea of pedestrianism as a mode that is self-consciously slow and 'out of step' might be traced to Raymond Williams's assertion that 'culture' emerged in the Romantic period as 'the normal antithesis of the market'²⁵—or, as E.P. Thompson wrote in his 1967 essay 'Time, Work-Discipline, and Industrial Capitalism', the connected phenomenon that

> a recurrent form of revolt within Western industrial capitalism, whether bohemian or beatnik, has often taken the form of flouting the urgency of respectable time-keeping.²⁶

In the attentiveness and sensitivity to environments that it fosters, Keiller, Sebald, and Sinclair's pedestrianism implicitly acts as an immanent critique of the 'space of flows' and the 'cinematic long shot': the act of travelling on foot strikes back against an incipient sense of the 'erasure of place by "space"', as the critic Phil Baker has put it.²⁷ Yet it is notable too that their pedestrianism and 'straying' is often of a kind that risks the subject's disorientation; and the exploration of a sometimes confusing and deceptive landscape, marred by an 'atmosphere of conspiracy' produced by the sometimes opaque activity of politics and finance at the end of twentieth century, opens up a vertiginous fault line within the 'space

---

²³ Michel Foucault, 'Fantasia of the Library', in Donald Bouchard (ed.) and Bouchard and Sherry Simon (trans.), *Language, Counter-Memory, Practice: Selected Essays and Interviews*, (Ithaca, NY: Cornell University Press, 1977), p.92.
²⁴ Solnit, *Wanderlust*, p.10.
²⁵ Raymond Williams, *Culture and Society 1780-1950* (New York: Columbia University Press, 1959), p.39.
²⁶ E.P. Thompson, 'Time, Work-Discipline and Industrial Capitalism', *Past and Present* No.38 (December 1967), p.95.
²⁷ Phil Baker, 'Psychogeography and the End of London', in Joe Kerr and Andrew Gibson (eds.) *London From Punk to Blair* (London: Reaktion, 2012), p.290.

of flows' just as it anticipates the phenomenon of that landscape's 'derealization'. If the 'space of flows' produces a sense of both presence and detachment—a melancholy experience that Heidegger termed 'a loss of rapport with things'— then it can also seem that even an unmediated encounter with the spaces of late twentieth-century England might not redeem it.[28]

The poets Paul Farley and Michael Symmons Roberts pleasingly captured this experience in their 2011 exploration of peripheral landscapes, *Edgelands*. The French philosopher Jean Baudrillard, they observed,

> defined hyperreality as 'the simulation of something which never really existed'. Although he probably wrote that line in between drags on a Gauloise in the corner of a café on La Rive Gauche, the penny might have dropped even sooner had he sipped an espresso bought from a barrow pushed by a man in authentic street-vendor costume at an English outlet village.[29]

The problem suggested here is a failure of authenticity: a breakdown in the sense of connectedness between people and place and of place with itself. In this respect, Farley and Symmons Roberts's point bears an interesting to relation to the remark made by Svetlana Boym in her 2001 book *The Future of Nostalgia* that 'a modern nostalgic can be homesick and sick of home, all at once', a contention paralleling Baudrillard's own more famous claim that 'when the real is not what it used to be, nostalgia assumes its full meaning'.[30] In the works examined in this book, this kind of disorientation, often manifested in the form of a certain world-weariness or melancholia, is framed as a symptom of the 'deregulation' associated with neoliberal monetarist economics in the late twentieth century. In various ways, Keiller, Sebald, and Sinclair suggest that these shifting social-economic relations, and the uncertainties they produced, could well have initiated a trend paralleling that noted by Margot and Rudolf Wittkower in their 1963 study of art and melancholia, *Born Under Saturn*. The melancholia that the Wittkowers describe, suffered by artists in Renaissance Italy during the uncertain period between the collapse of the medieval guilds and the rise of the Florentine academies, finds its analogue in the instability produced by late twentieth-century Britain's deregulated, laissez-faire economy and the travails of its 'flexible' workforce.[31]

---

[28] Martin Heidegger, 'Building Dwelling Thinking', in *Poetry, Language, Thought* (New York: HarperCollins, 1971), p.155.
[29] Paul Farley and Michael Symmons Roberts, *Edgelands: Journeys Into England's True Wilderness* (London: Vintage, 2012), p.219.
[30] Svetlana Boym, *The Future of Nostalgia* (New York: Basic Books, 2001), p.50; Jean Baudrillard, 'Simulacra and Simulations', trans. Paul Foss, in Mark Poster (ed.), *Selected Writings* (Cambridge: Polity, 1988), p.171.
[31] Margot Wittkower and Rudolph Wittkower, *Born Under Saturn: The Character and Conduct of Artists* (New York: New York Review Books, 2007), esp. Ch.4, 'Eccentric Behaviour and Noble Manners'.

In respect of these three figures' relation to twentieth-century 'nature' writing in England, one figure who stands out in this connection is Richard Mabey, whose extensive contribution ranges from the practical and didactic (including foraging handbooks like 1972's *Food for Free*) to meditative and reflective accounts of a life attuned to the flora and fauna of rural England. Mabey's 1979 book *The Unofficial Countryside* is particularly significant in relation to this study and the themes outlined in this introduction. The text begins with a revelatory visit to an overgrown and dilapidated canal, a visit set into relief by the melancholy sensation of detachment suffered by Mabey in the anodyne office environment he describes: 'I think it was my black frame of mind', he writes, 'that made the unexpected late fruitfulness of this place strike me with such intensity.'[32]

The figure of the melancholic naturalist as it is emblematically presented here is particularly interesting, in this study, for the problems that it might be expected to produce in relation to the idea of a stable or sturdy national culture and identity. In 1969, the art historian Kenneth Clark argued that anxiety, fear, boredom, and despondency produce decline and fall; 'civilisation' needs 'confidence', and 'civilised man [...] must feel that he belongs somewhere in space and time; that he consciously looks forward and looks back. And for this he needs a minimum of stability.'[33] Yet at the end of the twentieth century, Clark's contention was aggravated by a general sense of what Enzo Traverso has called 'the eclipse of utopias', rendering history as a 'landscape of ruins', as well as a specific sense of England itself having become peripheral or marginal, attached to the image of its own imperial decline.[34]

Citing Wallace Stevens, Frank Kermode has argued that the imagination 'is always at the end of an era', but the approach to the year 2000 does seem to have rendered this experience more acute—at least in the writing and film-making examined here.[35] Keiller's London, as his narrator insists, is not an imperial city but a 'colonial' one—'there was nothing here before the Romans came'.[36] In Sebald's work, Manchester, East Anglia, and East London are loci of both environmental decay and material dilapidation—'eastness', here, freighted by the significance deriving from Sebald's remarks on the 'westward drift of civilisation' in *The Rings of Saturn*.[37] Sinclair's interest in structures like the M25 and the grotesqueries of regeneration projects and schemes like the Millennium Dome provides a parallel vision of outer London as a marginalized, even decadent chaos rather than a coherent cosmos. Such perceptions, as this study shows, are

---

[32] Richard Mabey, *The Unofficial Countryside* (Wimborne Minster: Dovecote, 2010), p.18.
[33] Kenneth Clark, *Civilisation* (London: John Murray, 2005), p.12.
[34] Enzo Traverso, *Left-Wing Melancholia* (New York: Columbia University Press, 2016), p.5; p.20.
[35] Frank Kermode, *The Sense of an Ending: Studies in the Theory of Fiction* (Oxford: Oxford University Press, 2000), p.96.
[36] Patrick Keiller (dir.), *London* (British Film Institute: 1994).
[37] W.G. Sebald, *The Rings of Saturn*, trans. Michael Hulse (London: Harvill, 1998), pp.158–9.

constantly produced and re-produced by means of a dynamic relationship between the landscape itself and the melancholic subjectivity cultivated in the work. And even if Sinclair's writing is characterized by a venom that sometimes seems at odds with the more gentle reflectiveness of Keiller and Sebald, its structure (as Chapter 6 shows) comes increasingly to replicate Freud's 1917 diagnosis of melancholia as a neurotic cycle of 'unfinished mourning'.[38]

The common claim of Keiller, Sebald, and Sinclair's work, this book suggests, is that it is only by building on instability itself that a proper 'being in the world' can be cultivated: an immanent rebuttal of arguments like Kenneth Clark's. These three figures critique, adapt, and dislodge conventionalized notions of landscape and culture, producing a distinctive set of contemporary variations on the theme of the 'English Journey'. In so doing, they take a place in the 'off-modern' tradition that Boym, in suggestively topographical terms, sees as consisting of 'sideshadows and back alleys rather than the straight road of progress' and which, she continues, 'allows us to take a detour from the deterministic narrative of twentieth-century history'.[39] Perhaps, in the process, these works suggest the possibility of having realized Robert Macfarlane's recent call for a landscape writing that would not 'kowtow to the doubtful idea of a "national" literature' but rather take the form of 'a series of local writings, which concentrated on particular places, and which worked always to individuate, never to generalise'.[40]

Though this possibility remains an uncertain one, it does seem possible to contend that the work of Keiller, Sebald, and Sinclair variously articulates a certain dialectical relationship between dwelling and displacement, one which functions as a working-through of the condition of estrangement that tends towards some kind of reorientation—however provisional—of the subject. Martin Heidegger's notion that 'only if we are capable of dwelling, then can we build' is adjusted here, so that 'dwelling' means not physically residing in one spot but *dwelling on* the odd experiences produced by the tension between the spaces of 'flows' and those of 'interdict'.[41] In his 1936 essay 'The Storyteller', Walter Benjamin referred to the proverbial saying that 'when someone goes on a trip, he has something to tell about', and in the works examined in this book, travel certainly serves this purpose; at the same time, however, 'dwelling' as 'dwelling *on*' produces precisely the kind of boredom or *ennui* that, in the same essay, Benjamin termed 'the dream bird that hatches the egg of experience'.[42] Disaffection, alienation, and disorientation become the unlikely basis for a cultural critique of renewed urgency. The

---

[38] See Sigmund Freud, *On Murder, Mourning and Melancholia*, trans. Shaun Whiteside (London: Penguin, 2005).
[39] Boym, *The Future of Nostalgia*, p.xvii.
[40] Robert Macfarlane, '4x4s Are Killing My Planet', *Guardian*, 4 June 2005 (https://www.theguardian.com/books/2005/jun/04/featuresreviews.guardianreview32).
[41] Heidegger, 'Building Dwelling Thinking', p.148.
[42] Walter Benjamin, 'The Storyteller', in Hannah Arendt (ed.), *Illuminations*, trans. Harry Zohn (New York: Schocken, 2007), p.84; p.91.

result produces ideas of England and Englishness that might be seen as increasingly significant for the new millennium's experience of grappling with various stop-start processes of disintegration and devolution and the varying scales of 'imagined community' in relation to which a sense of 'belonging' might be felt. The 'affective topography' here opens up a wide field of enquiry into what belonging can mean and how it can function.

This book proceeds with two chapters devoted to each of its subjects. In each case, the first excavates and critiques particular early works that have some strong bearing on the themes and ideas explored more thoroughly in the later work, which is directly addressed in the second. The rationale behind this is simple: although I take these artists to be among the most significant of their period, none of them is so widely known that a knowledge of their diverse contributions might be taken as given. This approach also has the pleasing effect of developing a triptych portrait of three figures who have occupied the same time, and often overlapping spaces and places, producing work rich in family resemblances, whilst only rarely coming into direct contact with each other. Beginning with Keiller—perhaps the least well known of the three—it develops its inquiry by a process of accretion and reflection.

The opening chapter, 'The Camera-I: Patrick Keiller's Early Short Films and Essays', reconstructs Keiller's early career and his shift from architecture to filmmaking, reading the use of 'subjective camera' and the creation of 'subjective townscape' in his early experimental works as crucial to the developing sensibility of his later docu-narratives. Looking chiefly at *Stonebridge Park* (1981) and *Norwood* (1983), it explores the 'atmosphere of unemployed reverie' and paranoiac, noir methods that provided a footing for his later 'Robinson' series. At the same time, it offers a view of the exciting world of political agitation and film co-operatives that existed in 1960s London.

Chapter 2, 'A Vagrant Sensibility: Patrick Keiller's *Robinson* Films', casts new light on Keiller's later work, partly by considering it in relation to the idea of 'left-wing melancholy' and Boym's discussion of 'restorative' and 'reflective' nostalgia. If, as Raymond Williams wrote, 'there is usually principle in exile, there is always only relaxation in vagrancy', then this chapter shows how the vagrant wanderings of 'Robinson' through London and England are able to both 'luxuriate' and to produce a potent critique of capital, landscape, and culture.[43] Beginning by reading the Robinson of *London* (1994) as an urbanist swayed not so much by the ebb and flow of the Baudelairean crowd as the blips and dips of the free market economy, it ends by enquiring into Keiller's own critique in *Robinson in Ruins* (2010) of Heideggerian dwelling as the process of 'entering in simple oneness into things'.

---

[43] Williams, *Culture and Society*, p.309.

Chapter 3, 'W.G. Sebald's Early Writing: "A European At The End of European Civilization"', looks at the long poem *After Nature* (1988) as part of its exploration of what Markus Zisselsberger has called Sebald's 'original journey' from southern Germany to Manchester. It discusses and critiques his depiction of the city in that poem as well as in 'Max Ferber' (the final story of 1996's *The Emigrants*) and his early poem 'Bleston: A Mancunian Cantical' (1967). Reading these works as a set of variations on Manchester as the 'end of European civilization'—a phrase taken from Susan Sontag's review of *The Emigrants*—the chapter shows how fictional and factual histories are harnessed by Sebald to produce a rich texturology of place. At the same time, tracing Sebald's creative appropriation of the damaged histories of Jewish refugees from Nazi Germany, it stages his work in the context of Theodor Adorno's famous comment on the 'barbarism' of writing poetry after Auschwitz.

If, as Salman Rushdie has written (in an essay on Günter Grass), 'the migrant is, perhaps, the central or defining figure of the twentieth century', then Chapter 4, 'An English Pilgrim: Sebald's *The Rings of Saturn* and *Austerlitz*', explores how Sebald depicts spaces scored by both his own migration to England and that of the Jewish refugees he encounters there.[44] Placing his work into dialogue with regional history texts like Ronald Blythe's *Akenfield* (1969), this chapter also examines the ways in which Sebald's Suffolk becomes an exemplary setting for his saturnine account of the 'natural history of destruction' as well as his problematic depiction of 'heritage' spaces in *The Rings of Saturn* (1995). It goes on to show how *Austerlitz* (2001) frames its depictions of England within a network of other locations including Brussels, Prague, Paris, Marienbad (Czech Republic), and North Wales, cultivating a thickened sense of space and place by way of the profound and moving friendship that it recounts between Sebald's narrator and the fictional Jacques Austerlitz.

Chapter 5, 'Iain Sinclair's Early Writing: The Arcane Scholarship of Place', spends time exploring the influence of an eccentric 1914 text by Elizabeth Gordon entitled *Prehistoric London: Its Mounds and Circles* on Sinclair's occult-inflected poetic geographies of London. Examining his creative exchanges with other writers including Peter Ackroyd and Alan Moore, it explores the coterie atmosphere of Sinclair's early work before going on to navigate his increasingly venomous and toxic vision of East London and the Thames Estuary in the period spanning 1970 to 1994, adumbrating and critiquing the parallel development of what Patrick Wright has called the 'acid negativity' of his prose.[45]

---

[44] Salman Rushdie, *Imaginary Homelands: Essays and Criticism 1981-1991* (London: Granta, 1992), p.277.
[45] Patrick Wright, 'Downriver: From the Far Side of the Thames Estuary', Literary London Society Seminar 14 April 2015.

Sinclair's creative misreading of 'psychogeography' as 'psychotic geography' is central to Chapter 6, 'Crosses, Circles, and Madness: Iain Sinclair's *Lights Out for the Territory, London Orbital*, and *Edge of the Orison*'. Here, the neuroticism of Sinclair's later documentary narratives is foregrounded, showing how the idea of walking is ever more closely associated with madness and psychological instability. Exploring Sinclair's cultivation of 'secret' histories and 'obscenery' in *Lights Out for the Territory* (1997) and *London Orbital* (2002), its examination of *Edge of the Orison* (2005) arcs back to John Barrell's study of *The Idea of Landscape*, mentioned earlier in this introduction, by showing how Sinclair's attachment to the figure of John Clare finds his work 'haunted' by nothing so much as itself, returning constantly to the same themes and territories in a perverse parody of the picturesque mode.

This account is bound to take some interest in that which seems absent from it. Perhaps most striking is the absence of women, raising the question of whether 'English psychogeography' has been an exclusive, overtly male domain, centred on a 'romancing' of space that does little to disrupt regressive gender norms or binaries. The tradition of Parisian Surrealism, for example, is certainly significant here. André Breton's vision of Paris in the 1920s specifically feminized the city, and, as George Melly pointed out (himself in full agreement with Breton), in this reading Paris's 'femininity acted as the ideal Surrealist muse, a role the movement assigned, much to the indignation of some women liberationists, to "Woman" in general'.[46] The disparagement legible in Melly's use of the term 'liberationists', as if 'liberation' were some distasteful dogma, here betrays an unpleasant tone that reappears in unexpected places across this field. In his 1974 study *Topophilia*, for example, the geographer Yi-Fu Tuan—citing Erik Erikson's essay 'Genital Modes and Spatial Modalities' (1965)—claims that 'along with tall structures boys play with the idea of *collapse*; ruins are exclusively male constructions'.[47] A trend of male bias is also legible in the tradition of writing and thinking about melancholia: in her 2000 study *The Nature of Melancholy*, Jennifer Radden observes that 'melancholy, with its loquacious male subject, leaves little room for the mute suffering of women'.[48]

If these assertions seem sweeping, then the work of Keiller, Sebald, and Sinclair nevertheless does not go far to question them; indeed, it sometimes actually seems to expressly pursue the eviction of women from its purview. Their work is frequently centred on male-male friendships: between Robinson and the Narrator in Keiller's films; Sebald and each of his 'emigrants'; or Sinclair and his fraternity of fellow travellers in *Lights Out for The Territory, London Orbital*,

---

[46] George Melly, *Paris and the Surrealists* (London: Thames and Hudson, 1991), p.63.

[47] Yi-Fu Tuan, *Topophilia: A Study of Environmental Perceptions, Attitudes and Values* (Englewood Cliffs, NJ: Prentice-Hall, 1974), p.54.

[48] Jennifer Radden (ed.), *The Nature of Melancholy: From Aristotle to Kristeva* (Oxford: Oxford University Press, 2000), p.65.

and elsewhere. In this connection, it is notable that Solnit's woolgatherer or window-shopper—the figure who is able to 'flout the urgency of respectable time-keeping', as E.P. Thompson put it—is one that telescopes the vagrant and the gentle*man*, just as the value vested in amateurishness also plays into the hands of a perceived *gentlemanly* distaste for professionalism. Overall, the suggestion is that the production of 'affective topographies' at the end of the twentieth century remained a frustratingly male prerogative.

One other striking issue with the 'English Journey' descriptor is the amount of territory that is not included; a diagrammatic illustration of the territories covered by Keiller, Sebald, and Sinclair gives a clear indication of how closely circumscribed their journeys are (see Figure 0.1). Stephen Daniels's 1993 study *Fields of Vision: Landscape Imagery and National Identity in England and the United States* suggests one elegant explanation for this phenomenon. Discussing the emergence of landscape art, Daniels remarks that, at the height of English imperialism, the craving for 'cosy home scenery' at the same time as imperialism reached 'into alien lands' meant that while 'the British public gazed at global maps centred mathematically on Britain', 'inside Great Britain lurked Little England'.[49] This 'Little England' might be regarded as having renewed ideological significance today, as a result of both the debates surrounding Brexit and the persistent spectre of British devolution. The struggle to forge a legitimate, pluralist English identity that is robbed of one of its basic tenets—that is, the suppression of other identities—is part of the active dialogue into which the works studied here can be brought.

Another explanation is the anti-urban sentiment that can be traced through much English writing about landscape and which emerged forcefully in the political ideology of Thatcherism in the 1980s. The patriotic vision of 'cosy home scenery' described by Daniels nestles somewhere within the Home Counties but emphatically not in the capital city itself, a mode of thinking that relates to a conventionalized perception of London as paradoxically *un*-English. Ronald Blythe's avowal that town-dwellers in Britain have 'always regarded urban life as just a temporary necessity' is probably symptomatic here, even if there is a certain overzealousness to his comments in *Akenfield* on 'the almost religious intensity of the regard for rural life in this country' and 'the sense of guilt that so many people feel about not living on a village pattern'.[50] The powerful surge in this sentiment in the 1980s should be connected with the Conservative ideology of 'little England' and the specific attacks on cities that I discuss most directly in Chapter 2, in relation to Patrick Keiller's *London*. If the historian Roy Porter was right when he observed in a 1992 history of the capital city that 'I doubt if anyone thinks of themselves today as *citizens* of London', then my subjects' focus on

---

[49] Stephen Daniels, *Fields of Vision: Landscape Imagery and National Identity in England and the United States* (Cambridge: Polity, 1992), p.6.
[50] Ronald Blythe, *Akenfield: Portrait of an English Village* (London: Penguin, 2005), p.15.

Keiller   Sebald   Sinclair

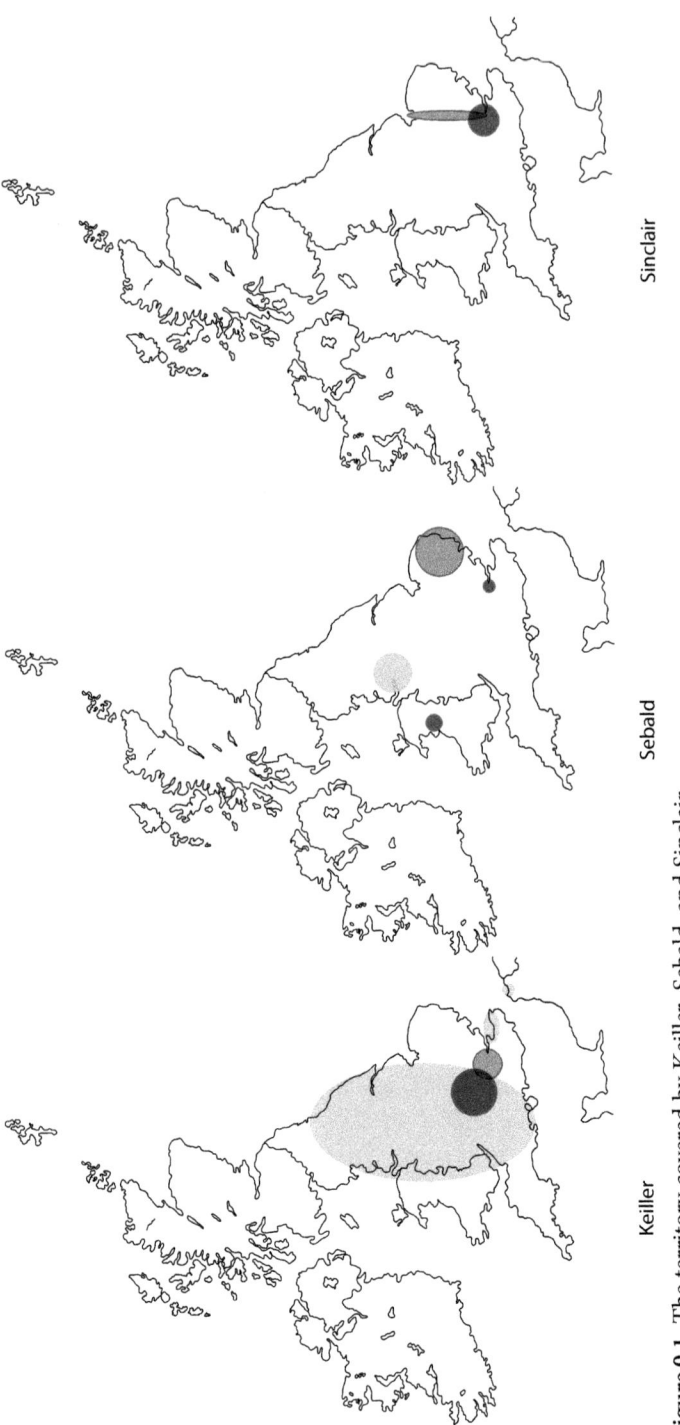

Figure 0.1 The territory covered by Keiller, Sebald, and Sinclair.

London should be read as a deliberately oppositional move.[51] In Keiller, Sebald, and Sinclair's work, London is neither the thrusting city of modernity nor a cesspit of decay but rather a layered, ruined, textured space, a space of both affection and alienation that is inscribed with profuse and productive histories.

Daniels's *Fields of Vision* is bookended by visions of the Thames. It opens by reflecting on the end of the nineteenth century and Queen Victoria's diamond jubilee, when 'the area around the west entrance of St Paul's was turned into an elaborate theatre, with grandstands, flags and illuminations' offering 'a parallel spectacle to the secular enlightenment projected by the Eiffel Tower'.[52] It concludes with a discussion of John Constable's painting *The Opening of Waterloo Bridge* (1829-31), arguing that 'the cultural power of London has impressed itself in the last decade, in various issues from high finance to heritage to homelessness'.[53] The riverine spectacle of St Paul's cathedral also acts as curious linking motif with which to characterize my own approach in this book, by way of a rather different scene: Gustave Doré's etching of 'The New Zealander' in his illustrations to Blanchard Jerrold's 1872 book *London: A Pilgrimage*. By means of a suggestive chain of connections, the 'New Zealander' of Doré's etching becomes an unlikely emblem of this study—a figure to close this introduction while opening up numerous threads for consideration later on.

The etching is significant, first of all, for the way in which it reveals the radical potential not of pomp and circumstance, or civic celebration, but rather of ruination, or of the decision to see something—in this case, London—*as* ruin. Themes of ruination and decay are recurrent in what follows. They coincide in the idea of the 'monument' as a vehicle of both historical understanding and nostalgic yearning: this is a point on which the critics Svetlana Boym and Enzo Traverso each reflect in their recent accounts of nostalgia, melancholia, and politics. Both Boym and Traverso discuss an essay written by Alois Riegl in 1903, entitled 'The Modern Cult of Monuments'; the former describes Riegl's distinction between

> 'historical value', which singles out 'one moment in the developmental continuum of the past and places it before our eyes as if it belonged to the present' [and] 'age value', which simply shows the traces of time, conferring on a monument the aura of a dead object.[54]

'Age value' here has a calming but anaesthetic quality, in common with Marc Augé's description of 'supermodernity' as a phenomenon that transforms 'the old (history) into a specific spectacle, as it does with all exoticism and all local particularity.'[55] 'Historical value', meanwhile, is disruptive and instructive,

---

[51] Roy Porter, *London: A Social History* (London: Penguin, 2000), p.3.
[52] Daniels, *Fields of Vision*, p.29; p.31. [53] Ibid., p.235.
[54] Traverso, *Left-Wing Melancholia*, pp.33-4. [55] Augé, *Non-Places*, pp.55-6; p.89.

strongly reminiscent of the approach of Walter Benjamin in the sixth of his famous 'Theses On The Philosophy of History' (1940), whereby

> [t]o articulate what is past does not mean to recognize 'how it really was' (Ranke). It means to take control of a memory, as it flashes up in a moment of danger. For historical materialism it is a question of holding fast to a picture of the past, just as if it had unexpectedly thrust itself, in a moment of danger, on the historical subject.[56]

Curiously enough, the 'Ranke' cited by Benjamin here had a hand in the creation of the 'New Zealander' figure, since it was in an 1840 review of Leopold von Ranke's *History of the Popes* that the Whig historian Thomas Macaulay first coined the term. This motion of coincidental circularity, highly appropriate to the practice of Keiller, Sebald, and Sinclair, is one reason why the 'New Zealander' forms such an apt emblem to this study. Another has more explicitly to do with the spectacle of ruination and memory, for it is precisely in its interest in the tension between Riegl's two forms of value that the work of Keiller, Sebald, and Sinclair offers its most compelling lesson in reading and experiencing space and place as a complex field where new understanding might 'thrust itself' unexpectedly into the present. If the 'curation' of space and its multiple narratives always threatens to objectify it, then these figures' cultivation of a dynamic relationship between landscape and subjectivity seeks to work in a counter-operative way. By roughening the experience of space and place and challenging the perception of history as smooth spectacle, the works discussed in what follows place dwelling and displacement into a fraught dialectical relationship. Interrogating this relationship, as this book hopes to show, might help contribute to some form of reorientation within the disorientating conditions produced by late twentieth-century modernity.

---

[56] Walter Benjamin, 'Theses on the Philosophy of History', in Hannah Arendt (ed.) *Illuminations*, p.255.

1
The Camera-I
Patrick Keiller's Early Short Films and Essays

Although he is best known for his *Robinson* series, comprising 1994's *London*, 1997's *Robinson in Space*, and 2010's *Robinson in Ruins*, Patrick Keiller's short films of the 1980s also present a richly conceived engagement with space, place, and subjectivity. These works combine images of landscape and townscape with idiosyncratic, often morbid narratives delivered in first-person voiceover that, while involving fictional personae, often incorporate highly self-reflexive allusions to the acts of travelling, observing, and film-making. In doing so they show that Keiller's later explorations of the 'transformative potential' to be found within 'images of the English landscape'—that is, ways that space and place can affect subjectivity—are built on a foundation of experiments in precisely the reverse process: the way that 'the adoption of a certain subjectivity [...] alters experience of the world, and so transforms it'.[1]

In all, Keiller made five significant short films in the 1980s—*Stonebridge Park* (1981), *Norwood* (1983), *The End* (1986), *Valtos* (1987), and *The Clouds* (1989). By revealing the nascent mechanisms of Keiller's 'subjective transformation' of space and place, these early works clarify his later use—in the *Robinson* series—of film-making as an experimental process of 'research' into the built environment. At their centre are the cultivation of a distinctively mordant narrative sensibility, the exploration of the 'camera-I' as an analogue or vehicle of consciousness, and the discovery of places, landscapes, and environments that seem to be receptive to the kinds of aesthetic speculation afforded by these techniques. In exploring these themes, this chapter looks specifically at Keiller's early photographic experiments and writings, elaborating on the aesthetic, cultural, and political contexts of his shift from architecture to film-making, before examining more closely the two films entitled *Stonebridge Park* and *Norwood*.

---

[1] Patrick Keiller (dir.), *Robinson in Ruins* (London: British Film Institute, 2011); Patrick Keiller, 'The Poetic Experience of Townscape and Landscape, and Some Ways of Depicting It', in Nina Danino and Michael Mazière (eds.), *The Undercut Reader: Critical Writings on Artists' Film and Video* (London: Wallflower, 2003), p.75.

Surrealism, the Situationists, and the Creative 'Acquisition' of Space

Graduating from the Bartlett School of Architecture in 1974, Keiller subsequently worked as both an architect and a lecturer on the subject at the North East London Polytechnic in Walthamstow. His move to image-making seems to have emerged principally from a sense of frustration at the architectural profession. 'My starting point', he wrote in his first published essay, 1982's 'The Poetic Experience of Townscape and Landscape, and Some Ways of Depicting It', 'was that of an architect, and my motivation the desire to find, already existing, the buildings that I wanted to build but for a number of reasons was unable to'.[2] He later dated this shift to 1977, when he began taking photographs of 'old industrial buildings, scaffolding structures, air raid shelters, and so on', describing how he felt them to be

> attractive as structures with striking architectural qualities that were not the result of conventional architectural activity, or, if they were, had perhaps not been seen by their designers in the way that I saw them.[3]

Keiller noted of these buildings that 'none were for sale, but even if they had been, acquisition seemed at first neither appropriate nor practical, so the collection consisted of 35mm colour slides'.[4] In this way, his 'encounters' with these structures marked the moment of his diversion from the actual construction of buildings to their subjective *reconstruction* in the imagination. His 'Poetic Experience' essay set out a rich heritage for this practice, running through Edgar Allan Poe's short stories, the '*flâneurs* and dandies' of Baudelaire and Apollinaire, the paintings of Giorgio de Chirico, the Surrealists' creative appropriation of sites in Paris in the 1920s, and the 'drifts' carried out in the same city by the Lettrists—later the Situationist International—in the 1950s and 60s. These are followed by a brief account of the depiction of space in cinema, particularly film noir.

Among all these influences, Keiller later asserted the primacy of Surrealism. In the introduction to *The View From The Train*, a collection of his writings published in 2013, he recalled a visit to the 1978 exhibition *Dada and Surrealism Reviewed*, at London's Hayward Gallery, placing particular emphasis on his reading of Roger Cardinal's essay 'Soluble City: The Surrealist Perception of Paris', which accompanied the exhibition and was reprinted in a special issue of *Architectural Design* alongside texts written by architects such as Bernard

---

[2] Ibid., p.75.
[3] Keiller, in Iain Sinclair (ed.), *London: City of Disappearances* (London: Hamish Hamilton, 2006), p.292.
[4] Ibid., p.292.

Tschumi, Rem Koolhaas, and others.[5] The exhibition, and Cardinal's essay, proved to be formative in Keiller's movement from architecture to film, seeming to grant validity to his original slide-making as a legitimate form of art practice and even 'prompting' his subsequent decision to apply to the RCA.[6]

Appearing to impart some uncanny sense of agency or even personality onto built space, Keiller's use of the term 'encounter' itself attested to the influence of a way of seeing informed heavily by Parisian Surrealism, tacitly alluding to its techniques: to Louis Aragon's animation of the Passage de l'Opéra and the Parc des Buttes Chaumont, and his meditations on the 'metaphysics of places', in his *Paris Peasant* (1926); to the encounters of André Breton and his friends with the strange objects at the Saint-Ouen flea market in *Nadja* (1928); or to Eli Lotar's photos of lined-up cows' hooves at the abattoirs of La Villette, a reproduction of which Keiller included in his 1982 essay. In each case, the inanimate is animated by a strange 'frisson' lent to it by the lens—a term Keiller borrowed from *Paris Peasant*, and which he found to be equally applicable to the sense in Eugène Atget's strangely unpeopled photos of nineteenth-century Paris streets (actually a by-product of the long exposure times necessary for his shots) that 'anything could happen'.[7]

At the same time, the term 'encounters' also suggests a subtly bathetic ironization of the artist in the guise of the explorer: putative 'discoverer' of things that were not necessarily 'lost' in the first place—at least not to anybody else. In this way it alludes to a subtle self-mockery highly characteristic of Keiller, whose narrator in *Norwood* describes the 'subjective transformation' of space as 'a talent of dubious value'.[8] A reference to Apollinaire's character the 'Baron d'Ormesan' (who appears in the 1910 story collection *L'hérésiarque et Cie*) is apt in this respect, since the Baron's 'art form', which he terms 'amphionism', is also characterized as merely the act of going for a walk. An ironic sense of the artist as a slacker or dilettante is key here, and, although Keiller doesn't elaborate on this story, his diffidence must also be partly informed by the fact that Apollinaire's 'Baron' is a fraudster: not only are his tours of Paris littered with errors, but he isn't even a real Baron, having changed his name from the plain 'Dormesan' to the noble-sounding 'd'Ormesan'.[9]

Keiller's activities also merited more serious theoretical justification. After all, his 'acquisition' of buildings not by means of deed and title but rather in the form of photographic slides echoed Susan Sontag's famous description of photography

---

[5] See Keiller, *The View From The Train* (London: Verso, 2013).
[6] Keiller, Personal Correspondence. [7] Keiller, 'Poetic Experience', p.78. [8] Ibid., p.78.
[9] See Guillaume Apollinaire, 'L'amphion faux messie', in *L'hérésiarque et Cie* (Paris: Stock, 2003), pp.199–204.

as 'the ideal arm of consciousness in its acquisitive mood', and the technique was as responsive to the idea of the *objet trouvé* and the 'ready-made' as to Joseph Addison's idea that an urban daydreamer can 'assume a kind of property in everything he sees'.[10] It also reflected trends in contemporary art practice. The British artist and theorist Victor Burgin, for instance, had written in his 1969 essay 'Situational Aesthetics' of how 'the artist is apt to see himself not as a creator of new material forms but rather as a co-ordinator of existing forms'.[11] Burgin's work applied this logic to space and environments, including installations of sculpture in urban parks, using photography to document the movement of objects through time as well as space. The 1969 installation *25 feet two hours*, a card index filled with photographs of its own movement around a room, is one rather dry example of this approach.

Burgin's ideas bore the stamp of Situationist theory: on the one hand, the notion of a creativity centred on appropriation and reuse of the already-existing, rather than creation *ex nihilo*, clearly bore some connection to the idea that, as one historian of Situationist thought has put it, 'surplus presents more fundamental problems for human societies than necessity'—an issue that had been approached by ideas like the Dutch architect Constant Nieuwenhuys's 'New Babylon' design, begun in the 1950s.[12] On the other, Burgin's contention that 'any path of consciousness through time' should be 'represented as a meander' bore the influence of Guy Debord's 1968 'Theory of the Dérive' as a movement though space involving 'playfully constructive behaviour and awareness of psychological effects', sharing Debord's conviction that the space in which to address these issues was that of the public realm.[13]

Keiller himself has described Christopher Gray's 1974 English-language compendium of Situationist writings *Leaving the 20th Century* as 'an essential text for any would-be-literate punk-rocker in the 1970s'.[14] His early ideas seem to have been highly responsive to a movement that, as Sadie Plant has observed,

[o]ut of the tradition which took letters out of words, inverted Notre Dame, and put urinals in galleries, [...] developed an armoury of confusing weapons

---

[10] Susan Sontag, *On Photography* (London: Penguin, 2008), p.2; Addison cited in Gregory Dart, 'Daydreaming', in Matthew Beaumont and Gregory Dart (eds.), *Restless Cities* (London: Verso, 2010), p.80.

[11] Victor Burgin, 'Situational Aesthetics', in Alexander Streitberger (ed.), *Situational Aesthetics: Selected Writings by Victor Burgin* (Leuven: Leuven University Press, 2009), p.9.

[12] McKenzie Wark, *The Beach Beneath The Street: The Everyday Life and Glorious Times of the Situationist International* (London: Verso, 2011), p.139.

[13] Burgin, 'Situational Aesthetics', p.8; Guy Debord, 'Theory of the Dérive' (1958), trans. Ken Knabb (http://www.bopsecrets.org/SI/2.derive.htm).

[14] Keiller, 'Imaging', in Matthew Beaumont and Gregory Dart (eds.), *Restless Cities* (London: Verso, 2010), p.150. See also Christopher Gray (ed.), *Leaving the 20th Century: The Incomplete Work of the Situationist International* (London: Rebel Press, 1974).

intended constantly to provoke critical notice of the totality of lived experience and reverse the stultifying passivity of the spectacle.[15]

The 'spectacle' here alludes to the 1967 tract *Society of the Spectacle*, a polemic penned by Debord that remains perhaps the single most significant work to emerge from the Situationist movement. Circulating around the idea that 'everything that was directly lived has receded into a representation', its idea of 'spectacle' refers to this general tendency as much as any particular image or set of imagery.[16] Keiller's response to such theorization was, similarly, less to do with any particular aesthetic than an avant-garde desire for life to follow the models suggested by art, as in 'New Babylon': that is, in this case, for political action to supplant aesthetics. After all, his activity wasn't simply about regarding functional buildings in aesthetic terms. Rather, as a kind of utopian horizon, it carried with it the imagined possibility of actually harnessing them for some alternative use: creative, hedonistic, or otherwise.

This mixture of refined aesthetic sensibility and utopian political commitment is highly legible in the case of the 'Nine Elms Coal Hopper', demolished in the winter of 1979–80 but which in 1977 was 'the last surviving structure of the Nine Elms Lane Gas Works' between Vauxhall Bridge and Battersea Power Station—an area that is now undergoing comprehensive redevelopment and has become home to the US Embassy, among other things.[17] This coal hopper was the subject of one of Keiller's slides, and an image of its demolition was included in the original printing of the 'Poetic Experience' essay, with an annotation but no explanation within the essay itself (see Figure 1.1). Only later did Keiller write of a specific 'effort to acquire the building and convert it to some cultural or hedonistic use', speculating on the sensation of possibility afforded by the dilapidated structure, whose site was at that time squatted by a car breaker.[18]

If not quite Constant's 'New Babylon', which was never built, Keiller might at least have had in mind projects like the Centre for Alternative Technology, an institution in Wales dedicated to 'demonstrating practical solutions for sustainability' where he had worked from 1973 to 1974.[19] Built on the site of the disused Llwyngwern slate quarry, the CAT had undergone something like a model transition from industrial to intellectual use. Keiller later made the connection with Tate Modern's transformation from a derelict power station, which closed in 1981, into an art gallery, which opened in 2000. Such a change would, in the case

---

[15] Sadie Plant, *The Most Radical Gesture: The Situationist International in a Postmodern Age* (London: Routledge, 1992), p.60.
[16] Guy Debord, *The Society of the Spectacle* (1967), trans. Ken Knabb (http://www.bopsecrets.org/SI/debord/1.htm).
[17] Keiller, in Sinclair, *London: City of Disappearances*, p.294.
[18] Keiller, 'Poetic Experience', p.76; Keiller, in Sinclair, *London: City of Disappearances*, p.294.
[19] See https://content.cat.org.uk/index.php/about-cat-what-do-we-do.

Figure 1.1 Coal Hopper, Nine Elms Lane, London, 1979, photograph, Patrick Keiller. Courtesy of Patrick Keiller.

of the coal hopper, have represented some sort of a return to the site's former purpose, given that 'several gas works were built on or near the sites of London pleasure gardens, most of which were on or near the river'. This was also true of the Tate, and there is a curious overlapping effect here, since—as Keiller observed—the Tate's collection contained 'examples of Bernd and Hiller Becher's photographs of industrial structures, including a series of coal hoppers'.[20]

Keiller's interest in the functional, industrial architecture typified by the coal hopper set the pitch of a recurrent note in his work: the Stockton Heath swing bridge on the Manchester Shipping Canal appears in both *The Clouds* and *Valtos*, where it is accompanied by imposing shots of what appears to be Fiddler's Ferry power station in Cheshire. Later, this attitude mutates into what might be termed the 'industrial nostalgia' of his *Robinson* films: the opening of *London* (1994), for instance, involves the search for a remembered image of 'a street of small factories backing on to a canal'—an exemplary light-industrial scene.[21] *Robinson in Space* (1997), its sequel, is motivated by similar concerns. Critiquing an England whose economic base, under the influence of laissez-faire neoliberal politics, had apparently shifted entirely towards service industries that do not produce material artefacts, the film is constructed as a search for residual traces of a manufacturing

---

[20] Keiller, in Sinclair, *London: City of Disappearances*, p.295.
[21] Keiller (dir.), *London* (London: British Film Institute, 1994).

economy 'based on appearances'—an economy capable, almost paradoxically, of providing a sufficient degree of visual pleasure for the passing aesthete.[22]

In the context of Keiller's early experiments, however, the Bechers' photographs are interesting for two main reasons. The first is related to the straight-on 'objectivity' of their framing. In the Bechers' case, this seems to emerge from a straightforward documentary impulse: their work began as a record of the vanishing industrial landscapes of the West German *Ruhrgebiet* in the 1950s, ultimately spanning Europe and America to gather vast 'typologies' of industrial structures. Yet, in its sheer scale, the Bechers' project ends up suggesting a kind of neurotic sensibility on the part of the artists: somewhere between childlike fascination and obsession, but either way eschewing an 'artistic' pose in favour of a 'scientific' one. In this respect, there is some commonality with the Parisian Surrealists assembled around Breton and Aragon, who styled themselves as earnest inquirers into the artistic potential of the unconscious mind, modelled their journal after the austere science periodical *La Nature*, and had themselves photographed in appropriately formal clothing to complete the image.

In the same way, the Bechers' images are often highly reminiscent of Surrealist photography: their work has often been connected with the loose tradition running through de Chirico and the Surrealists that Keiller cited in his 'Poetic Experience' essay. As Armin Zweite has written of the Bechers' *Typologies*, 'bereft of humans, purpose, or meaning, the structures mutate into anomalies'—his description remarkably reminiscent of Aragon's meditations on the 'enigmatic meanings' lent to certain objects by their appearance on the cinema screen.[23]

The second feature of the Bechers' work that is significant here is its subtle, rarely mentioned note of utopianism. In the catalogue to their show at the 1990 Venice Biennale (where they were awarded the prestigious Golden Lion), the Bechers wrote not only of attempting to see these functional objects in aesthetic terms but also of representing them as 'monuments to themselves, and at the same time symbols of a society organised around functionality and efficiency'.[24] In this way they positioned their work as both nostalgic and forward-looking, functioning as the wish-images of an unrealized, lapsed utopia that—if one looked for it hard enough—might yet still be recoverable.

In the particular historical context of Keiller's early slide collection, with Margaret Thatcher having been elected prime minister in 1979, such a utopian reorganization of society seemed unlikely to come to pass in Britain. In fact, what did happen seemed to many to be more like its perverse mirror image.

---

[22] Keiller (dir.), *Robinson in Space* (London: British Film Institute, 1997).

[23] Armin Zweite (ed.), *Typologies: Bernd and Hilla Becher* (Cambridge, MA: MIT, 2004), p.10; Louis Aragon, 'On Décor', in Paul Hammond (ed.), *The Shadow and its Shadow: Surrealist Writings on the Cinema* (San Francisco, CA: City Lights, 2000), p.52.

[24] Bernd Becher and Hilla Becher, *Tipologie, Typologien, Typologies* (Munich: Schirmer/Mosel, 1990), my trans.

26 LANDSCAPE AND SUBJECTIVITY

Keiller later discussed this in the essay 'Popular Science', a reflective piece written to accompany the British Council's 2000 touring exhibition 'Landscape'. Writing of the nearby Battersea Power Station, Keiller described its 1983 closure and subsequent sale to

> the owner of the most successful theme park in the UK who, with the explicit approval of the then prime minister, proposed to turn the structure into a theme park and invited her to return in two years time to open it.[25]

As in the 'Subjective Transformation' essay, he again reflected on the refurbishment of Tate Modern, noting that both buildings had been designed by Sir Giles Gilbert Scott. Battersea's reincarnation as a theme park represented a new use that—to employ his terms regarding the coal hopper—might have been 'hedonistic' but was hardly 'cultural': a warped parody of the 'playfully constructive behaviour' demanded by Guy Debord from practitioners of the 'dérive'. As the development went ahead, the effect was a 'sense of loss [...] partly mollified by observing these visible changes in the landscape as spectators at some sporting event might watch the opposition winning', Keiller's use of the term 'spectators' bleakly referring his reader to the deadening idea of the Situationist 'spectacle' and the correspondent collapse of genuine social interaction.[26]

The Royal College of Art and the London Film-Makers' Co-operative

The dread sense of disappointment implicit in Keiller's comments about Battersea Power Station was in tune with a wider political context: in *The Production of Space*, published in French in 1974, Henri Lefebvre referred to the events of May 1968, when mass protests in France were accompanied by a long-running general strike. These events, Lefebvre wrote, 'when students occupied and took charge of their own space, and the working class immediately followed suit, marked a new departure'. But, he continued, 'the halting of this reappropriation of space, though doubtless only temporary, has given rise *to a despairing attitude*' (my emphasis).[27]

Although he did not read Lefebvre's text until it was translated in the 1990s, this description neatly characterized Keiller's own sensibility and situation in the London of the 1980s: it is this sense that any real positive change in urban space is utterly unlikely which forms one reason for his characteristic diffidence about

---

[25] Keiller, 'Popular Science', in *Landscape*, ed. Anne Gallagher (London: British Council, 2000), p.92.
[26] Ibid., p.92.
[27] Henri Lefebvre, *The Production of Space*, trans. Donald Nicholson Smith (Oxford: Blackwell, 1991), pp.55–6.

film-making. The same attitude is legible, for example, in his later interview comment that in the same year as Thatcher's election, 'wandering around London taking pictures of funny buildings and what they did [...] I presented myself to a bit of the RCA [Royal College of Art] that no longer exists, [...] where one was allowed to think about those things'.[28]

Keiller enrolled at the RCA in October 1979 and remained there, in Peter Kardia's 'Department for Environmental Media', until June 1981. His 'collection' of 35mm slides facilitated his entry, and in this new context he sought—as he punningly put it in another interview—to 'develop the practice in some way'.[29] It was at the RCA that he made the crucial shift towards film and where he wrote the 'Poetic Experience' essay, which began life as his dissertation; he also studied alongside Julie Norris, who became his 'partner and sometime collaborator' and with whom he would work on all of his later films.[30] The transition from still to moving-image making was, at first, quite sudden, since the Department for Environmental Media possessed both a portable U-Matic colour video recorder and 'an old Bolex, a clockwork 16mm cine-camera'—the same kind used by Andy Warhol in his seminal 1960s films, such as *Sleep* (1963), *Empire* (1964), and *The Chelsea Girls* (1966). It must have been shortly after his arrival in the department that he went back to Nine Elms Lane to make a film of the coal hopper's destruction, in the winter of 1979–80. A 'short loop' recording the wrecking ball in action, this was 'the first film I ever exhibited', he wrote: 'it was projected on an unplastered white-painted brick wall, so that it looked as if the film was knocking the wall down'.[31]

The combination of 'subjective transformation' with a sense of crushing disappointment emerges forcefully here, in the form of a radical ambivalence: the fact of the wall only *seeming* to be knocked down asserts the role of imagination or altered perception in transforming environments, while also forming an ironical take on the unlikelihood of any actual transformation occurring. The ambivalence reflects the quotation from Raoul Vaneigem's 1967 Situationist text *The Revolution of Everyday Life*, which Keiller—via Christopher Gray's anthology—cited in his 'Poetic Experience' essay:

Although I can always see how beautiful anything could be if only I could change it, in practically every case there is nothing I can really do. Everything is changed into something else in my imagination, then the dead weight of things changes it

---

[28] Keiller, interview with John Wrathall, *Blueprint*, February 1999, p.11.
[29] Keiller, interview with David Martin-Jones, *Journal of Popular British Cinema* No.5 (2002), p.125.
[30] Keiller, *The View From The Train*, p.4.
[31] Keiller, in Sinclair, *London: City of Disappearances*, p.294.

back into what it was in the first place. A bridge between imagination and reality must be built.[32]

Keiller was clearly strongly attracted by the sensibility of these lines: they appeared again in *Robinson in Space*, alongside Lefebvre's elliptical contention in *The Production of Space*, echoing his thoughts on May 1968, that 'the space that contains the realised preconditions of another life is the same one as prohibits what those preconditions make possible'.[33] In each case, there is a strong sense of radical disappointment—a melancholy bound up with the act of settling for imaginative rather than actual change.

One way to solve this problem was inherent in film itself. In a section of the 'Poetic Experience' essay added for its publication in *Undercut*, the house magazine of the London Film-Makers' Co-operative (LFMC), before being excised again from its 2013 reprint in *The View from The Train*, Keiller wrote that, if the subjective part of space's transformation aligned with the cultivation of 'photography as a way of seeing', the task of communicating this experience was in part satisfied simply by film's mode of presentation. If the experience of exploring and film-making were, for Keiller at least, rather lonely ones, then 'the experience of having seen a film', he wrote, 'is nearly always a collective experience'.[34] His comments suggest the way that film could both channel a sense of creative isolation and also provide an escape from it, and the essay's first readers would likely have connected this idea less with a conventional cinema-going experience than with the quite specific atmosphere of the LFMC.

Underpinned by what A.L. Rees has described as an 'experimental' and 'underground ethos' and a subversive attitude redolent of the 1960s countercultural underground, carried over from its sister organization in New York (the New York Film Co-Operative had been established four years previously), the LFMC held regular screenings at various locations across London.[35] Many of these buildings were former industrial premises occupied by artists on a temporary basis, pending their demolition—a practical form of the creative re-appropriation of 'already existing' structures in which Keiller was engaged as an artist. They were, as Mark Webber has observed, uniformly 'desolate, cold, unwelcoming places', with 'no heating, broken windows, decrepit facilities. You had to want to be there.' But many aspiring film-makers did, for the organization offered one unique service to its members: 'by democratising the methods of production they bypassed the commercial laboratories and their connection to the film industry. They were free

---

[32] Raoul Vaneigem, *The Revolution of Everyday Life*, cited in Keiller, 'Poetic Experience', *The Undercut Reader*, p.79.
[33] Keiller, *Robinson in Space*; Lefebvre, *The Production of Space*, pp.189–90.
[34] Keiller, 'Poetic Experience', p.75.
[35] A.L. Rees, *A History of Experimental Film and Video: From the Canonical Avant-Garde to Contemporary British Practice* (Basingstoke: Palgrave Macmillan, 2011), p.70.

to explore new ways of creating films, in direct control of each stage of the process.'[36] In 1982, members of the Co-op could hire a cutting room equipped with a 6-plate Steenbeck editing machine for £6 a day or £25 a week, or a 4-plate model for £5 and £20.

The LFMC's small-scale, 'backwoods' set-up fed a radically retrograde approach to film-making. This was clearly, in part, necessitous, but it chimed in with the group's espoused wish to disrupt the dominance of commercial narrative cinema.[37] The consequence was an active engagement with the origins of the medium. Of the group's early work, Rees went on to write:

[T]hese films had no fictional narrative content; they seem to leap over the history of film, and back to the experiments of Demeny, Muybridge and Lumière. Here a line of descent is traced from the earliest cinema, with narrative as a grand detour.[38]

The result was a highly idiosyncratic style often marked by the film-makers' ability to manually intervene in the development process. Another key feature was artists' ability to work alone: as David Curtis, who became one of the group's chroniclers, observed in his *History of Artists' Film and Video in Britain* (2007), 'the common denominator shared by the films we watched, and the one to which we already attached great importance, was their emanation from a single imagination'. This fact radically widened the field of possibility open to aspiring, individual film-makers working on low budgets and set a tone for Keiller's own experiments with the use of the camera as an analogue and vehicle of consciousness.[39]

The LFMC's stripped-down set-up also seems to have informed its political identity. Writing retrospectively in 1996, Michael O'Pray would affirm that, in the early 1980s, 'the idea of the "underground" re-emerged with its implication for an art that comes from "below", from beneath the accepted culture, as opposed to leading from the front'.[40] This sense of a re-energized counterculture, whether conceived as 'underground' or 'avant-garde', was also fuelled by the contemporary political situation and the experience of marginalization felt by many artists under Thatcher's government. In his *History*, his tone perhaps softened somewhat by the passage of two decades, Curtis remarked that Co-op film-makers tended to be 'hostile to the commodification of the art object'.[41] This was putting the case

---

[36] Mark Webber (ed.), *Shoot Shoot Shoot: British Avant-Garde Film of the 1960s and 1970s* (London: Lux, 2006) (liner notes), p.7.
[37] See e.g. Peter Gidal's 'Theory and Practice of Structural/Materialist film', in Peter Gidal (ed.), *Structural Film Anthology* (London: BFI, 1976).
[38] Rees, *History of Experimental Film and Video*, p.81.
[39] David Curtis, *A History of Artists' Film and Video in Britain* (London: BFI, 2007), p.176.
[40] Michael O'Pray (ed.), *The British Avant-Garde Film, 1926 to 1995: An Anthology of Writings* (Luton: University of Luton Press, 1996), p.2.
[41] Curtis, *A History of Artists' Film and Video in Britain*, p.39.

mildly: in the context of a 1987 touring exhibition he had written in a far more urgent register about 'the social and political changes which have enveloped this country in the past ten years' and which fuelled LFMC work. 'The rise of a radical Conservatism', he noted in the catalogue of *The Elusive Sign*,

> and its economic consequences in the form of unemployment, the eradication of the old manufacturing centre, the squeeze on education (which includes Art schools where many avant-garde film-makers begin their careers), the return of the nuclear question, the virtual collapse of the Left, urban unrest and racial tension, are all factors which cannot be ignored and certainly provide the background to the work of such disparate film-makers as Derek Jarman, Black Audio Film Collective, Ian Bourn, Brett Turnbull, Patrick Keiller, Sally Potter and Cerith Wyn Evans. It is perhaps no accident that the fragmentation, the need for 'relevance' and 'content' and the desperate flight into fantasy felt so strongly at times in avant-garde film-making, should occur in the uncertain climate of Britain in the 80s.[42]

The description gives a powerful sense of the vibrant 'underground' from which Keiller's early film emerged, with the cinema itself a space of radical ideas and political ferment.

'Tape-Slide Assemblies' and 'Subjective Camera'

The vibrant, experimental context of the LFMC paralleled the kinds of interdisciplinary, 'unorthodox' developments instituted by Peter Kardia under the RCA's 'Environmental Media' umbrella. And, in fact, there was indeed a substantial overlap between the two worlds: the theorists and film-makers Malcolm Le Grice and Peter Gidal, for example, were prominent members of the Co-op and taught at Central St Martin's and the RCA respectively. Gidal's *Close Up* (1983) and Le Grice's *Finnegan's Chin* were both exhibited in the Department of Environmental Media's 1984 *Cross Currents* show, and the department's commitment to interdisciplinary investigation appears to have mirrored the 'non- (but not anti-) academic' atmosphere of the Co-op, as the critic Raymond Durgnat later characterized it.[43]

'Environmental Media' was interdisciplinary, but—as Curtis has written—in practice it 'attracted many artists who then gravitated towards film': the department

---

[42] Curtis (ed.), *The Elusive Sign: British Avant-Garde Film & Video 1977–1987* (London: Arts Council, 1987), p.10.
[43] Raymond Durgnat (writing in 1991), quoted in Curtis, *A History of Artists' Film and Video in Britain*, p.27.

was equipped with the country's only broadcast-level colour television studios outside the BBC, and audio-visual work acted as a common denominator. In 1984, writing of his department's apparently diffuse focus, Kardia himself commented that 'particular impetus does come from the need to use in fine art the products of communication technology', a 'need' framed around a broadly conceived notion of social and political engagement. 'One of the corollaries of the move into such a field of practice', he wrote, was a concern with 'those aspects of culture which reproduce and reinforce dominant interpretations of reality' and in turn the way in which fine art could attempt 'to restructure experience'.[44]

After the Nine Elms loop, Keiller's own experiments in the combination of image and text took the now near-obsolete form of the 'tape-slide assembly'. Such works were sequences of discrete images fed through a projector, accompanied by a soundtrack recorded onto magnetic audio tape. A parallel recording on the reverse side of the track emits, at predetermined intervals, a particular frequency that causes the projector to move on to the next slide. Twin projectors were often used to enable a crude 'dissolve' effect between frames. In the introduction to *The View From The Train*, and in 2010's 'Imaging', Keiller has referred obliquely to his tape-slide works, but neither is publicly available today, and he has chosen not to 'resurrect them in some more up to date format'.[45] Commentary on them is therefore speculative, but a certain amount of information appears on the flier for a 1982 exhibition at the Tate Gallery entitled *Drawings, Tape-Slide and Sound*. 'These are combinations of photographs or film', Keiller wrote there,

> with spoken narratives derived from them. It is not a rule, but the pictures are usually of place and weather, and the story tells the time and mood. There are often no people in the pictures, as this leaves more room for the narrator's creations, or would do had they not already left, for the stories are in the past tense and the connection can only be made in the imagination.[46]

Each about five minutes in length and overlaid with a single narrative voice, the works were entitled *The Tourists' Return, Episode 1* and *The View Behind Wormwood Scrubs Prison* (both 1980).

An echo of the tape-slide format is legible in the 'slide-show' effect of Keiller's later *Robinson* films, with their static camera shots, as well as the shorter films he soon went on to make, with their distinctive combination of images of space and first-person voiceover narration. *The View Behind Wormwood Scrubs Prison* in particular seems to have informed the ideas behind *Stonebridge Park*, which was

---

[44] Peter Kardia (ed.), *Cross Currents: Ten Years of Mixed Media* (London: Royal College of Art, 1984), p.8.
[45] Keiller, Personal Correspondence.
[46] Keiller, *Drawings, Tape-Slide and Sound* (London: Tate, 1982), p.1.

filmed only a few miles north-west of the same location. On the Tate flier, Keiller wrote of this work:

> While pursuing another matter, a man was obliged to remove his head, and then inspected the views through it. This is, no doubt, an allusion to the paradox of the camera's view.[47]

This 'paradox of the camera's view' reflects a question that clearly preoccupied Keiller in his early experiments with film and connects with his discussion of the Gothic and its cinematic inheritor, film noir, in the 'Poetic Experience' essay. There Keiller wrote of being keen to distinguish between 'depicting space, and depicting experience of space', although, he claimed, 'this is in a way an unnecessary distinction: nearly all films depict space and in doing so establish, if only inadvertently, a presentation of how that space is experienced, an atmosphere', the result of 'narrative, editing, camera movement and so on'.[48]

Asserting that 'the hollowness of space is what characterises the experience of it, and is what must be depicted in order to depict this experience', Keiller concluded that '[t]he first way that occurred to me [...] was the device known as "subjective camera"'—a device typical of film noir. 'The paradoxical, special-effect status of this view', he wrote,

> depends on the camera's impersonation of a character in the film, and is entirely appropriate to the special-effect, heightened-awareness mood in which a new inspection of everyday surroundings might best be carried out.[49]

Keiller seems here to have isolated a kind of schizophrenia in the experience and cinematic depiction of space, wherein the viewer is able to more closely relate to the non-eye-level representation of being within a space than the subjective one, which itself has a 'special effect' quality. Lastly, he mentions 'two films about memory'—Chris Marker's *La Jetée* (1962), which he had seen either at the Arts Lab or the Roundhouse in Chalk Farm, and Alain Resnais's *Toute La Mémoire du Monde* (1956), a highly stylized documentary about the Bibliothèque Nationale in Paris. These works, Keiller remarks, 'install the memory and dream quality of the view from above in the memory spaces of the museum of natural history in *La Jetée* and the library' (in Resnais). Resnais's film is replete with what Keiller calls 'moving linear camera at eye level' and over-the-shoulder shots, figuring the museum in an oddly noirish manner.[50]

The concerns and anxieties here suggest the narrative mood in all of Keiller's subsequent short films, where journeys often seem to be propelled by a curious,

---

[47] Ibid., p.2. [48] Keiller, 'Poetic Experience', p.81. [49] Ibid., pp. 81–2.
[50] Ibid., p.82.

often morbid subjectivity, drawing frequently on elements of the Gothic: 'The disease is my own', the narrator of *The End* (1986) ambiguously declares, 'the project is its cure—this journey'.[51] An opaque reference to 'the helmet' later in the same film seems to allude to Horace Walpole's fantastical Gothic romance *The Castle of Otranto* (1764), where an enormous helmet falls inexplicably from the sky, crushing the lord of the castle's son on his wedding day. In Keiller's film, environment and consciousness interpenetrate in a dreamlike manner suggested by this mode: 'I am walking', avows the narrator of *Valtos* (1987), 'in a place that has become the inside of my own mind'.[52] Each of these works features a curious motif wherein the narrator is haunted by a sense that he has been 'duplicated' and is now locked into pursuit of his 'true self', an idea recalling the Gothic trope of the double as it appears in tales like Edgar Allan Poe's 'William Wilson' (1839); Keiller's integration of this motif with the material processes of photographic reproduction is typical of the self-reflexive nuance of his early work.

In each of these early films, an anxious narrative subject transforms apparently indifferent spaces into ones of unease and uncertainty and, at the same time, reflects on the cinematic medium and its processes. They also centre on journeys that often cover significant ground. *The End* and *Valtos*, for instance, travel to Tuscany and Scotland respectively. Yet the remainder of this chapter looks not so much at these distant prospects as the near at hand, examining Keiller's cultivation of his distinctive narrative subjectivity in his first two films, *Stonebridge Park* (1981) and *Norwood* (1983). The experimentation with space and subjectivity in these films can be read as an elaborate inquiry into the technique of the 'camera-I', in which can be traced the formation of the anxious, essayistic manner of the *Robinson* series.

A Bridge between Imagination and Reality: *Stonebridge Park*

Stonebridge Park, which was shown both at Keiller's RCA graduation show and also in the LFMC's July 1981 Summer Show, marked his most thoroughgoing interrogation of the 'subjective camera' technique so far. Its genesis can be traced to an encounter with a location first seen from a train window on the main line out of Euston station in late 1980. Passing swiftly through north-west London, close by the LFMC's premises in Gloucester Avenue, on through Kensal Green and Harlesden and under the North Circular Road, Keiller noticed a site that 'seemed to present a curiously northern-looking landscape to find in outer London' and thought it might respond well to monochrome photography. Returning by bicycle, his attention was diverted by a footbridge, which he had not seen from the train.

---

[51] Keiller (dir.), *The End* (1986).   [52] Keiller (dir.), *Valtos* (1987).

Thirty years later, in the essay 'Imaging', he described this bridge's seductive effect—seductive in the fullest, Latinate sense of 'leading astray':

> About 200 metres long, it carries pedestrians over both the main line and a branch that passes underneath it, at an angle, in a tunnel. The longer of the bridge's two spans is oriented so that Wembley Stadium is framed between its parapets. The bridge's architecture suggested a renewed attempt at moving pictures: its long, narrow walkway resembled the linearity of a film; its parapets framed the view in a ratio similar to the 4×3 of a camera, and its elaborate articulation, with several flights of steps, half landings and changes of direction, offered a structure for a moving-camera choreography.

A few weeks later he returned with a handheld cine-camera to record a walk across this bridge: one continuous take lasting ten minutes, recorded on 120 metres of 16mm, monochrome film stock. Such a method recalled early cinematic 'actualities', silent works such as those of Alexandre Promio and the Lumière Brothers, although 'by this time', Keiller noted, 'I think I had already decided to write a fictional narration to accompany the picture'.[53]

The image-making itself was not yet complete, however: *Stonebridge Park* is, as its opening titles make plain, 'a film in two parts', and the footage so far accrued became its second part. The first, composed of two takes totalling just over eight minutes, was made in response to the discovery of another footbridge, this time over a nearby junction of the North Circular road. This other bridge's quadrilateral arrangement does not appear to be so instantly suggestive of the medium's 'linearity'. It is, however, rather more symmetrical, so that the 'choreography' of its space is oddly elegant (see Figure 1.2). In this part of the film the camera traces a circumlocutory path around the bridge, absorbing the surrounding landscape and the 'tin hulks' of the cars rushing below, before finally teetering over the railings towards the traffic in a highly unsettling manner. Yet the attentiveness to its narrow walkways still highlights the exceptionally close connection made by Keiller between the space being depicted and its suggestion of both the framing of the cinema screen and the material form of film. The sequence's solitary cut, made to enable the camera to cross the road, serves to highlight this smooth consonance by virtue of puncturing it so abruptly.[54]

Stonebridge Park begins with a muffled burst of Beethoven's third symphony, after which a first-person tale of theft, robbery, and attempted murder by a disgruntled and recently dismissed employee at a second-hand car dealership

---

[53] Keiller, 'Imaging', p.149.
[54] The practical necessity of this is discussed in a 1981 Funding Application to the Arts Council of Great Britain, held at the British Film and Video Artists' Study Collection, Central St Martins College of Art, London.

Figure 1.2 Footbridge above junction of Harrow Road and North Circular Road, London, 1981, frame from *Stonebridge Park* (1981), Patrick Keiller. Courtesy of Patrick Keiller.

gradually unfolds—a melodrama bearing the imprint of film noir's influence. The narrator's marginalized state of mind sits neatly with the location's anonymous peripherality, although an overtly philosophical, stoical register seems at first to be oddly bolted on to both the mundane turpitude of his acts and the striking ordinariness of the setting.

In fact, the film's narrative draws suggestively on Michael O'Pray's comments about avant-garde film as a 'marginal practice'.[55] And if O'Pray wrote that film-making had become 'a promiscuous activity', it is apt that *Stonebridge Park* begins with a dense meditation on precisely this theme:

> Promiscuity, in my case, results from an inability to recognise that it is not necessary to do all the things that I possibly could do. Such compulsive behaviour is not confined to acts that come about as a result of feelings of lust. Hate, greed, envy: all these passions can promote actions of a more or less consequential nature which may result in greater or lesser feelings of remorse. A thoughtless blow with a bottle; a casual theft; a hastily written fraudulent cheque; the

[55] O'Pray, *The British Avant-Garde Film*, p.2.

impulsive purchase of a desirable and inexpensive second-hand car; the subsequent disobeyance of a traffic signal, owing to its faulty brakes, and the resulting fatal injury to a pedestrian crossing the road. Any abandonment of oneself to sudden passionate desires can conventionally be reckoned to end in tears.[56]

The combination of profound despair and a measured, methodical tone here bears the stamp of Keiller's reading of Poe's *The Narrative of Arthur Gordon Pym of Nantucket* (1838), which he declared in his funding application to the Arts Council (addressed, in fact, to the same David Curtis mentioned above) to be the most significant influence on the film's script.[57] The film does not 'travel' to the extent of Poe's visionary work, which recounts a journey to the then still uncharted South Pole. Yet as the narrative of *Stonebridge Park* continues, the measured flow of images keeps pace with the narrative's digressiveness: the camera's 'walk' is more of a wander than a march, appropriate to Victor Burgin's idea of the 'path of consciousness through time' as a 'meander'.

The mesmeric effect of this sequence—compounded by the sensation of disembodiment effected by the handheld, walking camera—becomes particularly clear when the film is projected at anything approximating a full cinematic scale, when the effect is almost dizzying. As the camera works its way across the bridge, the space is sucked in as if by the vacuum cleaner that a passer-by carries (and to which the narrator alludes). Likewise, as the similarly disembodied voice-over (Keiller's own) relays the narrative, the sense of interiority effected by the 'subjective camera', compounded by a lack of environmental sound, becomes strongly reminiscent of the Surrealists' enthusiasm for 'film language as an analogue of oneiric thinking'.[58]

In his 1975 essay 'An Introduction to the Structural Analysis of Narratives,' Roland Barthes mentioned in a footnote that the 'signifiers of narrativity [...] are not readily transferrable from novel to film' and that the 'camera-I' technique was, for this reason, 'exceptional in the history of cinema'.[59] Yet it is precisely this technique that *Stonebridge Park* centres on. If Keiller's tape-slide assemblies, under the influence of *La Jetée*, had experimented with the relation between text and image, then the use of 'subjective camera' here should also be read as part of that interest. The film can be readily viewed as Keiller cultivating his distinctive essayistic voice on screen: Michel de Montaigne's phrase 'I revolve within myself', used to describe his state of mind when writing his *Essais*, already appears highly apt to its combination of disorientating motion, acute introspection, and material

---

[56] Keiller (dir.), *Stonebridge Park* (1981).
[57] Keiller, Funding Application, British Film and Video Artists' Study Collection.
[58] Hammond, *The Shadow and its Shadow*, p.9.
[59] Roland Barthes, 'An Introduction to the Structural Analysis of Narratives', in Susan Sontag (ed.), *A Barthes Reader* (London: Cape, 1982), p.292.

self-reflexivity, seeming to capture the relationship between the movement of thought and the revolutions of film within the camera or projector.[60]

While the film establishes a rhythm conducive to acute introspection, the marginal public space it depicts becomes an empty vessel into which private anxieties are poured. The setting becomes a 'crime scene' even if its relation to where the supposed 'crime' took place is only indirect: as our narrator contemplates the inescapability of his own sense of guilt, 'written everywhere on the surfaces of things around me', we scrutinize the image, confronted by the clash of intense narrative subjectivity and grey, indifferent objectivity of the everyday surroundings. In fact, for the narrator, the environment becomes not only a crime scene but a parallel of that 'prison-world' which film, as Walter Benjamin wrote in his canonical essay 'The Work of Art in the Age of its Technical Reproducibility', was supposed to have 'burst asunder'.[61] Keiller's technique seems to refer us not so much to the radical sense of freedom that, according to Benjamin, was the special capability of the cinematic medium as to the 'locked-in' experience explored by Poe when Arthur Gordon Pym becomes trapped in the noxious hold of a ship whose crew have mutinied. On Keiller's bridge, the unnerving experience is mollified only by the assertion that 'every man, after all, lives in his own prison to a greater or lesser extent, whether he knows it or not'.[62]

If Curtis wrote of how LMFC members 'attached great importance' to films' 'emanation from a single imagination', then here, as the 'prison' suggests, and as the device of the 'subjective camera' and the lack of environmental sound reinforce, the sense of this is brought to an extreme.[63] So trapped is the narrator within his private reverie that there is only occasionally a direct reference to what we can see. One of these comes at the point when the figure bearing the vacuum cleaner passes by, and the voiceover refers to people 'finding strange objects on which to fasten their desire' (see Figure 1.3). An allusion to the passer-by and, perhaps, to Keiller's own diversion into exploring these footbridges, this moment produces a vertiginous effect by suddenly telescoping the temporalities of text and image into unison with one another and responding to something that is visually depicted in the narrative present.

This is immediately followed by a renewed longing for a return to the 'safe', voyeuristic distance of retrospection and reflection. In tandem with the passing of a train in the upper part of the shot, the narrator mourns:

> Oh, how I longed to be on that train, in the safe world which exists only between railway stations, and demands only the passive acceptance of the view out of the

---

[60] Michel de Montaigne, *Essays*, trans. J.M. Cohen (London: Penguin, 1993), p.220.
[61] Walter Benjamin, 'The Work of Art in the Age of Mechanical Reproduction', in Hannah Arendt (ed.) and Harry Zohn (trans.), *Illuminations* (New York: Schocken, 1969), p.236.
[62] Keiller (dir.), *Stonebridge Park* (1981).
[63] Curtis, *A History of Artists' Film and Video in Britain*, p.176.

Figure 1.3 Footbridge above railway near Lyon Park Avenue, London, 1981, frame from *Stonebridge Park* (1981), Patrick Keiller. Courtesy of Patrick Keiller.

window. Why was it that existence always implied that one should intervene in the world? Why could one not somehow contrive to remain a spectator of the picturesque bunglings of others?

At this point, time, to the narrator, seems to be '*slowing down*, or more probably, I thought, my own frantic perception of it was speeding up'. And as the riveted sheets of the bridge move past in measured rhythm, we are reminded of the individual frames of the film passing through the projector and what Laura Mulvey has described in appropriately clandestine terms as cinema's 'secret, [...] hidden past'—the still photographic image.[64]

For the viewer, however, a different 'hidden past' may be traced here. Drawing on the metatextual suggestiveness of the vacuum-cleaner moment, the reference to the train can be readily inferred as an echo of Keiller's original encounter with his visual subjects. In this reading, the narrator's yearning to undo his 'crime' becomes synonymous with a desire to unravel the creative act of film-making itself and return to the 'hidden past' that was Keiller's original, indifferent glance from the train window (the 'view from the train' with which it all began); to be

---

[64] Laura Mulvey, *Death 24x a Second* (London: Reaktion, 2005), p.67.

disentangled from the troublesome project of constructing a film at all. If, in the 'Poetic Experience' essay Keiller wrote of the association made between Atget's photographs of Paris and the 'scenes of crime', then here this 'crime' might be read as the act of film-making itself—a kind of unwonted transgression, a superfluous act of dubious validity. The narrator's agonies thus become an ironic send-up of the aberrational act of making the film in the first place, drawing again on the notion of art-making itself as a hubristic, possibly even an anti-social, act.

Here we might read an echo of one of Keiller's favourite texts, *The Anatomy of Melancholy* (1621), in which Robert Burton repeats Plutarch's advice to 'seek not after that which is hid'.[65] This reading also draws on the overdetermined status of trains in spatial theory. Michel Foucault's concept of the 'heterotopia' described in his 1967 essay 'Of Other Spaces', for instance, took the train as one of its models: 'a train is an extraordinary bundle of relations', Foucault wrote, 'because it is something through which one goes, it is also something by means of which one can go from one point to another, and then it is also something that goes by'.[66] As cinematic spectator, our voyeuristic position corresponds with the train's heterotopian 'safe world', so at odds with that of the narrator, who is emphatically not 'going by'. At the same time, the suggestion of subjectivity as a 'prison' also recalls the writings of Michel de Certeau, whose 1974 study *The Practice of Everyday Life* characterized rail travel as an 'incarceration-vacation' that 'generalises Dürer's *Melancholia*, a speculative experience of the world'.[67] The *mise-en-scène* also seems to draw on the works of Giorgio de Chirico, where trains are often found passing by along the paintings' distant vanishing-points. His 1914 painting *Gare Montparnasse: Melancholy of Departure*, in which, as the Situationist Ivan Chtcheglov wrote in his 1953 'Formulary for a New Urbanism', 'an empty space creates a richly filled time', is typical of this.[68]

When the camera finally reaches the view of Wembley Stadium, the narrator experiences a moment of resolution consonant with the neat 'framing' of the stadium by the bridge's walls, and the subsequent escape from that frame as these walls slip out of view. At this moment, visual and narrative temporalities coincide conclusively, and the climactic effect is reinforced by the arrival of a satisfyingly coherent spectacle of landscape extending into the distance and resolving on the stadium itself. 'And then it hit me!' declares the narrator:

---

[65] Robert Burton, 'Democritus Junior to the Reader', *The Anatomy of Melancholy* (New York: New York Review Books, 2001), p.15.
[66] Michel Foucault, 'Of Other Spaces, Heterotopias', in *Architecture, Mouvement, Continuité* No.5 (1984) (https://foucault.info/doc/documents/heterotopia/foucault-heterotopia-en-html).
[67] Michel de Certeau, *The Practice of Everyday Life*, trans. Stephen Rendall (Berkeley: University of California Press, 1988), p.111.
[68] Ivan Chtcheglov, 'Formulary for a New Urbanism' (1956), trans. Ken Knabb (http://www.bopsecrets.org/SI/Chtcheglov.htm).

A revelation. Though it was perhaps less a revelation than a realisation that at last the panic had subsided. The boys who passed noticed my elation. I have never been a believer but I am bound to say that I felt it as a message from God. I would escape. My disconcerted ambitions were finally united to this end. I knew what I had to do. I was absolved. I gazed transfixed at the view, secure in the knowledge that I would now transcend the iron grip of history.

At this moment—alluding to the title of one of his tape-slide works—we might finally acknowledge the unassuming footbridges as elaborate visual puns on the 'bridge between imagination and reality' which the Belgian Situationist Raoul Vaneigem insisted 'must be built'. It seems highly likely that Keiller should have been thinking of this kind of ironical pun, particularly because of the way that his narrative, complete with its mock-serious intertitles like 'SOME TIME LATER' and its mimicry of Poe's prose style, veers constantly towards bathos. Fittingly, as *Stonebridge Park* comes to a close, the narrator's agonies turn out to have been largely unwarranted. His crime was 'perfect' in the sense that, like the act of film-making, it left no trace of itself—except, that is, the images themselves.[69]

'Unemployed Reverie': *Norwood*

Norwood (1983) takes up the same narrative thread as *Stonebridge Park*, although in the space between the two films the narrator has died and speaks, in the second, mostly not from Norwood at all but 'quite another plane'. Subtitled austerely 'an idyll', this film recounts the narrator's murder at the hands of an 'unscrupulous' builder, his 'haunting' of Norwood, and his subsequent reincarnation. In this way the narrative rearranges motifs from Arthur Conan Doyle's 1903 Sherlock Holmes story 'The Adventure of the Norwood Builder', where the titular figure cynically attempts to fake his own death before finally being revealed by the detective.[70] In the film, as Keiller wrote on his funding application to the Arts Council, he hoped to capture 'the atmosphere of unemployed reverie peculiar to certain parts of South London on sunny days. Hopefully', he added with playful urgency, 'this latter will not be autobiographical, as the film will need to be shot while the leaves are still on the trees'.[71]

In *Norwood* we soon learn that, while still alive, the narrator had returned to London and built up a substantial property portfolio, his financial assets having burgeoned in the 'criminal underworld' of Nice, France, where he had fled after

---

[69] See Jean Baudrillard, *The Perfect Crime*, trans. Chris Turner (London: Verso, 1996).

[70] See Arthur Conan Doyle, 'The Adventure of the Norwood Builder', in Richard Lancelyn Green (ed.), *The Return of Sherlock Holmes* (Oxford: Oxford University Press, 1993).

[71] Keiller, July 1981 Funding Application to the Arts Council of Great Britain, held at the British Film and Video Artists' Study Collection.

the events recounted in *Stonebridge Park*. After spending a long time there (latterly realized as 'unnecessary'), 'I packed up and came back to London, settling in Norwood, after the example of the painter Camille Pissarro, who had done so 111 years before'. His references to Pissarro here allude to the idea of 'seeing somewhere as somewhere else' or, indeed, 'seeing somewhere in terms of a picture of somewhere else' that Keiller set out in an essay written for *Undercut* the same year that *Norwood* was made; they also point forward to *London*'s retracing of French writers' and painters' presence in the city.[72]

Though inspired by Pissarro, the narrator is keen to counter the suspicion that 'I had any idea of a new life as an artist': 'I came not to paint the streets of Norwood', he adds, drily reversing the terms of Keiller's early slide collection, 'but to buy them, for I have never felt that a picture is really any substitute for the real thing'.[73] The narrative thus alludes to the kind of rampant property speculation represented in films like *The Long Good Friday* (1980) and to the idea of photography's 'acquisition' of the world. Yet *Norwood*'s narrator throws himself into the London property market only to be murdered during the failed redevelopment of a triangular cul-de-sac called Bloom Grove (a real place, about 100 yards north of West Norwood train station) (see Figure 1.4). The contractor turns out to be the brother of the former employer 'whose stolen money had become the foundation of my wealth. This unwitting benefactor was my murderer's brother – my death was his revenge.'

As with *Stonebridge Park* and the tape-slide works, *Norwood* does not actually show us these things but recounts them whilst depicting the sites on which they supposedly took place or which bear some oblique connection to them. Yet, unlike the characters of the tape-slide works, the narrator has not, at least not completely, 'already left': in this case his immanent position *as* the camera itself, 'haunting' the areas in which he has formerly lived, is explicit. Other motifs familiar from *Stonebridge Park* soon emerge. Norwood's anonymity, its marginal position in the south of the metropolis—beyond the South Circular Road and distant from the Underground network—acts as an analogue of the narrator's ambiguous state of existence on the threshold of physical form. At the same time, the narrator's subsequent comment that 'I have moved to quite another plane, but Norwood persists' marks a typical instance of Keiller's narrative alluding to the material processes of cinematic representation: it is not only Norwood the place but also *Norwood* the film that stubbornly persists and endures, albeit in celluloid form.

Structurally more complex than *Stonebridge Park*, with many more shots and cuts, *Norwood*'s internal rhythm of recurrence and return to already visited places

---

[72] Keiller, 'Atmosphere, Palimpsest and Other Interpretations of Landscape', in *The Undercut Reader*, p.206.
[73] Keiller (dir.), *Norwood* (1983).

Figure 1.4 Bloom Grove, West Norwood, London, 1982, frame from *Norwood* (1983), Patrick Keiller. Courtesy of Patrick Keiller.

is established early on by the structure of Handel's air, *I Know That My Redeemer Liveth* (from his 1741 oratorio *Messiah*). In this sequence the organ follows the vocal melody, always a short distance behind, as if tracing its steps. Following its use in the film's preamble, the same music recurs at the point in the narrative immediately after the narrator relates his own death-by-hammer. Later, at the point of his reincarnation—after realizing the true identity of his murderer—we witness an abrupt moment of formal self-reflection: 'There, I am observed!' he declares, accompanied by an incursion of the camera's matte box into the visible frame—something that occurs when it is moved forward to allow the lens to be changed. *Stonebridge Park* had made the spectator self-aware by its oblique references to voyeuristic visual pleasure separated from any need to 'intervene' and the tension between this experience and the narrator's subjectivity. Here, the process is embellished when the apparatus of film-making, its mechanical artifice, is suddenly revealed to the audience (see Figure 1.5).

This highly pronounced method of estrangement is heralded by a new, more explicit attention to visual experience itself. In this respect Norwood, as the 'site of my tragedy', might just as well be written as the 'sight of my tragedy'—reversing Giuliana Bruno's rendition of 'sight-seeing' as 'site-seeing' in her voluminous

Figure 1.5 Peabody Hill, London SE21, view through matte box, 1982, frame from *Norwood* (1983), Patrick Keiller. Courtesy of Patrick Keiller.

study of film *Atlas of Emotion* (2002).[74] The limitations that the camera places on conveying the fullness of experience are also emphasised by frequent references to non-visual perception, as in the summery sense-image of 'the smell of lavender'. 'I survey my former habitat with some detachment', says the narrator in the film's preamble, while the camera pans across an anonymous park,

> the Norwood of the sharp blow on the head – *against which one must maintain vigilance at all times with all senses other than the visual.* For our Maker, not anticipating such a threat, neglected to provide us with eyes in the backs of our heads. Instead, we must rely on the speedy recognition of the swish of the hammer as it passes through the air, and, if the wind is favourable, that faint whiff of male sweat from the armpit of the shoulder that swings it.

The unassuming 'all senses other than the visual' acts as a reminder of the spectator's situation, locked into the 'subjective camera' and a relation to the world that is mediated solely by visual means: as with *Stonebridge Park*, *Norwood*'s

---

[74] Giuliana Bruno, *Atlas of Emotion: Journeys in Art, Architecture and Film* (New York: Verso, 2002), p.15.

audio track was added in post-production, with no diegetic sound included. Later, the recurrence of 'the faintest smell of sweat' perpetuates this technique at the moment of the narrator's death, which, again, we only see the 'site' (or 'sight') of, rather than the event itself.

As in *Stonebridge Park*, *Norwood* pitches the 'iron grip of history'—figured as the inevitable forward movement of physical film, and time—against the narrator's capacity to slide between temporalities, existing beyond, between, and above them. 'The past is a closed book,' he declares (voiced, as in *Stonebridge Park*, by Keiller himself), but the point is that he is able to say it. It is in its cultivation of this abstracted temporal space occupied by the film, then, that *Norwood* is a 'reverie', a state of mind popular with the narrator's spectral 'fellow residents' in the building that is presented as his abode in the latter portion of the film (Frederick Gibberd's Pullman Court, in Streatham), which is imagined as a kind of ghost asylum where he takes refuge prior to his reincarnation.

The attempt to capture an atmosphere of '*unemployed* reverie' (my emphasis) also signals *Norwood*'s more direct relation to the social and political conditions of the early 1980s: the narrator's escapades in the world of business precipitate a more transparent commentary on the contemporary 'radical Conservatism' mentioned by Curtis than the passing reference in *Stonebridge Park* to the second-hand car market having, 'as a result of general economic circumstances that are now all too familiar', 'gone into recession'. In *Norwood*, the imagery is far more ominous. Indeed, in O'Pray's 1984 review of the film for the *Monthly Film Bulletin*, he claimed: 'Keiller manages to capture contemporary Britain with much more insight and "political" verve than most other films which claim as much.'[75] It is in this light that the narrator's mercantile intent 'not to paint the streets of Norwood, but to buy them' should also be read, pointing to a view of urban space as a commodity or asset to be purchased rather than an environment in which to live and think sociably.

The film's epigraph, taken from a letter written by Pissarro in June 1885 (misattributed as 1883) to his son Lucien, also a painter, renders the situation with some force: 'England, like France, is rotten to the core. She knows only one art, the art of throwing sand in your eyes.' These two caustic sentences foreground the arrival of ominous political imagery later on, when the narrator explains that there is 'evil afoot in this suburb':

> Dark thoughts and political atavisms abound, for this is the age of the small business. The petty bourgeoisie are in command, and the world has been told that Norwood does not like to pay its rates. Collectivity lies in ruins: children will tell you that the idea is unnatural, and even conversation is becoming inadmissible.

---

[75] Michael O'Pray, Review of *Norwood*, in *Monthly Film Bulletin* No.51 (October 1984), p.322.

He mourns an apparently lost sense of the cosmopolitan, having an 'interest in urbanism' that 'no doubt had its roots in a nostalgia for the promiscuity of the pavement, the irresistible possibility of a chance encounter with a desirable stranger'.

It is interesting to note the recurrence of the word 'promiscuity' here. In the preamble to *Stonebridge Park* this word characterized the doom-laden descent into a series of events unfolding outside of individual control. On one level, this idea does continue to obtain in *Norwood*, in terms of the narrator's overall trajectory—the failure of his marriage and his business, and his death:

> Those who make big decisions soon discover that, once made, they effect a destiny all their own, quite without regard for any administrative efforts on the part of the protagonist. So it was for me—the crime, once committed, determined all the subsequent moves.

Ultimately, this sense of gloom and fatalism prevails. At the same time, however, 'promiscuity' here seems to refer us to the Baudelairean 'chance encounter' and an aestheticized urban space such as that discussed in the 'Poetic Experience' essay. The narrator of *Norwood* might bemoan the contemporary social-political situation in London, but he adds that 'I think I can remember a time when things were not like that'. Whatever the case, the experience of 'falling in love in the street' becomes associated with a bygone age. Certainly a deliberate allusion to Baudelaire's famous poem *À Une Passante*, celebrated by Walter Benjamin in his writings on Paris, this moment sets the tone of *London*'s subsequent interest in Baudelaire and other French writers of the city.[76]

The 'Subjective Townscape' and Spatial Critique

Stonebridge Park and *Norwood* reveal various ways in which Keiller's cultivation of a distinctively mordant narrative sensibility, his exploration of the 'camera-I' as an analogue or vehicle of consciousness, and the discovery of places, landscapes, and environments that seem to be receptive to the kind of aesthetic speculation effected by these techniques, presage the use of the camera as 'an instrument of criticism' in his later work.[77] In doing so they indicate a remarkably consistent field of interest, undercutting the film scholar Anthony Kinik's contention that the

---

[76] Benjamin, 'On Some Motifs in Baudelaire', in *Illuminations*, p.166.
[77] Keiller, 'Architectural Cinematography', in *The View From The Train*, p.81.

tradition of literary urbanism outlined in Keiller's 'Poetic Experience' essay 'remained repressed for a decade after he got involved in filmmaking'.[78] In fact, as is by now clear, *Stonebridge Park* and *Norwood* offer convincing evidence of his creative interrogation of these sources from an early stage.

Further evidence for this is provided by a short 1982 essay for *Undercut* that was not subsequently included in 2013's *The View From The Train* collection or any other publications, in which Keiller characterized *Stonebridge Park* as a 'subjective townscape'. He also applied this phrase—his own coinage—to two other now obscure films, Clemens Klopfenstein's *Geschichte der Nacht* (1979) and Annik Leroy's *In Der Dämmerstünde, Berlin* (1980).[79] The 'subjective townscape' term certainly applies to *Norwood* too. Clarifying it, Keiller established a distinction from the tradition of 'city films': 'Walter Ruttmann's *Berlin, Symphony of a City* may be an influence', he wrote, 'but the didacticism of this or, say, [Dziga] Vertov's films is never called on. Instead the films contemplate and reminisce, they *moon* over what they portray.'[80]

The significance of the 'subjective townscape' term is revealed partly by what it excludes. In the late 1970s, the LFMC had been associated with a genre that came to be known as 'landscape film' and was associated with figures like Chris Welsby and William Raban, who managed the LFMC from 1972 to 1976. Their *River Yar* (1971–2) is symptomatic of this movement, which sought to explore film-making as a 'direct organic process'—*River Yar* was presented as a two-screen installation and used time-lapse effects to depict seasonal shifts. Though formally experimental, the work was politically disinterested—perhaps even uninterested. And it is notable that Keiller never refers to 'landscape film' directly in any of his writings, even when screenings of Welsby and Raban's work were listed immediately alongside his essays in *Undercut*. In fact, the 'subjective townscape' descriptor was probably intended, at least in part, as a device designed to distance himself from it. It suggested not so much an organic sense of connectedness and flow between nature and artifice as an interest in disjuncture, discord, and self-reflection: a quite specific combination of subjective 'reverie' and, because of its urban focus, an interest in the lived spaces of everyday life.

This lent the 'subjective townscape' a sharper political edge. Certainly, in his catalogue entry for 1984's *Cross Currents* exhibition at the RCA, where both films were shown, Keiller wrote of having 'taken up this tradition' running through the Surrealists and the Situationists

---

[78] Anthony Kinik, 'A Bridge Between Imagination and Reality Must Be Built: Film and Spatial Critique in the Work of Patrick Keiller', *Intermediality: History and Theory of the Arts, Literature and Technologies* No. 14 (2009), p.107.
[79] Keiller, 'In der Dämmerstunde, Berlin', *Undercut* No.5 (Summer 1982), pp. 45–6.
[80] Ibid., p.46.

with its knowledge that the appropriation of a (real) place in the service of a fiction is a political act, as the relation of private experience to public space is a political relation.[81]

If the phrasing here recalled the cadences of Situationist rhetoric, this was also appropriate to the genre and the other films selected by Keiller. For instance, Annik Leroy described *In der Dämmerstunde, Berlin*, which narrates a return to the city after two years' absence, as 'une dérive en noir et blanc'.[82] *Stonebridge Park* and *Norwood* show Keiller to be alert to these ideas too: the perambulations of the camera-consciousness certainly resemble the Situationist *dérive*, 'with its flow of acts, its gestures, its strolls, and its encounters', and the notion that 'urbanism renders alienation tactile'.[83] By 'laying bare the device', Keiller's cinematography in both *Stonebridge Park* and *Norwood* also sets out precisely the 'estrangement between man and his surroundings' that Walter Benjamin wrote about in his discussion of Surrealist photography, which defamiliarizes space in order to set the scene for its radical rediscovery.[84] In doing so, it draws on the 'tradition' that Keiller outlined in his 'Poetic Experience' essay, while reflecting on the artifice of cinema in a more politically charged manner than Welsby or Raban.

The sense and experience of marginality provides one other connecting thread between Leroy, Klopfenstein, and Keiller. By matching the isolation of the narrating consciousness with the marginality of the scenes depicted, Keiller's films allude to the Surrealists' interest in the Parisian 'zone'—the 'bastard countryside' separating central Paris from its suburbs that, today, is smothered by the *boulevard périphérique*—and to the spaces depicted in both Leroy and Klopfenstein's films. At the same time, they suggest the unnerving, eerie spaces of film noir: as Edward Dimendberg has written in his influential 2004 study *Film Noir and the Spaces of Modernity*, this genre was influenced by the post-war rearrangement of American urban space to follow a disparate, centrifugal rather than a concentrated, centripetal model, depicting figures on the urban 'periphery' who 'appear cursed by an inability to dwell anywhere', just as the narrator of *Stonebridge Park* and *Norwood* suffers from a restlessness and anxiety that is both produced by himself and which seems to be exacerbated by his environment.[85]

Stonebridge Park and *Norwood* can be seen to embellish this experience by elaborating on themes suggested by Keiller's interest in Surrealism. When reading

---

[81] Keiller, in Kardia (ed.), *Cross Currents*, p.34.
[82] Annik Leroy, 'In der Dämmerstunde, Berlin', *Le Soir* (Belgium), 25 April 1987 (copy held at the Brussels Cinémathèque).
[83] Debord, 'Theory of the Dérive'.
[84] Benjamin, 'A Little History of Photography', in *Selected Writings Vol. 2: 1927–1934*, ed. Michael Jennings, Howard Eiland, Gary Smith, and Rodney Livingstone, trans. Livingstone (Cambridge, MA: Belknap, 1999), p.519.
[85] Edward Dimendberg, *Film Noir and the Spaces of Modernity* (Cambridge, MA: Harvard University Press, 2004), p.7.

Aragon's thoughts on cinema in 'On Décor', Keiller would certainly have also read Paul Hammond's essay 'Available Light', which introduces the 1978 volume in which it was translated into English. Hammond's discussion elaborates on the idea of a tension between 'objectivity in time' and digressive thought: in film, he wrote, the Surrealists thought that 'objectivised subjectivity could transfigure and redeem our perception and experience of reality by letting us into the affective clandestine life of the material world'.[86] *Stonebridge Park* and *Norwood* build on the experience of marginality by cultivating this tension in cinematic terms, between what André Bazin described as 'objectivity in time' and the aberrant, digressive activity of subjective thought—somewhat analogous with Rees's idea of narrative in cinema as 'a grand detour', wherein the 'detour' also becomes a Situationist '*détournement*' of space against itself.[87]

Both *Stonebridge Park* and *Norwood* seem highly responsive to this idea, drawing on the Surrealists' notion of film-language approximating to the forms of dream-language and of man being 'soluble in his thought'. The two films' preoccupation with a 'haunted' sense of self, meanwhile, also reflects what Hammond remarked on as the 'magical materialism of film' with its power of 'making reality uncanny'.[88] It specifically recalls the agonized opening demand of André Breton's *Nadja* (1928): 'Who am I? Perhaps, if this one time I were to rely on an adage, perhaps everything would resolve itself on the question of whom I "haunt".'[89] Playing on the original meaning of the French 'hanter' as to frequent a place habitually or obsessively, just as his 'suis' (as in 'Qui suis-je?') punningly suggests that 'being' is also a kind of 'following', Breton's anxieties make their way into the fabric of Keiller's early short films.

This was certainly noticed by contemporaries: one review of *Stonebridge Park* noted the 'inevitable re-creation of a transformed world which comes into existence at the moment of re-counting'.[90] Of *Norwood*, Michael O'Pray emphasized the sense of a 'surrealism [...] where the stress is on the real'.[91] In a personal note sent to Keiller, Raymond Durgnat praised *Stonebridge Park*'s 'glassy-eyed schizo-lyricism'.[92] Meanwhile, the tension between fact and fiction that is established by the narratives' acute self-reflexivity is responsive to the way in which both *Nadja* and Aragon's *Paris Peasant* take the form not of fiction as such but rather stylized reportage: what Benjamin termed 'demonstrations, watchwords, documents, bluffs, forgeries', calling *Nadja* in particular 'a book with a banging

---

[86] Hammond, *The Shadow and Its Shadow*, p.10.
[87] André Bazin, 'Ontology of the Photographic Image', in *What is Cinema?* Vol. 1, trans. Hugh Gray (Berkeley: University of California Press, 1967), p.14.
[88] Hammond, *The Shadow and Its Shadow*, p.10.
[89] André Breton, *Nadja*, trans. Richard Howard (New York: Grove Press, 1994), p.14.
[90] Danino, Nina, 'On "Stonebridge Park", a Film by Patrick Keiller', in *The Undercut Reader*, p.105.
[91] O'Pray, Review of *Norwood*, p.323.
[92] Durgnat, loose leaf in CSM Study Collection, dated 2 February 1982.

door', on the threshold between imagination and reality.[93] By incorporating into his early narratives so many pregnant references to the activity of film-making and the materiality of film, Keiller produced work that seems highly responsive to this notion of the 'banging door', where fictionality is freighted with ironical ambivalence towards the very distinction between fiction and fact. In fact, it is this sense that cultivates Keiller's distinctive blend of the playful and the unsettling in these early films: if Vaneigem's 'bridge between imagination and reality' corresponds humorously with the physical bridges of *Stonebridge Park*, for instance, then Freud's suggestion that 'an uncanny effect is often and easily produced when the distinction between imagination and reality is effaced' is just as significant to these films' atmospherics.[94]

By building on the traditions picked out by Keiller, *Stonebridge Park* and *Norwood* form an idiosyncratic, critical and entertaining enquiry into space and subjectivity. But it is worth emphasizing that if these films '*moon over* what they portray', as in Keiller's 'subjective townscape' definition, then this suggests not only melancholy contemplation but also the subtle, warmer theme of a 'romance' with space that draws on the Surrealists' example. Ian Walker has written of how, in *Nadja* and *Paris Peasant*,

> a private city has been created within the public city, occupying the same space, only differently, more intensely. The physical geography of Paris is replaced by an affective topography, superimposing a sort of *carte du tendre* over the actual city.[95]

As in the case of the 'carte du tendre', a sense of a loving relationship with space is present here. If the unusual term 'moon' means 'to behave listlessly or aimlessly' and 'to daydream; to indulge in sentimental reverie', it also means 'to gaze adoringly' and to 'behave as if besotted'.[96] For all the mordant and paranoiac preoccupations of *Stonebridge Park* and *Norwood*, their exploration of marginal space and marginal consciousness, it is precisely this subtle *affection* for space—in spite of the frustrations it presents—that sets the tone for Keiller's return to the city for 1994's *London*, and which suggests the complex romancing of space undertaken by the figure of Robinson.

---

[93] Benjamin, 'Surrealism: The Last Snapshot of the European Intelligentsia', in Peter Demetz (ed.), *Reflections: Essays, Aphorisms, Autobiographical Writings* (New York: Schocken, 1986), p.180.
[94] Cited in Nicholas Royle, *The Uncanny* (Manchester: Manchester University Press, 2003), p.133.
[95] Ian Walker, *City Gorged With Dreams: Surrealism and Photography in Interwar Paris* (Manchester: Manchester University Press, 2002), p.53.
[96] OED.

2
A Vagrant Sensibility
Patrick Keiller's *Robinson* Films

In the 1990s, Patrick Keiller's film-making practice underwent a significant shift. The working title of his new project, echoing Louis Aragon's *Paris Peasant* (1926), was *London: or a feeling for nature*.[1] First screened in 1994 under the abbreviated title *London*, the film is over 80 minutes in length and in 35mm colour. It takes the form of a fictional documentary, which is to say that, although the footage consists of unstaged actualities, the film is structured around the peregrinations and preoccupations of two fictional characters: a disgruntled, disillusioned, yet urbane researcher named Robinson and a separate, accompanying Narrator figure who conveys his and Robinson's 'expeditions' and thoughts in laconic voiceover.

This fictional documentary model is sustained in *Robinson in Space* (1997) and *Robinson in Ruins* (2010), which complete a loose trilogy of witty and politicized, essayistic depictions of English landscape and townscape in a state of apparent disarray and disrepair. In each case, the alternately heated and listless lilt of the meditative voiceover recalls the first-person narrators of Keiller's earlier short films, as does the fact that neither Robinson nor the Narrator ever stray into the meticulously framed, almost exclusively fixed-camera shots—an absence that acts as a constant reminder of their fictionality.

Where the cinematography of Keiller's earlier work interrogated the idea of the 'camera-I', the 'Robinson' sequence and its sequels see those films' introspection re-articulated outwards, onto the spectacle of everyday life. At the same time, the 'Robinson' device means that the plight of individual 'private man' nevertheless continues to shape the three films' interrogations of space and place, which veer from the 'problem of London' to the 'problem of England' (in *Robinson in Space*) and ultimately the problem of 'nature' itself (in *Robinson in Ruins*).

Across these works, it is precisely through the prism of Robinson's fraught and disintegrating subjectivity that the spaces of England are transformed into an affective topography, and it is by this means that the films' distinctive take on space and place emerges. Robinson's disappearance at the end of *Robinson in Space*, for instance, dramatizes his affective response to market deregulation by means of his excessive dedication to a '*dérèglement*' or '*derangement* of the senses'

---

[1] Claire Barwell, 'Flanêur of London', in Ilona Halberstadt (ed.), *Pix*, No.2 (1997), p.159.

Landscape and Subjectivity in the Work of Patrick Keiller, W.G. Sebald, and Iain Sinclair. David Anderson, Oxford University Press (2020). © David Anderson.
DOI: 10.1093/oso/9780198847199.001.0001

inspired by the nineteenth-century French poet Arthur Rimbaud, his own disorientation seeming to be played out in the inconsistencies he discovers between the idea and reality of the English landscape. Later, in *Robinson in Ruins*, when his research is being collated in his absence, the ambiguity surrounding what has happened to Robinson forms a subtle critique of Martin Heidegger's formulation of 'dwelling' as entering 'in simple oneness into things'.[2]

It is partly by comparison with 2000's *The Dilapidated Dwelling*, a report on the condition of British housing that does away with the Robinson-Narrator arrangement and features head-on interviews to camera, that the effectiveness of the trilogy's distinctively digressive, meandering, maudlin, and often melancholic approach to space and spatial critique becomes clear. This chapter reconstructs that approach: focusing on the 'Robinson' trilogy, it shows how Keiller's work, informed by that of Walter Benjamin, elaborates a version of the melancholic's extreme 'loyalty to things' (presaging his later 'entering in simple oneness' into them) coloured heavily by Surrealism's 'metaphysical materialism' and its faith in the 'revolutionary energies that appear within the "outmoded"'.[3] In the process, it argues that, although Keiller's 'Robinson' films unfurl a vision of landscape and townscape scored by disarray, disrepair, and disorientation, they nevertheless discover in the same spaces the submerged possibility of radical, even utopian, change.

'A Fictional Journal about the Year 1992': *London*

London marked a pivotal moment in Keiller's film-making practice. His first feature-length film and his first to be shot in 35mm colour, it was also the first to garner significant funding, commissioned by the British Film Institute's Production Division with a budget of £160,000 (which was ultimately exceeded by £22,000).[4] Shot on a newsreel camera with assistance from Keiller's partner Julie Norris, the film is a rich and highly stylized account of the late-millennial city in social, material, and ideological decay, the 35mm format permitting a new level of sharpness to its depictions of space and place, matching the quality of his earlier slide collection. In the programme notes for its 1994 premiere at the Berlin Film Festival, Keiller described it as

> a film about a city in decline, and about the roots of that decline in culture and politics, in the form of a fictional journal about the year 1992. This saw the

---

[2] Martin Heidegger, 'Building Dwelling Thinking', in *Poetry, Language, Thought*, trans. Albert Hofstadter (New York: HarperCollins, 1971), p.157.
[3] Walter Benjamin, 'Surrealism: The Last Snapshot of the European Intelligentsia', in Peter Demetz (ed.) and Harry Zohn (trans.), *Reflections* (New York: Schocken, 1986), p.181.
[4] Iain Sinclair, *Lights Out for the Territory: 9 Excursions in the Secret History of London* (London: Penguin, 2003), p.300.

surprise re-election of the hapless John Major as Prime Minister; the renewal of the IRA's bombing campaign in mainland Britain; the "fall of the house of Windsor"; the bungled devaluation of the pound and its sudden withdrawal from the European Monetary System, and various other scandals, bankruptcies etc.[5]

Keiller's matter-of-fact description downplays the unusualness of the film, which, like its sequels, immediately strikes one as markedly at odds with conventional narrative cinema and almost as far removed from the supposed objectivity of documentary. In fact, for a film whose appearance, at least, suggests sober reportage, a mood of unsettlement strikes from the outset of *London*, when the opening of Tower Bridge is accompanied by the Narrator's wearied voice issuing a jeremiad on 'Dirty Old Blighty' and the 'horror of home'. Paul Scofield's narration is by turns affectionate and jaded, and we soon find ourselves caught up in what Iain Sinclair has termed 'a polemic that is half in love with the thing that it denounces', marooned in 'a fabulation backed by congeries of improbable fact'.[6]

London might well be read as a late addition to the 'city symphony' genre, in the tradition of Alberto Cavalcanti, Dziga Vertov, or Walter Ruttmann—or as a 'subjective townscape' expanded to this scale. A more recent precedent, though one with significant differences in style and tone, is offered by William Raban's 1986 *Thames Film: London 1984–86*, a maudlin account of the city's waterway narrated by John Hurt. With its self-conscious blend of fiction and fact, *London* might also be bracketed under the broad church of the 'essay film' as pioneered by figures such as Chris Marker: to be sure, the Narrator's early observation that 'it is not generally agreed that Montaigne lived for a time in London' both alludes to the progenitor of the essay form and—with Scofield's languid delivery gliding straight past the 'not'—functions as a marker of the narrative's wilful subjectivity and self-consciously devious approach to historical fact, recalling the dubious claims of Apollinaire's Baron d'Ormesan on his 'tours' of Paris.[7]

The film is shaped by Keiller's earlier time in London—the scenes more than likely collated from the slides of 'interesting buildings' he had been compiling from an early stage—and by the influence of Marker's *La Jetée*.[8] The impact of that film's still-image construction on *London* is certainly legible in a cinematography that seems to resemble moving postcards.[9] Partly a function of the laborious method of film-making undertaken by Keiller, with his heavy newsreel camera, this system is also significant in the way that it manages to invoke both *avant-*

---

[5] Patrick Keiller, 'Filming London Obliquely' (1995), p.54.
[6] Keiller (dir.), *London* (British Film Institute: 1994); Sinclair, *Lights Out for the Territory*, pp.302–3.
[7] See Keiller, 'The Poetic Experience of Townscape and Landscape, and Some Ways of Depicting It', in Nina Danino and Michael Mazière (eds.), *The Undercut Reader: Critical Writings on Artists' Film and Video* (London: Wallflower, 2003).
[8] Keiller, interview with Anna Price in *Artifice*, No.3 (1995), p.27.
[9] Keiller, 'On Chris Marker', *Artforum*, January 2013, p.156.

garde French cinema and the somewhat anorakish quality of the documentary slide-show. In this respect, Keiller's cinematography itself suggests the highly characteristic blend of high-art *bricoleur* and garden-shed 'tinkerer' in his film-making sensibility. At the same time, it permits comparisons with painted representations of the city such as Monet's scenes of the Thames, which the film at one point seeks to replicate. *London* is also heavily influenced by what Keith Griffiths referred to in 1994 as 'an important legacy of "poetic" documentary cinema' in whose spite 'the film still takes an audience by surprise': the stylized reportage of figures like Humphrey Jennings and John Grierson.[10] Keiller has written of his debt to Jennings; the brief appearance of the Queen Mother in *London* alludes to her cameo in Jennings's wartime documentary *Listen to Britain* (1942) even as her action—unveiling a statue of Arthur 'Bomber' Harris, head of RAF Bomber Command in WWII and the so-called 'Butcher of Dresden'—implicitly critiques post-war memorialization and uncritical patriotism.

The 'Problem' of Cities

If *London* doesn't document quite the physical destruction depicted in Jennings's wartime films, it nevertheless reveals striking levels of dilapidation. The Narrator deems the city 'all waste', and the camera lingers over its decrepitude. It is, we are told,

> under siege from a suburban government which uses homelessness, pollution, and the most run-down and expensive transport system of any metropolitan city in Europe, as weapons against Londoners' lingering desire for the freedoms of city life.

Returning home after seven years working as 'ship's photographer' on board a cruise ship (implicitly the one seen passing through Tower Bridge in the film's opening sequence), he 'is shocked by the increase in the number of people sleeping out' (see Figure 2.1) and by the population's blasé attitude to events such as the frequent bombings carried out by the IRA.

This decay and disenfranchisement are presented as symptoms of a subtler, more cynical destructiveness: that of London's civic cohesiveness and identity under the 'one-party state' of Conservative government, which Robinson sees as embodying English culture's supposed petty provincialism and antipathy to cities in general. Such an attitude can be seen to have emerged forcefully in the 1980s, during Margaret Thatcher's tenure as prime minister, and the reverberations of

---

[10] Keith Griffiths, 'Anxious Visions.' *Vertigo* Vol. 1 No.4 (1994), p.50 (https://www.closeupfilmcentre.com/vertigo_magazine/volume-1-issue-4-winter-1994-5/anxious-visions/).

Figure 2.1 People 'sleeping out' in Lincoln's Inn Fields, frame from *London* (1994), Patrick Keiller. Courtesy of BFI National Archive and Patrick Keiller.

Thatcher's laissez-faire 'monetarist' ideology form the basis of what the Narrator calls the 'problem of London'. That the historic centre of London—the City, with a capital C—was (and is) the epicentre of this ideology produces much of Robinson's frustration with the way that civic culture in England lacks an enlightened *polis* at its core, having instead only a barren 'civic void'.

Throughout the 1980s, the socialist administrations of Britain's cities had often been at odds with a prime minister who had referred to 'the pursuit of equality' as 'a mirage' and famously remarked that there was 'no such thing!' as society.[11] In 1985, a report on urban deprivation by Archbishop Robert Runcie delineated twenty-three points where the government 'was exhorted to improve its record on housing, homelessness, child benefit and other forms of support for children in poverty, and to support local councils grappling with inner-city decay', but it was largely ignored.[12] Indeed, the approach of Westminster politicians was cynical and destructive: the Greater London Council was dissolved in 1986, its offices at County Hall redeveloped as a hotel. Meanwhile, at a rare site of urban Tory

---

[11] Margaret Thatcher, 'Speech to the Institute of Socioeconomic Studies', 15 September 1975 (http://www.margaretthatcher.org/document/102769); Douglas Keay, Interview with Margaret Thatcher. *Women's Own*, 31 October 1987 (http://www.margaretthatcher.org/document/106689).

[12] Andy McSmith, *No Such Thing as Society* (London: Constable, 2010), p.223.

control, the Conservative leader of Westminster City Council, Dame Shirley Porter, was busy decanting social tenants out of marginal wards in order to protect her party's slim hold on power in the constituency of Westminster South.[13] Porter was only found guilty of gerrymandering in 1996; in 1992 London was still ailing. As the geographer Andy Thornley declared in his 1992 book *The Crisis of London*, the city was 'a mess,' crippled by untenable increases in transport costs, growing discrepancies of income, diminishment of the public realm, and the development of 'a fortress mentality based upon fear'.[14]

These concerns were paralleled by the problem of comprehending and representing the city—one that perhaps has deeper roots. At one point, Robinson argues that, just as London has become 'a city of fragments, no longer organised around the centre', it is now 'too thinly spread for anyone to know'. His turn of phrase is strikingly similar to the urbanist Ruth Glass's 1964 contention that London is 'too vast, too complex, too contrary and too moody to become entirely familiar' and that one of its chief problems 'is that of incoherence'.[15] And just as it recalls Glass's arguments, it anticipates the diagnoses of critics like Julian Wolfreys, who—looking backward from the new millennium—saw the London of the 1990s as characterized by a sense of its 'illimitable nature, and the experience of this condition'.[16]

London tackles these issues by bringing digressiveness into its essence. While Keiller depicts scenes of homelessness, for instance, quite directly (as in the shot of homeless people 'sleeping out' at Lincoln's Inn Fields), his film also incorporates this problem into its form. Robinson and the Narrator travel (on foot) as far upriver as the Thames's tidal limit at Teddington Lock; they visit Joshua Reynolds's house in Richmond just as they explore the Docklands, Brent Cross shopping centre, and beyond. The film is partly 'about' London, then, in this sense of moving or wandering about, and the two characters enjoy comparatively unrestricted movement through the city and its environs, although Robinson does note at one point that this is not a privilege shared by all of its citizens. 'In all the time he had lived in South London', the Narrator relates, while the camera observes a scene of a black driver being spoken to by police, 'he'd hardly ever seen them stop a motorist who was white'. This observation is left to hang pregnantly in the air, 1992 being a year of riots in the US after four white police were acquitted of brutally assaulting black motorist Rodney King in Los Angeles in March 1991, despite clear video evidence against them. Invisible as they are, Robinson and the

---

[13] See Nick Cohen, 'Dumping the Poor', *Independent*, 16 January 1994 (http://www.independent.co.uk/news/uk/dumping-the-poor-nick-cohen-unravels-the-homes-for-votes-scandal-engulfing-dame-shirley-porter-and-1407226.html).

[14] Andy Thornley, *The Crisis of London* (London: Routledge, 1992), p.4.

[15] Ruth Glass, with UCL Centre for Urban Studies, *Aspects of Change* (London: Macgibbon & Kee, 1964), p.xxvii.

[16] Julian Wolfreys, 'Undoing London or, Urban Haunts: The Fracturing of Representation in the 1990s', in Pamela Gilbert (ed.), *Imagined Londons* (Albany, NY: SUNY Press, 2002), p.193.

Narrator's skin colour remains ambiguous. Limitations on their vagrancy tend to result not from prejudice so much as misunderstandings, such as their untimely assumption that an inn located between Isleworth and Brentford might still offer accommodation to passing travellers.

At the same time, the Narrator speaks in a tissue of quotations drawn from diverse sources—principally those of writers exiled in the city such as Rimbaud and Apollinaire, whose activities in London are one recurrent point of interest for the film. He reads, for instance, Rimbaud's 1886 prose poems 'City' and 'Bridges' (which were written in London) in full, illustrating the latter poem with shots of London's river crossings. At another point, Leicester Square is 'imaginatively reconstructed as a monument to Laurence Sterne'—who is then, in passing, credited 'with the discovery of the cinema' for his gloss of John Locke's idea of duration and 'the succession of ideas' as resembling 'the images in the inside of a lanthorn turned round by the heat of a candle'.[17] In fact, in the disparateness, whimsicality, and frequent melancholy of these allusions, citations, and digressions, *London* presents a city not unlike another memorable contention of Sterne's *Tristram Shandy*: Tristram's claim that the world is a 'vile, dirty planet [...] made up of the shreds and clippings of the rest'.[18]

The Enigma of Robinson

These 'shreds and clippings' coalesce in the sensibility of their compiler: Robinson is a dandyish misanthrope who apparently carries on a 'bickering, sexual relationship' with the Narrator. Robinson, for all his vitriol, is a melancholic and simultaneously humorous figure. 'He isn't poor because he lacks money, but because everything he wants is unobtainable.' The scenes at the unveiling of Arthur 'Bomber' Harris's memorial, for instance, are cynical (Harris helped mastermind the 'saturation bombing' of cities like Hamburg, Cologne, and Dresden in the Second World War), but they are also drily funny: 'Robinson said afterwards that throughout the event he found it impossible to stop thinking about his father, but I've never met his father, so I didn't know what he meant.' If the two figures are so close, the viewer is forced to wonder why he could not simply have asked his companion for an explanation.

Though perhaps part of his self-fashioning as a *déclassé* intellectual, Robinson seems out of time and out of place, living in a council flat in Vauxhall but enthusiastic about the nineteenth-century city as it was depicted by French writers and artists. The number and variety of his enthusiasms recalls both Baudelaire's famous 'painter of modern life'—'an "I" with an insatiable appetite for the

---

[17] Laurence Sterne, *Tristram Shandy*, ed. Melvin New (London: Penguin, 1985), p.201.
[18] Ibid., p.40.

"non-I"'—as well as the sociologist Georg Simmel's idea that city life permits 'a kind and an amount of personal freedom which has no analogy whatsoever under other conditions'.[19] Yet he is oppressed by 1990s London, and although he often becomes an 'enthusiastic *flâneur*' when he is abroad, at home he falls periodically into sloughs of despondency.

Like Walter Benjamin, whose unfinished *Arcades Project*, composed in *Konvolute* or 'sheafs' of quotations and observations, offers a structural model for *London*, and who lived in a small apartment in Paris's 15th arrondissement before fleeing the Nazis in 1940, Robinson is trapped: in a small flat, with few friends. Seeing a 'small man reading from a book by Walter Benjamin' in Brent Cross shopping centre at one point, he embraces him, only to discover later that the telephone number he is given is that of a 'phone box in Cricklewood' and find himself unable to trace the man. This moment of fleeting, attenuated intimacy offers a model example of Robinson's London as an alienating 'ant heap' of a city, as the Narrator remarks, quoting the exiled nineteenth-century Russian anarchist Alexander Herzen—whose *My Life and Thoughts* is glossed parenthetically in the Berlin Film Festival programme as 'the motivating source which prompted the making of the film'.[20]

A part-time lecturer in art at the fictional 'University of Barking,' Robinson lives in Vauxhall, we are told, out of an enthusiasm for Sherlock Holmes. The precise connection remains unclear, bearing out his apparent susceptibility to interpretative errors or slippages, but his melancholic bent certainly recalls Holmes's famous tendency to slumps of 'brown study', just as the formal distinction between Robinson and the Narrator also draws on that between Holmes and Dr Watson. Robinson's characterization elaborates the maudlin and strangely dignified first-person narrators of Keiller's early short films like *Stonebridge Park* and *Norwood*, with their involuted tales of petit-bourgeois crime and meandering monochrome shots of indifferent suburban landscapes. Suggestive of Defoe's *Robinson Crusoe* (1719), his name might allude to the tradition of fictionalized accounts presented as fact—just as in another model offered by Defoe, his 1722 *Journal of the Plague Year* (to which Keiller's description of the film as a 'journal' of 1992 certainly alludes). The recurrence of the name in Chris Petit's 1993 novel *Robinson*, which tackles similar themes of urban disrepair and *anomie*, appears to have been sheer coincidence.

It seems clear that 'Robinson' is, to some extent at least, a mask for the filmmaker himself: throughout the film, we are invited to believe that the 'series of

---

[19] Charles Baudelaire, *The Painter of Modern Life and Other Essays*, ed. and trans. Jonathan Maybe (London: Phaidon, 1964), p.9.; Georg Simmel, *Simmel On Culture*, ed. David Frisby and Mike Featherstone (London: SAGE, 1997), p.184.
[20] Keiller, 'Filming London Obliquely', p.54; in the 2003 essay 'London in the Early 1990s' (in *The View From The Train*, London: Verso, 2013, p.86), however, it is merely 'one of the starting points'—a variation typical of Keiller's inconsistent comments on the film's genesis.

postcards of contemporary London' Robinson is making, which seem to transmute the city into a kind of 'collection' (alluding perhaps to Benjamin's famous writings on the affectations and affinities of collectors), are the images we are seeing. The idea of the character as a cipher, meanwhile, bears a clear relation with Keiller's comments on the choice of Scofield as the Narrator, selected not so much for the weathered urbanity of his voice as for its lack of clear class indication.[21] He remains stubbornly anonymous, with a name so chosen because it

> had seemed to me that Robinson was a name that someone who wasn't English might choose, either for a fictional character, or for themselves, should they wish to adopt an English name. It is found in many non-English contexts.

One of these 'non-English contexts' is Franz Kafka's unfinished 1927 novel *Amerika*, also known as *The Man Who Disappeared*, where it is specifically remarked upon as a pseudonym. Keiller has more than once referred to this as the source of the name.[22] Another potential source is the French verb *robinsonner*, Rimbaud's adaptation of the 'robinsonade', designating an imaginary journey or the process of letting the mind wander. This is perhaps the most significant reference point, reflecting the film's exploratory, arcane, non-systematic approach to knowledge acquisition. Robinson explicitly compares himself with the seventeenth-century diarist John Evelyn, whose Cabinet of Curiosities the pair witness at the Geffrye Museum in Hackney.

As Robinson and the Narrator travel about, their attempts to practise 'psychic landscaping' and 'drifting'—which begin with a search for 'the location of a memory' in Lambeth—clearly reflect Keiller's own interest in the Parisian Situationists of the 1950s and 1960s and their idea of 'psychogeography'. Defined by Guy Debord as 'the study of the precise laws of the geographical environment, whether consciously organised or not, on the emotions and behaviour of individuals', this has a key role in *London*, playing into the fickleness and bathetic sentiment that forms a counterpoint to Robinson's melancholy.[23] Indeed, his insights frequently suggest an alternative version of the city, 'imaginatively reconstructing' it in terms of an alternative set of memorials and waypoints which don't necessarily correspond with received wisdom—just as Leicester Square is not generally regarded, in its entirety, as a monument to Laurence Sterne.

One obvious example of this is the Monument—the huge column near London Bridge commemorating the Great Fire of London—which, although it does appear at one point, receives no comment; the easily-missed 'London Stone', meanwhile,

---

[21] Barwell, 'Flanêur of London', p.161.
[22] See Keiller, *The Possibility of Life's Survival on the Planet* (London: Tate, 2012), p.6.
[23] Guy Debord, 'Introduction to a Critique of Urban Geography', in *Les Lèvres Nues*, No.6 (1955) (http://library.nothingness.org/articles/SI/en/display/2).

Figure 2.2 The 'London Stone', Cannon Street, frame from *London* (1994), Patrick Keiller. Courtesy of BFI National Archive and Patrick Keiller.

a fragment nestled in a nearby wall facing Cannon Street station, is harnessed to suggest the slim possibility of renewed civic pride when Robinson designates the street a 'sacred' one and 'the number 15 a sacred bus route' (see Figure 2.2). Elsewhere, Robinson is constantly diverted by the fleeting prospect of a civic 'utopia', for instance at the bandstand of the Boundary Estate in Shoreditch, a pioneering social housing development built in 1900 on the site of the 'Old Nicholl' slum made famous by Arthur Morrison's 1896 novel *A Child of the Jago*.

'Shipwreck and Protestant Isolation'

Keiller has described *London*, somewhat offhandedly, as a 'joke about a man who thinks he would be happier if London were more like Paris'.[24] Robinson's enthusiasm for Rimbaud, Baudelaire, and the Situationists bears this out, but the comment also suggests that the 'problem of London' might, at least partly, be a problem with himself. This is foregrounded during a visit to Edgar Allan Poe's school in Stoke Newington and has to do with the peculiar esteem in which Poe

[24] Keiller, *The Possibility of Life's Survival on the Planet*, p.8.

was held by European writers of the nineteenth century: his short story 'The Man of the Crowd', explicitly set in London, fuelled its French translator Baudelaire's theorization of 'the painter of modern life' and in turn Walter Benjamin's designation of Paris as the 'capital of the modernity'. In the sense that it is about one man following another man through the city, it is also another formal model for *London*.

The trip to Stoke Newington, then, is a pilgrimage. To Robinson's dismay, however, he finds that Poe's school has been demolished, and 'opposite, just across the road, was the house in which Daniel Defoe had written *Robinson Crusoe*'. The moment is one of despair:

> Robinson was devastated by this discovery. He had gone looking for the man of the crowd, and found instead shipwreck, and the vision of protestant isolation. For weeks he read long into the night, until towards the end of August he began to venture out again with the fresh eyes of the convalescent.

This scene forms a crescendo. It was apparently unplanned by Keiller—who shot the film in an exploratory manner, 'essaying' in Montaigne's sense of the word as a trial or experiment, before composing the narrative around the images. The text's reference to convalescence echoes the state of the narrator in 'The Man of the Crowd', who is also recovering from illness and notes how 'the film from the mental vision departs' in the course of his betterment.[25] Perhaps Keiller was also aware that Benjamin formulated his own suicidal thoughts of 1931 expressly in terms of being 'a shipwrecked person, adrift in the wreck'.[26] In any case, Robinson's retreat to Vauxhall marks his confrontation not with the continental 'freedoms of city life' or any of the 'non-English contexts' of his name but with Defoe's vision of man as an island: the figure of whom Karl Marx wrote that 'necessity itself compels him to divide his time with precision between his different functions [...] and having saved a watch, ledger, ink and pen from the shipwreck, he soon begins, like a good Englishman, to keep a set of books'.[27]

'Necessity itself' hardly bespeaks dandyism, decadence, or 'utopia', and Robinson is brought back to the 'horror of home' with a bump. Yet such discords are a central feature of the film. The idea of a clumsily inartistic and inarticulate English culture is toyed with in the depiction of a sign reading 'Margritte' (for an exhibition of work by Magritte), and the same humour appears in the camera's deadpan focus on a McDonald's restaurant during a disquisition on Baudelaire's theory of Romanticism. Keiller's camera flattens high and low culture just as it

---

[25] Edgar Allan Poe, 'The Man of the Crowd', in David Van Leer (ed.), *Selected Tales* (Oxford: Oxford University Press, 2008), p.84.

[26] Barwell, 'Flâneur of London', p.160; Susan Buck-Morss, *The Dialectics of Seeing: Walter Benjamin and the Arcades Project* (Cambridge, MA: MIT Press, 1989), p.37.

[27] Karl Marx, *Capital*, trans. Ben Fowkes (London: Penguin, 1990), pp.169–70.

takes in both established spectacle, like Tower Bridge or the Trooping of the Colour, and odd things like the overlooked 'World Time Today' mechanical map display in Piccadilly Circus Underground Station or the gateposts at Vauxhall Park (to which Robinson 'listens'). The jarring effect of all this is mirrored by the film's score. A sequence from Beethoven's late string quartet No.15 in A minor, Op.132, is frequently repeated, becoming a kind of leitmotiv, but the studious sobriety of its long-held notes is offset by mock-bombastic incidental music from *The Lone Ranger* and a song by two Peruvian musicians named Carlos and Aquiles, apparently encountered by chance near the beginning of Robinson's research.

This 'flattening' technique also functions by defamiliarizing everyday scenes: footage of handprints in concrete or the ripples of rainwater in a puddle produces something like a poetics of loitering. As Iain Sinclair has claimed, this method—based around the pedestrian exploration of the city—cultivates a mood where 'we're ready to brood on stone until we become stone, until granite enters our veins'.[28] The technique, following the 'straight' documentary style associated with English Surrealist photographers like Tony Ray-Jones (and upon which Ian Walker has elaborated in his 2007 study *So Exotic, So Homemade*, which takes its name from a phrase contained in the Narrator's opening jeremiad), achieves an impression of composure and accident appearing to pun on the Surrealist principle of 'objective chance' or *hasard objectif*—where *objectif* can also mean 'lens'. Keiller's technique of composing the shots before writing a narrative around them has the effect of opening up his practice to the intervention of chance events; it also turns the process of filmmaking into a kind of primary 'research' in itself and the camera into an 'instrument of criticism'.[29]

This methodology makes *London* peculiarly alive to the city's shifting physical fabric and social character, its unexpected juxtapositions in keeping with Rimbaud's description of a city 'where all known taste has been avoided'. Where Keiller's camera replicates the perspectives of Monet's views of the Thames, for example (the extortionate price of his room at the Savoy Hotel, £4,000 a week, duly noted), it is equally drawn to a nearby poster advertising the 'Chippendales' male stripper show. In this way, high seriousness is constantly undercut by seediness and vulgarity, and the condemnation of contemporary culture is counterbalanced by a willingness to revel in its lurid decadence. In fact, it is precisely by means of this discordance that *London* might well be thought of—like Rimbaud's 'City' or 'Bridges'—as a 'prose poem' itself: 'musical without rhythm or rhyme, supple and choppy enough to accommodate the lyrical movement of the soul, the

---

[28] Iain Sinclair, *Lights Out for the Territory: 9 Excursions in the Secret History of London* (London: Penguin, 2003), p.302.
[29] Barwell, 'Flâneur of London', p.164; Keiller, 'Architectural Cinematography', in *The View From The Train* (London: Verso, 2013), p.81.

62 LANDSCAPE AND SUBJECTIVITY

Figure 2.3 The view of the Thames from Monet's hotel room, frame from *London* (1994), Patrick Keiller; the same scene as depicted in Monet's 'Charing Cross Bridge' (1903), one of a large series. Courtesy of BFI National Archive, Patrick Keiller, and the Saint Louis Art Museum.

undulations of reverie, the bump and lurch of consciousness', as Baudelaire put it in 1862 (see Figure 2.3).[30]

In these respects, and as with his work of the 1980s, Keiller's film is highly distinct from the contributions of contemporaries like William Raban, whose *Thames Film: London 1984–86* is particularly relevant. Taking a voiceover documentary form similar to *London*, this film adopts a self-consciously poetic approach to its subject. 'The river journey', declares Raban's narrator, voiced by John Hurt,

> unwinds a distant memory. Each moment has a particular meaning and relation to the past. Another time, different values, but the river transcends these changes [...] On this journey time is exposed. The past and present form one continuous pattern of unfolding experience.[31]

Raban's film also features recordings of T. S. Eliot reading from his *Four Quartets*, first published in 1943, giving explicit voice to the idea—expressed more subtly in Keiller's work—of distinct temporalities overlapping in the same space: time, to elaborate Raban's pun, 'exposed' not once but severally, in a complex layering of superimpositions.

There are a handful of visual overlaps between the two films, too. One scene in particular is almost identical—that of commuters walking along the pavement of London Bridge, as if visually echoing Eliot's 1922 *The Waste Land*. Raban's film ends with this sequence, which is its only non-waterborne shot. Yet the films are markedly distinct in their modes of subjectivity. The mordant, subversive wit of Scofield's monologue contrasts with the sombre tone of Hurt, a very different persona.

As an elegy for London's vanished docklands, Raban's film repeatedly swerves from contemporary scenes of industrial decay into transcendent formulations of Nature and Time, cutting archive footage from other films, books, and imagery together with its present-day scenes of drab decay. The gentle bobbing of the water-borne camera, approaching Tower Bridge, runs alongside Eliot's observation that 'I do not know much about gods; but I think that the river / Is a strong brown god.' Raban's Romantic construction of the city here recalls Wordsworth's 'Composed upon Westminster Bridge, September 3, 1802', with its sense of the morning as a space of eternal calm, transcending the city's busy actuality.

When asked in a 1998 interview about the 'landscape film' of Raban and Chris Welsby, Keiller remarked that although 'I very much admire' them, 'they are not part of the strand with which I attempt to connect. I try to maintain an ironical

---

[30] Charles Baudelaire, *The Parisian Prowler*, trans. Edward Kaplan (Athens: University of Georgia Press, 1997), p.129.
[31] William Raban (dir.), *Thames Film* (BFI: 1986).

attitude to the process of image making'.[32] It is this attitude that frequently marks *London*'s variance from *Thames Film*. This self-reflexivity is foregrounded during Robinson and the Narrator's own journey to 'the sources of English Romanticism', when the latter quotes from Baudelaire's 'Salon of 1846' that the Romantic project is seeing oneself 'from the outside, as if in a Romance'. An extra layer of irony is teased out of this scene by the way that Keiller's camera lingers on the garish spectacle of a McDonald's restaurant beside a busy road: high-brow and low-brow cohabit in a manner aptly illustrating Keiller's 'ironical attitude'.

London is also distinct from Raban's work in its professed intent not only to document its subject's affective capabilities but also to affect that subject in turn—echoing the interest of Keiller's former RCA tutor Peter Kardia in how artworks could be made to 'restructure experience'.[33] 'Robinson', we are told, 'believed that if he looked at the surface of the city closely enough, he could cause it to reveal to him the molecular basis of historical events, and in this way he hoped to predict the future'. This is seen as urgent in a city where the woeful effects of government policy are unmistakeable. For instance, while St Thomas's hospital is 'under threat of closure or amalgamation', a tunnel being burrowed under the Thames between MI5 and Terry Farrell's bombastic MI6 building—the two headquarters of the secret services—is subject to spiralling costs; the Narrator tells us that six general hospitals might have been built with the funds swallowed up by Farrell's MI6 building alone.

Since the government had at that time yet to officially acknowledge the existence of MI6, Robinson's sense of an 'atmosphere of conspiracy' attaching to this stretch of the Thames is deeply ironic. Later, his reaction to the election of John Major is one of straightforward 'spleen' (echoing Baudelaire) which begins with bathos but ends with the violent judgement that 'his job would be at risk and subjected to interference; his income would decrease; he would drink more and less well; he would be ill more often; he would *die sooner*'. Though it is ever perched on the edge of bathos—as in the film's opening scene when the Narrator remarks on being asked by Robinson to return 'before it is too late'—the gravitas is only partly tongue-in-cheek: after all, as Keiller observed in the 2000 essay 'Popular Science', 'we now know, on average, people in the DDR lived longer than Westerners—even wealthy Westerners—because they were more equal, and it is said that in advanced economies more people now die as a result of depression than in car crashes'.[34]

---

[32] Keiller, in Barbara Pichler, *Landscapes of the Mind* (Birkbeck, University of London: unpublished MA thesis, 1998), Appendix p.viii.

[33] Peter Kardia (ed.), *Cross Currents: Ten Years of Mixed Media* (London: Royal College of Art, 1984), p.8.

[34] Keiller, 'Popular Science', in *The View From The Train*, p.68.

The Redevelopment of Docklands

If Robinson is an urbanist swayed not so much by the 'ebb and flow' of the Baudelairean crowd as by the blips and dips of the free market economy, then the film's sequences in Docklands, an area deemed by Thornley 'the flagship for the Thatcherite approach to dealing with London's problems', are particularly interesting.[35] Once the heart of London's imperial trade, the Docklands of the 1980s were a vast, desolate space of industrial decay and poverty. Under Thatcher's administration, the area had been set to become an emblem of urban renewal; yet the governing 'monetarist' ideology meant that this did not follow a socially enlightened path. In fact, the government's creation of an 'enterprise zone' here in the 1980s had effectively lifted all planning restrictions and forced state-owned companies to sell their land in the area, so that the urban fabric became a peculiarly direct manifestation of free-market logic.

The result of this was often registered as disorientating. Iain Sinclair's 1991 novel *Downriver* depicted the Isle of Dogs as the 'Isle of Doges' or, in a not-so-subtle pun on 'value-added tax', as 'Vat City Plc', a city-state owned by the Vatican and occupied, in a nod to the association of Oswald Mosley's fascists with the nearby Cable Street riots of 1936, by 'blackskirts'. A contemporary sociological account of this area in Patrick Wright's *A Journey Through Ruins: The Last Days of London* (1991), meanwhile, was more sober but depicted a scene hardly less bizarre, describing lifelong Docklands residents who frequently found themselves lost or confused as street names and layouts changed rapidly and without warning.[36] The two writers here found themselves in unlikely accord with Prince Charles, whose 1989 anti-modernist polemic *A Vision of Britain* described the tower at 1 Canada Square, known metonymically as 'Canary Wharf', as 'a monument to the wrong thinking of the 1960s, but built in the 1980s'.[37]

For Robinson, 1 Canada Square becomes significant only when the development project falls into bankruptcy and stagnation, at which point he acerbically deems the phallic edifice a monument to Rimbaud, who had his own 'bickering' homosexual relationship with the poet Paul Verlaine during his time in London. Keiller's long-distance framing, which depicts the tower emerging from a distant shrubbery, renders it absurd, but the mood is nonetheless mournful: the stagnant tower, transformed into a stalagmite of reflection, seems to loom as a marker of mismanaged speculation and hubris (see Figure 2.4). In this it is akin to the idea of 'ruins in reverse' developed by the artist Robert Smithson in the 1960s: by opting to see a half-finished building as a ruin—rather like choosing to see a glass as half-

---

[35] Thornley, *The Crisis of London*, p.8.
[36] Patrick Wright, *A Journey Through Ruins: The Last Days of London* (Oxford: Oxford University Press 2009), p.227.
[37] Charles, Prince of Wales, *A Vision of Britain: A Personal View of Architecture* (London: Doubleday, 1989), p.54.

Figure 2.4 1 Canada Square emerging from a shrubbery, frame from *London* (1994), Patrick Keiller. Courtesy of BFI National Archive and Patrick Keiller.

empty rather than half-full—the artist is able to adopt a mood of melancholic subjectivity and critical reflection.[38] In this way Canary Wharf becomes a twin to the City office block pictured immediately after its devastation by an IRA bomb, with its window blinds fluttering in the wind.

The sequences detailed here make some sense of the otherwise opaque notion that Robinson's 'vision of the universe' is 'that of Lucretius'. The ancient Greek atomists' theory of vision was built on the idea that when we see things, a layer of the seen thing comes off and enters into the eye. Taken to its logical conclusion, this would mean that the act of observing something actually contributes to its ruination. Whether or not his subjects really are in a state of decay, the vision of Keiller certainly reproduces some version of this process, lending a patina of ruination to its subjects in order to provoke a mode of critical reflection inflected by melancholy. Such moments recall Gustave Doré's 1872 etching in which the imaginary 'New Zealander' regards the future ruins of London, offering the viewer chance to ruminate on the passing of time and the ephemerality of status and power.[39]

---

[38] Jackie Bowring, *A Field Guide to Melancholy* (Harpenden: Oldcastle, 2008), p.196.
[39] Gustave Doré, *Doré's London: All 180 Illustrations from London: A Pilgrimage* (Mineola, NY: Dover, 2004), p.98.

In an apt performance of *London*'s characteristic doubleness, it is at the very heart of the City that Robinson and the Narrator finally discover—or seem to discover—the 'conviviality of café life' and the ephemeral vision of Parisian sociability for which they have longed. The irony of its surfacing here, which elicits a flight of fancy from Robinson on the City falling into decay and ultimately being repopulated by artists, recalls Henri Lefebvre's reflection in *The Production of Space* that 'the spatial chaos engendered by capitalism, despite the power and rationality of the state', might 'turn out to be its Achilles' heel'.[40] At the same time, the Narrator dispiritedly reflects that it would probably be some time 'before the Bank of England re-opened as a discotheque'. The fact that the site depicted—the 'Café Libre'—is actually an abandoned film location lends a further layer of irony to this moment, while also alluding to the significance of film itself as a medium with the capacity to conjure imagined spaces out of real ones.

An Outmoded City: 'Reflective Nostalgia'

London comes to an abrupt close, with the Narrator stating that 'the next morning I woke at 5.30' and an intertitle announcing the date: 'December 9th, 1992'. The sudden disappearance of both Robinson and the Narrator, which amounts to a kind of vanishing act, is fitting: shortly beforehand, Robinson has reflected on London itself as 'the first metropolis to disappear'. The moment, shot from the portico of the Royal Exchange in an echo of a similar shot in Keiller's 1987 film *Valtos*, is as apparently dispiriting as a slightly earlier scene of bonfire night on Kennington common, where Beethoven's melancholy strings seem to mourn not only Guy Fawkes's failed attempt on power in 1605 but also, more subtly, the ineffectual Chartist meeting of 1848, which occurred on the same site.

Such moments might indicate a wholesale condemnation of the city. Laura Rascaroli and Ewa Mazierska take this view in their essay on *London*, arguing that 'Keiller's overall opinion of London's present is negative'.[41] In fact, the film's attitude is much more ambivalent. As Keiller himself declared in 1997, *London* constituted an attempt 'to make anew, to rediscover, to reconstruct' the city 'and reveal it as a place which might be in the wrong hands but is not irredeemable'.[42] Scenes of Notting Hill Carnival, of Diwali being celebrated in Southall, or of the hubbub of Ridley Road market in Dalston certainly depict lively social interaction worth defending and are at odds with the idea of the city as *only* an alienating 'ant heap'. This ambivalence is in key with Robinson's unconventional longings and

---

[40] Henri Lefebvre, *The Production of Space*, trans. Donald Nicholson Smith (Oxford: Blackwell, 1991), pp.62–3.
[41] Laura Rascaroli and Ewa Mazierska, *Crossing New Europe: Postmodern Travel and the European Road Movie* (London: Wallflower, 2006), p.61.
[42] Barwell, 'Flâneur of London', p.165.

the subtleties of his nostalgia. He mourns Gilbert Scott's red telephone boxes not for their iconic appearance, we note, but for 'the smell of cigarette ash and urine that used to linger'.

This is not the straightforward longing of works like *The London Nobody Knows*, Geoffrey Fletcher's 1960 book—which generated a 1969 documentary film starring James Mason—cataloguing fading fragments of the city and mourning the way certain areas had 'degenerated'.[43] In fact, the contrast illuminates *London*'s potency. If Fletcher's work, pining for some lost golden age, appeals to what the theorist Svetlana Boym has referred to as an uncritical 'restorative' mode of nostalgia, then what we find in *London* is more akin to her idea of an alternate, 'reflective' nostalgia. This, she writes, would be a 'sideways' nostalgia, characterized by a practice of 'lingering' and proceeding in a mode that is 'ironic, inconclusive and fragmentary'.[44]

London's patchwork structure, its experimental, essayistic methodology, and its melancholy subjectivity mark its allegiance to this mode. The subtle positivity here also brings the film into line with the transition that Boym describes between the nineteenth-century and late twentieth-century nostalgic: if the former 'dreamed of escape from the city into the unspoiled landscape', then the latter is 'the urban dweller who feels that the city itself is an endangered landscape'.[45] It is for this reason that the use of the camera as an 'instrument of criticism' is not wholly pejorative. As Keiller himself has pointed out, 'the whole point of making the film is rather optimistic in that the idea is to make everybody value the place'.[46] His use of 35mm film is significant in this respect: as he has remarked, 'people in London weren't used to seeing their everyday surroundings represented in 35mm cinema', which lent an added definition and 'unusual' sharpness to the scenes and sites depicted.[47] And audiences were encouraged to reflect on the space between actual experience of the city and its representation: as in Keiller's early loop of the destruction of the Nine Elms Coal Hopper, where the wall onto which the film was projected itself seemed to be demolished, *London* encouraged viewers to think creatively about the relationship between actual and imagined space. Viewers of early screenings at the ICA, for instance, would emerge directly onto the Mall, one of the film's locations, with the tension between real and projected spaces immediately suggested to them.[48]

Robinson's seeming nostalgia for a lost age cannot, therefore, be considered in any simplistic sense but rather has something in common with what Benjamin saw as Surrealism's 'substitution of a political for a historical view of the past' and parallels Giorgio Agamben's idea of the contemporary as 'that relationship with

---

[43] Geoffrey Fletcher, *The London Nobody Knows* (London: Penguin, 1962), p.55.
[44] Svetlana Boym, *The Future of Nostalgia* (New York: Basic Books, 2001), p.41.
[45] Ibid., p.80.   [46] Barwell, 'Flâneur of London', p.165.
[47] Keiller, Personal Correspondence.   [48] Keiller, 'London in the Early 1990s', p.84.

time that adheres to it through a disjunction and an anachronism'.[49] If the early 1990s, as Stephen Daniels claims, were a time when 'the cultural power of London has impressed itself [...] in various issues from high finance to heritage to homelessness', then Keiller's film dislodges any simplistic sense of nostalgia from its moorings, counteracting Prince Charles's yearning for 'long-established principles and values'.[50] Crucially, *London* doesn't create this tension by intercutting archive footage or overlaying old photographs onto present scenes, as in Raban's *Thames Film* or the centrepiece of *A Vision of Britain*, where a print of Canaletto's 1750-1 *London: The Thames from Somerset House* can be overlaid with a translucent photograph of the 1989 riverscape. Rather, *London* attempts some kind of resistance to congealing into established 'heritage'.

Rascaroli and Mazierska's criticism of *London* is based on the idea of the *flâneur* (Robinson) as a 'bygone figure'. In fact, the affectation of outmodedness was central to this figure even in nineteenth-century Paris—as Benjamin remarked, for the *flâneur* 'far-off times and places interpenetrate the landscape and the present moment'.[51] It is this kind of complexly layered untimeliness that is integral to the film's effect, including its submerged optimism. Untimeliness is also bound up with *London*'s documentary form. After all, as Julian Stallabrass has recently argued,

> [i]f in the early 1990s you had predicted that documentary work would come to make up a large and influential strand of contemporary art, the idea would have seemed absurd. It would have been said that documentary had surely had its day, perishing with the liberal politics that had nourished it; and along with it, naïve ideas about humanitarian reform and the ability of visual representation to capture reality.[52]

In fact, both Robinson and *London* should properly be regarded in terms of a deliberate outmodedness, aligning with the presentation of the city itself as a forlorn, decaying space. This actually contributes to the shadowy possibility of a radical change in its fabric, since the film is attuned to Benjamin's comments on 'the revolutionary energies that appear in the "outmoded"' within Surrealism, where a focus on the unfashionable or *passé* reveals the mutability of taste and culture, estranging the contemporary and revealing its instability.[53] As Keiller's camera travels around the city seeking out the forgotten, the overlooked, and the worn out, his film also cultivates utopian possibilities: for humanitarian reform or

---

[49] Giorgio Agamben, *Nudities*, trans. David Kishik and Stefan Pedatella (Stanford: Stanford University Press, 2010), p.11.
[50] Stephen Daniels, 'Paris Envy: Patrick Keiller's London.' *History Workshop Journal* No. 40 (Autumn 1995), p.7.
[51] Walter Benjamin, *The Arcades Project*, trans. Howard Eiland & Kevin McLaughlin (Cambridge, MA: Belknap, 2002), p.419.
[52] Julian Stallabrass, *Documentary* (Cambridge, MA: MIT Press, 2013), p.12.
[53] Benjamin, 'Surrealism', p.181.

even revolution; for the aestheticization of everyday life; for the solution thereby to the 'problem of London'.

Today, this veiled radicalism is doubly obscured by the patina of age, where 'restorative' nostalgia threatens to seep into the 'reflective'. It is notable, for example, that, in the 2003 essay 'London in the Early 1990s', Keiller repeated many of the formulations of the original 1994 Berlin Film Festival programme, yet he placed the word 'decline' into distancing quotation marks—'the film set out to document, among other things, the "decline" of London under the Tories'.[54] The subtle shift should alert us to the risk of the film becoming an object of uncritical nostalgia and remind us that its energies should be harnessed for a critical urbanism of the present. Yet it also highlights how ambivalent the film really is about its subject—'rather critical', certainly, but a profoundly sympathetic portrait of the city and its emblematically alienated citizen.

A Dissatisfying Success Story: *Robinson in Space*

Robinson in Space succeeded *London* after an interval of three years: it was filmed in 1995 and first screened in 1997. The film finds Robinson dismissed from his job and having suffered a period of 'deep depression'. It opens with a departure by train from London's Paddington Station to his new home of Reading, where he has latterly been commissioned by an unnamed advertising agency to produce a study of the 'problem of England'. The series of seven journeys that follow are separated by numbered, pastel-coloured intertitles and loosely follow the model of another of Daniel Defoe's texts, his 1724-6 *Tour Through the Whole Island of Great Britain*.[55]

Unlike Defoe's *Tour*, however, Robinson's excursions do not reach into Wales and Scotland: the specific object of his study is a perceived association of English 'gentlemanly capitalism' with industrial decline and dilapidation in the built environment. The film forms an attempt to qualify or correct Robinson's perception that 'poverty and dilapidation are the result of economic failure, and that economic failure is a result of the inability of UK industry to produce *desirable* consumer products'.[56] In this way it recalls Robinson's search for 'the location of a memory' early in *London*, which—as 'a vivid recollection of a street of small factories backing onto a canal'—took the form of a conventionalized light-industrial scene.

---

[54] Keiller, 'London in the Early 1990s', p.85.
[55] Patrick Keiller (dir.), *Robinson in Space* (BFI: 1997).
[56] Patrick Keiller, *Robinson in Space, and a Conversation with Patrick Wright* (London: Reaktion, 1999), p.36.

As Andrew Burke has observed, *Robinson in Space* 'begins with the vexing question, "What is England?" but insists that this question can only be answered after a spatial enquiry, a tour of the nation that will facilitate a piecing together of the system and the formulation of a larger organising logic, both spatial and temporal, behind it'.[57] Keiller himself has offered a more practical slant. In an interview appended to the 1999 book version of *Robinson in Space* (where the film's script is annotated with screenshots and asides), he pointed out that

> towards the end of *London* there is a line—'The true identity of London is in its absence'—to which the viewer might reply: 'Absence of what?' London began and grew as a port city; its port activity is now mostly absent, but it continues elsewhere. *Robinson in Space* was an attempt to locate some of the economic activity that no longer takes place in cities.[58]

Neither perspective fully captures the dynamic of the film as both a whimsical 'tour' and serious critique of political economy. Staging its enquiry into the 'problem of England' after the same formal mannerisms of *London*, *Robinson in Space* is structured around a deeply affective relationship with landscape and its traversal. Throughout, the subjective prism of Robinson's faltering psychology facilitates a distinctively melancholic mode, where a 'deeper sense of place' is arrived at through his own disorientation and disintegration. It is this method that forms the basis of rediscovering mid-1990s England as a profoundly dissatisfying success story.

'Space' and Spatial Theory

If it is the case—as in Svetlana Boym's analysis—that 'reflective nostalgia' proceeds in a mode that is 'ironic, inconclusive and fragmentary', then *Robinson in Space* sustains this mode with an irony lodged at its very centre. Although Robinson claimed in *London* that English responses to the French Revolution 'irretrievably diverted' English culture, he is himself perpetuating these responses by making an 'English journey', since one definite result of continental upheaval in the late eighteenth century was a rapid growth in domestic tourism. Political turmoil and a perception of danger in Europe led to a domestication of the so-called 'Grand Tour'. The construction of turnpike trusts in England helped facilitate a growing trend for travelling around the country, and the increasing fashion for self-

---

[57] Andrew Burke, 'Nation, Landscape and Nostalgia in Patrick Keiller's Robinson in Space', in *Historical Materialism* Vol.14, No.1 (2006), p.9.
[58] Keiller, interview with Patrick Wright in *Robinson in Space*, pp.223-4.

conscious 'pedestrianism' in the Romantic period, as critics like Robin Jarvis and Anne Wallace have shown, consolidated this shift.[59]

The journey of Keiller's film, conducted mostly by car, is an unconventional one and sustains the urbane and often absurdist humour of *London*. For instance, given Robinson's supposed cosmopolitanism and declared antipathy to the 'petty provincialism' of England in *London*, it seems ironic that the film's title appears to equate 'space' with the comparatively small area of England itself. A joke, perhaps, about Londoners' notorious regard for the rest of the country as completely alien, 'space' is also meant in a theoretical sense, setting the scene for readings of the Situationist Raoul Vaneigem, as well as Henri Lefebvre. The opening train ride finds the Narrator opening his copy of Raoul Vaneigem's 1974 *The Revolution of Everyday Life* and reading:

> Reality, as it evolves, sweeps me with it. I am struck by everything and, though not everything strikes me in the same way, I am always struck by the same basic contradiction: although I can always see how beautiful anything could be if only I could change it, in practically every case there is nothing I can really do. Everything is changed into something else in my imagination, then the dead weight of things changes it back to what it was in the first place. A bridge between imagination and reality must be built.[60]

The lines, which also appeared in Keiller's 1981 'Poetic Experience' essay, function as a hymn to the undulations of creative impotence. Here, they are matched with Henri Lefebvre's similar observation in *The Production of Space*, which had by now been translated into English, that 'the space that contains the realised preconditions of another life is the same space that prohibits what those preconditions make possible'.

These two quotations, setting the tone for the film, posit a space always on the cusp between the everyday and the ideal. In this way they appeal to a Surrealist conception of the 'convulsive' beauty to be found in the humdrum or mundane. At the same time, *Robinson in Space* perpetuates an English brand of Surrealism through wry humour and misunderstanding. Vaneigem's 'bridge' ends up being constructed from the strange concatenation of Robinson's preoccupations, errors, and desires. Indeed, Robinson's move to Reading, where he has been working as an English teacher, has itself been characterized by Keiller as a joke that plays on Robinson's propensity for autodidactic misconceptions, resulting from a misreading of another French theoretical text: Michel de Certeau's *The Practice of*

---

[59] See Robin Jarvis, *Romantic Writing and Pedestrian Travel* (Basingstoke: Macmillan, 1997); Anne Wallace, *Walking, Literature, and English Culture: The Origin and Uses of Peripatetic in the Nineteenth Century* (Oxford: Clarendon, 1993).

[60] Cited in Keiller, 'Poetic Experience', in *The Undercut Reader*, p.79.

Everyday Life (1974). As Keiller wrote in the person of Robinson for a 1997 interview with *Time Out* magazine (to date his only appearance 'as' Robinson), 'we started in Reading, because as Michel de Certeau has said: "Reading frees itself from the soil that determined it."'[61]

De Certeau is not mentioned in the film itself, but Robinson is explicitly on the tracks of Rimbaud. In Reading, he finds the 'coaching establishment' where Rimbaud worked as a French teacher in 1874 and praises the town 'with a euphoria reminiscent of that of Nietzsche for Turin'. The reappearance of Rimbaud (whose various dwellings formed a running motif in *London*) sets the scene for a bathetic clash of the plain and the picaresque, drawing on Enid Starkie's 1938 biography. Humdrum, suburban Reading is juxtaposed with the poeticization of everyday life represented by the poet.

As Kristin Ross argues in her 1988 study *The Emergence of Social Space: Rimbaud and the Paris Commune*, Rimbaud stood for a revolt against bourgeois docility and specifically the idea of craft or *métier*, which, as she observes, is 'that specialization, dating back to the justification of the division of labour in Plato's *Republic*', that is also 'simply the prohibition against doing anything else'.[62] Rimbaud's vagabond life stood for a flight 'from the idiotism of the *métier*'. His later works, she continues, 'stage the dialectic of the city and the desert (or the city and the sea in "The Drunken Boat")—the crowd and an absolute, vertiginous, nonhuman or more-than-human solitude: the Drunken Boat as incandescent atom'.[63]

To capture the method of *Robinson in Space*, Ross's case might be usefully juxtaposed with an essay in Roland Barthes's 1957 collection *Mythologies* that contrasts the aesthetic of 'The Drunken Boat' with nineteenth-century narratives of exploration epitomized by the work of Jules Verne. Verne's writing, claims Barthes, despite an 'obsession for plenitude', actually results in a vision of the world that is 'finite [...] full of numerable and contiguous objects':

> Verne in no way sought to enlarge the world by romantic ways of escape or mystical plans to reach the infinite: he constantly sought to shrink it, to populate it, to reduce it to a known and enclosed space, where man could subsequently live in comfort: the world can draw everything from itself; it needs, in order to exist, no one else but man.[64]

---

[61] Keiller, 'Longshots Special: Interview with Robinson', in *Time Out*, 8 January 1997, p.69.

[62] Kristin Ross, *The Emergence of Social Space: Rimbaud and the Paris Commune* (London: Verso, 2008), p.13.

[63] Ibid., p.21.

[64] Roland Barthes, 'The Nautilus and the Drunken Boat', in *Mythologies*, ed. and trans. Annette Lavers (London: Granada, 1973), pp.65–6.

For Barthes, the image of Captain Nemo's ship—the *Nautilus*—embodies this desire as the 'emblem of enclosure'; 'the most desirable of all caves'. Rimbaud's boat is its 'true opposite', 'the boat which says "I" and, freed from its concavity, can make man proceed from a psycho-analysis of the cave to a genuine poetics of exploration.'[65]

This perspective is acutely appropriate as a means of grasping Keiller's distinctive poetics in *Robinson in Space*, which imbricates the exploration of England with the fragmentation of Robinson's psychology. The Narrator declares himself concerned by Robinson's 'commitment to the "derangement of the senses"', and the film's exploration is ingrained with an atmosphere of homelessness, unease, and subjective bewilderment. The film meets its close by way of a transgression on Robinson's part—a theft of some aeronautical equipment seemingly motivated by his own slippage into madness: 'on the evening of the 23rd of October, he told me he was going out to steal a piece of equipment from one of the Saudi Arabian Tornados.' Later, 'on the 30th of October, without warning, we were told our contracts [with the advertising firm] had been terminated, and we heard on the car radio that a Tornado had crashed in the North Sea. I cannot tell you where Robinson finally found his utopia.'

Deregulation and the 'Derangement of the Senses'

In his response to *Robinson in Space*, Andrew Burke points out that Defoe characterized his own *Tour* as an 'essay'—a necessarily partial, exploratory, and subjective account.[66] If *Robinson in Space* is marked by a similar essayistic subjectivity, a sense of its own incompleteness (as Robert Mayer has observed, both *London* and *Robinson in Space* 'end inconclusively'), then this is also attributable to the disorientation of the subject.[67] The film also charts the decentring of economic life via the prism of Robinson's disintegrating subjectivity: Robinson's simulation of Rimbaud isn't only an elective affinity but a symptom of prevailing economic conditions. It seems to emerge from another implicit creative misreading, this time of Rimbaud's 'dérèglement' as 'deregulation' rather than 'derangement'. 'Deregulation', as Keiller later qualified in the 2001 essay 'Port Statistics', 'like repression, [...] inflicts pain and suffering. Unemployment, increased inequality, lower wages and longer working hours all lead to depression, ill health and shorter life expectancy.'[68]

---

[65] Ibid., p.67.   [66] Burke, 'Nation, Landscape and Nostalgia in Robinson in Space', p.13.
[67] Robert Mayer, 'Not Adaptation but "Drifting": Patrick Keiller, Daniel Defoe, and the Relationship Between Film and Literature', in *Eighteenth-Century Fiction*, Vol.16, No.4 (2004), p.807.
[68] Keiller, 'Port Statistics', in *The View From The Train*, p.48.

In his essay, Burke draws a useful comparison between Keiller and Defoe as both working at times when 'changing ideas of the nation are explicitly linked to radical changes in the workings of finance'.[69] Defoe, he remarks, worked 'at the moment of modern capitalism's accelerated early development'; Keiller 'at the end of the Thatcher-Major era, characterised by both the Tory party's jingoistic nationalism and leftist speculations on the imminent break-up of Britain'. But it is not sufficient to claim, as he does, that 'Robinson and his companion are wary of the process of privatisation and deregulation Thatcher insisted must underlie' the transformation of Britain into an economy based on heritage, tourism, financial services, and high-tech industries—even if he does acknowledge Robinson's encroaching 'paranoia'.[70] Rather, it should be emphasized that the shift enters into the very substance of the film and the beings of its two protagonists, throwing them into turmoil.

Anticipating the political scientist Wendy Brown's 1999 formulation of 'left melancholy', which she described as 'a failure of the left to apprehend this time' and associated with Walter Benjamin's cultivation of a 'mournful, conservative, backward-looking attachment to a feeling, analysis or relationship that has been rendered thinglike and frozen in the heart of the putative leftist', Robinson is conflicted by his yearning for a politics that, with its attachment to 'unified movements, social totalities, and class-based politics [...] literally renders itself a conservative force in history'.[71] His cynicism towards contemporary England's apparent devotion to finance and commerce, and its indifference to producing 'desirable' material things, is haunted by a sense of outmodedness. It is in this sense of untimeliness that the fleet of Routemaster buses, whose revolutionary design was modelled on that of World War II aircraft, can be understood as 'undeniably utopian'. Established tourist emblems, these buses are also part of the confusing spectacle of a lapsed future that is (or was) both technologically and socially progressive. These contradictions precipitate Robinson's psychological undoing.

The affective response of Robinson to the 1990s landscape inheres in both Robinson's characterization and the film's very form. *Robinson in Space* achieves 'a deeper understanding of space (place)'—the '*Stimmung*' referred to in Keiller's 'Poetic Experience' essay—by cultivating a mythology of place through a disorientating mélange of actual documentary footage and fictional histories, purloined and montaged mostly from literature.[72] After the train's arrival in Reading, for example, the camera settles on the 'Maiwand Lion' in the town's Forbury Gardens park, which we are told commemorates the battle after which 'Doctor

---

[69] Burke, 'Nation, Landscape and Nostalgia in Robinson in Space', p.16.   [70] Ibid., pp.23–4.
[71] Wendy Brown, 'Resisting Left Melancholy', in *boundary 2* Vol.26, No.3 (Autumn, 1999), p.23; pp.21–2; p.25.
[72] Keiller, 'Poetic Experience', in *The Undercut Reader*, p.75.

76 LANDSCAPE AND SUBJECTIVITY

John Watson was invalided out of the army and into his acquaintance with Sherlock Holmes'.

Later, Robinson takes the Narrator to see a declivity in Woking apparently left by H.G. Wells's Martians in *The War of the Worlds* (1898). Although this might be spurious, it is attended by the observation that '500 tonnes of Mars is estimated to land on earth each year'. The reference is to microscopic particles, but the context estranges this, becoming a typical example of fact and fiction interweaving in Robinson's subjectivity. On the road to Bristol, the pair hear a reading of Richard Jefferies's 1885 *After London* on the radio, thinking its apocalyptic vision to be a real report—'Robinson had been most affected by the book, which we'd heard one night being read on the radio, and had mistaken for a documentary'. This itself seems to allude to Orson Welles's famous 1938 radio broadcast of *The War of the Worlds*, which commenced as a mock news bulletin and was presented as factual. Later, in Whitby, we learn that 'it is about a hundred years since the *Demeter* arrived in Whitby harbour, its fifty great wooden boxes of earth consigned to Mr Samuel Billington, a Whitby solicitor, who had them sent on to Purfleet by train.' This portion of Bram Stoker's *Dracula* (1897) is presented as fact.

Robert Mayer has argued that this slippage between fact and fiction exemplifies Keiller's indebtedness to Defoe, even if this tour lacks the 'triumphalist air' of its forerunner.[73] As part of his argument that Keiller's films 'problematize the distinction between documentary and fiction films', Mayer points out that Defoe wrote at a time when 'the borderline that the new fictional form that would become the novel most frequently straddled was between fiction and history', comparing his practice with the 'autobiographical aspect' of W.G. Sebald's work.[74] In fact, this problematization of the generic 'borderline' marks an affinity with Defoe but is not new to *Robinson in Space*. Rather, it has to do with a way of seeing that has been a consistent concern of Keiller's: as he observed in the essay 'Architectural Cinematography' (2002), film space, because of its selectiveness, 'is always a fiction, even when the film is a documentary'.[75]

The *Stimmung* of *Robinson in Space* is also generated by splicing fictional references with practical observations on the presence of factories and power stations in the landscape—and on the difficulty of getting a good dinner. 'We very often ate in supermarkets', which have all the necessary facilities for 'the provincial spy or anyone in a hurry' (Robinson's self-fashioning as a spy again follows the model of Defoe). Yet the two still spiral into disarray. 'We were both ill from the cumulative effects of months of bad food and living in hotels', reports the Narrator, declaring of his friend that I 'did not think his move to Reading was a good one'. Despite Robinson's 'euphoria', he lives in a single room (before relocating to the Ramada Hotel), with poor pay, lacks job security or a circle of

---

[73] Mayer, 'Not Adaptation but "Drifting"', p.804.   [74] Ibid., p.805; p.803.
[75] Keiller, 'Architectural Cinematography', in *The View From The Train*, p.76.

acquaintances, suffers homophobic taunting, and is vulnerable. If Turin was where Nietzsche experienced his 'euphoria', moved by the same townscape that fed de Chirico's paintings, it was also where the philosopher finally went mad at the sight of a horse being killed. Aware, perhaps, of this gloomier side to the 'spirit of place', the Narrator is concerned for Robinson's psychological well-being: Robinson's autodidactic misconceptions are also a real inability to unpin fact from fiction, establishing a mythology of place that threatens common sense.

Appearance and Reality: 'Material Flows'

In the task of discovering precisely how the visual appearance of England relates to the functioning of the United Kingdom's economy, Robinson's bewilderment is frequently instated by an opaque thickness of incompatible or insoluble data. Discussing a moment when a new factory operated by Samsung is juxtaposed with Shandy Hall, where Laurence Sterne wrote *Tristram Shandy*, Andrew Burke observes that 'since neither Robinson nor the Narrator explicitly delineates the exact relation between Samsung and Laurence Sterne, the spectator is, by default, asked to speculate on possible connections'.[76] This is certainly true, and yet conjunctions like this are also clearly intended to disorientate, enacting Robinson's faltering state of mind: after all, there is no substantial deep channel of relevance between Sterne and Samsung apart from the subjectivity of the traveller and their spatial proximity. The search for a deeper principle of connection is sure to be in vain.

On a trip to Christ Church College, Oxford, where Robert Burton—writer of *The Anatomy of Melancholy*—was librarian, the Narrator explicitly connects this kind of disorientating search for an organizing logic or principle with disillusionment, placing a sense of alienation at the heart of an English melancholic tradition just as it takes refuge in facts about the building's history:

> 'The Jacobean melancholy, like our own', said Robinson, 'was the result of a disorientation. You and I are deeply disillusioned people.' Burton was vicar of St Thomas the Martyr between 1616 and his death in 1639. The porch is his addition.

'I think we were never so happy', the Narrator reflects, 'as on the day of our pilgrimage to the memorials of Robert Burton.' Yet although their melancholy is temporarily salved by his presence, disorientation quickly sets in again. At one point, a brief history of the 'Cliveden Set', the Profumo scandal, and Brunel's 1837

---

[76] Burke, 'Nation, Landscape and Nostalgia in Robinson in Space', pp.9–10.

78 LANDSCAPE AND SUBJECTIVITY

Figure 2.5 Brunel's bridge over the Thames at Maidenhead, frame from *Robinson in Space* (1997), Patrick Keiller; the same scene as depicted by Turner in *Rain, Steam and Speed—The Great Western Railway* (1844). Courtesy of BFI National Archive, Patrick Keiller and the National Gallery Picture Library.

bridge at Maidenhead—the site of J.M.W. Turner's 1844 painting *Rain, Steam and Speed*—are all passed through in a few minutes (see Figure 2.5). Later, we hear that 'Westland' has won a contract (worth £2.5 billion) to build army attack helicopters, 'in preference to the domestic options offered by British Aerospace and GEC. Westland is now owned by GKN.' The final acronym, which Scofield's delivery seems to freight with clandestine significance, is not decoded—although the expanded 'Guest, Keen and Nettlefolds' is hardly less opaque.

In fact, opacity is integral to the film's concern with how the UK can look so dilapidated and yet be the world's 'fifth-largest trading nation'. The Narrator quotes a maxim spoken by Lord Henry Wotton to Dorian in Oscar Wilde's 1890 novel *The Picture of Dorian Gray*: 'It is only shallow people who do not judge by appearances. The true mystery of the world is the visible, not the invisible.' A perpetuation of the tendencies exhibited in *London*, and Benjamin's enthusiasm for the Parisian arcades, this citation casts Robinson's interest in material things as an outlandish, even dandyish enthusiasm. Its wordplay also prepares us for the film's central, unexpected discovery: that England's ports and productive industries are actually doing 'rather well'. Observing the 'heritage' spectacle of Nelson's HMS *Victory* at Portsmouth, the Narrator remarks:

> Those of us aesthetes who view the passing of the visible industrial economy with regret, and who long for an authenticity of appearance based on manufacturing and innovative modern design, are inclined to view this English culture as a bizarre and damaging anachronism. But if so, it is not an unsuccessful one.

Looked at in this way, Robinson's disorientation is merely the disorientation of capitalism, under which—as Marx and Engels observed in the *Communist Manifesto* in 1848—'all fixed, fast-frozen relations [. . .] are swept away'.[77] It is, then, not so much a marker of 'decline' *tout court* as of a decline in the capacity of industry to produce an aesthetically rewarding spectacle in the eye of this unusual observer.

Robinson's reading of W.D. Rubinstein's 1993 study *Capitalism, Culture and Decline in Britain 1750-1990*, a staunchly revisionist account of British economic history, sustains this perception. Rubinstein's study argues against the so-called 'gentlemanly critique', which holds that Britain's economic decline in the nineteenth century was down to an anti-industrial culture whose roots were in the feudalist, aristocratic and anti-technological persuasion of the Public Schools—the perspective of critics like Stephen Daniels in his discussion of the shift from a 'north country' English identity to a 'south country' one in the 1880s, the period during which 'the industrial revolution came to be seen as an unEnglish

---

[77] Karl Marx and Friedrich Engels, *Manifesto of the Communist Party*, trans. Samuel Moore (https://www.marxists.org/archive/marx/works/1848/communist-manifesto/ch01.htm).

aberration' just as industrial might was being ceded to Germany and the USA.[78] Rubinstein's radical claim is in fact founded on a belief that the Industrial Revolution itself did not really take place, or at least not in a comprehensive way. The Thatcherite shift from 'industry to commerce' was 'entirely rational' because Britain, in the first place, 'was *never* fundamentally an industrial and manufacturing economy; rather, it was *always*, even at the height of the industrial revolution, essentially a commercial, financial, and service-based economy whose comparative advantage always lay with commerce and finance'.[79]

Rubinstein's account is certainly flawed. It relies on statistics that exaggerate and simplify a crude north/south binary, leaning on a 'south country' metaphor of its own that is unconvincing in its implication, for instance, that London had little or no role in industrial activity. Other statistics are equally misleading. An increase in owner-occupation of housing clearly does not necessarily indicate an increase in quality of life—even if, as Andy McSmith has observed, it did turn 'hundreds of thousands of Labour voters into Conservatives' by way of the 'Right to Buy' scheme introduced by Thatcher's government in 1980.[80] In this light, Robinson's reading of Rubinstein might well appear masochistic. After all, as the conservative politician and historian Ian Gilmour wrote in 1993, 'Rubinstein seems to be echoing official propaganda of the Eighties, when the damage the Government had done to manufacturing led it to extol the importance of the service industries.'[81]

Taking in the industrial spectacle, Robinson's professed aestheticism sustains an ironically melancholic posture: as the camera depicts cargo vessels approaching Southampton, the Narrator reads from Baudelaire's prose poem 'Sea Ports'. Reprising the appropriation of prose poems by Rimbaud and Baudelaire in *London*, he declares that 'a sea port is a pleasant place for a soul worn out with life's struggles'. Yet, as Keiller observed in 'Port Statistics', 'it is difficult to be certain, but judged simply by the numbers of people present, a modern port, for example, seems a reduced phenomenon compared with the sea ports of earlier times'.[82] The labour force in all cases has been hugely reduced, and the activity has become disparate. 'London', as Keiller notes, 'consists of the Port of London Authority's entire jurisdiction from Teddington Lock to Foulness—more than seventy miles of the Thames estuary.' Its largest single port is at Tilbury, 'but Tilbury itself is not a large port'. Efficiency has also increased: ships are sparsely crewed, and 'there are never many ships in even a large modern port; they don't

---

[78] Daniels, 'Paris Envy: Patrick Keiller's London', pp.214–15.
[79] W.D. Rubinstein, *Capitalism, Culture and Decline in Britain* (London: Routledge, 2002), p.24.
[80] Ibid. p.43; McSmith, *No Such Thing as Society*, p.235.
[81] Ian Gilmour, 'Napoleon Was Wrong', *London Review of Books* Vol.15, No.12, 24 June 1993 (https://www.lrb.co.uk/v15/n12/ian-gilmour/napoleon-was-wrong).
[82] Keiller, 'Port Statistics', in *The View From The Train*, p.73.

stay long, and crews have little – if any – time ashore, even assuming they have money to spend'.

Robinson in Space journeys to the kind of port activity found in 'out-of-the-way' places 'at the end of roads', and the sense of a certain disquieting shadowiness is replicated in the euphemistic language of the industries found there. At Sheerness, the Co-Steel plant is run by a Canadian firm that 'evangelises "total team culture"', but this does not mean a sense of camaraderie and mutual support. Rather, it is their term for conditions where 'overtime is unpaid and union workers fear identification'. The discoveries here anticipate those of Noël Burch and Allan Sekula in their polemical 2011 essay film *The Forgotten Space*, which charts the strange cosmopolitanism introduced by containerization, where huge volumes of commodities are on a constant global tour, operated by a migrant workforce that is all but invisible to those commodities' buyers and sellers.[83]

In fact, Robinson's (and Keiller's) findings in *Robinson in Space* do to some extent reflect Rubinstein's revisionism. As the film discovers, and as Keiller asserts in 'Port Statistics' (which is named after the same statistical publication of the Department for Transport to which Robinson refers in the film), while 'the UK's production of *desirable* artefacts is certainly lamentable [...] any perception of the demise of manufacturing industry based on its failure to produce technologically sophisticated, attractive consumer goods is bound to be overstated'.[84]

The crucial finding of *Robinson in Space*, then, turns out to be a discord between appearance and reality: 'the UK does not look anything like as wealthy as it really is. The dilapidated *appearance* of the visible landscape, especially the urban landscape, masks its prosperity.'[85] The 'spectacular dereliction' of the Liverpool docks, for instance (see Figure 2.6), seemingly 'symptomatic of a past decline in their traffic', is in fact misleading: 'in September 1995, when the images of Liverpool in the film were photographed, Liverpool's port traffic was greater than at any time in its history'.[86] The fact that the sacking of Liverpool dockworkers in the same month initiated a strike that would last until February 1998 showed that what had changed was the balance of labour relations and the sense of direct human connectedness with this industrial landscape—a prelude to the total mechanization seen at the ports in the south east. 'What has vanished', as Keiller observes,

> is not the working port itself, even though most of the waterfront is derelict, but the contribution that the port made to the economy of Liverpool. [...] The warehouses that used to line both sides of the waterfront have been superseded by a fragmented, mobile space.[87]

---

[83] See Alan Sekula and Noel Burch (dirs.), *The Forgotten Space* (Doc.Eye Film: 2010).
[84] Keiller, 'Port Statistics', in *The View From The Train*, p.45.   [85] Ibid., p.46.
[86] Ibid., p.37.   [87] Ibid., pp.40–1.

Figure 2.6 The 'spectacular dereliction' of the Liverpool docks, frame from *Robinson in Space* (1997), Patrick Keiller. Courtesy of BFI National Archive and Patrick Keiller.

Heritage and Stately Homes

In his essay 'Port Statistics', Keiller cited the work of cultural historian Patrick Wright, whose December 1994 *Guardian* article 'Wrapped in Tatters of the Flag' in turn referenced Anneke Elwes's report *Nations for Sale*, written the same year for the advertising agency DDB Needham. Robinson's own employment by an advertising agency in *Robinson in Space* might be taken as a specific allusion to this document, in which Elwes 'found Britain "a dated concept" difficult "to reconcile with reality"'.[88]

In his discussion of *Nations for Sale*, Wright explained that in Elwes's report 'our "brand personality" is entrenched in the past and, in America at least, has become almost entirely "fictionalized"'. He continued that 'Englishness, particularly, now often appears as a diminished and residual thing, arrived at only after all

[88] Keiller, *Robinson in Space*, p.196.

sorts of modern excrescences—from modern architecture to Europe—have been peeled away from it.'[89] This idea of an Englishness that has revelled in its own dilapidation ('since the Sixties, at least, we have lived and breathed disintegration, and found all sorts of creative opportunities there') is reflected in *Robinson in Space*, where Keiller notes, for instance, that the English music industry 'is one of the UK's most successful, and brings in more money from abroad than motor manufacturing, its products often characterized by sexual ambivalence, and a traditional English contempt for petit-bourgeois England'.

The context for Wright's critique of Englishness emerges from his 1983 study *On Living in an Old Country: The National Past in Contemporary Britain*, which deconstructed the idea of 'heritage' as a straightforward 'experience of identification' with a version of history that is mere 'gloss [...] an impression of pastness' or 'the new Biedermeier'.[90] Wright revealed how 'the national past—"our" common heritage—seems indeed to be identifiable as the historicised image of an instinctively conservative establishment', a fact made all the more sinister by the emphatic cross-party support for the 1980 Heritage Act, which allowed for property to be handed to the state in lieu of overdue taxation.[91]

'Heritage', Wright worried, seemed to promote the image of 'History' in the 1980s as a depoliticized, indisputable assemblage of truths. The issues that such a conception might generate are clearly pronounced in relation to the built environment, where a sense of the 'spirit of place' at some particular 'heritage' location might well segue into the impression of an unproblematical past and where the very idea of subjective bias would hardly make sense. This, as Wright showed, was integral to the project of Margaret Thatcher, who 'promised a radical break with the past, while simultaneously evoking a traditional idea of British identity and even history to be restored', and who proposed heritage and tourism—along with financial services—as a serious replacement for manufacturing industries.[92]

A key crisis point for Thatcher's seemingly contradictory desire was the stately home. Keiller does not mention Mentmore Towers, whose bungled sell-off in the late 1970s, when the government refused to accept the building instead of tax, precipitated the 1980 Act. But *Robinson in Space* does visit impressive houses, including Cliveden, Stowe, and West Green House, home of the former treasurer of the Conservative Party Alistair McAlpine, who lived there as a tenant of the National Trust. Outside the latter is an obelisk bearing an inscription which explains that 'this monument was built with a large sum of money which would have otherwise fallen, sooner or later, into the hands of the tax-gatherers'. An

---

[89] Patrick Wright, 'Wrapped in the Tatters of the Flag', *Guardian*, 31 December 1994 (http://www.patrickwright.net/wp-content/uploads/pwright-wrapped-in-the-tatters-of-the-flag-final.pdf).
[90] Wright, *On Living in an Old Country: The National Past in Contemporary Britain* (Oxford: Oxford University Press, 2009), pp.65–6.
[91] Ibid., p.43.   [92] Ibid., p.ix.

apposite quotation from Conan Doyle's 1892 short story 'The Adventure of the Copper Beeches' goes some way to shattering this obnoxiousness:

> 'It is my belief, Watson,' said Holmes, 'founded upon my experience, that the lowest and vilest alleys in London do not present a more dreadful record of sin than does the smiling and beautiful countryside.'

Such irony is at odds with the bombastic, neoclassical porticoes of suburban domestic architecture, and 'Robinson says that unless Labour wins a landslide victory in a general election there is always a Conservative majority in England.' Another inscription at West Green House reads 'Do What You Will'—a quotation from Rabelais—with the contemporary neoliberal veneration of the free market registered as a corruption of Rabelais's vision of an ideal libertarian society.

In the same vein, Robinson and the Narrator note the number of Jane Austen adaptations being filmed at that time, sending up the use of heritage as a mere 'style' and the use of 'History' as mere spectacle or 'the impression of pastness'. 'We knew of six Jane Austen adaptations under way, all involving country houses mostly in the west of England.' Keiller's ironic presentation of the Austen houses elicited the film scholar Paul Dave's suggestion in a 1997 essay that 'oppositions of old and new lead us to understandings of the relations between class, capitalism and historical change that lie outside the bourgeois paradigm' of progress and historical development—the Austen adaptations are recorded as 'non-agricultural land uses'—yet it also tacitly acknowledges that there is a serious economic activity going on here. Crass as the 'heritage' spectacle might seem, as a profitable industry it cannot be omitted from Robinson's study.[93]

Later, we are told that the stately home at Stowe, Buckinghamshire, is 'described by the National Trust as "Britain's largest work of art"', and it is there that Robinson pays his respects to Locke and Shakespeare, represented by busts in William Kent's 'Temple of British Worthies'. There is an irony at work here: Keiller's films seem to demand the aestheticization of the space, including the spaces of domesticity, and yet the National Trust's wider project renders the same desire suspect: as Wright observes, the organization's full name when it formed in 1895 was 'The National Trust for Places of Historic Interest and Natural Beauty', the two determinants confusingly overlapping so that 'historic interest'—a certain kind of historic interest, coupled with a privileging of the idea of private property—becomes part of that 'natural beauty'.[94]

The 'coalescence' of 'historic interest and natural beauty', as Wright claims in suggestively corporate language, risks producing 'a merger in which a

---

[93] Paul Dave, 'The Bourgeois Paradigm and Heritage Cinema', *New Left Review* Vol.1, No.224 (July–August 1997), p.111.
[94] Wright, *On Living in an Old Country*, pp.46–7.

conventional realism can be used to naturalise a bourgeois interpretation of history and society', eliding the way in which such houses—and the land associated with them—remain active forces in agrarian capitalism.[95] In this light, he concludes that 'the National Trust has become an ethereal kind of holding company for the dead spirit of the nation' where 'private property, the public interest and the national imagination seem to be so perfectly harmonised'.[96] This is precisely the miasma that Robinson seeks to critique, only to find himself frequently seduced and even overwhelmed by the view. At Cliveden, the Narrator notes that 'the view along the river was compared by Garibaldi with the mighty river prospects of South America'. The camera lingers on this privileged vista. If stately homes form an object of dismay, they are also havens for the affective sensibility; even if they do reveal Britain as a 'dated concept', their sheer seductiveness nevertheless seems to prevent the frisson of Surrealist 'outmodedness' from burgeoning into any revolutionary activity.

The Transformation of Space and the Fragments of an Imagined Future

In 1973's *The Country and the City*, Raymond Williams remarked that Jane Austen's novels cultivate a vision of an England constituted simply as 'a network of propertied houses and families', in which 'most people are simply not seen' and 'most of the country [...] becomes real only as it relates to the houses which are the real nodes'. Despite their weakness for an attractive river prospect, Keiller's characters' incorporation of Austen-like 'heritage' England into the humdrum mundanity of much of what they see and experience acts as a deft send-up of the period drama aesthetic.[97]

While maintaining this criticality towards constructed ideas of the 'national past', *Robinson in Space* also pays attention to visions of the future. At one point, the Narrator reads from the geographer Doreen Massey's 1994 study *Space, Place and Gender*:

> Amid the Ridley Scott visions of world cities, the writing about skyscraper fortresses, the Baudrillard visions of hyperspace, most people still live in places like Harlesden or West Bromwich. [...] Much of life for many people, even in the heart of the first world, consists of waiting in a bus shelter with your shopping for a bus that never comes.

---

[95] Ibid., pp.46–51.   [96] Ibid., pp.51–2.
[97] Raymond Williams, *The Country and the City* (Oxford: Oxford University Press, 1975), p.166.

Massey's wry remark shares the deadpan humour of Keiller's films, yet it is in one respect rather misleading: the environment of Scott's *Blade Runner* (1982) draws much of its power from the way in which a decaying, older urban fabric is simply overlaid with the new rather than being comprehensively replaced by it—a conventionalized noir depiction of Los Angeles intersects with an imagined cityscape. The ageing elements serve two main purposes: firstly, they make it clear that the city we are shown is in fact Los Angeles; secondly, they render this future more convincing because it seems to have followed the partial and inconsistent approach to urban renewal with which we are familiar in contemporary urban environments.

The cinematography of *Robinson in Space* cultivates similar disjunctions between drably outdated and 'futuristic' space. Its carefully framed scenes of the present often look oddly out of time: the bridges crossing the Tyne, for instance, with their different architectures and materials intersecting in a disorderly manner, present a seemingly haphazard and chaotic future cityscape even as they allude subtly to the perfectly functioning, stratified modernist city outlined in works like Le Corbusier's 1923 *Towards A New Architecture*. As in *London*, the suggestion is that the present consists partly of a lattice of incomplete, unrealized futures.

The molecules known as 'Buckminsterfullerenes' are central to this aspect of *Robinson in Space*, yet they have been overlooked in earlier discussions of the film. In his study of the essay film as a genre, for example, Timothy Corrigan writes as if they were people whom Robinson wishes to track down.[98] In fact, the term refers to an 'allotrope' of carbon discovered in the 1980s and named after the American architect Richard Buckminster Fuller, or 'Bucky', whose 'geodesic domes'—pioneered as a revolutionary architectural form in the 1940s—roughly anticipated their football-like truncated icosahedron shape.

Geodesic domes also stand for a lapsed vision of future landscapes: they are a recurrent trope of science fiction writing and are a prominent feature in texts like William Gibson's 1984 novel *Neuromancer*. In this respect, they form an implicit connection with the science-fiction allusions in *Robinson in Space* and also contribute to the suggestion of a landscape that, despite its dilapidation, is uncannily futuristic: just as Buckminsterfullerenes, Robinson finds, feature in 'more than one hundred patents in microelectronics, nanotechnology and other fields', structures closely resembling geodesic domes do actually appear in the landscape of *Robinson in Space*, at the US National Security Agency's 'listening station' at Menwith Hill (see Figure 2.7). Their strange, alien forms become a vector of problematic modernity—a vision of how the contemporary landscape might once have been expected to look.

---

[98] Timothy Corrigan, *The Essay Film: From Montaigne, After Marker* (Oxford: Oxford University Press, 2011), p.117.

Figure 2.7 The NSA's 'listening station' at Menwith Hill, frame from *Robinson in Space* (1997), Patrick Keiller. Courtesy of BFI National Archive and Patrick Keiller.

This problematized modernity also establishes itself through the film's use of trains. Even if Robinson and the Narrator travel mostly by car, train journeys figure prominently. A panning shot in Liverpool seems to replicate the train-bound swoop of Alexander Promio's early films there; like the trip out of Paddington Station at the film's opening, the moving camera literally 'sweeps us with it'. In the earlier scene, the dilapidated Victorian woodwork of the platform roofs at Paddington effects the same sense of temporal disjunction as the Tyne bridges and the Menwith Hill domes, and connects to what Hal Foster has described as the 'historical dimension of the uncanny' within Surrealism. The music over the announcements, which recurs later in the film, is connected with this: it is from *A Matter of Life and Death*, Michael Powell and Emeric Pressburger's whimsical 1946 film about a World War II pilot who, because of thick fog, is not scooped up into the afterlife but remains on earth after he has died, only to fall in love—all of which leads to protracted legal proceedings in Heaven.[99]

---

[99] See Emeric Powell and Michael Pressburger (dirs.), *A Matter of Life and Death* (Rank: 1946).

88 LANDSCAPE AND SUBJECTIVITY

Like trains, trams offered an early mechanism for moving-camera cinematography, and Keiller's work on this subject has discovered a contemporary urban scene uncannily similar in appearance to that found in the 'actualities' that were being made a century ago. His essay 'Tram Rides and Other Virtual Landscapes', as well as a 2007 exhibition at the British Film Institute called *The City of the Future* and another at Le Fresnoy, France, in 2005 ('Londres, Bombay'), picked up on this idea, inviting navigation through a 'virtual landscape' of around 1900 by means of films arranged on a series of interconnected maps. Drawing on the simultaneity of early cinematic depictions of space and the arrival of twentieth-century modernity, Keiller's work in these areas explored how the fact of 'virtual space' becoming 'much more pervasive' perhaps marked an early moment in the divergence of real and imagined space.[100] The publicity material for *The City of the Future*, for instance, included photomontages in which early film actualities were inset within a contemporary recording of the same location, demonstrating the 'relative stasis in city space' over the last century.[101]

In *Robinson in Space*, Keiller's own birthplace of Blackpool, with its flamboyant

Figure 2.8 T.H. Mawson's 'dream' of Blackpool, in *The Life and Work of an English Landscape Architect* (1927). Courtesy of British Library.

illuminations and brightly coloured trams, is described as holding 'the key' to Robinson's 'utopia'. The Narrator describes him quoting the architect and garden

---

[100] Keiller, 'The City of the Future', in *The View From The Train*, p.136.   [101] Ibid., p.140.

designer T.H. Mawson's statement that 'Blackpool stands between us and revolution'—in fact, as Keiller later noted in the 2002 essay 'The Robinson Institute', not Mawson's own phrase but that of 'an unidentified Lancashire businessman'.[102] Mawson's 1927 memoir *The Life and Work of an English Landscape Architect* describes his employment as the designer of Blackpool's Stanley Park in 1922 and his wider ambitions for renovating Blackpool as a whole. It includes an illustration of his bombastic neoclassical design for the civic centre and railway station, described as 'the town planner's dream' (see Figure 2.8).[103]

In the volume, Mawson admits that his feeling for Blackpool might result from the fact that 'I am a Lancashire man' but hymns the town as a resort for the region's workers:

> It may appear strange that in all the town-planning work of which I have dreamed, Blackpool appealed to me the most. The fact that I am a Lancashire man may account for this preference. Blackpool's unbroken stretch of golden sand, its bracing air, and the kaleidoscopic gaiety of its miles of promenade, combine to weave a spell of attraction.[104]

With the cadence of his prose curiously comparable to Baudelaire's 'Sea Ports'— 'the wide expanse of sky, the mobile clouds, the ever changing colours of the sea'— Mawson's text argues for Blackpool as an escapist paradise for the labouring classes. It is in this sense that it 'stands between us and revolution'. Keiller's own use of the phrase, however, seems to shift its meaning, so that the hedonistic atmosphere of Blackpool might actually *be* the 'revolution of everyday life' itself— Blackpool 'stands between' here and revolution in that it provides an unfinished model of liberated existence. As he remarked in conversation with Patrick Wright, 'Robinson says what he says in Blackpool because he is a Surrealist and believes in the carnivalization of everyday life. Blackpool is probably the nearest you get to that.'[105] This idealization of the town also revolves around the touristic gaze cultivated there: as Ian Walker pithily puts it in *So Exotic, So Homemade*, discussing the work of English Surrealist photographers like Tony Ray-Jones, 'it tells us something about Englishness that Blackpool can be both quintessentially English and not English at all, both central and marginal at the same time. Blackpool's exoticism is thoroughly homegrown.'[106]

---

[102] Keiller, 'The Robinson Institute', in *The View From The Train*, p.121.
[103] T.H. Mawson, *The Life and Work of an English Landscape Architect* (London: Batsford, 1927), p.343.
[104] Ibid., p.340.   [105] Keiller, *Robinson in Space*, p.230.
[106] Ian Walker, *So Exotic, So Homemade: Surrealism, Englishness and Documentary Photography* (Manchester: Manchester University Press, 2007), p.181.

90 LANDSCAPE AND SUBJECTIVITY

The *Ur-Past* as the Image of Hope

As Robert Mayer discerns, one key difference between *Robinson in Space* and Defoe's *Tour* is their confidence in what they set out to do:

> Defoe's 'gentleman'-narrator believes that he can both capture and render 'the *Present State*' of England and that the nation he surveys is both powerful and admirable. Robinson and his friend, by contrast, seem capable of doing little more than registering their peculiar vision of England and their highly personal feelings of distress, anger, and disorientation. At the end of *Robinson in Space*, Robinson himself is at best confused and at worst mad.[107]

In fact, Robinson's confusion and madness—as he sets off to sabotage the Tornado aircraft—is integral to both the method and outcomes of the film. It is clear that the discoveries or outcomes of *Robinson in Space* are owed precisely to

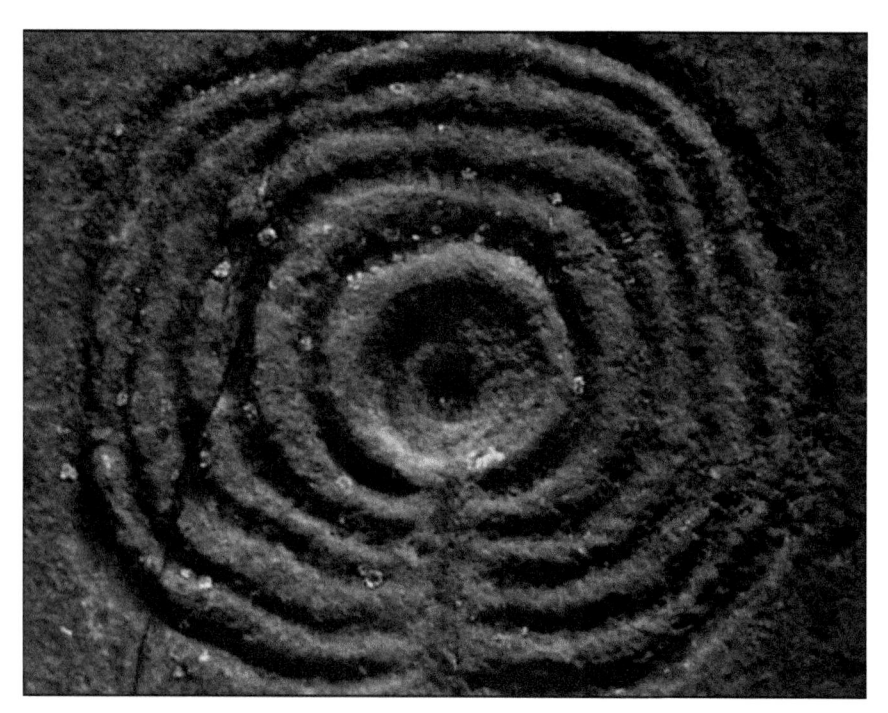

Figure 2.9 Rock art, Northumberland, frame from *Robinson in Space* (1997), Patrick Keiller. Courtesy of BFI National Archive and Patrick Keiller.

---

[107] Mayer, 'Not Adaptation but "Drifting"', pp.813–4.

the languourous disaffection and disorientation of its invisible protagonist, whose own psychological decay comes to embody that which he had expected to find in the landscape itself—and which he does find, only not on the terms he anticipated. This may be an 'inconclusive' ending, as Mayer contends, but it is not merely one of 'distress, anger, and disorientation'.[108] With Robinson's disappearance, the mood is still maudlin, emerging from a sense of decay and dilapidation into an unexpected, if deeply ambivalent, hopefulness. As the Narrator reports Robinson's transgression with the fighter planes, *Robinson in Space* closes with a series of images of Neolithic rock art in Northumberland (see Figure 2.9), reminiscent of rock art on Rombalds Moor, near Ilkley in Yorkshire, depicted in his 1989 film *The Clouds*. This sequence also captures Ian Walker's attention: he notes that Keiller 'had also wanted to make a specific study of them, linking them to some manifestation of the primitive in modern art', but makes no further comment.[109] In fact, this plunge into a Neolithic past also stands as part of the film's imagining of possible futures. It follows the pattern referred to in the 1935 exposé to Benjamin's *Arcades Project*, which plays on a quotation from French historian Jules Michelet to argue that 'wish images' for the future, in 'a positive striving to set themselves off from the outdated', react against the recent past by drawing their fantasies from the '*ur*-past'.[110]

In this context, such a conclusion marks Robinson's shaking-off of a present that has frustrated him. As Keiller later noted:

The presence of so many outstanding examples of this kind of art in the UK is very encouraging: rock art is abstract, international in its distribution (while also, in the UK, oppositionally northern); it was made by people who were mobile, and though they moved around within what we would consider a relatively small area—rock art has distinct local characteristics—it demonstrates a way of inhabiting landscape very different to that derived from long-term, essentially agricultural settlement, and the systems of landowning that have been developed from it in recent centuries.[111]

The rock art stands for an alternative version of the aestheticization of everyday life. And in so far as it also stands for a different mode of habitation, disrupting property relations, it represents a positive rendition of untimeliness: rather than the strange conservatism of 'left melancholy', here we at last have a nostalgia that looks forward as well as back—or, to put it another way, which looks back in order to look forward.

---

[108] Ibid., p.807.   [109] Walker, *So Exotic, So Homemade*, p.182.
[110] See Buck-Morss, *The Dialectics of Seeing*, p.114.
[111] Keiller, *The Possibility of Life's Survival on the Planet*, pp.18–19.

Domesticity and Decay in *Robinson in Ruins*

In his essay 'Port Statistics,' Keiller remarked that there was 'something Orwellian' about the effect of England's 'dilapidated everyday surroundings, especially when it is juxtaposed with the possibility of immediate virtual or imminent actual presence elsewhere, through telecommunications and cheap travel'.[112] In the essay 'The Dilapidated Dwelling', published in 1998 in advance of an eponymous film made for Channel 4 as 'a kind of pendant' to *Robinson in Space*—which has never received a general release—Keiller elaborated on the distinction between 'old space' and 'new space' in contemporary England:

> The dilapidation of *old space* seems to have increased, in an Orwellian way, with the centralisation of media and political power—by the disempowerment of local government, for instance. At the same time, experience of dilapidation is tempered by the promise of immediate virtual or imminent actual presence elsewhere, through telecommunications and cheap travel.

'As I stand at the bus stop carrying my bags in the rain', he continued, replicating Doreen Massey's image and alluding to his reading of Louis Aragon,

> I can window shop cheap tickets to Bali, or contemplate Hong Kong, Antarctica or Santa Cruz as webcam images on my Nokia; or I could if I had one – the virtual elsewhere seems, if anything, most effective as a mere possibility, as a frisson.[113]

Fittingly, at one point in the film itself, the Narrator and her partner consider having new insulation fitted to their home. Unable to afford the cost, they go on holiday instead.

If Rubinstein had argued for 'initially high and continuously rising standards of living throughout modern history' in Britain, then *The Dilapidated Dwelling* convincingly makes the case that this is not reflected in domestic architecture.[114] Constituting 'an attempt to anticipate the future' through 'an investigation of the predicament of the house in the United Kingdom', the film asserts this in part by running against an implicit connection that might be made between the 'insubstantiality' located in *Robinson in Space* and ideas of 'supermodernity' and the 'non-places' of contemporary logistics, arguing that 'modernity [...] is exemplified not so much by the business park or the airport, but by the dilapidated dwelling'.[115] It investigates why consumer culture's superabundance of relatively

---

[112] Keiller, 'Port Statistics', in *The View From The Train*, p.46.
[113] Keiller, 'The Dilapidated Dwelling', in *The View From The Train*, p.52.
[114] Rubinstein, *Capitalism, Culture and Decline*, p.40.
[115] Keiller, 'The Robinson Institute', in *The View From The Train*, p.122; Keiller (dir.), *The Dilapidated Dwelling* (Unreleased).

cheap commodities—the colour TVs, washing machines, and vacuum cleaners to which Rubinstein refers—is not matched by a ready availability of good-quality, affordable housing.[116] At one point, aping Tony Blair, Keiller's narrator purchases a Fender Stratocaster guitar, 'which didn't seem at all expensive', but the basic home improvements that she requires remain out of reach. Retail construction, as the film shows, is often industrialized (Tesco and McDonald's use prefabricated elements in the construction of their buildings), yet, apart from a few exceptions, the domestic landscape does not use industrialized methods of construction, and the cost of housing is disproportionately high.

As the Danish architectural critic Steen Eiler Rasmussen wrote in 1937, the English house from the late eighteenth century was a standardized object, a 'refined industrial product' that was built en masse without the need for architects and has become integral to the image of Englishness abroad.[117] And as Keiller avers in his film, 'the Georgian house was a prototype for urban dwelling until the middle of the nineteenth century'. Yet the problem with housing, he contends, is that it does not renew itself. Despite theoretical associations of modernity with movement, flux, and instability, the idea of the house seems associated with permanence. In this light, Heidegger's formulation of *dwelling*, appealing to the ideal of the Black Forest peasant's farmhouse, 'certainly sounds unfashionable'.[118] *The Dilapidated Dwelling* finds that where modern methods are used in housebuilding, such as at Richard Rogers's 'Montevetro' tower in Battersea, the products are prohibitively expensive.

If *Robinson in Space* can be read as an attempt to resuscitate a modernist poetic of trade, exchange, and movement—reflecting the preference of groups like the Futurists for 'big hotels, railway stations, immense roads, colossal ports, covered markets, brilliantly lit galleries'—then in its approach to the issue of domesticity *The Dilapidated Dwelling* anticipated the preoccupations of Keiller's subsequent film, *Robinson in Ruins*. This last instalment (to date) of the Robinson series rearticulates the 'problem of England' by eliding it with the problem of 'dwelling' in a deeper sense, approached by means of Robinson's own vagrancy and 'increasing insubstantiality'. Thematically, it revolves around Shelley's declaration in 1819's 'The Mask of Anarchy'—written in the wake of the Peterloo massacre— that 'All things have a home but one - / Thou, Oh Englishman, hast none!'[119]

Robinson in Ruins began as part of the Arts and Humanities Research Council's 'Landscape and Environment' project, undertaken alongside Doreen Massey and Patrick Wright. Massey's output was an essay circulating around the film's themes, while Wright's has been less concrete. In truth, the supposedly academic

---

[116] Rubinstein, *Capitalism, Culture and Decline*, p.43.
[117] Steen Eiler Rasmussen, *London: The Unique City* (London: Jonathan Cape, 1937), p.224.
[118] Keiller, 'The Dilapidated Dwelling', in *The View From The Train*, p.58.
[119] Keiller (dir.), *Robinson in Ruins* (BFI: 2011); Keiller, *The Possibility of Life's Survival on the Planet*, p.13.

and collaborative nature of this project must be taken in part as a pragmatic response to the decline in state funding for the cinema—which had underwritten all of Keiller's earlier work—and the exigencies of academic funding applications. As for the film itself, it documents a series of walks begun in January 2008 and is set against the political and economic background of the contemporaneous global financial crisis. In this atmosphere of heightened economic tension the film hopes, as Massey put it, to restage questions of landscape by asking not how we 'belong' to a certain place but rather 'to whom this place belongs'.[120]

The film opens with a tale of its own reconstruction from a set of film cans and a notebook discovered in a caravan. Robinson himself is absent. Having been released from Edgecott Open Prison—the fictional institution where he apparently served penance for the transgression with which *Robinson in Space* concluded—he went looking for a place to 'haunt' and found himself in a neo-Gothic house in Oxford, the city in which Keiller himself has lived since leaving London in the mid-1990s. Glossing Robinson's career so far, the film runs oddly against the assertion in *Robinson in Space* that Blackpool was his hometown. 'Of course,' states the Narrator, 'Robinson wasn't his real name, and he wasn't English. He'd arrived in London in 1966 from Berlin, before which his history was uncertain, having been attracted by the period's popular culture and the presence of so many prehistoric structures in the landscape.'

Robinson's absence (alongside that of Scofield, who died in 2008, as the Narrator) certainly weakens the cinematic artifice. There is no 'bickering' in this film, and Vanessa Redgrave's voiceover lacks something of the disaffected camp of Scofield's. As Paul Dave has argued, 'the absence of the indulgent intimacy sustained between Robinson and his former narrator-partner gives his present isolation and loneliness a sharpness lacking in the earlier films'.[121] The absence of incidental music, as Dave also points out, further 'acts to heighten our impression of his disconnection'.[122] As if to justify this decay of the original set-up, Keiller's writing on *Robinson in Ruins* placed a new emphasis on his protagonist's pseudonymity. In *The Robinson Institute*, a major 2012 exhibition at Tate Britain based on the film, and the accompanying book *The Possibility of Life's Survival on the Planet*, he mentioned the Robinson of Franz Kafka's unfinished *Amerika* (published posthumously in 1927) and the Misión Robinson, an anti-poverty initiative in Venezuela named after the pseudonym of the philosopher Simón Rodriguez during his 1806–23 exile.[123]

---

[120] Doreen Massey, 'Landscape/Space/Politics: An Essay' (with Keiller, *Robinson in Ruins*), p.12.

[121] Paul Dave, 'Robinson in Ruins: New Materialism and the Archaeological Imagination', in *Radical Philosophy* No.169 (September/October 2011), p.20.

[122] Ibid., 21.   [123] Keiller, *The Possibility of Life's Survival on the Planet*, p.6.

The 'Problem of Nature'

In spite of his absence, the Robinson of *Robinson in Ruins* is not necessarily dead. His 'increasing insubstantiality' should be read rather as a kind of dissolution into 'nature', conceived in broad terms that include the material remains of his films and notebook and the assortment of road signs, plants, and pillar boxes that make up his elective Oxfordshire cosmos. 'Nature' in *Robinson in Ruins* is highly inclusive—an attitude that reflects Keiller's arguments in the 2000 essay 'Popular Science'. As he wrote there,

> since pure science began taking a serious interest in the weather and other indeterminate, complex phenomena, the second law of thermodynamics has lost much of its melancholy allure, but phenomena like the fluctuations of the stock market have become part of 'nature'. Everything is 'nature'. Everything that exists in actuality, perhaps even every thought, dream or fantasy, must have some material basis or it wouldn't exist at all. Probably artists have always known this, but for many people it is distressing. How can human aberrations like nuclear power stations, neoliberal governments or uncomfortable clothing be 'natural' in the same way as wild flowers or thunderstorms? A spoilsport might assert that, though everything may be natural, not everything comes about in quite the same way; but that doesn't seem to diminish the sense of enlightenment.[124]

This attitude sets up a foil to the film's interest in the application of 'natural' metaphors to the logic of the free market. The 2008 financial crisis, whose echoes were still being felt acutely by the time of the film's release in 2010, renewed the pertinence of this concern. The Rabelaisian motif 'Do What You Will' is referred to again, and the crisis's roots in laissez-faire economics and misdealing in American mortgage markets connects to Keiller's earlier interest in deregulation, dwelling, and the shift to an economy based overwhelmingly on financial services and commerce rather than the production of material things.

The film is staged around the possibility that the 2008 crisis represents a 'historic shift' that might precipitate new modes of dwelling. At one point, on the site of a ruined cement works, Robinson 'encountered a moment of experiential transformation':

> A few days later, he made contact with our research team. He proposed that we establish an experimental settlement. In places of extraordinary biomorphic architecture, we would devise ways to transform land ownership and democratic

---

[124] Keiller, 'Popular Science', in *The View From The Train*, p.68.

government. We would pioneer the renewal of industry and agriculture after the decline of the global dollar and the disappearance of cheap oil.

We learn that Robinson has been reading Marx's doctoral thesis (on the differences between the Epicurean and Democritean theories of nature), as well as Fredric Jameson's more recent 'anticipation of the crisis'—his intimation in 1994's *The Seeds of Time* that 'it seems to be easier for us today to imagine the thoroughgoing deterioration of the earth and of nature than the breakdown of late capitalism; perhaps that is due to some weakness in our imaginations'.

Robinson in Ruins deals with this issue by positing an actual 'deterioration of the earth' to keep pace with the contemporaneous financial crisis. As Dave has asserted,

> whilst the earlier films take place within a context in which neoliberalism is so thoroughly naturalized that any revelation of the mechanisms of its ideological operations appears to offer a sustaining breakthrough for its opponents, the making of *Robinson in Ruins* accompanies a more extensive exposure of the frailty of that system in turmoil, and it consequently raises the possibility of genuine change emerging.[125]

And as Keiller himself has written, the 'ruins' of the film 'were of four kinds':

> architectural, in that a surprising number of the locations encountered were, in one way or another, ruins; personal, in that, by then, Robinson seemed physically depleted, if not actually a ghost; ecological, in that, in the narrative, he is enlisted by non-human intelligences anxious to preserve a long-term future for the biosphere; and economic, in that the film had been photographed during 2008, the year of long-awaited neoliberal crisis, its cinematography continuing until mid-November.[126]

Robinson, we learn, has taken a renewed interest in clockwork and solar-powered objects, with the objective of detaching himself from the national grid. Ironically living up to the 'vision of Protestant isolation' that was so horrifying in *London*, this appeal to the myth of complete self-sufficiency forms a mirror image of the neoliberal project and the perceived decay or non-existence of society as such, marking a renewed appeal to the idea of Robinson Crusoe as a template of economic man.

In a new development of Keiller's interest in Surrealism—already suggested by Robinson's 'haunting' of Oxford, as André Breton's *Nadja* 'haunted' Paris—we are

---

[125] Dave, 'Robinson in Ruins: New Materialism and the Archaeological Imagination', p.20.
[126] Keiller, *The Possibility of Life's Survival on the Planet*, p.10.

also told that 'as a Surrealist, he believed that the designers of artefacts should seek to emulate the morphogenesis of life forms, and pursued this and similar questions in encounters with flowers'. He reads from the journal *Nature*, which shares its name with that which the Surrealists' journal *La Revolution Surréaliste* sought to emulate (*La Nature*), and there is a great deal of 'straight' Surrealist cinematography in *Robinson in Ruins*. The camera lingers on the lichen on a road sign, primroses, opium poppies, orchids. These are often approached as if sentient: Robinson '*visited*' the lichen; later, he '*met* some primroses' on the verge of the A34 road, recalling Keiller's own 'encounters' with buildings in London in the 1970s and 1980s.

Robinson is also reading from Karl Polanyi's *The Great Transformation*, a 1944 work of economic history which traces the origins of modern capitalism's crises to the original emergence of market society in England. Polanyi's text, as Paul Dave writes, runs against the idea of laissez-faire capitalism as in any way 'natural', so that its involvement becomes part of the film's attempt 'not just to denaturalize capitalism (critique), but to see the non-human world and its relationship to the human one as an enlivening, incomplete, *strange commonality*'.[127] As a result, he explores alternative ways that nature and natural phenomena could provide models for economy and society: while the camera captures bees and butterflies rustling in flowers, we learn that 'he inclined to biophilia—the love of life and living systems—having discovered Lynn Margulis's view that symbiotic relationships between organisms often of different phila are a primary force in evolution' and had been inspired by Margulis's 'denunciation of neo-Darwinism and all capitalistic cost-benefit interpretations of Darwin'.

Robinson repeatedly returns to a road sign to Newbury, tracking the growth of a lichen around its lettering (see Figure 2.10). We are left to speculate on his initial attraction to the sign, but the hexagonal patterning of its reflective surface forms an oblique allusion to *Robinson in Space* and the Buckminsterfullerenes he sought there. 'Lichens', we are told, 'are examples of mutualism, in which all the partners benefit from their association. They are the dominant life form on about 8% of the earth's land surface. Many live in extreme environments. Some lichens are believed to be about 5000 years old, and among the oldest living things on earth.' They flourish 'in places exposed to nitrogen pollutants'—living, that is, on the waste produced by human activity.

As Richard Mabey declared in his 1979 study of marginal ecology *The Unofficial Countryside*, lichens 'are one of our most successful plant forms'. They are not seasonal, and they adapt to changing conditions. Observing a lichen in his local parish churchyard, Mabey explained that 'when there is plenty of nutrient-rich moisture trickling down the stones they are able to grow. When it is

---

[127] Dave, 'Robinson in Ruins: New Materialism and the Archaeological Imagination', p.23.

Figure 2.10 Details of road sign, Oxford, 2008, frame from *Robinson in Ruins* (2010), Patrick Keiller. Courtesy of Patrick Keiller.

dry they pass into a kind of petrified hibernation.' His book, a re-enchantment of peripheral and overlooked landscapes that should be seen as a forerunner of *Robinson in Ruins*, makes the case that 'the notion that a plant is a weed is the most effective barrier for stopping us looking at it closely'.[128] He specifically mentions *Xanthoria parietina*, the lichen found on the Newbury road sign, in what becomes a manifesto for new ways of looking at marginal plant and animal

---

[128] Richard Mabey, *The Unofficial Countryside* (Wimborne Minster: Dovecote, 2010), p.39.

life: many of his subjects eke out an existence just as fragile as Robinson in Keiller's film.[129]

Robinson's intense empathy with the lichen is striking. Later, it is described as his 'patron', to whom he describes his plans for a new settlement. These, apparently, are the 'non-human intelligences' that have 'enlisted' his services. The camera's narrow framing and extremely close-up focus invite us to forget that we are looking at a road sign, estranging the 'u' of the word 'Newbury' around which the lichen is clustered. Only the ambient sound of traffic serves as a reminder of the unexpected situation of this utopia, which otherwise carries a sense of post-human vibrancy obliquely recalling visions of landscape like that in Jefferies's *After London* or science fiction works like John Wyndham's 1960 novel *Trouble with Lichen*. In *Nature*, Robinson reads about a post-human planet, and the film takes up this idea by offering almost no images of people at all. Humans are barely seen outside of vehicles, and tend to be moving at pace, such as in the scene of a farmer running across a field to his tractor. The man's hasty progress across the frame produces an estranging effect, with a sense of the landscape itself as having become somehow uninhabitable.

As the geographer Matthew Gandy observed in a 2013 essay comparing Keiller's practice with that of Iain Sinclair and Chris Petit in *London Orbital* (2002), 'abandoned urban landscapes have frequently been venerated as places of reverie'. The 'marginal landscapes' of *Robinson in Ruins*, Gandy argues, are often presented

> as estranged or mysterious. [...] An enlarged aluminum street sign reveals a cellular surface pattern encrusted with lichens and other traces of life so that the familiar is rendered mysterious. The largely deserted locales recall science fiction scenarios in which modernity has dissipated into a new kind of wilderness.[130]

Yet *Robinson in Ruins* is more taciturn than its forerunners—the links made in Keiller's earlier films to works like *The War of the Worlds* and *After London* are suggested rather than explicitly remarked upon.

'Dwelling' and Heidegger's 'Simple Oneness'

Regarding the form of *Robinson in Ruins*, Keiller has discussed his reading of Edward Soja's 1989 *Postmodern Geographies* and particularly Soja's quotation from John Berger's essay 'The Changing View of Man in the Portrait'. Berger's

---

[129] Ibid., p.177.
[130] Matthew Gandy, 'Marginalia: Aesthetics, Ecology, and Urban Wastelands', *Annals of the Association of American Geographers* Vol.103, No.6 (2013), p.1310.

essay, written in 1969, posits a contemporary 'crisis' of individual identity and uses the analogous 'crisis of the modern novel' to describe how 'it is scarcely any longer possible to tell a straight story sequentially unfolding in time'. This, he claims,

> is because we are too aware of what is continually traversing the story line laterally. That is to say, instead of being aware of a point as an infinitely small part of a straight line, we are aware of it as an infinitely small part of an infinite number of lines, as the centre of a star of lines. Such awareness is the result of our constantly having to take into account the simultaneity and extension of events and possibilities.[131]

This quotation clearly had a strong effect on Keiller: in the exhibition at Tate Britain that was developed from *Robinson in Ruins*, the layout was originally planned in the form of stars of intersecting lines, ultimately figured in terms of the spaces between the objects on display.[132] Berger's essay had wider repercussions for the film, too. Tracing the history of portrait painting as an idealization of 'the chosen social role of the sitter' to the 'modern lonely desire to be recognized "for what one really is"', Berger avers that

> the measures, the scale-change of modern life, have changed the nature of individual identity. Confronted with another person today, we are aware, through this person, of forces operating in directions which were unimaginable before the turn of the century.[133]

It is this that gives way to his 'star of lines' analogy. Yet his concluding remark is that 'the demands of modern vision are incompatible with the singularity of viewpoint which is the prerequisite for a static-painted "likeness"'.[134]

The extended static-camera sequences in *Robinson in Ruins* might be read as an oblique confrontation with this problem, for, just as it discusses the question of markets and especially the idea of the free market as natural, ruminating on the 2008 financial crisis, *Robinson in Ruins* also stages and unfolds the complex question of 'dwelling'. Keiller's camera lingers or 'dwells' for improbable durations—on a field being harvested; on a spider building its web (while the mortgage market chaos is described). In the process, the 'cinematic thinking' developed in *London* reaches its apogee: frequent extended periods with no voiceover emphasize duration in and of itself, and the estranging effect of this is highly pronounced.

---

[131] John Berger, 'The Changing View of Man in the Portrait', in Geoff Dyer (ed.), *Selected Essays* (London: Bloomsbury, 2014), pp.101–2.
[132] Patrick Keiller, interview with David Anderson, in *The White Review*, January 2014 (http://www.thewhitereview.org/feature/interview-with-patrick-keiller/).
[133] Ibid., pp.100–1.   [134] Ibid., p.102.

The question of 'dwelling' is processed in other ways, too. One of the film's recurrent leitmotivs is the neo-Gothic house that Robinson 'haunts', which is being renovated rather than demolished and rebuilt—a process that offers a structuring rhythm to the film. Another is the somewhat dour sculpture 'Together', outside a branch of the German supermarket chain Lidl (which opened its first UK shop in 1994), sited where the Morris motor works once stood in Oxford—a location whose replacement of productive industry with commercial exchange and consumption makes it typical of Keiller's interests.

At one point, Robinson buys some alcohol from the store. In a characteristic blend of the low-brow and the high-brow, its label reminds him of Martin Heidegger's discussion of Black Forest peasants and his idea of 'dwelling' as the process of entering 'in simple oneness into things'. The phrase is from the essay 'Building Dwelling Thinking' ('*Bauen Wohnen Denken*'), a gnomic, incantatory text originally written in 1951 that discusses man's place in the 'fourfold' of earth, sky, divinities, and mortals.[135] Keiller had also quoted Heidegger's comments in the essay of 'The Dilapidated Dwelling', noting:

> This was the essay invoked by Kenneth Frampton towards the end of his *Modern Architecture: A Critical History* as a recognition of a quality of experience that many believed modern building had lost, and Richard Sennett, in a lecture of 1992, pointed out that Heidegger neglected the stupefying nature of *dwelling*, and that in fact *dwelling* and *thinking* are antithetical. The creativity of cities, said Sennett, arises from their being sites of unresolved conflict between *thinking* and *dwelling*.[136]

Sennett's idealization of the city, and his idea of 'dwelling' as 'stupefying', recalls the Futurists' sneering approach to stability and rootedness. Yet, in certain respects, Heidegger's text may not be so regressive as it initially seems. His fall from grace after the publication of the so-called *Black Notebooks* in 2014 (which evidenced his willing co-operation with the Nazi regime after 1933) must be circumnavigated a little here: the claim that 'only if we are capable of dwelling, then can we build' does not simply idealize the life of Black Forest peasants. 'Our reference to the Black Forest farm', he writes, 'in no way means that we should or could go back to building such houses; rather, it illustrates by a dwelling that *has been* how *it* was able to build.'[137] If his point is not to venerate any supposed rural harmony so much as to assert that an appropriate type of building should emerge from the mode of dwelling of a particular people, then this is something that

---

[135] Martin Heidegger, 'Building Dwelling Thinking', in *Poetry, Language, Thought*, trans. Albert Hofstadter (New York: HarperCollins, 1971), p.148.
[136] Keiller, 'The Dilapidated Dwelling', in *The View From The Train*, p.58.
[137] Heidegger, 'Building Dwelling Thinking', p.160.

Keiller's films, in their critique of domestic dilapidation, also call for. In the case of *Robinson in Ruins*, Keiller has also referred to Theodor Adorno's contention in *Minima Moralia* (1951) that 'dwelling, in the proper sense, is now impossible'.[138] Although Robinson (who in *London* was described as 'a modernist') might seem to share this view, espoused in 1944 when Adorno himself had fled the Nazi regime to live in America, his own material decay acts as an oblique criticism of the problems that a wholesale devotion to it can bring about. And if it is, as Adorno joylessly announced in the same fragment, 'part of morality not to be at home in one's home', then Robinson's dissolution might well be taken to represent the inevitable result of his attempt to hold to such a demanding proposition.[139]

Here we might find an unexpected logic behind Keiller's cinematic practice in *Robinson in Ruins*: just as Robinson himself is deprived of stability, rootedness, or dwelling, so these repressed needs are displaced into the camerawork of the film. Robinson's vagrancy itself precipitates the cinematic practice of 'dwelling *on*' things, as if some form of dwelling is ultimately inescapable. Many of the shots in the film are extremely long takes during which a whole sequence of subtle shifts in light can be fully registered by the viewer, the clouds moving slowly across the frame. Voiceover is also absent for long stretches, frustrating audiences attuned to the relatively rapid analytic montage of conventional narrative cinema, and drawing our attention to the form's pure duration. In a protracted sequence depicting the wheat harvest, as the sunlight filters through the shifting clouds, this in itself becomes a reminder of seasonality, juxtaposing the 'natural' shift of the seasons against the requirements of the marketplace and fears that early rain will render a harvest either less profitable or entirely worthless.

In her response to the film, Massey pinpointed precisely this relation between duration, stillness, and the global marketplace. 'These long takes', she wrote, 'give us, in the midst of the rush and flow of globalisation, a certain stillness. But they are not stills. They are about duration. They tell us of "becoming", in place.'[140] As she remarks of one scene, 'the camera stays on the butterflies working the teasel for four minutes and 15 seconds.' The long scenes of harvesting are paired with predictions of the weather and comments on the fluctuating value of the grain, but the spider weaving its web, which we see for a full two minutes and fourteen seconds during a description of the collapse of various banks, becomes both antidote to and oblique comment on 'the complexities of global capital; the pretensions and attendant subordinations of geopolitics'.[141]

Reminiscent of Keiller's interest in early film 'actualities' and the 'backwoods' activities of the London Film-Makers' Co-operative, one other effect of the shots' length is an increased sense of them as discrete elements or fragments, whose

---

[138] Theodor Adorno, *Minima Moralia: Reflections from Damaged Life*, trans. E.F.N. Jephcott (London: Verso, 2005), pp.38–9.
[139] Ibid., p.39.   [140] Massey, 'Landscape/Space/Politics', pp.2–3.   [141] Ibid., p.13.

tendency is a little at odds with that of film as a composite of montaged elements. In this way, Keiller's practice comes to form an imagistic counterpoint to Adorno's method in *Minima Moralia*, his 'melancholy science'. Reflecting critically on his choice of the aphorism form as a means to generate a fragmentary aesthetic, Adorno asserted that 'the attempt to present aspects of our shared philosophy from the standpoint of subjective experience, necessitates that the parts do not altogether satisfy the demands of the philosophy of which they are nevertheless a part'.[142] The tension described here could well be applied to the sense generated by Keiller's long takes in *Robinson in Ruins*, developing a disjunctive pressure between the whole and its component parts that forces the viewer to reflect on the artifice of the film-making process.

The practice in turn implicitly argues against Heidegger's idea (in 'Building Dwelling Thinking') that depression results from a 'loss of rapport with things': Robinson's 'increasing insubstantiality' and the displaced 'dwelling' that characterizes the film's form are in fact tied closely to his enthusiasm for material objects and phenomena, more akin to the 'loyalty to the world of things' found in Walter Benjamin's model of the melancholic figure in his 1924–5 *Origin of German Tragic Drama*; the way that 'the wisdom of the melancholic [...] is secured by immersion in the life of creaturely things'.[143] It is this that sustains Keiller's Surrealist aesthetic of 'metaphysical materialism', transfiguring often mundane material objects such as the 'Together' sculpture into the conduits of profound meditation on the interactions of human and non-human nature.

'Picturesque Views', Estrangement, and Expropriation

England, in *Robinson in Ruins*, is depicted as 'the location of a *Great Malady*, that I shall dispel, in the manner of Turner, by making *picturesque views*'. This desire is bound up with Keiller's choice of medium. On the one hand, the Narrator observes that Robinson's choice of analogue film was made on the basis that 'it would be more durable in the long term than any digital medium' and therefore better able to survive any loss or corruption of data or change in format or technology. On the other, as he remarked in the essay 'The City of the Future', 'an everyday landscape of 35mm cine colour images made by outstanding cinematographers compares very favourably with today's space routinely represented in indifferent electronic imagery'.[144]

---

[142] Adorno, *Minima Moralia*, p.18.
[143] Heidegger, 'Building Dwelling Thinking', p.155; Walter Benjamin, *The Origin of German Tragic Drama*, trans. John Osborne (London: Verso, 2009), p.157; 152.
[144] Keiller, 'The City of the Future', in *The View From The Train*, p.145.

In 1989's *A Vision of Britain*, Prince Charles had called for architecture to stick to humanized scales and gentle skylines in order to 'enhance the picturesque quality of our landscape'.[145] Yet if the framing and verdant scenery of *Robinson in Ruins* appeal to the tenets of the picturesque, the film's tendency towards much longer shot durations—by alerting us to the artifice—nevertheless means *Robinson in Ruins* has an estranging effect, rubbing up against Charles's notion that picturesque beauty is a 'natural' state and something other than a 'style'. In fact, as Christopher Hussey observed in his canonical study, the idea of estrangement was wrapped up within Uvedale Price's original schema for the picturesque style. A person uninitiated in the characteristics of the picturesque might even, at first glance, 'be amazed by their ugliness'. In a comment that strongly suggests Keiller's method of focusing on the seemingly trivial, Hussey states:

> Such objects in real life that the person had previously passed by without observing, he might now begin to look at with increasing interest, remembering how Ruysdael or Teniers, Waterlo or Hobema, Salvator or even Claude had treated, or might have treated, such a scene. At length he would scarcely be able to stir abroad without recognizing scenes and objects with which pictures had familiarized him; none of them beautiful or sublime, but all of them intrinsically and objectively picturesque.[146]

It seems here that the picturesque might well be thought of as generating the same sort of appreciation that Viktor Shklovsky wanted through the process of '*ostranenye*' (estrangement), even if this is generally thought of as a modernist principle. In fact, it makes perfect sense: if the cult of the picturesque emerged from the vogue for domestic tourism in the early eighteenth century, as a turning-inwards of the 'Grand Tour', then the 'making foreign' of the English landscape can be seen partly as a straightforward carrying over of the desire to see actually foreign places and scenes.

It might well be observed that this dedication to 'estrangement' could terminate in a disorientating experience for the picturesque traveller. This, in fact, is also a remarked-upon feature of the tradition. In his 1997 study *Romantic Writing and Pedestrian Travel*, Robin Jarvis discussed the 'disorientation of the personality' risked by the picturesque traveller whose 'strong mental and emotional investment' in space shifts into the condition of an 'erotic adventure' that shares in 'the destabilising power of those mutual identifications of subject and object that characterise all desire'. The 'sensuous excesses' resulting from this, and their destructive effect on the traveller himself (Jarvis's perspective is always

---

[145] Charles, *A Vision of Britain*, p.79.
[146] Christopher Hussey, *The Picturesque: Studies in a Point of View* (London: Cass, 1967), p.14.

masculine), help explain how Robinson's disorientation in *Robinson in Space* vaults into a 'physically depleted' state in *Robinson in Ruins*.[147]

For Hussey, this disorientation was connected with the contemporary flowering of the 'Theory of Association' described in Archibald Alison's 1790 *Essays on the Nature and Principle of Taste*, which held that anything was beautiful that set in train an association of pleasant ideas. The idea of this, at least, is presented as radically democratic: 'according to it, every man's taste is as good as another's [...] So long as a picture or building aroused an agreeable train of thought, it must be beautiful.' The scheme backfires, however, when the subject concerned is overly suggestible. As Hussey glosses, 'the stronger the imagination of the beholder, the more insignificant might be the objects that roused him to a fine frenzy'.[148]

All of these senses are present in *Robinson in Ruins*, as a correlative for Robinson's own enthusiasm for networks and connectedness, as well as the notion that 'every mode of individuality now relates to the whole world', as Berger had it in 'The Changing View of Man in the Portrait'. In *Robinson in Ruins*, the picturesque appearance of landscape is obliquely undermined by the actual usage of space, often for semi-clandestine military purposes. The pleasing ruination of the rural scene turns out, like the appearance of dilapidation in *Robinson in Space*, to be profoundly misleading, setting decidedly *unpleasant* associations of ideas in train. Pipelines underneath the ground are marked by quaint coloured

Figure 2.11 USAF fire hydrant, Greenham Common, 2008, frame from *Robinson in Ruins* (2010), Patrick Keiller. Courtesy of Patrick Keiller.

---

[147] Jarvis, *Romantic Writing and Pedestrian Travel*, pp.53–61.
[148] Hussey, *The Picturesque*, p.15.

Figure 2.12 Satellite earth station, Enslow, Oxfordshire, 2008, frame from *Robinson in Ruins* (2010), Patrick Keiller. Courtesy of Patrick Keiller.

hats in the style of gabled roofs, but they are owned by pension funds whose foreign ownership is not only unexpected (and largely unknown) but also at least partly accountable for the 2008 crisis, with their dogged pursuit of private profit over the common wealth. Pipework also suggests other disagreeable variations on globalization in the form of the US Air Force pipe, a residual trace of the former base on Greenham Common where protests against nuclear weapons took place in the 1980s (see Figure 2.11).

Weaponry features more heavily in the associated book and exhibition (*The Robinson Institute*) than the film itself. Both are pre-occupied with the abortive 'Blue Streak' missile programme, which would have made the United Kingdom a 'credibly independent' nuclear power rather than an American 'client state'. Keiller's claim is that this is effectively what it became after the 1963 Polaris Sales Agreement, which supplied Britain with US-built nuclear missiles but locked it into the framework of NATO, so that the weapons 'could be used independently only in situations of extreme national emergency'.[149] The Spadeadam facility in Cumbria, where fragments of the earlier Blue Streak development programme remain, does not feature in the film, which is tied to an 'ellipse' of land in Oxfordshire, but it does garner comment in the book as the precise location where Robinson was arrested at the close of *Robinson in Space*.

At another point in the film, a landscape that appears to be militarized transpires to have a quite unexpected radical history. A disused quarry where the telecoms company Cable and Wireless have their communications satellites is

---

[149] Keiller, *The Possibility of Life's Survival on the Planet*, p.23.

at a site formerly known as Enslow Hill, where a carpenter named Bartholomew Steer had planned an uprising against enclosure in 1596 (see Figure 2.12). (One of those who accompanied Steer, who preached 'the politics of Cockayne', was named Robert Burton—not the writer of melancholy but a local mason, later arrested, examined, tortured, charged with treason, hanged, drawn, quartered, and finally executed at Enslow Hill.) A field full of satellite dishes, purchased and privatized by an international corporation, suddenly becomes a site of unexpected political contemplation here. This estranges it, just as the pipelines of foreign militaries and pension funds literally 'en-foreigns' the landscape, while offering unexpected networks and connections running through it.

In Christopher Hussey's view, the estranging activity of the picturesque was bound up with the acquisition of painted landscapes as part of huge collections. This, in its turn, formed an analogue to the actual enclosure and sale of estates—as William Cowper put it in *The Task* (1785), 'estates are landscapes [...] gaz'd upon awhile and auctioneered away'.[150] *Robinson in Ruins* comments on the picturesque as a mode and a style by illuminating both these aspects: its own 'picturesque views' are used as a means to approach the actual estrangement of the contemporary English landscape, both by foreign ownership and concealed complicity with the upheaval of the 2008 crisis. The move perversely short-circuits Robinson's escapist desire to be 'elsewhere' by turning the familiar *into* the elsewhere. In the process, the landscape becomes 'uncanny' in a very full sense—'*unheimlich*' as both shorn of its secrets and, literally, 'unhomely'.

At this point, politics and aesthetics meet in a manner that is highly characteristic of Keiller, even if his films' imaginative acquisition of landscape (and landscapes) in the form of images acts as a constant argument against the need to actually possess territory in legal terms. His aesthetic appropriation of it, in fact, comes to act as an alternative to the 'possessioning' of the landscape carried out, for instance, at Otmoor in June 1830, where local residents walked the circumference of the moor to reject its enclosure. It is ultimately in this way that *Robinson in Ruins* persuasively reframes the question of 'belonging', conceived through the lens of Robinson's fragile subjectivity, and Keiller leaves us with a convincing articulation of Adorno's contention that 'in the period of his decay, the individual's experience of himself and what he encounters contributes once more to knowledge'.[151]

In 'Popular Science', Keiller wrote:

In the UK, the subjective transformation of landscape seems to offer the individual a way to oppose the poverty of everyday surroundings. As individuals, we

---

[150] William Cowper, *The Task* (London: John Sharpe, 1817), Book III.
[151] Adorno, *Minima Moralia*, p.23.

can't rebuild the public transport system, or re-empower local democracy, but we can poeticise our relationship with their dilapidation.[152]

In his characteristically diffident style, Keiller underplayed the value of the 'Robinson' trilogy here. The series marks an important, extended moment in landscape art and landscape-thinking, excavating radical energies from the urban and rural environments of England. Staging their enquiries through the affective prism of their invisible and faltering protagonist, the films follow a vagrant and essayistic mode of thought. Activating a productive slippage between fact and fiction, and balancing sincerity with irony, they establish mythologies of place that interrogate the problems of dwelling and displacement.

As Paul Dave has observed, one way to organize *London*, *Robinson in Space*, and *Robinson in Ruins* is in terms of the dates of the 1992, 1997, and 2010 British General Elections.[153] Even if this is at least partly down to a certain *hasard objectif* on Keiller's part, the films and their accompanying essays nevertheless stand out as crucial documents of their era. In parallel, they respond to Keiller's ambition to 'raise the issue that the UK landscape is not really seen imaginatively at all, there's no contemporary imagination of it'.[154] By means of its distinctively affective mode, the *Robinson* series forms a compelling reimagination of that landscape and the experience of it. Activating melancholia and estrangement as radical tools, the act of observing the landscape 'as spectators at some sporting event might watch the opposition winning' is recalibrated as a convincing politicization of aesthetics.

---

[152] Keiller, 'Popular Science', in *The View From The Train*, pp.71–2.
[153] Dave, 'Robinson in Ruins: New Materialism and the Archaeological Imagination', p.19.
[154] Keiller, 'Photogenie', *Scroope: The Cambridge Architectural Journal* No.8 (1996/7), p.37.

3

W.G. Sebald's Early Writing

'A European at the End of European Civilization'

In 1992, while Patrick Keiller was filming *London*, the German émigré writer and academic W.G. 'Max' Sebald 'set off to walk the county of Suffolk'.[1] This, at least, is the timetable attested to in *The Rings of Saturn*, which forms the idiosyncratic, digressive document of his journey. Published in German in 1995 and in English three years later, the text bears a strong family resemblance to the mode of landscape-thinking or 'affective topography' practised contemporaneously by Patrick Keiller. Merging the mannerisms and form of documentary with a distinctly melancholic, reflective subjectivity, it offers a rich and nuanced account of space and place as a densely woven texture of loss, suffering, and ruination. Its scholarliness, digressiveness, and frequent harnessing of the overlooked or peripheral as prompts to subjective reflection all parallel Keiller's meditative 'mooning over' space and place, mixing estrangement and attachment to produce a distinctive atmospherics.

The year 1992 was also when Sebald published *The Emigrants*, a set of four 'lange Erzählungen' or 'long stories' recounting meetings between Sebald—in the guise of an anonymous narrator figure—and four refugees whose traumatic biographies this figure shapes into narrative form. Although his second substantial work of non-academic prose after *Vertigo* (De. 1990, Eng. 1999), *The Emigrants* was the first to be translated into English. When it was, in 1996, Susan Sontag celebrated it in the *Times Literary Supplement*: 'I know of no book', Sontag wrote,

> which conveys more about that complex fate, being a European at the end of European civilization. I know of few books written in our time but this is one which attains the sublime.[2]

Sontag's majestic reception, taking the 'end of European civilization' for granted, might have as much to say about her own attitude to Europe as it does about Sebald, but it has proved symptomatic in the English-speaking literary world; indeed, since then, critical veneration of Sebald has arguably made him into a curious reflection of Alfred Döblin, who—as Sebald wrote in his 1973 PhD thesis—was regarded after

---

[1] W.G. Sebald, *The Rings of Saturn*, trans. Michael Hulse (London: Harvill, 1998), p.3.
[2] Susan Sontag, 'A Mind in Mourning', *Times Literary Supplement*, 25 February 2000, p.14.

Landscape and Subjectivity in the Work of Patrick Keiller, W.G. Sebald, and Iain Sinclair. David Anderson,
Oxford University Press (2020). © David Anderson.
DOI: 10.1093/oso/9780198847199.001.0001

the publication of *Berlin Alexanderplatz* in 1929 as 'a veritable *paysan de Berlin*' (a suggestive allusion to Louis Aragon's 1926 Surrealist text *Paris Peasant*) 'who symbolized modern existence in his person and work'.[3]

In this light, Jon Cook's observation that Sebald's death in 2001 'has not been used as an excuse to stop reading him' is misleading in so far as it might well be seen to have had the opposite effect, hastening the kind of 'canonization' that the writer himself seems to wryly anticipate in sequences like *The Rings of Saturn*'s meditation on St Sebaldus of Nuremberg.[4] A scene near the close of Grant Gee's 2012 documentary film *Patience: After Sebald* toys with this phenomenon, when a firework set off by the artist Jeremy Millar at the point on the A146 road where Sebald suffered his fatal stroke produces a billow of smoke in which the author's face possibly, momentarily, appears (see Figure 3.1).[5] The quasi-religiosity of this scene is interesting, too, for its indication of how the poised, Keiller-esque self-ironization in Sebald's writing seems often to have become somewhat lost in the earnest sobriety of his epigones.

The way that responses to Sebald's work are subtitled 'after' him, 'searching' for him, or even 'stalking' him attests to this strange phenomenon, as does the frustratingly opaque mode that Sebald has excited in some critics.[6] Deane Blackler's 2007 monograph *Reading W.G. Sebald: Adventure and Disobedience*, for example, is fraught with 'episodes' from her own reading of Sebald, aping tendencies that she perceives in her subject: 'I shall be more essayist than theorist,' writes Blackler, engaging

> in the kind of transgression which has no place in a scholarly monograph, a kind of disobedience, blurring the boundaries between orthodoxy or convention and imaginative or creative license, that errant 'I', that restless traveler, that ambulant, writerly voice.[7]

Blacker's insight to Sebald's 'errant' and 'ambulant' voice does at least point us to the kind of essayistic vagrancy—both in terms of exploration of space and attitude to form—that Sebald's work shares with Patrick Keiller's *Robinson* films, entangling the creative and the critical. Yet at the same time it symptomizes an approach that both venerates and implicitly undervalues Sebald's achievement,

---

[3] Sebald, *The Revival of Myth: A Study of Alfred Döblin's Novels* (unpublished PhD thesis) (Norwich: University of East Anglia, 1973), p.3.

[4] Jon Cook (ed.), *After Sebald: Essays and Illuminations* (East Anglia: Full Circle, 2014), p.9; Sebald, *The Rings of Saturn*, pp.86–8.

[5] Grant Gee (dir.), *Patience: After Sebald* (SODA: 2012).

[6] See Cook and Gee; as well as Phil Smith, *On Walking:—And Stalking Sebald: A Guide To Going Beyond Wandering Around Looking At Stuff* (Axminster: Triarchy, 2014); Lise Platt (ed.), *Searching for Sebald: Photography After W.G. Sebald* (Los Angeles, CA: Institute of Cultural Enquiry, 2006).

[7] Deane Blackler, *Reading W.G. Sebald: Adventure and Disobedience* (Rochester, NY: Camden House, 2007), p.40.

Figure 3.1 The apparition of Sebald's face in Jeremy Millar's 'A Firework for W.G. Sebald' (2005), frames from *Patience: After Sebald* (2012), Grant Gee. Courtesy of Grant Gee.

as if any scholar who includes some subjective reflection and 'scene setting' with their critique might produce comparable work.

In fact, Sebald's canonization has left several blind spots. His concern with the reverberations of German twentieth-century history, for instance, which reached their most forceful and direct in the series of lectures that became *Luftkrieg und Literatur* or *On The Natural History of Destruction* (De. 1999, Eng. 2003), have partly to do with this, focusing critical attention towards Germany and away from

England, where his narrators' epiphanic encounters and historical realizations actually, on the whole, take place.[8] In spite of his long-term habitation in England (travelling through Italy in *Vertigo*, for instance, he is repeatedly taken to be English), Sebald's preoccupation with the traumatic consequences of Nazism and the Holocaust can seem to remove anxiety safely across the North Sea—or, as Sebald archaically styles it, the 'German Ocean'. England is the eccentric but basically safe and reasonable place where Jewish refugees arrive; it is Germany that 'has something curiously unreal about it, rather like a never-ending *déjà vu*', as he put it in a 1996 speech accepting the offer of a place in the 'Deutsche Akademie für Sprache und Dichtung'.[9]

Indeed, for all its apparent anguish about Germany, a text like *On The Natural History of Destruction* should also be remarked upon for the strikingly unproblematic picture it paints of contemporary Britain, drawing a rather binary distinction between the writer's original and adopted homelands. At one point, for instance, Sebald remarks:

> In spite of the strenuous efforts to come to terms with the past, it seems to me that we Germans today are a nation strikingly blind to history and lacking in tradition. We do not feel any passionate interest in our earlier way of life and the specific features of our own civilization, of the kind universally perceptible, for instance, in the culture of the British Isles.[10]

The sense here is of a remarkably coherent British culture, untainted by mnemonic lacunae, moral aporia, suffering, or destructiveness—even when the *Natural History* itself discusses the morbid machinations of the RAF's Bomber Command in creating the firestorms that swept through German cities like Hamburg in the Second World War. The comment certainly downplays what has sometimes been seen as a problematic British 'obsession' with the war and the sense that the journalist Paul Gilroy characterized in a 2008 article as a 'lingering pathology of imperial greatness' that has clouded historical understanding and self-criticism in Britain.[11] Although the Allied policy of 'area bombing' is implicitly condemned in *On The Natural History of Destruction*, Sebald does not strike an attitude anything like Keiller's cynicism at the unveiling of Arthur 'Bomber' Harris's statue in *London*: rather, a certain genteel reserve advances a sense that such an attack might be improper or gauche, perhaps even *un-English*.

Such reserve is also legible in the studied formality or politeness of Sebald's register in the English translations of his texts that, as a fluent speaker of the

---

[8] See Sebald, *On The Natural History of Destruction*, trans. Anthea Bell (London: Penguin, 2004).
[9] Sebald, *Campo Santo*, trans. Anthea Bell (London: Penguin, 2005), p.217.
[10] Sebald, *On The Natural History of Destruction*, pp.viii–ix.
[11] Paul Gilroy, 'A Land of Tea Drinking, Hokey Cokey and Rivers of Blood', *Guardian* 18 April 2008 (https://www.theguardian.com/commentisfree/2008/apr/18/britishidentity.race).

language, he closely supervised. In the 'Max Ferber' story of *The Emigrants*, for instance, the narrator refers to the way that 'one is quite dreadfully crammed in together with one's fellow passengers' when travelling by aeroplane.[12] On the one hand, the narrator's diction here recalls Keiller's choice of narrator in the first two *Robinson* films, of which he observed: '[F]or some reason I find it difficult to place Paul Scofield's voice in class terms. It has a kind of European quality to it.'[13] It is an English whose precision implies or at least suggests that it may have been learned in adult life. On the other, we might detect the traces of Sebald's own reading of texts like J.B. Priestley's *English Journey* (1934) and a subtle attempt to situate his own works within a loose domestic tradition of a somewhat ruffled, gentlemanly cynicism. In his own copy of the *Journey*, now preserved deep in an underground bunker at the German Literature Archive (DLA) in Marbach, Sebald repeatedly marked out examples of Priestley's stoical grumpiness, such as his assertion of Newcastle that 'the whole town looked as if it had entered a penniless bleak Sabbath' or of Liverpool that 'I find it impossible to imagine what the city looks like in clear bright sunshine'.[14]

Sebald's preoccupation with 'eccentric' English people, the bizarre traditions of private schools, and the picturesque decay of stately homes all suggest that his notion of what is 'universally perceptible [...] in the culture of the British Isles' might well be rather more shaded by his own preoccupations and disposition than has hitherto been acknowledged. English readers of *The Rings of Saturn* might be surprised, for instance, to discover that the original German edition is specifically marketed as not only a 'journey through the decline-history of culture and nature' but also, by means of 'its many portraits of extraordinary and singular Britons, a loving homage to the type of the English eccentric'.[15] Seeing the text in this light calls for new attention to be paid to the sometimes rather jaded image of 'heritage' Britain that undergirds Sebald's depictions—and which for readers like Sontag might tessellate seamlessly with a wider imagination of European civilization at its last gasp.

The following chapter, focusing on *The Rings of Saturn* and *Austerlitz*, develops this point. This one explores Sebald's early articulations of landscape as a nexus of mournful subjectivity, centring on instances where Sebald's approach to space and place is more nuanced than the above account might suggest but which have nevertheless not been much discussed by critics. In this vein, it focuses on his depiction of the city of Manchester in the long poem *After Nature* (De. 1988, Eng. 2003), in 'Max Ferber' (last of the four 'long stories' of *The Emigrants*), and in the

---

[12] Sebald, *The Emigrants*, trans. Michael Hulse (London: Random House, 2002) p.149.
[13] Keiller, in Claire Barwell, *Pix*, No.2 (London: British Film Institute, 1997) p.161.
[14] J.B. Priestley, *An English Journey* (London: Penguin, 1997), p.296.
[15] My (literal) translation. Sebald, *Die Ringe des Saturn* (Frankfurt: Fischer, 1998), p.2.

poem 'Bleston', found in the early typescript entitled 'Poemtrees' and included with the collection *Across the Land and the Water* (De. 2008, Eng. 2011). By reading these three texts as an ensemble that repeatedly work and rework Sebald's experience of Manchester, where he was a *Lektor* at the university in 1966, and developing the commonalities and overlaps both between them and with other key texts like Michel Butor's 1956 'Manchester Novel' *Passing Time*, this chapter shows how Sebald renders space and place as a dizzyingly prismatic palimpsest of experience and recollection, writing and rewriting, where—as Sebald put it in the introduction to his as-yet untranslated collection of essays *Die Beschreibung des Unglücks* (De. 1985)—'the description of unhappiness includes within itself the possibility of its own overcoming'.[16]

Genre, Form, and Motion: Sebald's Transgressive Essayism

As if mirroring his own straying beyond national frontiers or the physical migration of his narrator and characters from place to place—a theme that also fed his critical interest in Austrian literature—Sebald's works constantly transgress conventional formal boundaries.[17] In her *TLS* review, Sontag described *The Emigrants* as 'an unclassifiable book' because it was 'at once autobiography and fiction and historical chronicle', even employing the suggestive coinage '*roman d'essai*' to describe the characteristic slippage in Sebald's works between diaristic critical writing, documentary reportage, and a fiction whose fictionality can often seem translucent, like a thin cloak or gauze cast over lived experience.[18] Part of Sebald's attempt, after post-war German writers like Hans Erick Nossack, to disrupt the 'culture of the novel' and its 'bourgeois concepts', this transgressiveness has much in common with Giuliana Bruno's notion of 'errare' as both a physical 'straying' as well as a formal and stylistic vagrancy.[19] Though by nature often self-occluding, this slippage is highly pronounced, and tends to have an academic flavour: Sebald's critical essays often read as if they might have been inset narratives within his 'fictional' works, which themselves employ a noticeably documentary, enumerative style, employing a wordplay on the German '*Erzählung*' that parallels, in English, the presence of 'counting' in 'recounting' and the subtler duality of a word like 'telling'.

One element of this is the way that Sebald's texts are loaded with documentary data—principally photography but also fragments of paintings, drawings, and other found material. The deployment of this material to create what Blackler

---

[16] My translation of Sebald, *Die Beschreibung des Unglücks* (Frankfurt: Fischer, 2001), p.12.
[17] Regarding Austrian literature, see *Beschreibung des Unglücks*, p.10.
[18] Sontag, 'A Mind in Mourning', p.14.
[19] See Giuliana Bruno, *Atlas of Emotion* (New York: Verso, 2002), p.15.

has termed 'fictionally reconstructed reality' problematizes the relationship between the imagined and the reported, often producing a vertiginous, uncanny sensation, since the data employed in a fictional context must necessarily depict some 'real' person or scene distinct from the fictional framework and ultimately unknowable to the reader.[20] It is linked to the documentary impulse that Martin Swales has called 'a kind of encyclopaedic constatation of places, of cities, buildings, houses, of landscapes'—a delight in 'circumstantial specificity, in naming things and objects, thereby acknowledging their testable thereness'—which has such a pronounced bearing on Sebald's depiction of space and place.[21] A marked attentiveness to the local and the particular is fused into an extensive saturnine scheme of decay, destruction, and finality.

Another, connected feature is the fact that, if the 'spatial anxiety' that Dora Osborne has noted in Sebald's work is structured around his depiction of migratory characters who share 'an ambivalent relationship to spaces of habitation and travel', then one of these 'migratory characters' is himself: all of his works feature a sublated narrator figure that Rüdiger Görner has termed the 'Sebald-Ich', incorporating 'a good deal of shared identity with the author'.[22] In this sense, the subjectivity of the 'essai' as an exposition of and coming to terms with the self, after the model of Montaigne, emerges clearly. Sebald's narrators certainly build profoundly empathic relationships with other characters, but, as J.J. Long observes in his Foucauldian analysis of Sebald's work, *Image, Archive, Modernity*, although 'Sebald's peripatetic narrators repeatedly encounter new places, people and things', they also perpetually encounter ciphers of the narrating self.[23] The effect is prismatic, thickening the experience of environments by means of intersecting, emotive biographical accounts of loss and departure. Space and place are here shorn of straightforward narratives of belonging and instead become the nodes of vast, variegated, polyglottic texts of dislocation and estrangement. In this way, the 'ambivalence' that Osborne describes emerges as something quite distinct from the 'indifference' associated with the spaces of transit and movement identified by Marc Augé as 'non-places'. Rather, it is a vital and stimulating ambivalence between the seductiveness of particular environments and the oppressive, estranging uneasiness that they can provoke.

---

[20] Blackler, *Reading W.G. Sebald*, p.117.
[21] Martin Swales, 'Intertextuality, Authenticity, Metonymy? On Reading W.G. Sebald', in Rüdiger Görner (ed.), *The Anatomist of Melancholy: Essays in Memory of W.G. Sebald* (München: Iudicium, 2003) pp.81–2.
[22] Dora Osborne, *Traces of Trauma in W.G. Sebald and Cristoph Ransmayr* (London: Legenda, 2013), p.105; 'Sebald–Ich' from Görner, 'After Words: On W.G. Sebald's poetry', in *The Anatomist of Melancholy*, p.79.
[23] J.J. Long, *W.G. Sebald: Image, Archive, Modernity* (Edinburgh: Edinburgh University Press, 2007), p.6.

'An Elementary Poem': *After Nature*

These features are all highly discernible in Sebald's first substantial published work, a long, three-part narrative poem entitled *After Nature*, which, although published in German in 1988, wasn't translated into English until 2002. This text might seem like something of an anomaly: in a 1997 interview, Sebald remarked that 'mein Medium ist die Prosa' ('my medium is prose'); when asked during a radio interview given eight days before his death in 2001 if he had been influenced by German poetry, he replied 'no, not at all', adding that he felt a stronger affinity with the 'nineteenth-century German prose writing' whose style he often imitated.[24] Yet if his later work can be regarded as a particularly refined and even poetical prose, painstakingly honed in a process of composition that involved numerous handwritten drafts, then *After Nature* is—in the best sense—a kind of prosaic poetry. It also occupies an important space in reconstructing the development of Sebald's literary practice and the idiosyncratic knitting together of place and biography that is such a distinctive feature of his work.

After Nature's subtitle, 'Ein Elementargedicht' (an 'elementary' or 'elemental' poem), as with later works, is omitted from the English translation. It may be an allusion to the German Romantic notion of the 'Elementargeist' or 'elemental spirit'; being an 'utterly unconventional genre-description' (as the critic Thomas Anz has termed it), it is also an appropriate characterization of the way that the poem forms a kernel of Sebald's later concerns, broaching topics that would become sustained, 'elementary' preoccupations.[25] As Rüdiger Görner has observed, Sebald's 'literary prose of the late 1980s and 1990s elaborated on key-words and motifs that his epic poem had already supplied, such as the increasing incongruity between man and nature, the history of melancholy, the hardship of emigration, and the betrayal of emotions'.[26] Marcus Zisselsberger, in his study of the 'poetics of travel' in Sebald's work, concurs, remarking that 'one might ask whether the border-crossing in *Nach der Natur* from the "physical" world into an imagination of disaster is not in fact Sebald's "original" journey'.[27] Lise Platt, meanwhile, whose 'search' for Sebald barely mentions *After Nature*, nevertheless wonders if the poem's 'numerous borrowings, cobblings, and [...] (dis)associative processes' might not make it 'the shibboleth of Sebald's method'.[28]

---

[24] Sigrid Löffler, '"Wildes Denken" Gespräch mit W.G. Sebald', in *Porträt 7: W.G. Sebald*, ed. Franz Loquai (Eggingen: Edition Isele, 1997); Sebald, interview with Michael Silverblatt, *Bookworm*, KCRW Radio, 6/12/2001 (https://www.youtube.com/watch?v=pSFcTWIg-Pg).

[25] 'Eine ganz ungebräuchliche Gattungsbezeichnung', Anz, Thomas, 'Feuer, Wasser, Steine, Licht' in *Porträt 7: Sebald*, p.58.

[26] Görner, *Anatomist of Melancholy*, p.75.

[27] Marcus Zisselsberger, *The Undiscover'd Country: W.G. Sebald and the Poetics of Travel* (Rochester, NY: Camden House, 2007), p.6.

[28] Platt (ed.), *Searching for Sebald*, p.23.

The three parts of *After Nature*—whose title in German as in English suggests both a work copied from nature and one that, in some apocalyptic sense, comes after it—originally appeared separately in the Austrian journal *Manuskripte*, from 1984 to 1987.[29] Unlike later works, the poem does not contain visual material, although the front and end papers of the German edition feature six photographs by Thomas Becker: desolate, unpopulated seascapes and landscapes included unobtrusively before and after the text, rather than incorporated within it in the manner for which Sebald is better known. The text is nevertheless preoccupied with visual experience. Its first part, 'As the Snow on the Alps', narrates the life of the painter Mathias Grünewald and reads as an ekphrastic elaboration of his most famous works: the altarpieces at Lindenhardt and Isenheim and the Basel *Crucifixion*. The second narrates the life of the botanist and explorer Georg Wilhelm Steller; the third recounts elements of Sebald's own biography and particularly his experience of moving to Manchester in 1966.

The poem's structure is indebted to models from visual art: not only does it form a kind of 'triptych' (recalling other, shorter works like 'Erinnertes Triptychon einer Reise aus Brüssel'); its use of interconnecting inset narratives might also be seen to reflect the very form of altarpieces like Grünewald's, whose wooden panels can be opened and removed to reveal new layers and scenes nested within.[30] Techniques like the 'nesting' of narratives, the long and digressive subclause, and the effect of the '*mise-en-abyme*' (sometimes known as the 'Droste' effect of dizzying images-within-images or infinite regression) all resurface frequently across Sebald's later work. One notable theme that also recurs is the omnipresent sense of death and the fragility of life. Another is that of both human suffering in itself and of the Sebald-Ich's profoundly empathic identification with anguish and loss experienced by others—specifically the real historical figures of Grünewald and Steller. This is particularly true in the poem's first part, where John Berger's 1963 account of the Isenheim altarpiece, in which he recounts having become 'convinced [...] that for Grünewald disease represented the actual state of man [...], the condition of life', might just as well apply to Sebald's narrator, for whom a lunar eclipse is tantamount to 'the secret sickening away of the world'.[31]

In contrast with contemporaries like Albrecht Dürer, with his famous monogram, Grünewald is an elusive figure whose life is not well documented; even his name has been a subject of uncertainty. Sebald's account—meditating on the absence of reliable information—renders this elusiveness as a Christ-like self-effacement, making of

---

[29] 'And if I Remained by the Outermost Sea' (October 1984), 'As the Snow on the Alps' (June 1986), and 'Dark Night Sallies Forth' (March 1987)'.

[30] See Sebald, *Across the Land and the Water: Selected Poems 1964–2001*, ed. and trans. Iain Galbraith (London: Hamish Hamilton, 2011), p.10.

[31] John Berger, 'Mathias Grünewald', in Geoff Dyer (ed.) *Selected Essays* (London: Bloomsbury, 2001), p.135; Sebald, *After Nature*, I.VI.35

118 LANDSCAPE AND SUBJECTIVITY

Grünewald an archetypal suffering artist figure who has endured misfortune not only in life (displaced by the German reformation) but also in death, at the hands of a deceptive historiography tainted by Nazism. Sebald discusses a monograph on Grünewald written by the historian 'W.K. Zülch DPhil' (whose qualification appears in pompous contrast to the imputed modesty of the artist) and published 'in the year 1938 for Hitler's birthday', which makes no reference to the possible Jewishness of Grünewald's wife.[32] As if to set himself pointedly apart from this example of corrupted scholarship and its pretence of objectivity, Sebald foregrounds the subjectivity of his own work. The idiosyncratic reference to a marginal figure sharing his name, for instance, introduces a note of Surrealist *hasard objectif* into the frame of historical meticulousness—the arbitrariness of personal affiliation—while also foregrounding the partiality of the narrating figure and the inherent bias of all historical accounts.

One way that the poem's second part (an account of the botanist Georg Wilhelm Steller's ill-fated role in the 1741 Bering expedition) connects with the former is through the recurrence of place: the appearance of the city of Halle, for instance, to which Grünewald moved in the year 1527 to build waterworks for its salt springs, forms a connecting filament with the preceding part of the poem. Another is its attention to the visual and the apparatus of seeing: at Steller's frozen expiration in the far east of Russia—an event deferred agonizingly by the botanist's profound devotion to progress and 'the constructs / of science'—the experience of confronting death is imagined as seeing it somehow reflected in a monocle.[33] The harrowing scene, in which the distortion of images effected by a monocle's convex lens becomes somehow monstrous, recalls the close of the first part, which imagines that to 'peer ahead sharply' is to risk the optic nerve tearing and the entire visual field turning 'as white as / the snow on the Alps'.[34]

Sebald's 'Original Journey' from Germany to England

Marcus Zisselsberger's comments on *After Nature* as Sebald's '"original" journey' begin to make sense in the poem's third part, 'Dark Night Sallies Forth', which begins by asking 'How far, in any case, must one go back / to find the beginning?'[35] Reflecting at this point on the poem's repeated references to looking either back or forwards in time, the reader suspects some suggestion of mystical, metempsychotic connectedness between Grünewald (who lived at the turn of the fifteenth century), Steller (1709–46), and Sebald himself, whose birth and early life are the poem's next subject. His 'journey' in both this and later texts is his flight from the

[32] Sebald, *After Nature*, I.III.49.   [33] Ibid., II.XIII.20–21.   [34] Ibid., I.VIII.33; 43–4.
[35] Ibid., III.I.15–16.

Allgäu region of southern Germany, via Switzerland, to northern England, where he became a 'Lektor' at the University of Manchester in 1966.

Sebald's birthplace of Wertach im Allgäu and the town to which his family later moved, Sonthofen, appear frequently in his writings, thinly encoded into the initials W. and S. in the same manner that he chose to abbreviate the overtly Germanic 'Winfried Georg' of his name to 'W.G.'. These places are frequently a cause of unease in his work. In the last section of *Vertigo*, 'Il Ritorno in Patria', for instance, the narrating figure remarks during a journey home to Wertach that

> the more images I gathered from the past [. . .] the more unlikely it seemed to me that the past had actually happened in this or that way, for nothing could be called normal: most of it was absurd, and if not absurd, appalling.[36]

Crystallizing as another moment that might be read as a 'shibboleth' of Sebald's method, it is striking that this observation, apparently made in conversation with his former childhood acquaintance Lukas, comes shortly after a description of a huge fire at a sawmill—a scene which is also narrated in *After Nature* and establishes the tenor of the Sebald-Ich's preternatural sensitivity to destruction by fire. This fire acts like the original shock whose reverberations can be traced throughout Sebald's later work—in his comments, for instance, on the Hamburg firestorms in *On The Natural History of Destruction* or in his reflection in *The Rings of Saturn* that 'combustion is the hidden principle behind every artefact we create'.[37]

The blaze at the sawmill, we learn in *After Nature*, 'lit up the whole valley'.[38] Yet the striking thing about Sebald's account of his birthplace is the uncanny way in which, in spite of the 'dreadful course' of the closing phases of the Second World War, he himself was raised, as if sealed off from history, 'without any / idea of destruction'.[39] That this should be uncanny results from the fact that, in retrospect at least, Sebald clearly came to see his life as defined by destruction, combustion, and his own affective relationship with them—a relationship tainted by the suspicion that his own early memories had been somehow 'unlikely' or even deliberately falsified by his parents' failure to communicate their experiences to him. The sawmill fire stands out in his memory because it seemed to be exceptional—a destructive scene from which he was *not* deliberately kept in ignorance by his family and those around him. As he later realizes, it was the exception proving the rule of the period surrounding his conception and birth.

---

[36] Sebald, *Vertigo*, trans. Michael Hulse (London: Random House, 2002), p.212.
[37] Sebald, *The Rings of Saturn*, p.170.   [38] Sebald, *After Nature*, III.II.19.
[39] Ibid., III.II.23–24.

Describing this period, Sebald writes of how fifty-eight planes attacked Nuremberg on 28 August 1943. In the narrative 'now' of the poem, his mother, despite having witnessing this spectacle of destruction, cannot remember either the moment of witnessing itself or her subsequent emotional response to it. However, the same night, she realizes that she is pregnant, and when Sebald later sees a picture of the same fire in a Viennese museum, he dwells on the unnerving sense he has of having already seen it.

The impression is that in some obscure way, the speaker has inherited the memory that his mother seems to have striven, or at least chosen, to forget. At the same time, it is significant that the scene plays to the Sebald-Ich's capacity for uncanny, vertiginous experiences in front of certain works of art. 'I nearly went out of my mind', he reports, presaging similar moments in later works such as his dizzying, profoundly empathic response to the anatomized corpse of the thief Aris Kindt in Rembrandt's 1632 painting *The Anatomy Lesson of Dr Nicolaes Tulp*, discussed in *The Rings of Saturn*.[40] The narrator seems to be endowed with a preternatural *visual* memory, in stark reversal of the lack of visual recall exhibited not only by his mother (in the above sequence) but also by his father, who, having departed for Dresden on the 27th of that same August, 'retains no trace' of that city in his memory. Given that the destruction of Dresden—well known to anglophone readers through texts like Kurt Vonnegut's *Slaughterhouse-Five* (1969)—was a notorious instance of irrational mass destruction, not seeming to serve any clear tactical purpose, this sequence links the idea of visual blindness to the theme of historical blindness first approached in the discussion of Zülch's monograph on Grünewald.

In the subsequent stanza, Sebald's birth on Ascension Day of 1944 is recounted. The scene is freighted with ill omens. Outside the family home, the fire-brigade band plays while the fields are blessed. Sebald's mother initially takes this as a positive omen, but the narrator corrects her: she is not aware of the influence of 'the cold planet Saturn' and its role in an impending storm that will take the life of one of the canopy bearers in the blessing ceremony.[41] As in Susan Sontag's famous 1978 characterization of Walter Benjamin, Sebald is here born 'under the sign of Saturn'. It is a significant allusion, since, although Benjamin is not an explicit subject of *After Nature* and is not specifically mentioned, the presence of his thought permeates the text. Most clearly, the mood of both *After Nature* and Sebald's later writings is heavily inflected by Benjamin's 1940 'Theses on the Philosophy of History' and specifically the ninth thesis, which imagines Paul Klee's 1920 painting *Angelus Novus* as representing the 'angel of history'. A figure whose 'face is turned towards the past', this angel sees history not as 'the appearance of a chain of events' but rather as

---

[40] Ibid., III.I.118; Sebald, *The Rings of Saturn*, pp.12-17.   [41] Sebald, *After Nature*, III.II.8.

one single catastrophe, which keeps piling wreckage upon wreckage and hurls it in front of his feet.[42]

'A storm is blowing from Paradise', Benjamin's thesis mystically continues;

> it has got caught in its wings with such violence that the angel can no longer close them. This storm irresistibly propels him into the future to which his back is turned, while the pile of debris before him grows skyward. This storm is what we call progress.[43]

If Grünewald's and Steller's lives are depicted as bound up with immense suffering caused by 'what we call progress', then it is the figurative and actual firestorm of Nazi Germany whose gusts, in *After Nature*, implicitly hurl Sebald to the far-flung post-industrial wasteland of Manchester in 1966—the city whose oxymoronically 'fallow / Elysian fields' appear gathered round with portents of blindness, fire, and forgetting.[44] This sequence opens by referring to Benjamin Disraeli's proclamation of nineteenth-century Manchester as a 'celestial Jerusalem'.[45] Yet the Manchester that Sebald encounters weighs down on the opposite side of that success, under the heavy ruins of the nineteenth century. Rambling through its careworn urban spaces, the Sebald narrator finds himself 'wondering' at the state of the decay and the 'work of destruction', taking in the spectacle of redundant industrial infrastructure and the vast brick-built structures.[46] The language richly evokes a decayed cityscape of towering, crumbling masonry and industrial effluvium strongly recalling works like Gustave Doré's 1872 etching of *The New Zealander*, depicting a future traveller who gazes at a ruined London. Like Doré's imagined pilgrim, Sebald here depicts himself as a figure far from his 'remote home'.[47] Manchester is unhomely, its infrastructure wasted, toxic—sick as the syphilitic patients at Isenheim's monastery of St Anthony, where Grünewald's altarpiece was originally situated.

The description here bears the imprint of J.B. Priestley's *English Journey*, where Manchester is rendered as an 'Amazonian jungle of blackened bricks' and 'what has been left us, to mourn over, by the vast, greedy, slovenly, dirty process of industrialization for quick profits'.[48] Yet is also clear that, for Sebald, the experience of wandering through this post-industrial city catalyses what has hitherto been only a latent sensitivity to destruction and decay; one that has, as it were, lain dormant since his birth. Staging this experience as a moment of sudden retrospective recognition—in which the past, as in Benjamin's sixth thesis, 'flashes up

---

[42] Benjamin, 'Theses on the Philosophy of History', in *Illuminations*, p.257.
[43] Ibid., pp.257–8.   [44] Sebald, *After Nature*, III.IV.13–14.   [45] Ibid., III.IV.6.
[46] Ibid., III.IV.14–15.   [47] Ibid., III.IV.9.   [48] Priestley, *English Journey*, p.239; p.238.

122 LANDSCAPE AND SUBJECTIVITY

at a moment of danger'—the speaker traces a trajectory not as things were at the time but as they seem to him 'now'.[49] Firmly situating this moment of present reflection in relation to past events, he narrates a time that is '[h]alf a life ago now' and goes on to describe the Mancunian working classes who degenerated into a 'race of pygmies' recruited into special military units during the war because of their inaptitude for conventional service.[50] These 'pygmies', obliquely echoing J.B. Priestley's description of the way that in Manchester 'you always seem to be moving, a not too happy dwarf, between rows of huge black square warehouses', are emblematic: 'part of the obscure crowds / who fuelled the progress of history'.[51] Their souls are imagined as populating the desolated space of Sebald's Manchester like 'will-o'-the-wisps', and the Sebald-Ich thinks that he can see them haunting the rubbish tips which rear up like a 'smouldering / alpine range' reaching into 'the beyond'.[52]

This final 'beyond' recalls the eye that 'peer[s] ahead sharply' in the poem's first part, only to sheer the optic nerve and produce a gulf of whiteness. It is particularly significant that the penumbral imagery incorporates the already-established presence of the Alps of Sebald's Allgäu homeland into a crepuscular Mancunian dreamscape. Just as mountains and rubbish dump merge into a single imaginative *topos*, the 'beyond' seems to function in a way that blurs the spatial with the temporal. In an extension of the scene, the image of the revenant pygmies morphs into that of crashed warplanes being lifted, under the watchful searchlight beams of bulldozers, from the wasted, boggy cityscape. As 'brothers', the humanized aeroplanes are brought onto a level with the ghostly pygmies; as searchlights 'pierced the void', the notion of journeys into the primeval unknown, so present in the rendition of Steller's Bering expedition, modulate into the Sebald-Ich's own state of mind, encumbered by the burden of history's 'pile of debris' and replicating the ephemerality of these restless souls, navigating the smouldering wasteland with the aid of their tiny lanterns.[53]

This uneasiness of mind precipitates a corresponding bodily restlessness in the speaker, who is pushed by the 'images' he describes (visual experience again taking centre stage) into a profound melancholy set to the 'incessant monotonous / vibrations of a Jew's harp'.[54] It is this melancholy that forces the speaker out of doors to wander through the city, rendered as a procession of 'infernally / glittering hostelries': 'Liston's Music Hall', 'Gospel Chapels', and Strangeways prison (whose star shape seems to nod forward to the interest in star-shaped

---

[49] Benjamin, 'Theses on the Philosophy of History', in *Illuminations*, p.255.
[50] Sebald, *After Nature*, III.IV.8; III.IV.38.
[51] Priestley, *English Journey*, p.241; Sebald, *After Nature*, I.IV.47–8.
[52] Sebald, *After Nature*, III.IV.50; III.IV.53–5.   [53] Sebald, *After Nature*, III.IV.59.
[54] Sebald, *After Nature*, III.IV.67–68.

fortifications in *Austerlitz*).[55] Manchester has by this point in the poem emerged as a thickly inscribed, brooding place, where the traumatic experience of coming to terms with the repercussions of Nazism are played out amid the haunting industrial ruins of Northern England. This is particularly clear when, as the narrator explores the city, he wanders through its now uninhabited former Jewish quarter. Scheduled to be imminently bulldozed to the ground for reconstruction, the German-Jewish shop signs in these ruined streets elaborate a mordant pun on Disraeli's idea of the city as a 'Jerusalem'.

As Sebald remarks in *Vertigo*, his childhood experiences had led him to think of destruction as a 'natural condition of larger cities'. But it is with his movement into one—with the first-hand experience of Manchester in *After Nature*—that his melancholy vocation, the path by which he has reached this point, is suddenly clarified, 'flashing up,' as in Walter Benjamin's sixth thesis, 'at a moment of danger'.[56] Amid the ruins of this decaying metropolis, the poem describes an encounter with a certain Mr Deutsch, born in Kufstein, Austria, in 1938. Mr Deutsch has never mastered English but watches television all day in the seeming hope for some kind of revelation that, implicitly, is surely never to arrive. If Sebald has observed of modern Germany that there is 'something curiously unreal about it, rather like a never-ending *déjà vu*', then the appearance of Mr Deutsch reconstructs an epiphany that he remarked on in an interview given shortly before he died, saying that

> in Manchester, I realised for the first time that these historical events had happened to real people. [...] You could grow up in Germany in the postwar years without ever meeting a Jewish person. There were small communities in Frankfurt or Berlin, but in a provincial town in south Germany Jewish people didn't exist. The subsequent realisation was that they had been in all those places, as doctors, cinema ushers, owners of garages, but they had disappeared – or had been disappeared.[57]

The morbid phrase 'had been disappeared' here is a particularly noticeable imitation of the grossly euphemistic character of totalitarian bureaucratese. At the same time, Sebald's observation clarifies the sense in which Manchester, while producing its own uncanny effects, acted for Sebald as a catalyst of historical consciousness and the determinant of his project of 'restitution'.[58]

---

[55] Ibid. III.IV.81–82; 83; 90. [56] Benjamin, *Illuminations*, p.255.
[57] Sebald, interview with Maya Jaggi, 'The Last Word', *Guardian* 21 December 2001 (https://www.theguardian.com/education/2001/dec/21/artsandhumanities.highereducation).
[58] Sebald, 'An Attempt at Restitution', 2001 speech at Stuttgart House of Literature, in *Campo Santo*, pp.206–15.

'A Steady Production of Dust': Memory and Place in 'Max Ferber'

If Görner, Zisselsberger, and Platt all argue for the significance of *After Nature* as an 'original', or a 'shibboleth', supplying 'key words' for Sebald's later work, then it is clear that the place or 'site' through which to trace this is Manchester. Sebald depicts the city not only in *After Nature* but also in the 'Max Ferber' story of *The Emigrants*—which restages his arrival there by plane and documents his friendship with the refugee Jewish artist who lends the story its name—and in his early poem 'Bleston. A Mancunian Cantical'. Considered together, these texts produce a palimpsestic rendition of the city's space and Sebald's journeys to and through it, offering keys to the entanglement of place, biography, and the working-through of trauma in his later work. 'Max Ferber' and 'Bleston' also provide case studies of Sebald's characteristic imbrication of the work of other writers into his own. This can be thought of either in terms of the 'borrowings' and 'cobblings' identified by Platt or Sebald's own, somewhat dandyish, description of having

> always tried, in my own works, to mark my respect for those writers with whom I have felt an affinity, to raise my hat to them, so to speak, by borrowing an attractive image or a few expressions.[59]

In this vein, Sebald's Manchester in 'Max Ferber' and 'Bleston' is underwritten by the work of, among others, the German-Jewish émigré painter Frank Auerbach and the French *nouveau romancier* Michel Butor.

Revisiting Sebald's arrival in England, 'Max Ferber' opens with the narrator declaring that he had never travelled further than five or six 'Zugstunden' or 'train-hours' from home until he was twenty-two years old.[60] Emphasizing the temporal experience of distance, one effect of this description is to naturalize train travel as part of Sebald's childhood and to estrange the implicit 'Flugstunden' ('flight-hours') of his journey to England. Making these measures of time and distance oddly incompatible with one another foregrounds the unusualness of this experience for the narrating subject and the uneasiness it provokes. Although the narrator's airborne elevation in this opening scene, in a twilit plane sparsely populated by passengers 'in ihre Mäntel gehüllt' ('wrapped in their coats')— might reflect the 'high-up' perspective that Marc Augé characterised as symptomatic of the contemporary experience of travel, it is hardly the one of blissful, deific serenity that Augé describes.[61] England is introduced by the 'orangefarbener

---

[59] Sebald, 'Le promeneur solitaire: A remembrance of Robert Walser', in *A Place in the Country*, trans. Jo Catling (London: Penguin, 2014), p.128.
[60] Sebald, *The Emigrants*, trans. Michael Hulse (London: Random House, 2002), p.149.
[61] See Marc Augé, *Non-Places: An Introduction to Supermodernity*, trans. John Howe (London: Verso, 1995), p.xvi.

Sodiumglanz' or 'orange-coloured sodium glare' of its street lighting, and the narrator glides above

> the strangely ribbed flank of a long, bare mountain ridge seemingly close enough to touch, and appearing to me to be rising and sinking like a giant recumbent body, heaving as it breathed.[62]

Of Manchester itself, the first thing that the narrator notices is not lamplight but 'a faint glimmer, as if from a fire almost suffocated with ash'—the guttering glow of 'one of the nineteenth century's miracle cities' being rendered in terms of physical discomfort.[63] Some time later, the proprietor of the 'soot-blackened' Hotel Arosa, where the narrator checks in after a protracted passage through customs and a taxi-ride through the city, clarifies her surname as Irlam, 'like Irlam in Manchester'—this clipped observation, probably not of much use to someone who has only just arrived in the city, perpetuating a sense of space that is simultaneously humanized and estranging.[64]

It is not Irlam, however, who comes to form the centrepiece of Sebald's humanization of the ruined city. This role falls instead to the artist 'Max Ferber'. Ferber's departure from Germany in 1933 maps onto that of Sebald's narrator, as does the strange experience of his arrival in Manchester as a kind of homecoming—as Ferber discusses the Jewish history of the city, he remarks that 'though I had intended to move in the opposite direction, when I arrived in Manchester I came home, in a sense.'[65] Like Keiller's 'fabulations backed by congeries of fact', Ferber is an imagined character who is a composite of real-life figures. His family's story, the writing-up of which from a bundle or 'Konvolut' of documents comes to be the narrator's special task and which ultimately takes him to the Bavarian spa town of Bad Kissingen, is drawn from the family memoirs of Sebald's friend and landlord, the architect Peter Jordan. The German Literature Archive holds copies of these, as well as a 1987 note in which Jordan remarks to Sebald how he feels compelled to show him the documents, having never previously encountered a German who enquired after what happened to his family—a communiqué that must have cemented Sebald's sense of vocation.[66]

Ferber himself, meanwhile, bears a strong resemblance to Frank Auerbach, the German-Jewish painter who fled to England in 1939, at the age of seven, and whose parents were both victims of the Holocaust. The original German edition of the text features a drawing by Auerbach and, later, a photograph of one of his eyes. These were excised from later editions, and from the English text, apparently at the request of the painter, whose name was also changed from 'Aurach' to the less

---

[62] Sebald, *The Emigrants*, p.150. [63] Ibid., p.150. [64] Ibid., pp.151–2.
[65] Ibid., p.192.
[66] Peter Jordan, letter to Sebald dated 17 February 1987, German Literature Archive.

126   LANDSCAPE AND SUBJECTIVITY

confusable 'Ferber'.[67] Auerbach is famous for having made London, and especially the area around his studio in Camden Town, the principal subject of his work over many years; for instance, the sign reading 'TO THE STUDIO' in the wasteland near Trafford Park, which first alerts the narrator to Ferber's presence, directly recalls Auerbach's studies in paint of the space around his studio, near Mornington Crescent Underground Station, made in the early 1980s. Sebald's 'translation' of him and his work to Manchester, making of the city a composite space structured partly around these London images, is symptomatic of the way that place and biography emerge as the products of creative reassembly in Sebald's work.

Ferber's introduction is accompanied by the description of his studio space, full of 'mountains of papers', materials, and equipment, with an easel at its centre lit by 'grey light that entered through a high north-facing window layered with the dust of decades'. The floor, we read, 'was covered with a largely hardened and encrusted deposit of droppings, mixed with coal dust, several centimetres thick at the centre and thinning out towards the outer edges', which resembles a floe of lava and which Ferber believes to be 'the true product of his continuing endeavours and the most palpable truth of his failure'.[68] Echoing here not only the work of Auerbach but also that of artists like Anselm Kiefer, Ferber's method of production involves an intense attachment both to his materials and to the by-products of his constant dissatisfaction: above all, the dust. Emphasizing this, the narrator remarks that all of Ferber's production 'really amounted to nothing but a steady production of dust, which never ceased except at night'.[69] Ferber's 'love' of the dust makes of him a parallel to the 'pygmies' physically deformed by their labour, his skin taking up a 'metallic sheen' when he has been working with charcoal.[70] And this sense of sickening as a result of one's labour is foregrounded by Ferber's anecdote about a photographic assistant who, as a result of silver poisoning, suffered a condition whereby his skin went blue under strong light—'or, as one might say, developed'.[71] This story becomes a kind of prophecy, since Ferber himself—when the narrator revisits him years later and receives the 'Konvolut' of his family's memoirs—has been hospitalized by pulmonary emphysema.

Ferber's art practice resonates closely with that of Auerbach, who is famous for constantly reworking drawings and paintings, sometimes hundreds of times, either scratching into the image or plying it with ever more pigment. In his early depictions of London bomb sites—which interestingly, given Sebald's later preoccupation with the air war, are not adapted into Ferber's practice—his technique involved heaping up such improbable amounts of oil paint that the

---

[67] See Schütte, Uwe, *W.G. Sebald* (Liverpool: Liverpool University Press, 2018), p.119.
[68] Sebald, *The Emigrants*, p.161.   [69] Ibid., p.162.   [70] Ibid., p.164.   [71] Ibid., p.165.

works are often over an inch thick in places, and took years to dry. The dark tonal schemes that characterize Auerbach's earlier work in this vein lend a penumbral quality to these scenes, which often only reveal themselves to the viewer after protracted observation, thereby seeming to have a durational quality akin to the way a photograph takes time to develop. In these works and others, Auerbach tends to use a wide brush—about two inches across—as he works into the paint on the canvas, as if dramatizing, in the most readily perceptible way, the inevitable clumsiness and failure with which man attempts to produce a veracious depiction of reality.

Working in a reverse manner, in some examples of Auerbach's drawings the paper itself, already very thick, has been worn away and patched together at certain points (this is exemplified in the image included with the original text of 'Max Ferber' but removed from later editions, the 1980 drawing *Head of Catherine Lampert VI*). Worked into so heavily that it bulges in places, threatens to fray apart at others, the paper itself develops a sculptural quality. The activity of Auerbach here closely matches Sebald's description of Ferber continually re-inscribing his paper with new variations of a particular image, re-enacting the processes of destruction and creation until the work has the impression of having 'evolved from a long lineage of grey, ancestral faces, rendered unto ash but still there, as ghostly presences, on the harried paper'.[72] In these images we seem to see the shadowy figures of Sebald's Manchester—the fires and children playing in the distance on the flattened blocks and the 'bustling characters' or 'hastiges Männervolk' of the obviously fairly seedy Hotel Arosa, 'clad almost without exception in tattered gabardine coats or macs'.[73]

In Sebald's story, Ferber's working schedule, 'ten hours a day, the seventh day not excepted', suggests a man possessed.[74] Yet witnessing this possession forms an antidote to the narrator's experience of *dis*possession: his Sunday walks from the hotel are undertaken out of 'a sense of aimlessness and futility' (in the German an 'überwaltigenden' or 'overwhelming' sense).[75] His job or occupation is never mentioned, but his later struggle with the task of writing up Ferber's family history—that is, the actual set of documents given to Sebald by Peter Jordan—sets in train an activity that reproduces Auerbach's/Ferber's working method. Of this 'arduous task', the narrator remarks that 'often I could not get on for hours or days at a time, and not infrequently I unravelled what I had done, continuously tormented by scruples that were taking tighter hold and paralysing me'. Before long, he adds, 'I had covered hundreds of pages with my scribble, in pencil and ballpoint. By far the greater part had been crossed out, discarded, or obliterated by additions.'[76]

---

[72] Ibid., p.162. [73] Ibid., p.155. [74] Ibid., p.160. [75] Ibid., p.156.
[76] Ibid., p.230.

128 LANDSCAPE AND SUBJECTIVITY

Mirroring Ferber's (and Auerbach's) practice, this 'Versuch' at authenticity also forms an oblique contrast with Sebald's use of photography and indeed comes to seem ethically necessary when Ferber recounts an uncle's obsession with a forged photograph of a Nazi book-burning—of which his Uncle remarks 'just as that document was a fake [...] so too everything else had been a fake, from the very start'.[77] By way of analogy with Ferber's practice, both Sebald's own project and that of his narrator come to function in explicit contradistinction with this kind of duplicitous documentary: the very flatness of the photographic image, so visibly at odds with the texture of Auerbach's work, is lent a treacherous or deceptive quality. At the same time, the sequence points to Sebald's own self-consciousness and anxiety about the inherent fakery of literary artifice and aesthetic representation, and the ethical dilemmas this produces when dealing with material such as the Jordan family memoirs: the anxieties of 'Max' Ferber are also those of 'Max' Sebald.

'Bleston' and Michel Butor's *Passing Time*

In his wanderings through the wastelands of central Manchester—an area that, echoing the description in *After Nature*, 'I came to think of as the Elysian Fields'—and his meetings with Ferber both at his studio and the strangely out-of-place transport café known as the 'Wadi Halfa', run by a Sudanese migrant, Sebald depicts Manchester as a city that 'displayed the clearly chronic process of its impoverishment and degradation to anyone who cared to see'.[78] In this respect he follows a loose but established tradition of German visitors to Manchester, running from the high point of the Industrial Revolution to the late twentieth century. The literary critic Hans Georg Schenk, for instance, refers to a certain Dr Carus of Saxony, 'who visited England and Scotland in 1844, was [...] appalled by the sight of Manchester', and wrote:

> At the side of every coal-pit a quantity of finer parts that are thrown out is perpetually burning, and the effect produced by the earth, thus apparently everywhere on fire, both the machinery used and the men busied with it, was horrible.

Carus's observation that 'it seemed as if I were in Dante's shadowy world' is certainly apt to Sebald's vision of 'a city spread across a thousand square kilometres, built of countless bricks and inhabited by millions of souls, dead and

---

[77] Ibid., pp.183–4.   [78] Ibid., p.156.

alive'.[79] Friedrich Engels's horrified encounter with the city in his 1845 *The Condition of the Working Class in England* sustained this heritage, reflected in responses to the post-industrial city over a century later. In the late 1960s, the American urbanist Jane Jacobs described Manchester as 'the very symbol of a city in long and unremitting decline', lamenting what she saw as its over-specialization in the textile industries during the nineteenth century and its consequent inability to adapt to shifting 'market forces' in the twentieth.[80]

When Sebald's narrator returns to Manchester, after many years' absence, to visit Ferber in hospital, he walks through housing estates 'which had been rebuilt in the early 1970s and had now been left to fall down again'.[81] The photographs included with the text contrast the rectilinear blocks of the Hulme estate, where Kevin Cummins's famous photographs of the band Joy Division were taken in late 1970s, with the decaying Victorian warehouses and the imposing Gothic-revival façade of the Midland Hotel where, following in the tracks of Priestley's *English Journey*, he checks in. Eschewing both the modernist straight lines of Hulme and the industrial decay it shares space with, the hotel is met by Sebald's narrator with something like rapture. He soon falls into a marvellous reverie at the prospect of its famously advanced plumbing, echoing Priestley's comments on its 'almost tropical' interior.[82]

In his meditations on and in the hotel, the narrator seems surrounded by a very different version of decline to that encountered in the wastelands around Ferber's studio. He ruminates on the risk that this once mighty institution might become a 'Holiday Inn', before the scene vaults into a strange vision of *Mitteleuropa*. Conjuring a seemingly imagined nostalgic image of a well-to-do past in this quarter of the city, the narrator thinks, while in the 'turret room', that

> (though it was utterly impossible) I heard the orchestra tuning their instruments, amidst the usual scraping of chairs and clearing of throats, in the Free Trade Hall next door; and far off, far, far off in the distance, I also heard the little opera singer who used to perform at Liston's Music Hall in the Sixties, singing extracts of *Parsifal* in German.[83]

Though this imagined sequence is unprecedented, it is in keeping with the earlier suggestion that part of Manchester's uncanny quality inheres in the sense of a certain theatricality. During his first stay in the city, the narrator remarks that the disused buildings give the impression of being 'surrounded by mysterious façades

---

[79] Hans Georg Schenk, *The Mind of the European Romantics* (Oxford: Oxford University Press, 1979), p22. N.b., ref. to Carus is from *England und Schottland im Jahre 1844* (Berlin, 1845), Vol.II, p.145.
[80] Jane Jacobs, *The Economy of Cities* (New York: Random House, 1970), p.88.
[81] Sebald, *The Emigrants*, pp.231-2.   [82] Priestley, *English Journey*, pp.242-3.
[83] Sebald, *The Emigrants*, p.234.

or theatrical backdrops', and Ferber describes the former sight of great ships on the shipping canal, far taller than the houses, peering out of the fog as an 'utterly incomprehensible spectacle' ('Schauspiel' or 'play' in the German).[84] These scenes, he remarks, 'moved me deeply' and were part and parcel of the 'irreversible decline' of the city's shipping traffic.

The music hall reminiscence also brings with it an odd sense of intertextual déjà vu to parallel those of the narrator and Ferber: although 'Max Ferber' contains no earlier references to this place where the narrator apparently saw 'the heroic tenor Siegfried' belting out *Parsifal*, the event *is* recounted in both *After Nature* and the shorter poem 'Bleston. A Mancunian Cantical', which features in the sheaf of writings entitled 'Poemtrees' and appeared in the posthumous collection *Across the Land and the Water*. This five-part poem, whose title is given in English even in the original German version, incorporates fragments of Latin and French. There are English elements in the original too, denotative references to places and signs whose linguistic difference—as is common in Sebald's work—is occluded by the translation back into English. These are 'Lewis's Big Warehouse' in part I (on whose sills starlings sit closely together but, apparently, without sleeping); the reference to Bleston's/Manchester's 'Breast-like hills' in part II (a pun on the meaning of Manchester's Latin name, *Mamucium*); the lines referring to the healing of sick people at 'Sharon's Full Gospel' in part III; and part V's comment on the 'verstellten / Büchern' or 'misplaced books' that escape even the comprehensiveness of the Dewey Decimal cataloguing system.[85]

As a 'cantical' (this spelling is used in both English and German versions), 'Bleston' might well have been influenced by Sebald's reading of the journalist Karl-Heinz Bohrer, with whom he was in brief correspondence in the mid-1980s. Working as British correspondent for the *Frankfurter Allgemeine Zeitung*, Bohrer made Manchester the subject of an eccentric and equally liturgical-sounding 'Litanei' on the Industrial Revolution in an idiosyncratic 1977 article. 'Are you like the terrible mountain which presaged the Fall of the House of Usher in rock?' Bohrer asked, alluding to Edgar Allan Poe's 1839 short story, before going on to meditate on the 'surreal forest of stone remnants' presented by the city's spectacle of industrial decay.[86] The source of the word 'Bleston', meanwhile, is identified by the critic Richard Sheppard in his essay 'The Sternheim Years: W.G. Sebald's *Lehrjahre* and *Theatralische Sendung* 1963-75'. Sheppard explains how

> the acute culture shock and sense of isolation that Max suffered during his first term at Manchester could not have been helped by his Baudelairian/Benjaminian

---

[84] Ibid., p.157; p.166.
[85] Sebald, 'Bleston. A Mancunian Cantical', in *Across the Land and the Water*, pp.18–22.
[86] My translation. Karl-Heinz Bohrer, *Ein Bißchen Lust Am Untergang* (Munich: Hanser, 1979) p.23.

flâneries through scenes of slum clearance and urban decay [...] or by his reading of Michel Butor's *L'Emploi du Temps* (*Passing Time*),

adding in a footnote that

> Butor had been a French *lecteur* in Manchester 1943–51, and while living in Chorlton in November 1966 Max was reading *L'Emploi du Temps*, which deals with Butor's experiences in Manchester. His heavily annotated copy (Paris: Éditions de Minuit, 1957) is among his books in the DLA.[87]

The poem's clearest borrowings are from this text: the title of the fourth section, 'Perdu dans ces filaments', the reference to the 'fil d'Ariane' (Ariadne's thread), and the intimation that Bleston's 'Stunde / Zwischen Sommer und Winter' is 'der Plan meiner Zeit' ['Bleston's hour / between summer and winter [...] is the plan of my time'] all attest to this: the first two being direct quotations from Sebald's French edition of the novel, the last a German ventriloquism of its title.[88]

Passing Time is an extraordinary text, reading like something placed halfway between Jean-Paul Sartre's *Nausea* (1938) and Alain Robbe-Grillet's *The Erasers* (1964) but set in industrial northern England. Imagining Manchester as 'Bleston', it is organized as a set of diary entries made by the character Jacques Revel during a year spent as a clerk at a firm known as Matthews and Sons. It documents Revel's discovery of a murder-mystery novel called *The Bleston Murder*, which becomes his guide to the city, and whose narrative bears uncanny similarities to events and people that he encounters in real life. As the increasingly alienated Revel starts to notice these similarities, the text's diaristic structure becomes complicated by his neurotic rereading and rewriting of earlier entries; and as he grapples with the problem presented by *The Bleston Murder*, *Passing Time* gradually becomes an address to Bleston itself, which exerts an ever more oppressive psychic presence. When *The Bleston Murder*'s pseudonymous author George Henry Burton is accidentally unmasked and almost killed in a car accident, Revel begins to feel culpable and, in turn, holds the city itself responsible.

In her 2012 essay 'Sebald's Encounters with French Narrative', Judith Ryan discusses Sebald's personal copy of *Passing Time* (held at Marbach). She notes that the dating of his annotations seems to show that he read it almost immediately upon arrival in Manchester, when 'he cannot have had much time to settle in the city'.[89] Sebald, she also points out, underlined Revel's description of writing as

---

[87] Richard Sheppard, 'The Sternheim Years: W.G. Sebald's Lehrjahre and Theatralische Sendung 1963–75', in Joe Catling and Richard Hibbitt (eds.), *Saturn's Moons: W.G. Sebald: A Handbook* (London: Legenda, 2001) p.66; p.100.

[88] Sebald, 'Bleston', in *Across the Land and the Water*, p.21.

[89] Ryan, 'Sebald's Encounters with French Narrative', in Zisselsberger, *The Undiscover'd Country*, p.125.

being 'comme une petite vengeance' against Bleston and his description of his writing desk as 'mon rampart contre Bleston', summing up that the 'gloomy and forbidding city that forms the novel's backdrop, its labyrinthine character, and the narrator's sense of being imprisoned within the confines of its complicated streets are elements that Sebald repeatedly marks in his copy'.[90] It is worth explaining at this point that the pages of *Passing Time* are headed by the consecutive months of Revel's year in Bleston, to which other months are increasingly added in a non-consecutive order to indicate his neurotic revisiting of earlier events, playing literary detective with his own text as the evidence. By itself this is already highly disorientating; Sebald's addition of further dates marking his own reading of the text both interacts with and exacerbates the confusion.

Sadly, a close look at Sebald's copy of *Passing Time* reveals it not to be especially heavy with other annotations. Those that do appear, however, testify to the way that his interest in the novel emerged from a specifically negative response to the urban space of Manchester. At the moment when Revel discusses his growing inability to communicate with other characters, for instance, mentioning that he purchased a copy of *The Bleston Murder* as a way of pursuing 'une petite vengeance' against the city, Sebald has not only underlined the phrase but also written 'j'ai commencé à lire l'emploi du temps par cette raison' ('I began to read *Passing Time* for this reason'). The annotation, seeming to be oddly directed at future scholars, somewhat spookily mandates Ryan's later comment that 'Sebald seems to have been very conscious of the scholarly attention his works would receive.'[91] It also makes clear the profound connection that Sebald felt with Butor's work, which attended to his sense of *anomie* while also offering the model for the creative engagement with urban space that he required: for the development of narrative structures involving the presence of texts submerged within texts, for close identification with other individuals, and for characterizing the attempt to achieve verisimilitude as an agonized activity of constant revisiting and reworking.

Abyss to Abyss: Writing and 'Translation' after Auschwitz

The use of fragments of several languages in Sebald's poem 'Bleston' (English, French, and Yiddish are all incorporated into the German text) is an interesting point and one with a bearing on Sebald's attempts, while and by means of processing his experience of Manchester, to come to terms with the horrors of German twentieth-century history. In this connection it is significant that, at the time of his Manchester residence, Sebald was in correspondence with Theodor

---

[90] Ibid., p.125.
[91] Sebald, in his copy of Michel Butor, *L'Emploi du Temps*, p.78; Ryan, in Zisselsberger, *The Undiscover'd Country*, p.125.

Adorno, enquiring about Adorno's confusing mention of Carl Sternheim in one of the fragments of 1951's *Minima Moralia*.[92] The closeness of Sebald's reading of Adorno is borne out by an interesting feature of the fifth part of 'Bleston'—a citation that appears to be from Pascal but is in fact, as Iain Galbraith points out in a footnote to his translation, a quotation of Adorno's *mis*quotation in his 1962 essay 'Commitment'.[93] It was Adorno who famously remarked that 'nach Auschwitz ein Gedicht zu schreiben, ist barbarisch'—'to write a poem after Auschwitz is barbaric'.[94] In 'Bleston', it might perhaps be said that Sebald's allusive borrowing or 'translation' of material from other works into his own—while often refraining from actually translating it into German—tentatively explores an opportunity submerged within Adorno's maxim, drawing on the etymological suggestiveness of 'barbarisch' as meaning spoken in unknown tongues. Sebald's creation of a patchwork of citations in various languages could be read as an attempt to carve out a new, and at points deliberately incomprehensible, language in which to speak.

Translation from one language into another has a sometimes unexpected bearing on anglophone readers' experience of Sebald's work. For instance, it is notable that reading the English version of 'Bleston' obscures the way that the names of sites like 'Sharon's Full Gospel' and 'Lewis's Big Warehouse' are transcribed directly in English in the original German text, since the surrounding text is in English too—a side effect of translation that effaces the defamiliarizing effect perhaps intended in the original. Set aside only by their capitalization, in Galbraith's English version of the text the linguistic difference of these phrases is traceable, like Ferber's recollection of the German language, 'as no more than an echo, a muted and incomprehensible murmur'.[95] Yet a consideration of 'Bleston' alongside Sebald's other representations of Manchester also suggests other ways in which 'translation' structures his depiction of place, not in terms of the movement from one language to another so much as this kind of direct, denotative movement of motifs between texts and places: a 'borrowing' or 'cobbling' that, as is clear from his creative engagement with both Auerbach's and Butor's work, extends both within and beyond Sebald's oeuvre and often results in a striking effect of uncanny recurrence and allusive reverberation.

One particularly important example of a recurrent motif, given Sebald's sensitivity to combustion, is ash: it is present in *After Nature*, 'Bleston', 'Max

---

[92] This appears in fragment 99, subtitled 'Gold Assay' in Jephcott's 1974 translation (London: Verson, 2005); Sebald and Adorno's brief correspondence is printed in Marcel Atze and Franz Loquai, *Sebald: Lektüren* (Eggingen: Edition Isele, 2005).
[93] Sebald, 'Bleston', in Meyer (ed.), *Über das Land und das Wasser* V.13 (p.26); Galbraith in Sebald, W.G., *Across the Land and the Water: Selected Poems 1964-2001*, ed. and trans. Iain Galbraith (London: Hamish Hamilton, 2011), p.180.
[94] Adorno, 'Cultural Criticism and Society', in *Prisms*, trans. Samuel Weber and Sherry Weber (Cambridge, MA: MIT Press, 1967), p.33.
[95] Sebald, *The Emigrants*, p.182.

134 LANDSCAPE AND SUBJECTIVITY

Ferber' (in the artist's 'ashen' appearance, his studio, and the city itself imagined as a fire 'almost suffocated in ash'), and *Passing Time*, where Revel at one point symbolically burns his map of the city and finally leaves the place with the words 'farther away from you, Bleston, as you lay dying, Bleston, whose dying embers I have fanned'.[96] This recurrence is especially resonant for its suggestion of Paul Celan's 1948 poem 'Todesfuge' ('Death Fugue'), where the 'golden' and 'ashen' hair of two figures named Margarete and Sulamith is incorporated into a hymn-like, circulatory structure, which lacks punctuation and can surely be regarded as a key stylistic model for 'Bleston'. If Celan's poem is one of the best-known German-language attempts to come to poetic terms with the Holocaust, Sebald's depictions of Manchester might be considered in a similar way, suggesting the moves that Sebald was making towards his own 'literature of restitution' both by adapting the frustrations of Revel to the experience of narrativizing traumatic pasts (those of the occluded German-Jewish histories he encountered in the English city, including the Jordan family memoirs, as well as his own) and by engaging creatively with critical theorists who were themselves Jewish refugees, above all Adorno and Benjamin.

Witnessing the recurrence of 'ash' and the repeated references to particular places in Manchester offers a clear view of the system of 'Bastelei' or 'bricolage' by which Sebald self-consciously worked, 'gathering together discoveries, raking them around until they somehow rhyme together' in a manner that suggests no 'final' arrangement but rather seems to keep the motifs of memory and place in constant motion.[97] It also offers a compelling example of the ways that Sebald's work engages in a constant act of 'translation' in the sense of editing, moving, and rearranging motifs and themes—shifting objects and characteristics from one text to another, from one person to another, and from one place to another, creating resonances without any ultimate point of resolution.

The process is replicated in the variant appearance of elements of the Mancunian cityscape in different texts: by the names of buildings and derelict Jewish shops in 'Bleston', for example, which parallel the vacant shops listed in *After Nature* and in turn reappear in the 'Max Ferber' story of *The Emigrants* in Manchester's 'one-time Jewish quarter'. The reference in 'Bleston' to the city's libraries, meanwhile, overlaps with a section in *After Nature* that describes reading the works of the Swiss Renaissance thinker Paracelsus in the university library, and particularly Paracelsus's negative view of northerly things.[98] In the same way, 'Sharon's Full Gospel' forms a variation on the 'Gospel Chapels' that sit between Liston's Music Hall and Strangeways prison in *After Nature*, where the speaker himself witnessed the euphoric healing of the sick and, notably, the blind.[99] Later,

---

[96] Michel Butor, *Passing Time*, trans. Jean Stewart (London: John Calder, 1965), p.310.
[97] Sebald, in Sigrid Löffler, '"Wildes Denken" Gespräch mit W.G. Sebald', p.132 (my translation).
[98] Sebald, *After Nature*, III.IV.63–70 (pp. 97–8).   [99] Ibid., III.IV.82–87 (p.98).

the description of ships that seem to hover in the distance recalls those on the Manchester Shopping Canal which, for Max Ferber, formed 'an incomprehensible' but strangely moving spectacle; elsewhere, the narrator's encounter with a child requesting a 'Penny for the Guy' also appears in both *After Nature* and 'Max Ferber'.[100]

The working and reworking of space and place here can be read as an analogue of Sebald's (and his narrator's) struggles with the writing-up of the sensitive and traumatic histories that he uncovered in England, like the Jordan family memoirs. It also reinforces the close connectedness in Sebald's writing between place and affective experience. A telling example of this appears when Ferber recounts his own trip to see Grünewald's paintings in Isenheim and Colmar—a journey he undertakes in spite of never having managed 'to master my fear of travelling' and which finds us circling back thematically to the account of Grünewald's work in the first part of *After Nature*. Recounting his visit, Ferber describes the 'monstrosity of that suffering' depicted by Grünewald—the 'Ungeheuerlichkeit' in the German also directly recalling the 'ungeheuer' or 'uneasily' resting body of the mountain range near Manchester at the story's opening.[101]

This sequence is particularly important, since it leads us into another way of comprehending the activity of translation and the recurrence of motifs described above. Meditating on the terrible sense of suffering in Grünewald's figures, Ferber remarks that 'mental suffering is effectively without end': 'One may think one has reached the very limit, but there are always more torments to come. One plunges from one abyss into the next.'[102] It is an arresting image, and this description of moving 'from one abyss into the next'—literally a process of *mise-en-abyme*—is multiply significant. First, it is striking for the way that it subtly reveals Sebald's self-consciousness about the activity of translation in all of the senses described above. Though unattributed, the sequence reworks a phrase from Walter Benjamin's 1923 essay 'The Task of the Translator' in which, referring to Hölderlin's translations of Sophocles, Benjamin remarks that 'in them meaning plunges from abyss to abyss until it threatens to become lost in the bottomless depths of language'.[103] Bearing this in mind, Ferber's remark draws attention to the way that Sebald's work often involved oddities of translation: in this case, working the stories of figures encountered in England (and often, though not always, in English) back into German; only to then closely supervise the translation (effectively a kind of *re*-translation) into English again at a later stage, covering his translators' typescripts with pencil annotations. Second, it is significant for the more general way that it suggests the effect of 'vertigo' produced by the activity of assembling so much testimony into narrative form, appropriating, editing, and reworking it in what could easily become an ethically dubious activity.

---

[100] Sebald, *The Emigrants*, p.166.   [101] Sebald, *The Emigrants*, p.170.   [102] Ibid., p.170–1.
[103] Benjamin, 'The Task of The Translator', in *Illuminations*, pp.81–2.

In this way Ferber's remark, itself an appropriation, can be understood as Sebald reflecting on the activities of borrowing, rearranging, and rewriting—both of his own work and that of others—as processes that are fundamental to his depictions of memory, narrative, and affective experience.

A *mise-en-abyme* effect is itself generated here not only by the way that the agonies of Grünewald, Ferber, and the Sebald narrator in their aesthetic tasks are all layered up onto one another—and in turn centre on a submerged allusion to a strikingly melancholic observation by Benjamin—but also by the way in which the narration takes place: the narrator recounts his conversation with Ferber, who in turn recounts his experience of Grünewald, who in turn depicts yet other scenes. Thus the sequence functions in a way that sees the final 'object' of the activity—perhaps the characterization of 'mental suffering' itself—seem constantly to recede from grasp. The framing of all this within Ferber's dust-laden studio in a desolate part of post-industrial Manchester is integral to the overall effect. A narrative *topos* constituted by the connected, multiple representations in *After Nature*, 'Max Ferber', and 'Bleston', this urban landscape provides acts as a crucible for the productive interference between place and biography that is so integral to all Sebald's later writing. Resonating and reverberating between variant renditions, its sites and spectacles are at the centre of a dizzying account of recollection and reconstruction.

4

An English Pilgrim

Sebald's *The Rings of Saturn* and *Austerlitz*

W.G. Sebald's *The Rings of Saturn* was first published in German in 1995 and in English three years later. It documents a series of walks apparently begun in 1992, when, as its narrator declares in a characteristically sombre image, 'the dog days were drawing to an end', and he 'set off to walk the county of Suffolk, in the hope of dispelling the emptiness that takes hold of me whenever I have completed a long stint of work'.[1] It ends with the declaration that 'today, as I bring these notes to a conclusion, is the 13th of April 1995', so that the text's purported duration, precisely circumscribed, closely overlaps with that of Keiller's *London* and *Robinson in Space*.[2]

The works share further parallels: an essayistic form that resembles an elaborate and highly idiosyncratic travelogue; an obsessive interest in often run-down spaces and topographies and their apparently overlooked features; and a tendency to digress unexpectedly from the apparently mundane and familiar to the exotic and remote. And they each have at their centre an eccentric, by turns melancholic figure who moves about almost exclusively on foot, and whose saturnine disposition is channelled through, and shaped and correlated by, the landscape. In *The Rings of Saturn*, these features generate a practical tension between physical movement through space and the countervailing tendency to dwell, unravel, and explore—to dig down, as it were, from space into place—so that the concrete and the abstract, the local and the remote, are placed into frequently unexpected constellations. The result produces not only a familiar theoretical interplay between depth and surface, but a sensitive and stylized account that combines personal experience of the spaces of East Anglia, and elsewhere, with a profound meditation on the woeful and destructive effects of humanity's 'Wissensdrang' or 'thirst for knowledge'.[3]

A 'Prose Book of an Indeterminate Sort': *The Rings of Saturn*

In attempting to brush history, following Walter Benjamin's advice, 'against the grain', *The Rings of Saturn* immediately generates interpretative issues on a formal

---

[1] W.G. Sebald, *The Rings of Saturn*, trans. Michael Hulse (London: Random House, 2002), p.3.
[2] Ibid., p.294.
[3] Sebald, *Die Ringe des Saturn* (Frankfurt: Fischer, 2008), p.74; *The Rings of Saturn*, p.57.

level.[4] Separated into ten numbered parts, each recounting a specific phase of Sebald's walking tour while circulating around a particular historical theme, the text is rather at odds with established narrative convention. Significantly, the German text is subtitled 'Eine englische Wallfahrt' or 'an English pilgrimage'. As in the case of *The Emigrants*'s 'Vier lange Erzählungen' or *After Nature*'s 'Ein Elementargedicht', this has not appeared on English editions, although the untranslated, epigraphic citation of an 1890 letter by Joseph Conrad, in which he refers to 'ces âmes malheureuses qui ont élu de faire le pèlerinage à pied' ('those unhappy souls who are elected to make the pilgrimage on foot'), does act as a submerged allusion. The 'pilgrimage' descriptor, which, as Rebecca Solnit has observed, is 'almost universally embedded in human culture as a literal means of spiritual journey', helps to explain the text's apparent ambivalence between purposefulness and drift—or between strict plotting and vagrant, essayistic digressiveness.[5]

Sebald's first English publisher, Harvill, categorized *The Rings of Saturn* as 'Memoir/Travel/History', making it the only one of his four major prose texts not to be pitched explicitly as a work of the imagination. A sheet of paper in the writer's *Handschriftensammlung* at the German Literature Archive contains a list of phrases including 'Naturgeschichte' ('natural history'), 'Trauerübung' (sorrow-exercise), 'Lebens & Reisebeschreibung' ('life and travel memoir'), and 'Mikrologie und Kosmologie' ('micrology and cosmology'), among others—as if Sebald were feeling around for an appropriate term for his text.[6] In a 2001 interview he called it simply a 'Prosabuch unbestimmter Art' (a 'prose-book of an indeterminate sort').[7] Going on to connect this with his work as a literary scholar, he explained how, tiring of academic writing, he increasingly 'felt drawn to write in a much more tentative sort of way', moving 'from the straight monograph to essayistic exploration, dealing with my subjects in an elliptical sort of way'.[8] Some echoes of 'conventional academic writing' remain clear, however. For instance, the ten numbered sections of the text are listed in the contents pages with an overview of their subject matter ('Schiphol airport—The invisibility of man—The Sailors' Reading Room) that apes a slightly archaic scholarly form, the eccentricity of the subject matter pushing this similarity into relief.

---

[4] Walter Benjamin, 'Theses on the Philosophy of History', in *Illuminations*, trans. Harry Zohn (New York: Schocken, 2002).

[5] Rebecca Solnit, *Wanderlust: A History of Walking* (London: Verso, 2001), p.46.

[6] Handschriftensammlung, German Literature Archive.

[7] Sebald, interviewed in *Der Spiegel*, November 2001, pp.228–34 (quoted Deane Blackler, in *Reading W.G. Sebald: Adventure and Disobedience* (Columbia: Camden House, 2007), p.88).

[8] 'That temptation to work with very fragmentary pieces of evidence, to fill in the gaps and blank spaces and create out of this a meaning which is greater than that which you can prove, led me to work in a way which wasn't determined by any discipline. It wasn't history, it wasn't literary criticism, it wasn't sociology, but it was all of these things together' (Sebald in Christopher Bigsby, *Writers in Conversation* (Norwich: Arthur Miller Centre, 2000), pp.151–2).

The fact that the text is commonly shelved alongside novels arguably only exaggerates this problem of genre, since it is the novel form that Sebald seems to militate most directly against. 'I have an aversion to the standard novel', he remarked in an interview with James Atlas of the *Paris Review*: 'there's something trite about it. You can feel the wheels turning.'[9] The expression recalls André Breton's aggravated demolition of the novel form in the first *Manifesto of Surrealism*, with its descriptions that are 'nothing but so many superimposed images taken from some stock catalogue' and its effect of rendering 'experience [...] increasingly circumscribed'. In this light, Sebald's choice of a highly idiosyncratic travelogue form—as well as his use of photography—can be read as an avant-garde gesture mimicking that of Surrealist texts like Aragon's *Paris Peasant* or Breton's *Nadja*, which Benjamin called 'a book with a banging door'.[10] The travelogue form, permitting a kind of formal spaciousness after the model of walking itself, allows room for Sebald's distinctively mordant narrative persona; it also opens up this kind of variously submerged interaction with the work of critics like Breton, Benjamin, and Adorno. Sebald's mode of 'discreet or tender subjectivity', germane to his predilection for themes of drift, decay, and destruction, certainly recalls Theodor Adorno's remark in *Minima Moralia* (1951) that 'in the era of his decay, the individual can once more contribute to knowledge'. Rejecting the novel form, it might be said, is precisely what allows this redemptive activity to take place.[11]

The Structure of Space: Threads, Mazes, and Elective Affinities

If figures like Adorno and Breton exercise a certain influence on Sebald's choice of form, then marginal figures dredged from the East Anglian landscape itself have an equally significant role in shaping the text. It is partly through direct personal and indirect elective affinity with such characters that East Anglia exerts its presence in Sebald's writing. In the final part, for instance, the narrator writes with admiration of the Huguenot weavers of eighteenth-century Norwich, of the 'indescribable beauty' of their pre-industrial creations, and particularly of 'the marvellous strips of colour in their pattern books, the edges and gaps filled with mysterious symbols'.[12] Though his monochrome reproduction flattens the colours, Sebald includes a double-page image from one of these volumes, remarking that they 'seem to me to be leaves from the one true book which none of our

---

[9] James Atlas, 'W.G. Sebald: a Profile', *Paris Review* No.151 (Summer 1999), p.282.
[10] André Breton, *Manifestoes of Surrealism*, trans. Richard Seaver and Helen Lane (Ann Arbor: University of Michigan, 1974), p.8; p.10.
[11] Rüdiger Görner, *The Anatomist of Melancholy* (Munich: Iudicium, 2003), p.79; Theodor Adorno, *Minima Moralia: Reflections from Damaged Life*, trans. E.F.N. Jephcott (London: Verso, 2010), p.17.
[12] Sebald, *The Rings of Saturn*, p.283.

textual or pictorial works can begin to rival'—although his own proclivity for alluding to or ventriloquizing other writers and cataloguing events and histories, in its tendency towards a 'pattern book' aesthetic, seems to constitute some kind of attempt.[13]

The sense of the text itself as a fabric, seeming to toy with the idea of 'weaving' a story or 'yarn', is significant here. In one reminiscence during the course of his third walk, Sebald's narrator recalls himself as a child watching the swallows flying 'in the last light' through 'the valley'—the direct article offering a sense of privacy and familiarity to the digression, as if Sebald's reader knows precisely which valley he means. 'I would imagine', the narrator writes of the careering swallows, 'that the world was held together by their courses through the air'.[14] Later, these imaginary threads seem to be actualized in one of Sebald's most striking photographs, which he arrives at while discussing the

> networks of a complexity that it goes far beyond the power of any one individual to imagine, from the thousands of hoists and winches that once worked the South African diamond mines to the floors of today's stock and commodity exchanges, through which the global tides of information flow without cease.[15]

Later still, in the course of the seventh part, Sebald's sense of affinity with the émigré German poet Michael Hamburger, arrived at through unexpected mutual acquaintances in their pasts, is paralleled textually by the way that surreptitious allusions to Hölderlin (with whom Hamburger himself has a strong sense of affinity) and to *King Lear* are included during an earlier discussion of Dunwich Heath, long before the writer and the text are explicitly mentioned during a discussion with Hamburger and his wife. The technique lends an unnerving déjà vu to parallel Sebald's own sense of having been in Hamburger's house before.

The disquieting experience of becoming lost in a maze on Dunwich Heath is embroiled with this trickery, leading to a dream where the yew maze of Somerleyton Hall is superimposed onto the Heath. At this point, the narrator remarks that 'I knew [...] with absolute certainty' that the maze's pattern 'represented a cross-section of my brain'. The moment forms a remarkably clear statement of the way in which subjectivity is layered onto place in this text, paralleling the uncanny way in which mazes, as Rebecca Solnit has remarked, elide real and imagined space by 'blurring the difference between map and world', offering 'the possibility of being real creatures in symbolic space'.[16] If Solnit is right in her suggestion that the mazes depicted on the floors of certain medieval churches 'offered the possibility of compressing a pilgrimage into the compact space of a church floor, with the difficulties of spiritual progress represented by the

[13] Ibid., p.286. [14] Ibid., p.67. [15] Ibid., pp.91–2. [16] Ibid., p.173.

twists and turns', then the Dunwich Heath incident also acts to replicate the 'pèlerinage' in miniature.[17]

Sequences such as this establish a sense of the text's conception as an elaborately intricate fabric, constantly suggesting connections with other places and texts—something that has been noticed by artists like Barbara Hui, whose electronic 'map' of *The Rings of Saturn* appears in Grant Gee's 2001 documentary film *Patience: After Sebald*.[18] Such connections also run between Sebald's own works, too: an unexplained allusion to 'various enquiries at Bad Kissingen' in part IV, for instance, is clearly a reference to the journey described within the 'Max Ferber' story in *The Emigrants*, though the allusion is deliberately opaque.

Strikingly, the sense of strange or unexpected affinity appears in the very maps that Sebald used, at least partially, in his actual navigation of rural Suffolk. His archive contains copies of hand-drawn walking maps of East Anglia, whose author is identified only as 'Wilfrid George'. On one of these, Sebald has playfully added an 'S', but, although 'Wilfrid George' sounds uncannily like an anglicization of 'Winfried Georg', the real Wilfrid George is not Sebald. Still, the coincidence (and Sebald's playful 'S') suggests one way that the writer may have been provoked to consider this landscape in terms of affinities and doppelgängers. This forms another example of J.J. Long's observation that 'Sebald's peripatetic narrators repeatedly encounter new places, people and things' but that these are often ciphers or analogues of the Sebaldian self, multiplying and filtering his presence in the text.[19] Figures like Thomas Browne, Joseph Conrad, Roger Casement, Edward FitzGerald, Algernon Swinburne, and Chateaubriand are all significant examples of this effect in *The Rings of Saturn*, as is Sebald's deceased colleague Janine Dakyns, whose office is described as a 'paper landscape' and who, amidst mountains of notes and documents, apparently 'resembled the angel in Dürer's *Melancholia*, steadfast among the instruments of destruction'.[20]

The saturnizing gaze, as we might term it, that seems to connect these figures is embellished by the presentation of writing as an extremely arduous, perhaps pointless pursuit. 'Of all the individuals afflicted with the disease of thought,' Sebald averred elsewhere in an essay on Rousseau, 'the writer is perhaps the most incurable.'[21] Almost all of the writers with whom Sebald establishes an affinity in

---

[17] Solnit, *Wanderlust: A History of Walking*, p.70.
[18] Barbara Hui, 'Litmap', http://barbarahui.net/litmap/#.
[19] J.J. Long, *W.G. Sebald: Image, Archive, Modernity* (Edinburgh: Edinburgh University Press, 2007), p.6.
[20] Ibid., p.8.
[21] From his essay on Rousseau, published in *A Place In The Country*, trans. Jo Catling (London: Hamish Hamilton, 2013), p.54. Of the Norwich weavers and their looms, Sebald remarks on the 'peculiar symbiosis' between them and, in turn, how 'we are able to maintain ourselves on this earth only by being harnessed to the machines that we have invented', so that 'weavers in particular, together with scholars and writers with whom they had much in common, tended to suffer from melancholy and all the evils associated with it'. Clearly reflecting onto himself, Sebald continues that this was 'understandable given the nature of their work, which forced them to sit bent over, day after day,

The Rings of Saturn seem to suffer from a similar melancholy proclivity: Conrad and Casement witness and engage in the savage wastefulness of colonial exploitation in the Belgian Congo, while Chateaubriand, in an episode borrowed from his autobiography *Mémoires d'Outre Tombe*, is depicted as caught in a hopeless love affair whilst exiled to Suffolk during the French Revolution. Non-writers are also significant: the farmer and model-maker Thomas Abrams's model of the Grand Temple of Jerusalem—a real project built by a real Norfolk farmer named Alec Garrard—is described as a 'never ending, meaningless and pointless project', which 'because of my increasingly accurate knowledge [...] now seems in every respect more difficult to complete than ten or fifteen years ago'.[22] Abrams's/Garrard's turn of phrase here is conspicuously similar to Sebald's own in an interview with Christopher Bigsby, remarking that 'people who tend to have rather blithe views of life often consider that writing is a form of self-therapy. I don't particularly think so. Rather, I believe the more you turn your mind towards things the more difficult it gets.'[23]

In this relation, one thing that is highly noticeable in *The Rings of Saturn*, as in all of Sebald's work, is the way in which these networks of empathic understanding are established almost exclusively between men. The doomed romance between the Chateaubriand and Charlotte Ives is exceptional in being one of the text's rare instances of profound affinity between a man and a woman, and Sebald's colleague Janine Dakyns is the only woman to be directly associated with melancholia as such.[24] Homosocial friendships, by contrast, such as those between Swinburne and Theodore Watts-Dunton, FitzGerald and William Browne, are often significantly couched in terms of repressed longing: Sebald writes of his brief car journey with Thomas Abrams, for instance, that 'I wished that the short drive through the country would never end, that we could go on and on, all the way to Jerusalem,' and it is not until after this point, over three quarters of the way through the text, that a mention of his wife 'Clara' appears. Her role: to pick the author up in her car and drive him home.[25] Seen in this light, *The Rings of Saturn* does little to dislodge the idea that melancholy and a taste for ruination are distinctly male prerogatives, and Jennifer Radden's observation that

---

straining to keep their eye on the complex pattern they had created. It is difficult to imagine the depths of despair into which those can be driven who, even after the end of the working day, are engrossed in their intricate designs and who are pursued, even into their dreams, by the feeling that they have got hold of the wrong thread' (Sebald, *The Rings of Saturn*, p.283).

[22] Ibid., pp.244–5; Abrams readily discusses the appearance of madness generated by his task, until the point at which it was in some sense validated by the arrival of Lord Rothschild in a limousine. 'Ever since then', he remarks, 'even the family have looked on me as a scholar engaged in serious study.' The observation clearly suits Sebald's ironic self-fashioning as an anachronistic, eccentric figure, as well as the diligent craftsman 'afflicted' by his work.

[23] Bigsby, *Writers in Conversation*, p.145.   [24] Sebald, *The Rings of Saturn*, pp.250–60.
[25] Ibid., p.249.

'the loquacious male subject' of melancholia 'leaves little room for the mute suffering of women' certainly seems to apply.[26]

Literacy, Topography, and Destruction

One particularly important analogue to the 'Sebald-Ich' is William Hazel, the gardener at Somerleyton Hall. Hazel describes having been fascinated by the enormous number of bombing raids flying from East Anglia to Germany during the Second World War, and his account forms an oblique reflection of Sebald's own biography.[27] He explains how he possessed a map of Germany in which single images of particular landmarks were used to denote each city. In a strange, unsettling elision of map and territory, this memory darkly recalls how major landmarks like Cologne cathedral would often be left standing by Allied bombers during the Second World War in order for them to act as waypoints for navigators. The image also strongly recalls Sebald's description of a card game known as 'Cities Quartet' that he possessed as a child, and which he discussed in a 2001 lecture reprinted under the title 'An Attempt at Restitution' in the volume *Campo Santo* (De. 2003, Eng. 2005). This game was 'based on pictures of the cities of Germany', by means of which he both learned to write and cultivated what became a 'passion for geography' and a 'delight in topography' that was implicitly bound up with destruction and horror.[28]

Creative self-fashioning or not, this presentation of a coincidence between literacy, topography, and destruction is clearly highly significant for Sebald's work. Hazel goes on to describe how later, as a soldier in Lüneburg with 'the army of occupation', he learned to speak German 'so that I could read what the Germans themselves had said about the bombings and their lives in the ruined cities', and his discovery that

> to my astonishment [...] the search for such accounts invariably proved fruitless. No-one at the time seemed to have written about their experiences or afterwards recalled their memories.[29]

Setting his anecdote in Lüneburg, where a significant German surrender was signed by the German Admiral von Friedeburg in May 1945, Hazel's anecdote anticipates Sebald's 1997 lectures that became part of *Luftkrieg und Literatur* (translated in 2003 as *On The Natural History of Destruction*). This work was his caustic assessment of German writers' failure to come to terms with the air war

---

[26] Jennifer Radden (ed.), *The Nature of Melancholy: From Aristotle to Kristeva* (Oxford: Oxford University Press, 2000), p.65.
[27] Sebald, *The Rings of Saturn*, pp.38–40.
[28] Sebald, 'An Attempt at Restitution', *Campo Santo*, p.207. [29] Ibid., p.39.

and the associated area-bombing of Germany—and, in turn, the wider sense of a conspiratorial silence about the atrocities committed under National Socialism.

In *On The Natural History of Destruction*, Sebald lauded the approach of Alexander Kluge, whose 1970 account of the bombing of Halberstadt in his *Neue Geschichten* series consisted of what Sebald called 'archaeological excavations of the slag-heaps of our collective existence', taking a documentary mode that presents an array of testimony in the form of evidence, with minimal accompanying remarks or explanation.[30] Sebald's own method in *The Rings of Saturn* runs in parallel, flattening the distinction between fact and fiction and the provenance of testimony. His use of other characters as doubles or filters of the narrating self is embellished by the decision (here as in other works) not to use quotation marks for direct or reported speech. Thus Sebald and Hazel seem to merge during conversation, as the 'I' shifts perpetually back and forth between narrator and interlocutor. This effect is exaggerated in the English edition of the text (in the original, Hazel's speech is sometimes left untranslated, making the shift obvious).[31] The same technique means that allusions to and extracts from texts like Borges's 1940 short story *Tlön, Uqbar, Orbis Tertius* (which itself features a narrator who, like Sebald in the text's first part, is apparently translating Thomas Browne's *Hydriotaphia*) are introduced and discussed without any direct indication of whether they are factual or not.

The disorientating effect that is produced by this mirrors the confusion between map and territory described above, rendering East Anglia as a landscape scored by a lattice of empathic connections laid onto the text and the space it documents. If Sebald assembles his characters and allusions like a 'pattern book' or 'catalogue of samples', then his text becomes a haphazard index to the landscape of East Anglia, which begins to emerge as a kind of fabric of their stories—matching Doreen Massey's conception of a space that is 'open, multiple and relational and always becoming' at the same time that it frequently refers us back to the subjectivity of the first-person explorer-narrator.[32]

The Religion of a Doctor: Thomas Browne

In his *English Journey*, J.B. Priestley described a wish for Norwich to become

> a literary and publishing centre, the seat of a fine school of painters, a city in which foreigners exiled by intolerance may seek refuge and turn their sons into sturdy and tolerant East Anglians.

---

[30] Sebald, *On the Natural History of Destruction*, trans. Anthea Bell (London: Hamish Hamilton, 2003), p.60.
[31] Sebald, *The Rings of Saturn*, pp.38–9.
[32] Doreen Massey, *For Space* (London: Sage, 2008), p.59.

The sequence could well be read as a stimulus to *The Rings of Saturn*, which, though focused on walks conducted in Suffolk, frequently tends back towards themes and personae with a close connection to Norwich, where Sebald worked and near to which he lived.[33] Norwich's 'Stranger's Hall'—where the silk pattern-books were kept before being moved to their present location, the Bridewell Museum—is a significant locality in this respect. One of its artefacts is a portrait of the very same Thomas Browne whose 1658 text *Hydriotaphia* Sebald's narrator, like Borges's in *Tlön, Uqbar, Orbis Tertius*, is busy translating, and whose intricate works, including *The Garden of Cyrus* (1643) and *Religio Medici* (also 1658), were an object of devotion for writers including Edgar Allan Poe, as well as Borges.

Sebald emphasized the role of locality, although not the Strangers' Hall, in his own discovery of Browne's work, claiming to have first encountered him via a statue situated outside the Norwich branch of C&A—a rather Keiller-esque conjunction that has the effect of grounding the two writers' connection in a mutual association with the same place and an apparently chance encounter. This may be apocryphal: Philippa Comber, a psychoanalyst whose sensitive memoir of Sebald, *Ariadne's Thread*, was published in 2014, avers that she herself introduced Sebald to Browne in December 1981.[34] More significant than this, for *The Rings of Saturn*, is the way that Browne's distinctively reflective and exploratory approach to knowledge dwells as long with the arcane, mythic, or fantastical as with the apparently rational—or confounds these distinctions: the mention in *Religio Medici*, for example, of the 'strange and mystical transmigrations' of silk worms, which 'turned my Philosophy into Divinity' and clearly inspired Sebald's extensive digression on the history of sericulture.[35]

It is clear that *Hydriotaphia*, a 'potted' history of cremation, was particularly important to Sebald, too. In this text, in a mournful and curiously detached manner (Sebald describes a 'sense of levitation' when reading), Browne discusses a set of burial urns discovered in a field in Old Walsingham, Norfolk, thought by him to be Roman but in fact of Saxon origin.[36] The text combines profundity with eminently practical comments on the benefits of cremation, which has the useful effect that our remains 'do abate a notable proportion', escapes the problem of grave robbers, and sidesteps the otherwise thorny eschatological problem of what posture the dead should assume.[37]

The improbable 'odyssey' of Browne's own remains—which Sebald describes in detail—retains a startlingly *outre-tombe* quality: in *Hydriotaphia* Browne expatiates, for instance, on the idea that seeking total control over one's memory is nothing but a 'superannuated peece of folly', as if somehow anticipating the

---

[33] Priestley, *An English Journey*, pp.366–7.
[34] Philippa Comber, *Ariadne's Thread: In Memory of W.G. Sebald* (Norwich: Propolis, 2014).
[35] Thomas Browne, *Major Works*, ed. C.A. Patrides (Harmondsworth: Penguin, 1977), p.58.
[36] Sebald, *The Rings of Saturn*, p.19.   [37] Browne, *Major Works*, p.292.

strange and hapless course that his own skull would follow—buried in St Peter Mancroft church, accidentally disinterred two centuries later, and passing (via a city councillor) to the hospital's museum before being subsequently reburied in 1921.[38] This in turn reflects the oddly uncanny sense that some critics have had when reading Sebald's own work. Geoff Dyer, for instance, has noted that 'the first thing to be said about W.G. Sebald's books is that they *always* had a posthumous quality to them'. It is certainly the case that Sebald's discussion of *Hydriotaphia* can read like part of an involuted literary joke about the 'death of the author' famously announced by Roland Barthes in 1967—a provocative and playfully academic conjunction of ideas that is typical of Sebald's work.[39]

Particularly relevant for *The Rings of Saturn*'s suggestion of the unexpected interconnectedness and patterns to be found in the 'decline-history' of nature and culture is Browne's 'quincunx', a tessellating five-point structure that he 'identifies [...] everywhere' in nature (not unlike Robinson's Buckminsterfullerenes) and whose form he describes in *The Garden of Cyrus*. The quincunx acts as a model for the way that experience and reminiscence freely intersect within *The Rings of Saturn*'s digressive form, contributing to its fabric-like quality. Built around a process which J.J. Long sees as relying on a 'hermeneutics of resemblance', this informs the intricately linked structure of Sebald's work, where coincidence and similarity often form the basis of otherwise abrupt shifts between subject matter.[40] The compendious result links significantly with the motif of the cabinet of curiosities: if, in Keiller's *London*, Robinson saw his task as similar to that of the diarist John Evelyn, then it is significant that in his own copy of a 1993 article by Anthony Batty Shaw in the *Journal of Medical Biography*, Sebald put a line alongside the comment that

> [o]n a visit to Browne's Norwich home in 1671, John Evelyn described 'his whole house and garden being a paradise and cabinet of rarities, and that of the best collections, especially medals, books, plants and natural things'.[41]

In all of these ways, Browne's presence in *The Rings of Saturn* is evidence of how the text is inflected by the East Anglian landscape even before the place, as such, has been discussed. The system of the quincunx and the 'hermeneutics of resemblance', meanwhile, accounts for a curious problem in discussing the text: if its thematic structure resembles a kind of fabric (or the silk cocoons that Sebald describes in a digression on sericulture) then the critic focuses on a particular point only to be inevitably drawn away from it—as if, in picking at one thread, one

---

[38] Ibid., p.308.
[39] Geoff Dyer, 'W.G. Sebald, Bombing and Thomas Bernhard', in *Working The Room* (Edinburgh: Canongate, 2010), p.231.
[40] Sebald, *The Rings of Saturn*, p.20; Long, Image, Archive, Modernity, p.33.
[41] German Literature Archive.

is forced to account for all those which are woven through it and have been disturbed: a process that parallels the travelling narrator's own vacillation between dwelling and displacement as he moves through this landscape 'am äußersten Rand der Erde', or 'at the outermost limit of the earth'.[42]

East Anglia, Rambling Tours, and the Idea of Englishness

At the bottom of Sebald's list of projected genre descriptions in the German Literature Archive's *Handschriftensammlung* is the phrase 'Rand des Deutschen Ozeans' or 'Edge of the German Ocean'. This sense of peripherality, figuring East Anglia as an 'edgeland' not only of Britain but also of Europe, even of civilization at large, permeates the text. It echoes the apocalyptic tenor of its second epigraph, from the *Brockhaus Encyclopedia*, which explains that the rings of Saturn are 'in all likelihood [...] fragments of a former moon that was too close to the planet and was destroyed by its tidal effect'. The East Anglian landscape also serves as a correlate to the text's preoccupation with themes of drift, decay, and destruction and the idea—given as part of the so-called 'Corsica Project' that Sebald began in the early 1990s but abandoned in favour of *The Rings of Saturn* and *Austerlitz*— that 'collective catastrophe marks the point where history threatens to revert to natural history'.[43] It is rendered as a forlorn and desolate region, riven with 'traces of destruction, reaching far back into the past'.[44]

As Christian Moser has pointed out, '[b]oth Marcilio Ficino in his *De vita* and Robert Burton in his *Anatomy of Melancholy* recommended the "*deambulatorio per amoena loca*" (walk in pleasant places) as an effective cure against the spleen'. Yet, in many ways, the East Anglian landscape hardly seems like an appropriate setting for such an enterprise.[45] In his essay on Sebald and the tradition of the 'literary walk', Moser develops this point by arguing that 'as a cure for melancholy, the journey along the East Anglian coastline seems ill-conceived' and 'more apt to produce melancholy than to cure it'.[46] In fact, Sebald's depiction of East Anglia enlists it as an analogue to his narrative self's frayed and tangential sense of identity, presenting a correlate to his melancholic condition. *Walking* through these spaces, in this respect, offers a perfect opportunity for '*working* through' his condition or temperament. The medieval port town of Dunwich, for instance, of which only a few crumbling ruins now remain, precipitates a mournful commentary on the inevitable process by which its inhabitants 'abandoned their hopeless

---

[42] Sebald, *Die Ringe des Saturn*, p.67; *The Rings of Saturn*, p.52.   [43] Sebald, *Campo Santo*, p.85.
[44] Sebald, *The Rings of Saturn*, p.3.
[45] Christian Moser, 'Peripatetic Liminality: Sebald and the Tradition of the Literary Walk', in Markus Zisselsberger (ed.), *The Undiscover'd Country: W.G. Sebald and the Poetics of Travel* (Columbia: Camden House, 2010), p.39.
[46] Moser, in Zisselsberger (ed.), *The Undiscover'd Country*, p.39.

struggle, turned their backs on the sea, and, whenever their declining means allowed it, built to the westward in a protracted flight that went on for generations'.[47]

The local history books and pamphlets in Sebald's library, held at the German Literature Archive, dwell on accounts of destruction and images of places like Dunwich and Orford in ruins after storms. Sebald marks, for instance, a description in Jean and Stuart Bacon's 1988 *Dunwich Suffolk* of how 'human bones can often be seen protruding from the cliff face and after a cliff fall many bones are strewn across the beach' and, later, of how at All Saints' Churchyard in Dunwich 'sometimes a white skull can be seen staring out to sea'.[48] He must certainly have been struck by the very clear difference between All Saints Church as it is depicted in an 1880 photograph in *Dunwich Suffolk* (see Figure 4.1) and the reduced version of it that he encountered on his visit. The fact that he adopts the same framing for his own photograph certainly suggests this. The North Sea erosion, effected by the tides and therefore, in turn, by the moon, here acts as a very visible version of the 'tidal effect' that, according to Sebald's epigraphic citation, destroyed Saturn's former moon and thereby produced its distinctive rings.

One effect of the East Anglian setting is to situate Sebald pointedly against the current of 'progress'. He seems to identify strongly with figures like the isolated fishermen on the beach known as 'Shingle Street' who camp out like 'the last stragglers of some nomadic people'.[49] The photograph of their tents along the strand, fading to an indeterminate vanishing point, embroiders the description. Reminiscent, perhaps, of the 'horizon of the sea in the background of Dürer's *Melencolia*', which Walter Benjamin focused on as an allusion to 'the melancholic's inclination for long journeys', this also carries a certain science-fiction suggestion of something like J.G. Ballard's 'terminal beach'. Replicated in others of the images included in the text, the bleached horizon produces a subtle sense of some uninhabitable, post-apocalyptic future.[50]

Later, the science-fiction suggestiveness is more emphatic at Orford Ness: a vast spit created by longshore-drift which seems to appeal to the narrator as a place created by the waste products of natural process. Its strange, otherworldly concrete 'pagoda' structures, however, part of an atomic weapons testing facility left in place when the National Trust took charge of the site in 1993, lend it a residual 'extraterritorial quality': the narrator imagines himself 'amidst the ruins of our own civilization after its extinction in some future catastrophe'. Soon afterwards, he looks back at the mainland and imagines seeing the windmills and pumps that

---

[47] Sebald, *The Rings of Saturn*, p.158.
[48] Jean Bacon and Stuart Bacon, *Dunwich Suffolk* (Marks Tey, Essex: Segment, 1988), p.12; p.30.
[49] Sebald, *The Rings of Saturn*, p.51.
[50] Walter Benjamin, *The Origin of German Tragic Drama*, trans. John Osborne (London: Verso, 2009), p.149.

All Saints Church, Dunwich, c. 1880. By kind permission of Mr. H. H. Lanman.

Figure 4.1 Photograph of All Saints Church, Dunwich, c.1880 by H.H. Lanman, reproduced in Jean and Stuart Bacon's *Dunwich Suffolk* (1988). Courtesy of Stuart Bacon.

are themselves described, in the second part of the text, as 'ruined conical brick buildings, like relics of an extinct civilization'.[51]

Sebald's approach to place and imagination in *The Rings of Saturn*, as elsewhere, has excited disparate opinions. Deane Blackler has written that 'place in Sebald is a series of stations, each a transit stop in this kind of pilgrimage of the mind and never really a destination'; and that 'Sebald's accounts of places are far less scrupulously indexed than they seem'.[52] J.M. Coetzee, meanwhile, has complained that Sebald frequently fails to

> lift off from the biographical or the essayistic—the prosaic in the everyday sense of the word—into the realm of the imaginative. [...] Chapters on Joseph Conrad, Roger Casement, the poet Edward FitzGerald, and the last empress of China, all of whom—surprisingly—have links with East Anglia, remain anchored in the prosaic.[53]

---

[51] Ibid., p.233; p.237. Christopher Woodward discusses the Trust's 'brave decision' to preserve the military structures in his book, *In Ruins* (London: Random House, 2002), p.223.

[52] Blackler, *Reading W.G. Sebald*, p.190.

[53] J.M. Coetzee, in *After Sebald: Essays and Illuminations*, ed. Jon Cook (Woodbridge: Full Circle Editions, 2014), pp.87–8.

By the one measure, Sebald is too imaginative; by the other, he is not imaginative enough. This opposition seems to emerge partly from the diverse expectations with which readers must arrive at the text (expecting either 'Memoir/Travel/ History', guide book, philosophical treatise, or novel). It neatly characterizes a tension whose roots might be traced to an article written by Sebald for the 'Travel' section of the German newspaper *Die Zeit* in July 1974, entitled 'Die hölzernen Engel von East Anglia: Eine individuelle Bummeltour durch Norfolk and Suffolk' ('The Wooden Angels of East Anglia: An Individual Ramble through Norfolk and Suffolk'). This article was accompanied by photographs, a map of the writer's itinerary, and useful information on ferry crossings.[54] The 'angels' it mentions, a distinctive feature of many East Anglian churches, remain unmentioned in *The Rings of Saturn*, although the subtle double meaning of 'englische' in the text's subtitle ('eine englische Wallfahrt') as 'angelic' might be read as a submerged allusion.

As Sebald averred in a later interview with the *New Yorker*, *The Rings of Saturn* emerged from his 'idea of writing a few short pieces for the [...] German papers in order to pay for the extravagance of a fortnight's rambling tour'.[55] The account is notable for its espoused individuality: the region's waterways might be described as a 'Freizeitparadies' (a 'free-time paradise') after the manner of a mass-market travel brochure, but holidaymakers are schooled away from established sights like Cambridge or the Saxon Burial mound at Sutton Hoo and towards places like Southwold and the old creaking inns that Sebald will patronize in *The Rings of Saturn*. In this way, the article is interesting in that it says directly what is only implicit in the final text: the supposed melancholic atmosphere of the region is rendered rather as a special flavour or mood to be cultivated than a morbid predisposition to be borne. A description of the taste of smoked eel, for instance, segues neatly into 'den Geschmack der ostenglischen Melancholie' ('the taste of East Anglian melancholy'). Other differences, like the straightforward use of 'Nordsee' and 'nördlichen Meer'—where *The Rings of Saturn* often employs the more affected, archaic term 'German Ocean'—give a sense of the latter text's subtle stylization.[56]

It is notable that the compound term 'Bummeltour' here summons not only an idea of rambling, strolling, or wandering but also a Kerouacian sense of idling, drifting, or loafing: the walk here must be qualified as seeming more than slightly dilettantish. Likewise, the text's provenance in the 'travel' section of a liberal

---

[54] A translation by Richard Sheppard appeared in *Journal of European Studies* 41.3-4 (2011), pp.243-54.
[55] Quoted by Macfarlane in Cook, *After Sebald*, p.23.
[56] Jo Catling and Richard Hibbit (eds.), *Saturn's Moons: W.G. Sebald—A Handbook* (London: Legenda, 2011), p.320.

newspaper affects Sebald's claim in the same *New Yorker* interview that it was the 'advantage of walking' that he would 'find things by the wayside'—a 'tiny little museum' or the 'odd details' that proliferate in *The Rings of Saturn* (like the museum at Strangers' Hall where the weavers' pattern books are kept). Such sites begin to seem not so much the objects of the melancholic's elective affinity as that most desirable of all touristic objects or 'experiences'—whatever can be found that still remains unblemished by tourism.

Critics have sometimes seemed keen to occlude this provenance, which makes Sebald out more as Benjamin's debonair, bourgeois 'collector' than his down-at-heel 'ragpicker'. Long, for instance, pointedly fails to mention Orford Ness's 1993 preservation as a 'heritage' site by the National Trust, seeing Sebald's visit as

> the episode in which the contrast between the embodied practice of the narrator and the normative expectations encoded in cartographic representations is most marked. Rather than gravitate towards the numerous tourist attractions or places of local interest with which the Ordnance Survey maps are generously sprinkled, he visits the unmapped, abandoned terrain of the military base that is only accessible by boat.[57]

In fact, Sebald's penchant for the strange, desolate, and undeveloped, which he will then 'invest [...] with myriad cultural meanings', might well be seen merely as part of the familiar cycle of tourism's appropriation and exploitation of the unspoilt.[58] In the light of its actual recuperation into heritage spectacle, the conspicuous absence of Orford Ness's military ruins from the outmoded Ordnance Survey Map included in the text actually seems to play out this process—seeming to make it into the literally 'uncharted' territory that, in actual fact, it had stopped being. In this context, too, Christian Moser's assertion that walking, as 'an outdated mode of travelling', 'marks a gesture of distinction [...] from the dominating travel-form of mass tourism' might then be read with a new emphasis on the word 'distinction'; its attempt 'to experience the country in a different, more intensive way than ordinary travellers' reimagined not only as a highly sophisticated and even elitist pursuit but also a part of tourism's inevitable appropriation of new modes of travelling and bearing witness.[59]

Registering this helps clear a path towards thinking about Sebald's sometimes uncritical relation with England and Englishness. One of the critiques of Sebald that Robert Macfarlane notes is 'that his characters, including his narrators, are a dynasty of Miss Havishams, living out a gossamery, granular existence, cherishing decay, falling joylessly to bits': figures like the 'Onkel Toby', an allusion to Sterne, mentioned in the poem 'Holkham Gap', or the invented recluse George Wyndham

---

[57] Long, *Image, Archive, Modernity*, p.134.   [58] Ibid., p134.
[59] Moser, in Zisselberger (ed.), *The Undiscover'd Country*, p.37.

152 LANDSCAPE AND SUBJECTIVITY

Le Strange, who leaves his vast estate to a housekeeper.[60] The rambler and dramaturge Phil Smith directly criticized what he saw as Sebald's class-blindness in his 2014 book *On Walking:—And Stalking Sebald*. 'Is Sebald's problem when confronting catastrophe', asked Smith, '—nuclear war, ecological devastation, depredation of species, Nazism—that he sees everything but the catastrophes of class?'[61] Staying in an unnamed inn in Lowestoft and chatting with a heavily drinking couple from Essex, he remarks: 'Sebald would have done better to stay here, inexpensively, rather than spend money on the faded glory of the now defunct Albion.'[62]

In her memoir, Philippa Comber observes that Sebald seemed always to have thought himself a 'guest' in England but that 'for all that, he had always taken pleasure in immersing things in all things English; and gone a long way to adopt an English way of life at the Old Rectory in Poringland'. Comber adds that in retrospect 'it seems likely that it was my very "Englishness"—*roots and family connections*, no matter how remote—that formed the cornerstone of his interest in me' (my emphasis).[63] Comber's father taught at Wellington College; her uncle, a missionary, is in the process of being canonized; she is even related to John Evelyn. Her testimony might help to explain Sebald's opinion that British culture is characterized by a 'passionate interest in our earlier way of life', the 'history' and 'tradition' that he saw as so absent and problematic in Germany, but it also, more subtly perhaps, betrays an uncritical repackaging of 'Englishness' and Sebald's incorporation within it. Quoting the Spanish novelist Javier Marías, Comber later defines 'Englishness' as 'the traditional aversion to the speculative and theoretical, inherent in the education and mind of the English', apparently correlating this with Sebald's own favouring of the circuitous, the inefficient, and the disorderly and overlooking his own interest in a more general human 'thirst for knowledge' and order.[64]

Despite Sebald's own quotation of the arrogant mottoes of figures like the Victorian businessman Cuthbert Quilter ('Plûtot mourir que changer' / 'sooner die than change') or the FitzGerald family ('Stesso sangue, stessa sorte' / 'same blood, same fate'), Comber's account absorbs Sebald's professed inclination to 'potter about' at home into a supposed liberal English antipathy for abstract principles, or the ideology of being supposedly un-ideological. Indeed, the suggestion is that perhaps it was in this sense that Sebald saw his 'pilgrimage' through a landscape characterized by ruination and decline as being specifically 'English'— as the wilfully inefficient opposite of 'Vorsprung durch Technik'.[65]

---

[60] Macfarlane in Cook (ed.), *After Sebald*, p.30.
[61] Phil Smith, *On Walking... and Stalking Sebald* (Triarchy, 2014), p.70.   [62] Ibid., p.72.
[63] Philippa Comber, *Ariadne's Thread*, p.123.
[64] Ibid., p.206 (quoted from Marías's *Your Face Tomorrow 1: Fever and Spear*).
[65] Sebald, *The Rings of Saturn*, p.224, p.197; On 'pottering about', see Sebald's comments in *Paris Review* No.151, p.282.

Social Documentaries: *Akenfield* and Lowestoft

Philippa Comber's remarks point us to the fact that while Sebald's text has often enough been used to counterpoint the desolation of the East Anglian landscape with a wider, international pattern or 'natural history' of loss and ruination, the relation of this landscape to England itself, as well as the idea of 'Englishness', has rarely been sufficiently problematized. In fact, the reverse has often happened: as Will Self has pointed out, referring to the 'Bakelite touches English critics find so reassuring', there is often an element within English responses to Sebald that seems to actually simplify the complexities of the history he deals with; a sense that, as Self writes,

> Sebald's onetime presence among us—even if we would never be so crass as to think this, let alone articulate it—is registered as further confirmation that we won, and won because of our righteousness, our liberality, our inclusiveness and our tolerance. Where else would the Good German have sprouted so readily, if not from our brown and nutritious soil?[66]

One way to address these dilemmas is by means of a more pointed enquiry into locality, which otherwise seems to risk becoming, like Janine Dakyns's office, a mere 'paper landscape'. In fact, for all that the Suffolk Sebald depicts is a dislocated, outlying place, it is not a mere lacuna. Rural Suffolk might seem to be the 'functionally irrelevant' landscape that Long describes in his monograph *Image, Archive, Modernity*, but, even apart from its actual functional and economic significance in terms of agriculture, it is culturally and symbolically significant in a way that gives added importance to Sebald's presentation of England and Englishness: a kind of *ur*-England and an extension of the north Essex 'Constable country' discussed by Stephen Daniels in his study *Fields of Vision* (1993).[67]

One half-imagined place that forms a key precedent to Sebald's work in this respect is the village depicted in Ronald Blythe's 1969 text *Akenfield: Portrait of an English Village*, later adapted into a 1974 film by Peter Hall. Blythe's account is set in a composite location based on his home village of Debach, Suffolk, and whose name, as he explained in a 1998 preface, is derived from the Old English word for oak and the local village of 'Charsfield'.[68] Debach is just a few miles inland from Orford Ness, and Edward FitzGerald, who features in Sebald's text and whom

---

[66] Will Self, in Cook, *After Sebald*, pp.106–7.
[67] Long, *Image, Archive, Modernity*, p.19; Stephen Daniels, *Fields of Vision: Landscape Imagery and National Identity in England and the United States* (Cambridge: Polity, 1992), Ch.7.
[68] Ronald Blythe, *Akenfield: Portrait of an English Village* (London: Penguin, 2005), p.8.

Blythe mentions, is buried 'in Boulge churchyard, just a mile or two from my house', so the territory is much the same as Sebald's.[69]

Blythe's text takes a composite form, as a compilation of ghostwritten testimonies from villagers of the fictionalized village. It offers a brief philosophy of 'Englishness' very much in line with the kind of anti-urbanism that would feed into Margaret Thatcher's rhetoric of the 1970s and 1980s. Blythe states in no uncertain terms that 'the townsman envies the villager his certainties and, in Britain, has always regarded urban life as just a temporary necessity'. He writes of 'the almost religious intensity of the regard for rural life in this country' and fittingly depicts Akenfield as both rugged and eternal.[70] Of the 'countryman's life', Blythe writes: 'The earth itself has its latest drugs and fertilizers poured into it to make it rich and yielding, but it is still the "old clay".' His tone becomes almost mystical, imparting consciousness to this clay itself, as he goes on that 'in both its and his [the countryman's] reality, the elemental quality remains uppermost', before making the bizarre conclusion that, for the village-dweller, 'science is a footnote to what he really believes'.[71]

Akenfield is certainly a remote place and home to great suffering. One villager describes having gained weight after joining the army in wartime:

> They said it was the food but it was really because for the first time in my life there had been no strenuous work. I want to say this simply as a fact, that village people in Suffolk in my day were worked to death. It literally happened. It is not a figure of speech. I was worked mercilessly. I am not complaining about it. It is what happened to me.[72]

The theme of suffering recurs in the speech of the Welsh Reverend, who remarks on the intense hardship that made Suffolk a place of mass exodus to the new world in the late nineteenth century and of the persecution of unionised labour after the war. Even in the 1930s, this figure avers, this was 'a part of Suffolk where the old feudal system was dying hard'—the residual system of tied cottages, which made it very difficult for farm labourers to move about, was one example of this.[73]

The history presented in *Akenfield* is composite, seeing its subject from many social angles, but placed next to Sebald's account it is the 'from below' that stands out. As Blythe points out, 1960s Suffolk was as socially polarized as it had been before 1914—at his time of writing,

> 183,200 of England and Wales's farms employ no workers at all; they are cultivated entirely by the farmer and his family. 24,600 employ only part-time

---

[69] Ibid., p.9.   [70] Ibid., p.15.   [71] Ibid., pp.14–15.   [72] Ibid., p.38.
[73] Ibid., p.67.

help. And of the 116,000 which employ whole-time workers, over ninety per cent employ less than five.[74]

In fact, in the Canadian Craig Taylor's 2004 *Return to Akenfield*, although all the 'old professions [...] are dead' the population has actually increased (from 298 in 1961 to 358 in 2001). New arrivals are 'commuters and entrepreneurs and retirees from other parts of the country. The family names in the local graveyard are no longer the surnames of the people living in the houses.'[75]

There is little of this kind of data in Sebald. The nearest we get is his depiction of Lowestoft, whose apparent decline catches the narrator off guard:

> I thought I remembered a town that had become something of a backwater but was nonetheless very pleasant; so now, as I walked into Lowestoft, it seemed incomprehensible to me that in such a relatively short space of time the place could have become so run down.[76]

Precipitating a reflection that it is something different to read about 'unemployment blackspots' and to witness them first-hand, this sequence elicits a solitary reference to contemporary British politics, and the 'inflated' hopes for prosperity from North Sea oil 'during the hardline capitalist years of Baroness Thatcher'.[77] Yet Sebald's decision that, ultimately, 'all that might be said for Lowestoft was that it occupied the easternmost point of the British Isles' shears off local specificity and ties Lowestoft into a grander scheme of civilization's 'westward drift'—as if making the shift from 'history' to 'natural history' by force. A passing funeral procession acts as an emblem for this, as well as 'enacting' within the scene the prose of Thomas Browne, whose 'labyrinthine sentences' Sebald has earlier described as 'resembling a funeral cortège in their sheer ceremonial lavishness'.[78]

For all Sebald's local sensitivity, Lowestoft seems here to have been enlisted in the service of an abstract principle. Some English writers have reacted violently to this: the artist and activist Stewart Home, in his abrasive 2001 novel *69 Things to Do with a Dead Princess*, maintained that

> among other things, Sebald claimed to have difficulty imagining that tourists and business travellers would choose to visit Lowestoft. As Alan [Home's protagonist] observed, it was through this type of half-baked rhetorical trick that the voyeuristic professor attempted to place himself outside the social system that his

---

[74] Ibid., p.81.
[75] Craig Taylor, *Return to Akenfield: Portrait of an English Village in the Twenty-First Century* (London: Granta, 2006), p.xv.
[76] Sebald, *The Rings of Saturn*, p.41.   [77] Ibid., pp.41–2.   [78] Ibid., p.19.

snobbish comments demonstrated he would never escape by dint of his own efforts.[79]

Phil Smith's oppositional view of Lowestoft in September 2011 followed suit, declaring the place to be

> a vibrant, working-class seaside town; yes, the odd shop is empty, but there is a rowdy buzz on the street, speeded by the unseasonably hot weather. [...] The town carries the distinguishing marks of New Labour investment; the High Street is ornamented inarticulately with numerous tiles and plaques from a succession of uncoordinated public art projects.[80]

Sebald's narrator's comments about the fish he is served for dinner, that had 'doubtless lain entombed in the deep-freeze for years', certainly sound a little facetious, 'entombed' slightly over-egging the melancholy obsession with death and dying. Replicating as they do the bad dinners endured by J.B. Priestley in his *English Journey*, many of which Sebald had marked in his edition, these contribute to the cultivation of a well-heeled persona reminiscent of Priestley's own.[81] Smith and Home are, however, ultimately accusing Sebald of snobbery, and this does not seem to be a fair assessment. As the ironic self-fashioning of the narrator figure should make clear, Sebald the author is not roundly condemning Lowestoft. Its fate is merely to have been necessarily reduced in scale as a feature of an account which, for all its focus on details, must also be allowed recourse to some broader brush strokes. If its weakness is in its depiction of contemporary social conditions, then this is also in keeping with the professed melancholic subjectivity of its narrator and the half-ironic sense of anachronism or untimeliness he brings with him.

In any case, Sebald's discussion incorporates the lavish excesses of grand country houses in Suffolk in a convincing way, making use of the sometimes whimsical ideas contained in local history pamphlets. In Sebald's own copy of John Greaves Hall's *Great Yarmouth and Lowestoft, a Handbook for Visitors and Residents* (1866), he marked out the author's descriptions of winter gardens that seemed to have been 'evoked by a magician's wand' and the observation that 'Coleridge may have seen it, when in his charmed opium slumber, he dreamed of the Abyssinian Maid and the palace of Kubla Khan.'[82] These observations are transferred directly to *The Rings of Saturn*'s account of Somerleyton Hall. Later,

---

[79] Stewart Home, *69 Things To Do With A Dead Princess* (Edinburgh: Canongate, 2003), p.96.
[80] Smith, *On Walking...*, p.68.
[81] For instance, the 'poor meal' Priestley has in Coventry or the night in Hull where he 'disliked my dinner so much I almost gave it up as a bad job' (J.B. Priestley, *An English Journey* (London: Penguin, 1997), p.75; p.337).
[82] German Literature Archive.

his discussion of Ditchingham Park, laid out in a way 'which enabled the ruling elite to imagine themselves surrounded by boundless lands where nothing offended the eye', is caustic in its approach to the way privilege is inscribed into landscape by means of picturesque 'improvements'. The account of the lavish balls on the pier off Lowestoft likewise presents a memorable and miserable image of the poor local people watching on from their boats like so many ghosts, unwelcomed by the decadent revellers inside.[83] Even if such figures remain comparatively silent in Sebald's account, the image is nevertheless a memorable one.

Illumination, Enlightenment, and Combustion

The Rings of Saturn, preoccupied as it is with the legacy of industrial and colonial exploitation, might be read as a negative history of enlightenment. Recording humanity's 'thirst for knowledge' and 'relentless conquest of darkness', it inverts Robinson's attempt in *London* to imagine the city 'as if the nineteenth century had never happened'.[84] Its attempt to demolish 'progress' as myth seems as responsive to André Breton's observation that 'our brains are dulled by the incurable mania of wanting to make the unknown known, classifiable' as to Adorno and Horkheimer's more direct assertion in 1947 that 'enlightenment is totalitarian'.[85] Approaching these issues with a conviction of the 'impossible business of ascertaining truth', as Sebald put it in the foreword to his as-yet-untranslated 1985 essay collection *Die Beschreibung des Unglücks*, local and global concerns are broached in unexpected ways.[86]

If this perspective recalls the 'standpoint of redemption' occupied by Walter Benjamin's 'Angel of History' and his description of 'progress' as a 'storm', then Sebald's account of Rembrandt's 1632 painting *The Anatomy Lesson of Dr Nicolaes Tulp* in the Hague's Mauritshuis museum (established by a man whose own hubristic motto 'Even unto the limits of our world' matches those of Quilter and FitzGerald) is also significant.[87] Focusing on the violence done to the body of the thief Aris Kindt not only by Dr Tulp but also by Rembrandt's representation—the tendons of Kindt's hand are painted incorrectly—Sebald then meditates on the connection between art patronage and the exploitative history of the sugar

---

[83] Sebald, *The Rings of Saturn*, pp.261–2; pp.47–8.
[84] Ibid., p.59; Keiller (dir.), *London* (BFI: 1994).
[85] André Breton, *Manifestoes of Surrealism*, trans. Richard Seaver and Helen Lane (Ann Arbor: University of Michigan, 1974), p.9.; Theodor Adorno and Max Horkheimer, *Dialectic of Enlightenment*, ed. Gunzelin Schmid Noerr and trans. Edmund Jephcott (Stanford: Stanford University Press, 2002), p.4.
[86] Sebald, *Die Beschreibung des Unglücks*, p.11.
[87] Benjamin, 'Theses on the Philosophy of History', in *Illuminations*, p.257; Sebald, *The Rings of Saturn*, pp.193–4.

trade (as in the case of Tate), associated in its turn with slavery.[88] These histories are bound together like the flat landscapes of the Netherlands and East Anglia, which seem to merge into one another in Sebald's discussion with the Dutchman Cornelius de Jong—in which context these thoughts emerge. As de Jong eloquently observes, in another instance of striking cognitive harmony between the Sebald-Ich and one of his interlocutors, 'at times it seems to me [...] as if all works of art were coated with a sugar glaze or indeed made completely of sugar'.[89]

In tracing the vanishing-point between 'history' and 'natural history', *The Rings of Saturn* closes with an account of the destruction of trees in the so-called Great Storm of 1987. This reflects the same concerns that appeared in the essay 'The Alps in the Sea', in which Sebald describes the thick primeval forest that once covered that island of Corsica and its destruction by both deforestation and fire.[90] If this was an intended theme of Sebald's unfinished 'Corsica Project', then it is consummated in *The Rings of Saturn* by rendering combustion as the symbolic and actual consequence of enlightenment and the means by which historical catastrophe becomes 'natural' catastrophe ('now, as I write', intones Sebald in the text's final paragraphs, '[I] think once more of our history, which is but a long account of calamities').[91]

Combustion becomes a recurrent theme in *The Rings of Saturn*—it might even be considered precisely the 'metaphor or allegory of collective history' that Sebald felt could not be achieved by writing straightforward historical monographs and which drove him to more unconventional approaches.[92] On the subject of Brazil, for instance, Sebald's narrator remarks that 'our spread over the earth was fuelled by reducing the higher species of vegetation to charcoal, by incessantly burning whatever would burn':

> From the first smouldering taper to the [...] sodium lamps that line the Belgian motorways, it has all been combustion. Combustion is the hidden principle behind every artefact we create. [...] From the earliest times, human civilization has been no more than a strange luminescence growing more intense by the hour, of which no one can say when it will begin to wane and when it will fade away.[93]

The intricacy of the description recalls the imagery of *After Nature* and Michel Butor's 'Bleston'. Ash and embers do indeed recur constantly in Sebald's work in various forms. One example appears in a reminiscence of a journey through rural Ireland, where Sebald's narrator recalls having stayed with the 'Ashbury' family,

---

[88] Sebald, *The Rings of Saturn*, p.16. [89] Ibid., p.194. [90] Sebald, *Campo Santo*, p.36.
[91] Sebald, *The Rings of Saturn*, p.295.
[92] Sebald, in Sigrid Löffler, '"Wildes Denken" Gespräch mit W.G. Sebald', p.133 (my translation).
[93] Ibid., p.170.

whose names give away their frail and etiolated condition. Another comes in the unlikely form of the herring, whose shoals, we are told in a striking image, glisten on the sea's surface like 'ash or snow'.[94]

The herring fits into Sebald's wider scheme of dissolution and decay and becomes a negative symbol of 'natural history'. A cultural link with northern Europe and once 'a popular didactic model [...] the principal emblem, as it were, of the indestructibility of nature'—Sebald includes a postcard showing a prodigious haul at Lowestoft, apparently in the early twentieth century—the herring now risks becoming a victim of human destructiveness. Chemical deposits in rivers, the narrator informs us, mean that the fish are now frequently deformed. Increasingly unable to breed normally, their 'ritual patterns of courtship' have become 'no more than a dance of death'.[95] This, combined with the devastating impact of exploitative fishing practices, means that the herring's reasons for being a 'didactic model' are now completely reversed. Rather than a symbol of nature's superabundance, the fish is now an emblem of the woeful effects of what has since been termed the 'anthropocene'.

The herring is also significant for the way in which it appears to evade scientific certainty: as the narrator remarks, 'the routes the herring take through the sea have not been ascertained to this day'. This trope recalls that of the eel in Graham Swift's 1983 novel *Waterland*, also set in East Anglia, where the lack of scientific certainty about eel-spawning forms a thread in the narrative's ambivalent presentation of 'History'—with a capital H—and writing. Eels in fact spawn in the Sargasso Sea, a region known for its circular currents where huge swathes of weed collect (including the Sargassum, which takes its name from the place), and Swift's text establishes an implicit parallel between the two outlying regions.[96] As if to cement his point, Sebald actually draws the herring into a discussion not only of 'enlightenment' in a symbolic sense but also the actual history of artificial illumination. Relating a curious story about two English scientists, named 'Herrington and Lightbown', who discovered that the fish glows briefly at the moment of its death, the narrator explains how these men

> investigated the unusual phenomenon in the hope that the luminous substance exuded by dead herrings would lead to a formula for an organic source of light that had the capacity to regenerate itself.

The collapse of this 'eccentric undertaking', Sebald continues, 'as I read some time ago in a history of artificial light, constituted no more than a negligible setback in the relentless conquest of darkness'.[97]

---

[94] Ibid., p.56.   [95] Ibid., p.53.   [96] See Graham Swift, *Waterland* (London: Picador, 1984).
[97] Sebald, *The Rings of Saturn*, p.59.

160   LANDSCAPE AND SUBJECTIVITY

The image of a fish included at this point in the text is not, in fact, a herring (the transfiguration of the image itself into a 'red herring' here provides one example of Sebald's devious sense of humour). In like manner, Herrington and Lightbown are Sebald's fabrications. Yet, amazingly, the theory of the herring's bioluminescence does have a basis in fact, albeit owing to the activity of a particular bacteria rather than the fish itself. Likewise the apparently outlandish 'history of artificial light': the indistinct photograph of the Boulevard des Italiens in Paris (coincidentally, where Louis Aragon's 'Passage de l'Opéra' was located) is reproduced from Wolfgang Schivelbusch's 1983 study *Lichtblicke: zur Geschichte der kunstlichen Helligkeit im 19. Jahrhundert*, translated in 1988 as *Disenchanted Night: the Industrialisation of Light in the Nineteenth Century*.

At the point in his text where this image appears, Schivelbusch is describing the transition from gas to electric lighting in European cities and remarks on the real way in which electric 'arc-light *was*, in fact, a small sun' since it offered a level of brightness that allowed one to see with the retinal cones (which can distinguish colour), as in daylight. Gaslight had only ever stimulated the so-called 'rods' of the eye, which differentiate chiefly between light and dark and which the eye naturally uses at night-time anyway. Arc lights were in fact so bright that they ushered in the hitherto unheard-of problem of 'dazzling'.[98] As a result, they needed to be placed out of the direct field of vision and ideally high up, so that plans were produced to place them in large towers, illuminating whole districts or even cities after the manner of the ancient lighthouse at Alexandria—a vision that predated the technical possibility afforded by electric light.

The actual horror of Sebald, or the affected horror of his narrative persona, at totalizing systems, large buildings, and what Schivelbusch describes as 'technical monumentalism' would surely have been excited here.[99] Schivelbusch describes one such project offered to Napoleon in 1799, where a main tower was to be constructed on the Place de la Révolution, now the Place de la Concorde, and arranged in concert with other edifices so as to eradicate all shadows.[100] Another plan for a 'sun tower' to be built for the 1889 Paris Exposition, which ultimately lost out to the Eiffel Tower in the competition for a monumental building, would have used electricity in an attempt to achieve this and represents the 'projects for the total illumination of our cities' to which Sebald refers.[101]

In Sebald's discussion, the dim glow supposedly afforded by the expiring herring offers a channel into a mode of historical enquiry that seeks to cast a gentle rather than glaring light over its subjects, as well as revealing certain lacunae of historical understanding. The light of herring is emphatically not 'dazzling' but rather risks being overlooked, offering the kind of light which, in the terms of

---

[98] Wolfgang Schivelbusch, *Disenchanted Night: The Industrialisation of Light in the Nineteenth Century*, trans. Angela Davies (Oxford: Berg, 1988), p.120.
[99] Ibid., p.127.   [100] Ibid., pp.121–3.   [101] Sebald, *The Rings of Saturn*, p.58.

Michelet, maintains the 'darkness, into which thought can withdraw'.[102] The absurd hubris of the 'sun tower', meanwhile, which was even intended to contain bedrooms where suffering neurasthenics could take the clean air, makes the glow of the herring seem like an entirely reasonable analogue for the wrong turns made in the name of 'progress' and totalizing systems, scientific or otherwise.

One particularly morbid example of these wrong turns comes via the conjunction between the images described above and another that appears soon afterwards, spread arrestingly across two pages, and which the reader assumes to be a representation of dead bodies at Bergen Belsen concentration camp (whose 'liberation' by the regiment of the eccentric local nobleman Le Strange in 1945 has just been described). In Grant Gee's film *Patience: After Sebald*, Lise Platt notes the way that the herring's scales are formally replicated by the image of the Boulevard des Italiens, and in turn the photograph of the enormous catch at Lowestoft seems to bear some dark connection with the image of the corpses at the concentration camp. If this is an example of the Long's 'hermeneutics of resemblance' at work, it is notable that the system of oblique connections produces ripples that seem to move off the page entirely. For example, in Claude Lanzmann's seminal 1985 film about the Holocaust, *Shoah*, a camp survivor describes bodies having to be buried 'like herrings, head to foot' ('disposé comme des harengs') due to the sheer number of dead. The suggestiveness of Sebald's method of oblique correspondences and visual resemblances seems to invite its connection with other texts, and particularly a text like this, whether or not he was consciously referring to it.

The Contrasting Perspectives of Pedestrianism

The herring offers a measurable example of the allusive richness with which Sebald's text imbues the particular and the apparently insignificant, as well as the way in which fictional digressions—red or 'read' herrings—are embroidered into the ostensibly factual 'natural history' of East Anglia in an intricate and fairly convincing, if disorientating, way. But the history of 'lighting towers'—which were employed in the 1880s in cities like Detroit but 'turned out to be a mere episode in the history of lighting'—suggests another way in which the text occupies itself with the tension between intricacy, abstraction, and folly: by the interrelation of clashing perspectives.[103]

In her account of Sebald's work, Blackler writes that we are 'unable to map the space in which one dwells because there is no godlike perspective of its beginning and its end'.[104] Yet contrasts between 'godlike' and grounded perspectives—both

---

[102] Quoted from Michelet's *Le Peuple* (1826), Schivelbusch p.134.
[103] Schivelbusch, *Disenchanted Night*, p.126.   [104] Blackler, *Reading W.G. Sebald*, p.11.

metaphorical and actual—are clearly present in *The Rings of Saturn*, whose very opening in the Norwich hospital inaugurates the recurrent theme of what Gillian Beer has called a 'panoramic sweep that exterminates the human'.[105] In this instance, Beer's claim is literally and darkly true: it is from the 'high up' perspective of the hospital window that the death of Sebald's colleague Michael Parkinson is recounted.[106] Yet the perspective inaugurates a wider theme of reality's all-too-easy transformation into a model of itself: not a model like that of Thomas Abrams's Grand Temple, conducive to critical reflection on the futility of model-making, but one that tends rather towards abstraction and inhumanity. And this tendency seems to be nurtured by the very flatness of the Suffolk landscape.[107]

This process reflects that which Michel de Certeau described in the first volume of *The Practice of Everyday Life* (1980). Writing of an imaginary spectator at the top of New York's World Trade Center, de Certeau explained that

> his elevation transfigures him into a voyeur. It puts him at a distance. It transforms the bewitching world by which one was 'possessed' into a text that lies before one's eyes. It allows one to read it, to be a solar Eye, looking down like a god.[108]

As if in performance of this phenomenon, almost all of the photographs of East Anglia that Sebald includes in *The Rings of Saturn* are dominated by the horizon. The scenery, in this way, lends itself to what seems like a perspective of overview or survey—gesturing towards the strange quietness noted by the pilots of bombing raids in the Second World War and later described in *On The Natural History of Destruction*.[109] In fact, it is when he is flying back over the similarly flat landscape of the Netherlands that Sebald's narrator looks down and contemplates 'one of the most densely populated regions in Europe', where '[o]ver the centuries the land had been regulated, cultivated and built on until the whole region was transformed into a geometric pattern'.[110] People are invisible in this depiction,

> and yet they are present everywhere upon the face of the earth, extending their dominion by the hour, moving around the honeycombs of towering buildings and tied into networks of a complexity that goes far beyond the power of any one individual to imagine.[111]

These lines, which precipitate the mention of the South African diamond mine discussed earlier in relation to Thomas Browne's 'quincunx', suggest a world of

---

[105] Gillian Beer in Cook, *After Sebald*, p.38. [106] Sebald, *The Rings of Saturn*, pp.5–6.
[107] Sebald references Diderot's comment, regarding Holland, that 'the most modest rise gave one the loftiest sensation' and clearly intends the description to reflect back onto East Anglia.
[108] Michel De Certeau, *The Practice of Everyday Life*, trans. Rendall (Berkeley: University of California Press, 1984), p.92.
[109] Sebald, *On The Natural History of Destruction*, pp. 90–1.
[110] Sebald, *The Rings of Saturn*, p.90. [111] Ibid., p.91.

remarkable connectedness, always threatening to exceed comprehension and to subjugate the individual by weight of sheer complexity—networks not so much of gossamer threads as of the heavy, oppressive chains of slavery and exploitation.

De Certeau's alignment between space and text in *The Practice of Everyday Life* corresponds with an observation made by Walter Benjamin in *One-Way Street* (1928) that

> the power of a country road is different when one is walking along it from when one is flying over it in an aeroplane. In the same way, the power of a text is different when it is read from when it is copied out.[112]

Sebald's text, as instances like the scene on Dunwich Heath make clear, exacerbates these distinctions. Yet it also frustrates them, since the 'godlike' perspective is itself a feature of the narrator's melancholic self-fashioning, situating himself at one remove from immediate reality. This variation on the deific position—located in Saturn rather than Heaven—is an attribute not so much of the omniscient author or the indifferent artist ('within or behind or beyond or above his handiwork' in James Joyce's famous statement) as the oblique, melancholic narrative disposition, at one remove from immediate experience.[113] In this respect, the Sebald-Ich seems again to respond to both Benjamin and Thomas Browne, who, he remarks, 'sought to look upon earthly existence from the things that were closest to him to the spheres of the universe, with the eye of an outsider, one might almost say of the creator'.[114]

The attraction of the 'godlike' perspective is that of enlightenment more generally: of dwelling in the abstract and the rational in place of the frayed and contingent. This becomes, as it were, a kind of home: the projection of an ordered, unquestioned cosmos implies the presence of a secure position from which it is observed. As Sebald remarked in a later essay, the 'cosmic perspective' can be 'the source of the sovereign serenity', removed from 'the vagaries of human destiny'.[115] Yet while the 'honeycombs' seen from the aeroplane might have given way to a positive image—they explicitly recall the imagery used by Dante in the *Purgatorio* to characterize *amore naturale*, the variety of love which acts as a propulsive force in every living thing and which is 'always without error'—these 'networks of complexity' are often bitter.[116] They are precisely those that run 'from the

---

[112] Walter Benjamin, *One-Way Street*, in *Reflections*, ed. Peter Demetz and trans. Edmund Jephcott (New York: Schocken, 1986), p.66.
[113] James Joyce, *A Portrait of the Artist as a Young Man* (London: Penguin, 2000), p.233.
[114] Sebald, *The Rings of Saturn*, p.19.
[115] Sebald, 'A Comet in the Heavens: On Johann Peter Hebel', in *A Place in the Country*, p.14.
[116] Dante, *Purgatorio*, XVII.94, ed. and trans. John D. Sinclair (London: Oxford University Press, 1971). The same image appears in Casanova's *History of My Life* ('The bee making its hive, the swallow building its nest, the ant digging its hole, the spider weaving its web would never have done anything without a previous eternal revelation') which Sebald had read: he refers in *Vertigo* to Casanova's escape

thousands of hoists and winches that once worked the South African diamond mines to the floors of today's stock and commodity exchanges, through which the global tides of information flow without cease'.[117] They are, as it were, intimately tied to the 'natural history' of exploitation and destructiveness, and the image, registering this, modulates into a characteristically vertiginous depiction: 'if we view ourselves from a great height', remarks Sebald's narrator, again emphasizing the position of elevation,

> it is frightening to realize how little we know about our species, our purpose and our end, I thought, as we crossed the coastline and flew out over the jelly-green sea.

As in the case of the herring images, the 'hermeneutics of resemblance' here has a disturbing, alienating effect. Yet contrary to Blackler's claim, it is precisely the presence of this perspective in *The Rings of Saturn* against which Sebald consistently sets the view of the pedestrian subject into relief. The maze on Dunwich Heath, for instance, is presented as a harrowing experience for the narrating subject, but afterwards, looking back, it seems to form 'a pattern simple in comparison with the tortuous trail I had behind me'.[118]

Robert Macfarlane has usefully characterized the clash of aerial and grounded perspective in Sebald's work as that between 'scholarship' and 'testimony'.[119] It is also that between the principles of the neat, abstracted pattern and the disorientating particularity of immediate experience: between the smooth authority of the map and the seductive or harrowing roughness of the territory. Sebald's narrating subject is constantly caught up in the balance between these two things. By virtue of this, it constitutes both a response and an antidote to assertions like Blythe's remark, in *Akenfield*, that 'the twentieth century, with its great comforts and its great crimes, has produced immense alienation experiences. People need the seasonal design of country time to remind them of what they are.'[120] *The Rings of Saturn* addresses this sense of alienation whilst seeking also to acknowledge the dilemmas of 'design'. Mobilizing a fraught narrative subjectivity, it places hearth and horizon into a tangled warp and—for all that it elides certain aporia related to ideas of England and Englishness—forms an act of resistance to the idea that the interconnected threads of 'progress' and suffering can be straightened out without doing an act of violence to the process of historical representation and understanding.

from the Doge's palace in Venice, and in *Austerlitz* to his writing of his memoirs in Bohemia, spending his last years lonely and isolated at the castle of Count Joseph Karl von Waldstein.

[117] Sebald, *The Rings of Saturn*, p.91.   [118] Sebald, *The Rings of Saturn*, p.173.
[119] Macfarlane, in Cook, *After Sebald*, p.21.   [120] Blythe, *Akenfield*, p.267.

The Fifth Emigrant: *Austerlitz*

Austerlitz, W.G. Sebald's last major prose work, takes a form much closer to that of the conventional novel than any of its predecessors. It recounts the story of a fictional character named Jacques Austerlitz, brought to England as a Jewish refugee from Nazi-occupied Prague as part of the *Kindertransport* programme and raised (under the name of 'Dafydd Elias') in an atmosphere of ascetic Calvinistic Methodism in the rugged landscapes of Bala, Wales, before becoming an architectural historian based at an unspecified institute of the University of London.

If this is the *histoire* of the text—using the structuralist narratological distinction—then its *récit* has two distinct layers. The first is Austerlitz's own rediscovery of his emigrant past, kept obscure from him by his Welsh foster-parents. The second is the process by which this experience of rediscovery is mediated through his relationship with an unnamed narrator figure. Seemingly the familiar 'Sebald-Ich' (although much less explicitly delineated as such), this narrator lives and works in East Anglia but finds himself unexpectedly encountering Austerlitz on a number of occasions. Not lacking a certain sense of providence and spiritual vocation, his transcriptions of Austerlitz's speech and mediation of his testimony, interwoven with reflections on this activity, form the substance of the text. This role—closer to the Barthesian 'scriptor' than the ironically anachronistic 'author' of *The Rings of Saturn*—resuscitates a familiar mnemonic pattern: Sebald himself claimed of *Austerlitz* that 'you might almost describe it as a sequel to *The Emigrants*'.[121]

One key aspect of Sebald's 'scriptor' role, drawing heavily on the practice of both *The Rings of Saturn* and *The Emigrants*, is that this layering of *histoire* and *récit*, and the sense of deep empathic connection between the two men, is arrived at through an extreme attentiveness to place. Certain recurrent *topoi*—train stations, fortifications, and burial grounds—merge into one another, confusing past with present and establishing an ever-increasing network of connections between significant locations in Belgium, London, Wales, Paris, Prague, and beyond. This is frequently bound up with a self-conscious sense of interaction with earlier writers' and film-makers' depictions of the same sites, so that the narrator often seems to be consciously *re*-writing or *re*-searching them. The result is a disorientating and kaleidoscopic sense of space and place, where subjectivity and environment bleed into one another in moving and unsettling ways and—as in *The Rings of Saturn*—the spaces and places of England are dragged into much wider contexts.

---

[121] Bigsby, *Writers in Conversation*, p.162.

The Uncanny Experiences of Belgium: Antwerp, Brussels, and Breendonk

Austerlitz and the narrator first meet by chance in Antwerp in the 1960s, in the waiting room of the central train station. This inaugurates the text's preoccupation with spaces of transit, with Liverpool Street Station in London and the Gare d'Austerlitz in Paris later figuring centrally. The earliest portions of the narrative unfold from conversations had in Antwerp and after an array of chance meetings in Brussels, Liège, Terneuzen, and Zeebrugge. Belgium, in each case, is rendered as the crucial site of the bourgeois era's perceived inhumanity. Its bombastic architecture is depicted as constituting a kind of modern antiquity, recalling the constatation of Manchester in *The Emigrants* and, in turn, the classical symbolism of Ariadne's thread in Michel Butor's *Passing Time* and Sebald's poem 'Bleston'.

As an architectural historian specializing in the buildings of high-bourgeois, late-nineteenth-century Belgium, Austerlitz's characterization makes him an oblique analogue of Walter Benjamin, whose unfinished study of nineteenth-century Paris, *The Arcades Project*, sought to capture the 'prehistory of modernity'.[122] But the meeting of Austerlitz and the narrator in Antwerp might also suggest a parallel with Thomas More's *Utopia* (1516), which, like *Austerlitz*'s opening sequence, is presented as a factual account of a conversation had in Antwerp between More himself and an ambiguous traveller figure. The similarity is certainly sustained by *Austerlitz*'s interest in totalitarian systems ostensibly based on principles of reason and rationality, however warped. The text, and its protagonist's biography, are ultimately determined by the atrocities and 'crazed administrative zeal' of Nazi Germany, but—perpetuating a theme developed in Sebald's discussion of Joseph Conrad and Roger Casement in *The Rings of Saturn*—this is framed by its presentation of Belgian architecture of the late nineteenth century as the articulation of a deeper history of inhumanity and barbarism, centring on colonial exploitation of the Congo.[123]

In its sheer scale, Antwerp Station seems to attest to the hubris of colonial domination and the correspondent verve for civic bombast at home. Later, the Palace of Justice in Brussels follows suit: its endless, uncharted corridors that apparently lead nowhere, reminiscent of the courtrooms in Kafka's *Trial*, seeming to be the hallmarks of an ill-conceived project that has spun out of all control (we learn, for instance, that it is the world's largest accumulation of stone blocks on a single site). In each case, Sebald's depiction of these buildings makes them reminiscent of Edward Said's comments on Napoleon's 1809–28 *Description de l'Égypte*, which—as Said pointed out in *Orientalism* (1978)—with its twenty-three

---

[122] Benjamin, *The Arcades Project*, trans. Howard Eiland and Kevin McLaughlin (Cambridge, MA: Belknap, 1999).
[123] Sebald, *Austerlitz*, trans. Anthea Bell (London: Penguin, 2011), p.337.

volumes and metre-square pages seemed to express the idea that 'the project and the size of the page had been thought of as possessing comparable scale'.[124] The *Description*, for Said, characterized an axiomatic correlation between the twin aspirations to complete knowledge and complete domination—a process of objectification expressed in the crudest of terms. Like it, these examples of Belgian architecture are presented by Sebald as the grotesquely swollen products of an inhumane exploitation.

In a typical example of Sebald's cultivation of narrative connections based on contingency, resemblance, and proximity and exacerbated by the act of remembering, Antwerp Station in *Austerlitz* is associated closely with the adjacent zoo—a more obvious product of the colonial enterprise. In a kind of spatial interference, the description of the zoo's 'Nocturama', in particular, bleeds into that of the waiting-room or '*Salle des pas perdus*', where the narrator takes 'refuge' from 'uneasy thoughts'. Observing how the assembled creatures' eyes are open wide, as if dazzled by the glare of enlightenment, he compares these with the eyes of 'certain painters and philosophers who seek to penetrate the darkness which surrounds us purely by means of looking and thinking'.[125] As J.J. Long observes, Sebald's presentation 'conflates station and zoo'; like the creatures in the Nocturama, the travellers in the waiting room seem to be 'somehow miniaturized' by the vast scale of the space, threatened by a dominating architecture that seems to exert some malicious energy.[126]

The type of penumbra that prevails in the station—as in the Palace of Justice— is different. Although the two structures' sheer bulk seems to manifest the aspiration towards total order and domination integral to colonial exploitation, the presence of forgotten, decaying spaces within them opens up the opportunity of perceiving them as ruins: as relics of an uncritical will to power. The *Salle des pas perdus* might be grandiose and extravagant, but it is accessed through a 'severely dilapidated foyer'.[127] The labyrinthine corridors of the Palace of Justice, meanwhile, have apparently been occupied by small businesses unofficially opening 'in one or other of the empty rooms in that great warren'.[128] The atmosphere, reminiscent of fallen Rome, is informed by Austerlitz's notion that 'somehow we know by instinct that outsized buildings cast the shadow of their own destruction before them': an acute statement not so much of the objective truth of these structures but of his own subjective, maudlin gaze on them.[129] This way of seeing buildings will become a recurrent trope in the text: by projecting a sense of ruination onto particular sites, Sebald attempts to expose the aporia of the ideologies they

---

[124] Edward Said, *Orientalism* (London: Penguin, 2003), p.85.
[125] Sebald, *Austerlitz*, pp.2–3.
[126] Long, *Image, Archive, Modernity*, p.42; Sebald, *Austerlitz*, p.6.
[127] Ibid., p.5.
[128] Ibid., p.40.
[129] Ibid., p.24.

168 LANDSCAPE AND SUBJECTIVITY

seem to represent, as well as turn them into mnemonically significant spaces for Austerlitz himself.

The term by which Antwerp Station's waiting room is known—the *'Salle des pas perdus*' or 'hall of lost steps'—is not unusual in French, but here it conspicuously echoes André Breton's essay collection *Les Pas Perdus* and the moment in his *Nadja* (1928) when the eponymous subject (supplied with a copy by Breton himself) exclaims 'Lost steps? But there's no such thing!'[130] If Nadja, in that text, becomes an embodiment of the Surrealist taste for the unsettling and eccentric, then the barmaid in Antwerp Station's restaurant, 'constructed like a mirror image of the waiting room', fulfils a similar role. Austerlitz deems her the 'Goddess of Time Past', and she presides over the strange contradiction at the heart of the space's atmospherics: although, as Austerlitz declares, the station monumentalizes the nineteenth century's submission to time as the 'supreme', 'standardized' determinant of modern life, the waiting room and restaurant now seem—like the very idea of waiting—to be somehow outside of this order.[131] With its faded extravagance, the space is a fragment of the past reaching oddly into the present, much like the strange *objets trouvés* collected at the Saint-Ouen flea market in *Nadja*, or the Passage de l'Opéra in Aragon's *Paris Peasant* (1926).

In his criticism of these Antwerp sequences, Long claims that 'the fact that the narrator is drawn to the Nocturama and devotes significant portions of text [to] listing the exotic animals kept there signals a fascination that is not entirely compatible with a critical agenda'.[132] Yet it is precisely the seductive *attractiveness* of this ordered world that is the point—like the 'sovereign serenity' Sebald detected in the work of Johan Peter Hebel, where 'every military campaign is followed by a peace treaty, and every puzzle has a solution'.[133] This is implicit in Sebald's depiction of the Nocturama, as it is in the case of the train station and the Palace of Justice, which, despite their alienating scale, are imbued with an odd sense of domesticity. The barmaid's complete ease in her setting, 'enthroned on a stool behind the counter [. . .] filing her nails [like Joyce's god of all creation] with complete devotion and concentration' attests to this, as does the mythic presence of 'a tobacconist's, a bookie's, a bar'—all unofficial—deep in the cavernous spaces of the Palace of Justice.[134]

In Long's view, the racoon that the narrator sees in the Nocturama is 'engaged in washing a piece of apple time and time again as though its actions could liberate it from its unreal, artificial environment'. Again, the precise point seems to require a subtly different inflection.[135] As the racoon's German name of *Waschbär* (or 'wash bear') suggests, the real sadness of the Nocturama is that this unhomely

---

[130] André Breton, *Nadja*, trans. Richard Howard (New York: Grove Press, 1960), p.72.
[131] Sebald, *Austerlitz*, p.14; on time, see Long, *Image, Archive, Modernity*, pp.96–7.
[132] Long, *Image, Archive, Modernity*, p.43.   [133] Sebald, *A Place in the Country*, p.13.
[134] Sebald, *Austerlitz*, p.8; p.40.   [135] Ibid., p.43.

place—effectively a prison—should host a creature apparently so at home, literally acting out its name in a manner reminiscent of Kipling's 'Just So' stories. How is it, Sebald's text seems to ask us, that a space which seems to have so much in common with the cosy domesticity of works like Hebel's *Kalendergeschichten*, aspiring to something like Noah's ark, can also be so disquieting? The *Waschbär* is both at home and not at home; its washing of the apple is *unheimlich* both in the sense of seeming strange, unsettling, or peculiar, and in this impression of a fundamental, even 'transcendental', homelessness.[136] In this way, its situation parallels the condition of Austerlitz as someone forced to become a migrant. It also reflects on the situation of the narrator, whose precise reasons for being in Belgium in the first place are never made clear but who also seems to be driven there by a kind of existential restlessness.

It is principally in terms of the *unheimlich* that the closed spaces of Belgian war fortifications, to which the text pays special attention, form another analogue to the *Salle des pas perdus* and the Nocturama. The narrator visits Breendonk, near Antwerp, where a 'nauseating smell of soft soap' reminds him of 'the bizarre German word for scrubbing-brush, *Wurzelbürste*, which was a favourite of my father's and which I had always disliked'.[137] Assailed by homely images in this fundamentally unhomely place, this sequence marks the most explicit incursion of Sebald's own biography into the text. The narrator describes a room reminiscent of 'our laundry room at home in W.' (i.e. Wertach im Allgäu, abbreviated here as it is elsewhere in Sebald's texts).[138] An image included at this point indicates that this space is the 'Folterkamer', which isn't rendered in English as 'Torture Chamber' but would be as obvious to a German reader as a Flemish one (the same is probably true of 'Lijkenkammer' for 'corpse chamber'/'mortuary'). Later, a hook attached to the ceiling recalls 'the image of the butcher's shop I had always passed on my way to school.'[139] The space becomes one where

> I could well imagine the good fathers and dutiful sons of Vilsbiburg and Fuhlsbüttel, from the Black Forest and the Bavarian Alps, sitting here when they came off duty to play cards or write letters to their loved ones at home. *After all, I had lived among them until my twentieth year.* [my emphasis][140]

The inhumanity of Breendonk is also developed in relation to the 'science' of fortifications, which Austerlitz and the narrator discuss at a new location, Antwerp's Glove Market or 'Handschoenmarkt'—an attractive cobbled street in the city's touristic centre. Antwerp itself, he explains, is a model of how these often

---

[136] N.b. In his essay on Peter Handke's play Kaspar, Sebald refers to Nietzsche's comment in *The Gay Science* on man wishing that animals tell him why they are happy.—'why do you just look at me instead of telling me about your happiness?'—'Because I always immediately forget what I wanted to say' (quoted in Sebald, *Campo Santo*, p.55).
[137] Sebald, *Austerlitz*, p.33.   [138] Ibid., p.32.   [139] Ibid., p.33.   [140] Ibid., p.29.

embodied a 'fundamentally wrong-headed idea'—its own fortifications having been continually expanded even after, in 1859, 'the entire Belgian army would have been insufficient to garrison' them.[141] The continued building, as if by inertia, forms a profane recurrence of the *Waschbär* motif in its suggestion of the perpetual repetition of a pointless action.

Breendonk itself is part of this narrative, pinned to the Second World War and particularly the association of bunkers with Nazi Germany.[142] In his 1994 study *Bunker Archaeology*, Paul Virilio discussed the 'Atlantic Wall' project, undertaken from 1942 to 1944, in which the Nazi administration planned to station concrete forts or bunkers, built to a set of predetermined designs, along the entire western coast of mainland Europe. 'The immensity of this project' as Virilio observed, 'is what defies common sense; total war was revealed here in its mythic dimension.'[143] The literally 'monolithic' ('single-stone') form of the bunkers has had a curious effect on their subsequent decay: today they are often found intact but upside down, fallen or teetering off the edge of sand dunes in France, Denmark, and elsewhere.

Sebald's insights give the lie, however, to Virilio's statement that prior to the Atlantic Wall 'fortifications had always been oriented toward a specific staked-out objective'. Instead, the German occupation of the fort is pinned into a wider and deeper narrative of 'wrong-headed' ideas.[144] Yet his sensations at Breendonk—'a monolithic, monstrous incarnation of ugliness and blind violence'—correspond with Virilio's in the bunkers of the Atlantic Wall, where, 'like a slightly undersized piece of clothing that hampers as much as it enclothes, the reinforced concrete and steel envelope is too tight under the arms and sets you in a semiparalysis fairly close to that of illness'. The tourist visiting such a place, he remarks, 'is beset with a singular heaviness; in fact he is already in the grips of that cadaverous rigidity from which the shelter was designed to protect him'.[145] The description of the bunkers as a kind of oppressive clothing matches the sense of uneasiness and disarray experienced by *Austerlitz*'s narrator at Breendonk, peering into the pit of the 'Folterkamer'.

Sites of Memory and Myth: England and Wales

Austerlitz closes with the narrator reading Dan Jacobson's late autobiographical work *Heshel's Kingdom* (1988) at Breendonk—a text apparently given to him by Austerlitz. Returning to the location thirty years after his initial visit, he is struck

---

[141] Ibid., p.17; p.22.
[142] See, for instance Joachim Fest, *Inside Hitler's Bunker* (London: Pan Macmillan, 2004).
[143] Paul Virilio, *Bunker Archaeology* (New York: Princeton Architectural Press, 1994), p.12.
[144] Ibid., p.11.   [145] Ibid., 15–16.

by no particular changes except a greater number of tourists. Yet the description in *Heshel's Kingdom* of similar fortifications in Kaunas, Lithuania, is highly suggestive of how places and particular types of building act as points of contact between narrative threads. One fort seems to connect to another, just as Jacobson's rediscovery of his Jewish ancestors in *Heshel's Kingdom* overlaps with the themes of *Austerlitz* more generally, suggesting the kind of *mise-en-abyme* effect discussed in relation to 'Max Ferber', where 'translation' in language and space involves plunging endlessly 'from one abyss to the next'.

The figure of the fort or fortress generates motifs that recur throughout the text: on Austerlitz's street in London there is 'a low block of flats like a fortress standing on the corner'; later, he dreams restlessly of being 'in the innermost heart of a star-shaped fortress'; and later still the text becomes preoccupied with Terezín in the Czech Republic—a fortified town that became the Theresienstadt Ghetto, to which his mother was deported.[146] Plans of the structure, included with the text, make this connection emphatically, and Terezín's star-shaped walls are in turn repeated in a 'star-shaped house' once owned by an Archduke Ferdinand of the Tyrol that was his parents' 'favourite destination'. In a similar way, the fact that the narrator visits Breendonk alone but that Terezín only appears through Austerlitz's description also demonstrates the subtlety with which the two characters' empathic relation and mutual understanding is sustained throughout the text, with substantial slippage or 'migration' of motifs and preoccupations between their testimony.

The form of the fortress or bunker also acts as a more general model for mnemonic space in *Austerlitz*, heavily informing Sebald's depictions of space and place in England and London. The stately homes that Austerlitz describes having visited with his former history teacher André Hilary are notable in this respect. They are presented—to borrow the phrase Ivan Chtcheglov used to describe Giorgio de Chirico's paintings of Turin—as spaces of 'richly filled time'.[147] Of 'Iver Grove', for instance, Austerlitz remarks that it

> seemed largely intact, at least from the outside. Nonetheless, as we paused on the broad stone steps which had been colonized by hart's-tongue ferns and other weeds and looked up at the blind windows, it seemed to us as if silent horror had seized upon the house at the prospect of its imminent and shameful end. Inside we found heaps of grain in one of the large ground-floor reception rooms, as if the place were a barn. In a second great hall, ornamented with baroque stucco work, hundreds of sacks of potatoes leaned against each other.[148]

---

[146] Sebald, *Austerlitz*, p.166; p.196.
[147] Chtcheglov, 'Formulary for a New Urbanism' (1953), trans. Ken Knabb (http://www.bopsecrets.org/SI/Chtcheglov.htm).
[148] Sebald, *Austerlitz*, p.147.

172   LANDSCAPE AND SUBJECTIVITY

Austerlitz claims to have been interrupted by the landowner before being able to take any photographs at Iver Grove, though one is included of the sumptuous room that he describes.

The dilemma that this presents is not an unusual one, since the photographs included with the text are only rarely described directly, functioning rather as a kind of evidence—as in Breton's *Nadja*—that complements and intersects with the text rather than forming its subject. Although they are ostensibly drawn from Austerlitz's own papers, entrusted to the narrator at the close of the narrative, it soon becomes clear that some are additions made by the narrator himself (the images of Breendonk, for instance, which correspond with observations made independently of Austerlitz). There is therefore some scope for interpretative variation concerning the Iver Grove photograph. Perhaps Austerlitz discovered the image after his visit, or the narrator found it and made the connection himself: either possibility is viable within the premises of the text.

What is certain is that 'Iver Grove' does refer to an actual house, if by a false name. In Sebald's own copy of *No Voice from the Hall*—a memoir by the architectural historian and defender of country houses John Harris—the same image is marked out for inclusion in *Austerlitz*. Although Harris's memoir does discuss an actual house called Iver Grove, in Buckinghamshire, the image itself is taken from his reminiscences of Burwell in Lincolnshire and was taken in 1957, the year before Burwell was demolished. Sebald marks the point where Harris describes his entry into the house: 'I tried the door, it opened—and suddenly, as if caught up in a torrent, I was engulfed by a flock of sheep.'[149] Later, he also marks the passage that clearly supplied the data of Austerlitz's incursion: 'In several rooms', he writes,

> were hundreds of sacks of potatoes and mountainous heaps of grain (no more sheep), and family portraits were hanging on the walls, covered in cobwebs, an added theatricality.[150]

This photograph in fact made its first appearance in Roy Strong and Marcus Binney's *The Destruction of the English Country House 1875–1975*, published in 1974 to coincide with a major exhibition at the Victoria and Albert Museum (of which Harris was a co-curator). It appears in this text without any elaboration, aside from a note that the sacks in fact contained not potatoes but grain. In Harris's later account, his chapter on Burwell concludes with an account of his return to the house in April 1958, only to find it in flames—'What a sight met my eyes! [...] I remembered London in the Blitz.' In his own copy, Sebald made a

---

[149] John Harris, *No Voice from the Hall: Early Memories of a Country House Snooper* (London: John Murray, 1998), p.181.
[150] Ibid.

pencil mark next to the closing lines: 'I was black with rage. As a single act of destruction, the burning of a masterpiece at the National Gallery would have been no worse.'[151]

Harris's elision of private and public patrimony here is characteristic, but it is striking that in Sebald's rendition, too, Austerlitz's journey is uncoloured by the 'heritage' debate of which Harris was a part. The polemical setting of *The Destruction of the Country House* does not translate to Sebald's text, where Burwell serves to add precisely the unproblematic patina or 'impression of pastness' that Patrick Wright complained about in his 1985 critique of formulations of the 'national past' *On Living in an Old Country*.[152] Indeed, as in the case of *The Rings of Saturn*, there is a sense in which the text incorporates a highly cultivated type of 'ruin tourism', evincing a fairly uncritical relationship with English class relations. Among the many words circled by Sebald in his copy of *No Voice From The Hall* is Harris's description of Langley Park, Buckinghamshire, as a 'Wunderkammer' and Hungerhall Lodge, Kent, as a 'Cabinet of Curiosity', and it seems clear that in his attraction to the apparently eccentric or bizarre—locked rooms and reclusive residents, for instance—Sebald systematically overlooks the oppressive role of such landed estates in agrarian capitalism.[153] He largely fails to 'stand at any point and look at that land', 'at what those fields, those streams, those woods even today produce', as Raymond Williams suggested in *The Country and the City*, and consequently fails to 'think it through as labour and see how long and systematic the seizure must have been, to rear that many houses, on that scale'.[154] In this case, in the shadow of his critique of Belgian colonialism, the result can seem a little inconsistent.

Excising this image from its polemical setting, Sebald seems to run with Harris's own description that 'the traveller through England after 1945 journeyed through a dream-like landscape, so many empty mansions standing forlornly in their parks'—he underlined this sentence in his own edition of *No Voice From The Hall*, as well as points like Harris's description of such houses' state of 'surreal limbo'.[155] In fact, it is telling that Sebald circled some of the most strikingly anaesthetic phrases in Harris's text, such as his description of one house as a 'distillation of history'.[156]

The motif of the locked room plays a significant role here. Iver Grove, Sebald's fictionalized version of Burwell, is described as having a billiards room that has rested undisturbed for over a century, its owner, named 'Ashman', having hidden it behind a false wall before the house was requisitioned by the state during the Second World War: in this room, the present owner's ancestor seems to have

---

[151] Ibid., p.182.
[152] Patrick Wright, *On Living in an Old Country: The National Past in Contemporary Britain* (London: Verso, 1985), p.65.
[153] Ibid. pp.36–7; p.87.   [154] Williams, *The Country and the City*, p.105.   [155] Ibid., p.2.
[156] Ibid., p.157.

engaged in an absurd, long-running tournament against himself: 'under the rubric of Ashman vs. Ashman, [he] had entered all the games won or lost against himself in a fine curving hand'.[157] The image, while arresting, becomes utterly benign, wrapped up in Sebald's long-standing preoccupation with imagery of ash, embers, and entropy and shorn of any further interrogative desire. The effect is that, although Belgian buildings are monuments to wanton colonial destructiveness, their English analogues—and their occupiers—are reduced to mere oddity or heritage spectacle. It is as if the elegance of a 'fine curving hand' provides enough aesthetic pleasure to offset any more troublesome issues of patrimony and power.

If *Austerlitz*'s narrative here derives its force partly from the tension between the emotive specificity of subjective experience and a more diffuse sense of historical richness, then this is analogized within the text by the way in which certain places are depicted in an insistently detailed way, while others function in rather more mythic, symbolic terms. The billiards room at Iver Grove, for example, remains a stock image, a stage set rather than an object of inquiry. This is probably how we should make sense of recurrent motifs like the phrase 'ans Karnevalistische grenzend' (bordering on the carnivalesque), which is used here to describe Austerlitz's private school just as it was applied to that of Max Ferber in *The Emigrants*. The schools are merely stock locations, standardized images of eccentric, exclusive institutions which apparently embody 'Englishness'—just as the occupants of country houses are people like John Harris's unusual Uncle Sid,

> who was learned in the writings of Richard Jefferies [...] and like that naturalist was a pantheist who would lie on the grass sward of ancient earthworks or tumuli, listening to the voices of the earth.[158]

Sid's supposed eccentricity and apparent harmlessness here is emblematic of the way that Sebald makes use of 'Exzentrizität' more generally. Turning his characters into charming oddballs tends to elide the elitism and even violence that they and their institutions represent, neutralizing social critique.

In a similar way, Austerlitz's childhood home in Wales seems to form a parallel to the depictions of W. and S. (Sebald's home villages of Wertach and Sonthofen) as, in Sebald's words, 'more of symbolic significance than anything', mere 'imaginary locations'—an issue discussed in detail by the Welsh scholar Mererid Puw Davies in her 2018 article 'On (Not) Reading Wales in W.G. Sebald's *Austerlitz*'.[159] If the freezing 'manse' where Austerlitz was brought up by the preacher Emyr Elias and his wife Gwendolyn is *bad*, the glorious, verdant 'Andromeda Lodge', the home of his schoolmate Gerald, is *good*.

---

[157] Sebald, *Austerlitz*, p.152.   [158] Harris, *No Voice from the Hall*, p.6.
[159] Bigbsy, *Writers in Conversation*, p.141; Mererid Puw Davies, 'On (Not) Reading Wales in W. G. Sebald's *Austerlitz* (2001)', *Oxford German Studies* Vol.47, No.1 (2018).

The obverse of this simplicity is the mythopoeic sheen that is lent to such locations. This is sometimes built around Sebald's more arcane research. His depictions of Mid Wales, for instance, seem to be strongly informed by a small leaflet on the history of Llanwddyn and Lake Vyrnwy, which can be found in his library at the German Literature Archive. *Austerlitz*'s photographs of the village of Vyrnwy before it was sunk beneath a reservoir are drawn from this volume, whose author, the Rev. T.H. Evans (Sebald underlines the seven previous vicars of Llanwddyn with the same surname), maintains an apparently sober narrative poise while discussing the various ghosts that were banished by vicars even up to the nineteenth century, and the 'Yr Ellyll Dan (the Fire Fiend)'—glossed as 'the well known phenomenon called "Will o' the Wisp"'.[160] Later Evans recounts how, in the preparation work for the reservoir, no local man would agree to help move a particular boulder under which a particularly troublesome ghost named Yspryd Cynon had apparently been placed years earlier by the local 'Dyn Hysbys' or 'wise man'.[161] It seems clear enough how Sebald would have developed an idea of Wales as a semi-mythic 'other' world of austere religious devotion, dramatic landscapes, stately homes, and magic.

'I am a Kind': Liverpool Street Station and East London

Austerlitz bristles with places that are more intricately depicted and where temporalities intersect in a much more complex way. One of these is Liverpool Street Station in the City of London. It is here that Austerlitz arrived as a child on a *Kindertransport* train as a refugee in 1942; here that, in the 1990s, he is shaken by a sudden re-emergence of the suppressed memory of that experience. It is also here that he and the narrator then meet by chance after two decades without contact and where Austerlitz begins to reveal his biography to the narrator in the 'saloon bar' of the Great Eastern Hotel adjoining the station; and where, in a room of the hotel, the narrator begins to write up this first substantial portion of Austerlitz's biography. So it is that numerous temporalities seem to hover or overlap palimpsestically on this site.

It is likely that Sebald's interest in Liverpool Street reached back some time before he began to write *Austerlitz*. It is certainly clear that the area held a genuine fascination for him, and it must have featured in his actual itineraries, travelling between Norwich and London by train. The descriptions of the 'flat, almost treeless landscape' on the way into Liverpool Street—listing 'the Colchester water-tower, the Marconi factory in Chelmsford, the empty greyhound track at

---

[160] T.H. Evans, *Llanwddyn and Lake Vyrnwy: Centenary Edition* (German Literature Archive), p.10.
[161] Ibid., p.15.

Romford'—recall his poem 'Day Return'; the return journey also appears in the final pages of *Vertigo*. Similarly, the reason for Sebald's narrator's visit, a sudden blindness in his right eye, draws on motifs of blindness in *After Nature*; allusions to this poem also appear in the narrator's phrasing.[162] Adding to a sense in which this space is richly inscribed or overwritten, nested quotations from 'one of my favourite poems'—'Fragment' by Sebald's friend, the East London poet Stephen Watts—also appear while the narrator muses on the city in the ophthalmologist's waiting room.[163]

Long notes that 'the foundational moment in Jacques Austerlitz's life-*story* is not the moment of his birth or even that of his separation from his parents, but rather several acts of archival destruction perpetrated by the German Luftwaffe during the Blitz and by Austerlitz's guardian Emyr Elias'.[164] 'The text's epiphanic moment', in his reading, is 'the moment when Austerlitz finally succeeds in discovering his mother's image in the theatrical archives of Prague'.[165] Yet he appears to have been waylaid by his overall argument about archival logics in Sebald's work. In fact, it seems clear that the mnemonic moment recounted at Liverpool Street is the text's critical fulcrum, placed conspicuously at its figurative and actual centre. It is in Sebald's densely palimpsestic rendering of Liverpool Street that he depicts Austerlitz finding—albeit accidentally—what Patrick Keiller's Robinson was looking for in Lambeth: 'the location of a memory'. It is this space where, as Benjamin wrote of the Parisian Surrealists' use of architecture and objects, 'the immense forces of "atmosphere" concealed in these things' is brought 'to the point of explosion'.[166]

As Martin Modlinger has shown in a 2012 essay, Sebald borrowed large parts of Austerlitz's story and characterization from the biography of the real-life *Kindertransport* refugee Susi Bechhöfer, also raised in Wales by a religious minister under a false name, whose account of her life details the traumatic experience of the rediscovery of her identity in a manner with which Sebald's 'fictional' account bears a number of striking similarities. Modlinger's—and Bechhöfer's—ethical complaint is that Sebald failed to ask permission to do this, failing to exercise the supposed sensitivity and the 'absolute moral respect' for which, they claim, he has been unduly lauded by critics.[167] But what is clear is that the identity of 'Austerlitz' is not *solely* borrowed from Bechhöfer; rather, Sebald's fictionalizing process, as we have already seen in the case of Max Ferber, is one of translating, patching together,

---

[162] Sebald, *Across the Land and the Water*, ed. Iain Galbraith (London: Penguin, 2012), p.92.
[163] Sebald, *Austerlitz*, p.50. [164] Long, *Image, Archive, Modernity*, p.152.
[165] Ibid., p.161.
[166] Benjamin, *Selected Writings Vol.II*, ed. Michael Jennings, Howard Eiland, and Gary Smith (Cambridge, MA: Belknap, 1999), p.210.
[167] Martin Modlinger, '"You can't change names and feel the same": The Kindertransport Experience of Susi Bechhöfer in W.G. Sebald's *Austerlitz*', in Andrea Hammel and Bea Lewkowicz (eds.), *The Kindertransport to Britain 1938-39: New Perspectives* (Amsterdam: Rodopi, 2012), p.227.

and amalgamating real histories—thereby problematizing the very distinction between fiction and fact.

It is certainly true that Liverpool Street, as the London terminus of the *Kindertransport* trains, bears a heightened significance in all accounts of the refugees' experience. In Sebald's archive, amidst the material collected together under *The Emigrants*, is an article from *Die Zeit* of 28 July 1989 and entitled 'I am a Kind', in which the writer highlights various phrases, including the refugee Paul Eisler's description of being collected by his uncle, 'am Bahnhof Liverpool Street Station, den er sein ganzes Leben lang hassen wird' ('which he would hate for his entire life').[168] Sebald's depiction of the space in *Austerlitz*, then, underwent a long gestation period. Austerlitz's mnemonic experience surrounds his arrival in the 'Ladies Waiting Room', a setting that provokes readerly associations with the complex network of impressions and associations cultivated at Antwerp Station. Descriptions of skaters on the frozen ground in former times also connect the two cities; crucially, the earlier description of that station's *Salle des pas perdus* are implicitly carried forward, acting as another channel between places and times. The 'labyrinthine vaults' of the station, with its 'dusty grey light', recall the 'subterranean twilight' of the Antwerp waiting room, and each forms a kind of bunker or fortress—also by this point established in their association with repressed memory.[169] The term 'vaults', which is repeated, is not insignificant, bringing forward the motifs established earlier at Breendonk and running ahead to Terezìn.

Comparisons with other figures also suggest themselves. As Blackler points out, the tiled floor—a distinctive feature of masonic temples like the one concealed within the Great Eastern Hotel, and which Sebald mentions—bears 'the pattern used by Dutch painters and by [Jan Peter] Tripp to create, and distort, perspective'. This is where, as Austerlitz explains, 'the endgame would be played', and the depiction seems specifically to recall Samuel Beckett's one-act play *Endgame* (1957) with its stage-description 'Bare Interior. Grey light.'[170] Meanwhile, the fact that the waiting room is depicted 'a few weeks at most before it vanished for ever in the rebuilding' seems to allude to the condition of the Parisian arcades both in Benjamin's depiction of them and in Louis Aragon's *Paris Peasant*, where they are described as 'places that were incomprehensible yesterday, and that tomorrow will never know'.[171]

This point in particular is emphatic, since the condition obtains both in the space Austerlitz is recollecting (the Ladies' Waiting Room) and the one in which he is *doing* the recollecting (the Great Eastern Hotel), which itself is 'soon to be

---

[168] Susanne Mayer, 'I am a Kind', *Die Zeit* 28 July 1989 (http://www.zeit.de/1989/31/i-am-a-kind).
[169] Sebald, *Austerlitz*, p.192.   [170] Blackler, *Reading W.G. Sebald*, pp.201–2.
[171] Louis Aragon, *Paris Peasant*, trans. Simon Watson Taylor (London: Cape, 1971), p.29.

thoroughly renovated'.[172] Of the former, Austerlitz remarks that 'in the middle of this vision of imprisonment and liberation I could not stop wondering whether it was a ruin or a building in the process of construction that I had entered'.[173] The layering of this motif emphasizes a sensation of the structure itself being in flux and thus, in some way, particularly receptive to a memory and imagination that is also in the process of being radically restructured. This sense of atmosphere is also set out by Sebald in his wider depiction of the City and East London. For example, a walk through 'the towering office blocks of the Docklands area' and through the foot tunnel to Greenwich Observatory prompts Austerlitz's 'disquisition' on time itself as 'by far the most artificial of all our inventions'—clearly drawing on the significance of Greenwich as the place to make such an remark. His observation that even 'in a metropolis ruled by time like London [...] it is still possible to be outside time' is clearly apt to the atmospheric layering of temporalities and his feeling for sites that seem somehow removed from the present moment—like Iver Grove, of which Austerlitz is brought to think at this point because he remembers it containing a panorama of Greenwich Park.[174] The narrator's comment that it 'was around three-thirty in the afternoon' when the two leave the Observatory punctures the atmosphere with just the hint of a raised eyebrow.

In fact, the way in which Austerlitz's subjective experiences are threaded through a broader sense of objective local-historical richness is precisely what gives these sequences much of their emotive force. On his way into Liverpool Street, as the train winds 'through a narrow defile' and into a space resembling 'an underground columbarium', Sebald's narrator imagines streets 'crowding ever more closely together' and 'one reef of buildings above the next', emphasizing a sense of the stratification of place.[175] Later, the description of railway lines on a map resembling 'muscles and sinews in an anatomical atlas' gives a sense of this humanization of the setting; and, as Austerlitz describes the area, there is a sense of historical data coagulating like blood through this figurative connecting tissue.[176] Observing that part of the site now occupied by the station was once taken up by the Bedlam, the insane asylum, the narrator wonders with Austerlitz 'whether the pain and suffering accumulated on this site had ever really ebbed away'.[177] The atmosphere is thickened by the description of 'bleachfields' on the site, where fabrics were dyed by 'the diminutive figures of weavers and washerwomen'.[178]

All of this becomes part of Austerlitz's ruminations on the place 'where the dead were buried once the churchyards of London could hold no more'.[179] At Broad Street Station, which preceded the present structure, we learn that 'examinations during the demolition work of 1984 brought to light over four hundred skeletons underneath a taxi rank', and the sequence is followed by a full-page

---

[172] Sebald, *Austerlitz*, p.57. [173] Ibid. p.191. [174] Ibid. p.140; p.141; p.143.
[175] Ibid. pp.49–50; p.51. [176] Ibid. p.186. [177] Ibid. p.183. [178] Ibid. p.184.
[179] Ibid. p.184.

photograph of decaying skulls that seem to peer out from the ground.[180] The connection with the buildings of Brussels here runs between texts, recalling the description in *The Rings of Saturn* of how they are 'erected over a hecatomb of black bodies'.[181]

Pulling into the station, for the narrator, is like pulling into the classical underworld. He observes that 'I always feel particularly apprehensive on the last stretch of the journey', and Bishopsgate was indeed one of the Romans' two major extramural burial sites in London. The Museum of London holds remains that were buried there alongside useful tools for the afterlife such as lamps, coins for the boatman Charon, food, and drink. Likewise, the priory of St Mary of Bethlehem—as a blue plaque on the site attests—really was here, and a nearby street named 'Tenter Ground' acknowledges the history of 'bleachfields' and weaving industries in this area which, like Norwich, was a centre for immigrant Huguenot weavers in the seventeenth century. Sebald would surely have been intrigued by this connection; he may even have had this *topos* suggested to him by Thomas Browne's mention of burial urns found at Spitalfields ('*Spittle* Fields by *London*' as he calls it) accompanied by tear-phials known as 'Lacrymatories' as well as 'lamps, Bottles of Liquor, and other appurtenances of affectionate superstition'.[182]

Yet as in the case of Lake Vyrnwy, the more significant influence seems to derive from the local history pamphlets that can still be found in his archive. In this case, the volume *Broadgate and Liverpool Street Station* by Penelope Hunting, published by Rosehaugh Stanhope Developments in 1991, is a clear source.[183] Various images, including that of the 'anatomical' train lines, are derived from here, as well as anecdotes such as that of the human remains found beneath a taxi rank. The text describes the frozen marshes on which citizens would skate, the Priory of St Mary Bethlehem (Bedlam) and the 'Tenter Grounds'. Sebald's inquisitive annotation of these as 'Bleichfelder?' ('bleach fields?') seems to indicate that he had not encountered the distinctively local term prior to reading this volume, which also includes suggestive cross-section illustrations of the adjoining site of the former Broad Street Station, emphasizing the location's archaeological richness.[184]

Sebald was clearly interested in the extravagances of the Great Eastern Hotel—with its vast fish store and 'pastry makers who came in every night to bake thousands of buns and cakes'—as a feature of the nineteenth century's excesses. It is also notable that, as if remarking on the capacity of this site to provoke

---

[180] Ibid. p.185.   [181] Sebald, *The Rings of Saturn*, p.122.
[182] Browne, *Major Works*, p.279.
[183] Sebald would surely have noted the mythic appropriateness of the name 'Penelope' in this context—a name which becomes that of the proprietor of the Bloomsbury shop in which Austerlitz overhears a radio broadcast relating to the *Kindertransport*.
[184] Penelope Hunting, *Broadgate and Liverpool Street Station* (London: Rosehaugh Stanhope Developments, 1991), p.27.

melancholy speculation, he marked with a double line Hunting's rather bleak analysis that 'the railway demolitions of the 1860s continued inexorably until London was a place of arrivals and departures and a place where nobody lived'.[185] Yet it is striking that Sebald's pencil markings in the text cease after the section on Liverpool Street's history. Characteristically, he seems uninterested in the site's contemporary significance as, according to *Chartered Surveyor Weekly*, 'one of London's largest projects since the Great Fire of 1666', and a flagship development project of the 1980s, visited by Thatcher herself.[186] He veers off instead into the imaginary space and the topology of the 'Ladies' Waiting Room'; and it is the way that accurate historical information and imagined space intersect here that forms the distinctive character of his depiction of space.

Another example of Sebald's long-running interest in this part of London comes from his 1989 sketch for a film entitled *Leben Ws* (first published April 1989 in the *Frankfurter Rundschau* and included in *Saturn's Moons*) where Ludwig Wittgenstein and Ben Richards wander through the 'Londoner East End', observing 'die vielen jüdischen Ladenschilder. Waiselfisch, Spiegeltheater Solomon etc.' ('the many Jewish shop-signs. Waiselfisch, Spiegeltheater Solomon etc.').[187] Jewish names echo through this landscape as they did in the deserted quarter of Manchester depicted in *The Emigrants*.[188] They read like the names of the gravestones in the Jewish section of Montparnasse cemetery, described later in the text.

Austerlitz's own house—which seems to be based on an actual building that perfectly fits Sebald's description, although it is on 'Alderney Road' rather than 'Alderney Street'—really does border a Jewish cemetery enclosed within high walls, open to visitors by appointment only. The larger Tower Hamlets cemetery nearby, where Austerlitz walks in a state of intense anomie and observes the way in which 'some of the graves themselves had risen above the ground or sunk into it, so that you might think an earthquake had shaken this abode of the departed' is a short distance away.[189] In Sebald's use of this *topos*, the 'testable thereness' referred to by Martin Swales can be felt emphatically. As with Liverpool Street, a

---

[185] Ibid., p.62; p.60.
[186] The periodical's article 'Maggie digs Broadgate', included in the 'Press Comment' chapter of *Broadgate and Liverpool Street Station*, records the prime minister's visit to the site and trumpets that she 'proved adept at the controls of the digger as at the helm of the ship of state [...] Perhaps extensive experience at political site-clearing provided a good background for her brief stint.' (*Broadgate and Liverpool Street Station*, p.99).
[187] Joe Catling and Richard Hibbitt (eds.), *Saturn's Moons: W.G. Sebald: A Handbook* (London: Legenda, 2001), p.330.
[188] In his copy of *Baedeker's London* (Leipzig, 1905), otherwise unmarked, Sebald placed a line next to the entries for Whitechapel, Bethnal Green, and Spitalfields (p.62 under 'XVI, Topographie und Statistik'). Of the latter it is remarked that this was 'ein früher großenteils von Seidenwebern bewohnter Fabrikbezirk' ('an area earlier occupied largely by silk-weavers'). That these were Huguenots expelled from France after the Edict of Nantes was revoked in 1685 forms a subtle ligature with the 'Strangers' Hall' of Norwich.
[189] Sebald, *Austerlitz*, p.320.

visitor to these locations has an acute sense of Sebald having himself attended closely to their actual situations, and it is this sensitivity that becomes such a pronounced feature of their *unheimlich* quality in the text itself.

For instance, the 'wingless' monument whose photograph is included in the text, bearing the text 'Until the day break, and the shadows flee away', but no other attribution, can be found relatively easily. This monument itself offers a model of Sebald's method as a compositor of history and fiction, as well as history *as* fiction: in fact, as becomes clear on closer inspection of the image, the angel does not match with the base, and the part that once must have stood there is pushed to one side. In the real-life visit to this site that Sebald's description provokes, the difference in the texture and appearance of the stone is immediately clear. This itself reads as a subtle and slightly uncanny commentary on the montage-like quality of the text, whose depiction of places that are both imagined and real is consistent with its condition as a fiction woven out of a surfeit of factual data, and whose protagonist's experience of trauma itself hinges precisely on elements of his own 'factual' biography having been revealed as fictions.

Austerlitz's 'Research' in Paris

Just as Sebald's depiction of London is affected by that of Brussels, Antwerp, and Breendonk, so it bleeds into his rendition of Paris. It is later in *Austerlitz*, when the text actually shifts to Paris (where Austerlitz is searching for traces of his father), that the overlaps with Walter Benjamin also become more pronounced. Austerlitz tells the narrator, for instance, that in 1959 he was focusing on the book *Paris, ses organes, ses fonctions et sa vie dans la second moitié du XIXème siècle* by Maxime du Camp, a volume which provided myriad fragments for the *Arcades Project*. At the same time, Austerlitz's descriptions of the old Bibliothèque Nationale, on the Rue Richelieu in the centre of Paris, are strongly reminiscent of Benjamin, recalling in particular the 1937 photograph in which, as Susan Sontag put it in her essay 'Under the Sign of Saturn', he sits 'taking notes for the book on Baudelaire and nineteenth-century Paris he had been writing for a decade'.[190]

Austerlitz's description of the library when he had been working there in the 1950s (this is also a site that the text visits and *re*-visits) presents it as an apt home to arcane and possibly futile research. 'My neighbour', he recounts, seeming to allude to Benjamin's unfinished work on the *Arcades Project*,

> was usually an elderly gentleman with carefully trimmed hair and sleeve protectors, who had been working for decades on an encyclopaedia of church

[190] Susan Sontag, 'Under the Sign of Saturn', in *Under the Sign of Saturn* (New York: Random House, 1981), p.110.

history, a project which had now reached the letter K, so that it was obvious he would never be able to complete it.[191]

When Austerlitz returns to Paris in the 1990s, he finds a place less amenable to this kind of activity. The new library on the Quai François Mitterand, opened in 1996, is presented as highly 'resistant', even 'useless' in his search for 'traces of my father', who escaped here from Prague in the 1940s and was, we presume, sent back east again to his peril.[192] This new library is inscribed with this sense of inhumanity and loss, an archive that frustrates the attempt at finding things. Austerlitz declares that

> both in its outer appearance and inner constitution [it is] unwelcoming if not inimical to human beings, and runs counter, one might say, to the requirements of any true reader.[193]

This sense of unapproachability seems to deliberately recall Borges's 'Library of Babel', 'a sphere whose exact centre is any one of its hexagons and whose circumference is inaccessible': the librarian Henri Lemoine (who recognizes Austerlitz from the 1950s) pointedly describes the new structure as 'Babylonian'.[194] The hubristic scale of the edifice recalls that of Antwerp Station and the Brussels Palace of Justice, and if, as Virilio called them, the bunkers of the Atlantic Wall were 'one of the rare modern monolithic architectures', then this structure also represents a newer manifestation of that form, appearing monolithic in the way it is utterly at odds with its environment.[195] Austerlitz imagines it as a vast boat at imminent risk of becoming unmoored from its surroundings, and he juxtaposes it, in passing, with Alain Resnais's extraordinary 1956 short film *Toute La Mémoire du Monde* (to which Keiller also referred in his 'Poetic Experience' essay), where the old library is presented as a natural organism, its various rooms anatomized in human terms.

If Sebald's depictions of space here owe something to Benjamin's ruminations on cities, then the latter's 1924 essay on Naples perhaps offers a clearer link than his writings on Paris. In this text, 'porosity' is seen as the key to authentic memory and humanity. The nineteenth-century buildings of Liverpool Street Station and the old Bibliothèque Nationale both exhibit this. Yet the glass monumentalism of the new Bibliothèque Nationale, its impermeable form, is implicitly contrasted with the permeability of the nearby Austerlitz station. There, as Austerlitz later remarks,

---

[191] Ibid., pp.363–4.   [192] Ibid., p.393.   [193] Ibid., p.386.
[194] Jorge Luis Borges, *Labyrinths*, ed. Donald Yates and James Irby (Harmondsworth: Penguin, 1970), p.79; Sebald, *Austerlitz*, p.401.
[195] Virilio, *Bunker Archaeology*, p.37.

AN ENGLISH PILGRIM: SEBALD'S *THE RINGS OF SATURN* 183

> I was particularly fascinated by the way the Métro trains coming from the Bastille, having crossed the Seine, roll over the iron viaduct into the station's upper storey, quite as if the façade were swallowing them up.[196]

While at the library,

> several times, said Austerlitz, birds which had lost their way in the library forest flew into the mirror images of the trees in the reading-room windows, struck the glass with a dull thud, and fell lifeless to the ground.[197]

The contrast, whose invocation of the denatured animals recalls the condition of the *Waschbär* in Antwerp's 'Nocturama', marks a critique of architectural modernism: if Walter Gropius wrote in his 1919 *Bauhaus Manifesto* of future structures that would 'one day rise towards heaven from the hands of a million workers like the crystal symbols of a new faith', then Sebald's depiction seems to have more in common with later critiques of glass and steel architecture.[198] Victor Burgin's 1998 description of 'the transparent wall, used by modernists such as Gropius to unite interior with exterior' having 'become the very index of capitalised corporate exclusivity' certainly seems closer to the mark.[199]

It is this sense of alienation that, in Sebald's depiction, the new library at the Quai François Mitterand exudes. But it is not fair to claim, as Long does, that the new Bibliothèque 'is designed to deter, dehumanise and intimidate'.[200] Long effectively presents Sebald's account—which is inseparable from the affective subjectivity of Austerlitz himself—as if it were simply true. Sebald does encourage us to resent the new library and architectural modernism in general: an image of Montparnasse cemetery, for instance, is presented with the widely despised Tour Montparnasse looming foggily in the background like an unwelcome interloper. The tenor of his case, in fact, strongly recalls Prince Charles's famous attack on the redeveloped British Library in London as resembling 'an assembly hall for an academy of secret police'.[201] Yet his criticisms should be seen as part of Austerlitz's private frustrations. After all, in Resnais's film, even the old library in the Rue Richelieu is described using a figure with pointedly negative connotations in Sebald's topographic scheme: employing a brooding, *noir* aesthetic with ample use of rather paranoiac 'subjective camera' shots, the narrator presents the constant accumulation of knowledge as a harrowing prospect: 'faced with these

---

[196] Sebald, *Austerlitz*, p.406.   [197] Ibid., 392.
[198] Walter Gropius, *The Bauhaus Manifesto* (1919) (http://michaellaiskonis.typepad.com/files/bauhaus-manifesto-and-program-walter-gropius-1919.pdf).
[199] Victor Burgin, 'The City in Pieces', in *The Actuality of Walter Benjamin*, eds. Laura Marcus and Lynda Nead (London: Lawrence and Wishart, 1998), p.60.
[200] Long, *Image, Archive, Modernity*, p.82.
[201] Charles, *A Vision of Britain: A Personal View of Architecture* (London: Doubleday, 1989), p.65.

bulging repositories', he declares, 'man fears being engulfed by this mass of words. To safeguard his freedom, he builds fortresses.'[202]

The new library on the Quai François Mitterand is revealed as part of a spatial choreography quite as dense as that which is established around Liverpool Street in London. The Jardin des Plantes (a botanical garden containing a dilapidated zoo), the Salpêtrière hospital, and the Austerlitz train station are even closer to one another than Alderney Street and Liverpool Street, so that the narrative is written into a very specific corner of Paris. Austerlitz's friend Henri Lemoine reveals to him that the new library is in fact embroiled in a layering of topographic significance, located on the site where Jewish possessions were assembled after having been looted in the 1940s in an 'extensive warehousing complex' known by the nauseating label 'Les Galeries d'Austerlitz' (punning obscenely on the 'Galeries Lafayette', a famous department store).[203]

The combination of transit, suffering, and stratification here seems to connect these parts of Paris and London, and the Bibliothèque Nationale keys in with other significant architectural typologies in Sebald's work, too. It is, for instance, described as resembling an ocean liner, and in this respect it specifically connects with the description of Theresienstadt, where, Austerlitz imagines, 'when the day's work was over, the residents of the town flocked out in their thousands on the ramparts and bastions to take the air, almost as if they were passengers enjoying an evening stroll on the deck of an ocean-going steamer'.[204] Likewise, the view from the top of the library over 'the entire urban agglomeration' recalls the same elevated perspective from Norwich Hospital in *The Rings of Saturn*. Christopher Gregory-Guilder characterizes the Bibliothèque Nationale as one of Sebald's 'unlikely vessels whose helms pierce through successive spatio-temporal frames'; in these ways, by picking up on motifs already developed at Antwerp Station and Liverpool Street, the very form of the library also seems to pierce through the text itself.[205]

Theresienstadt and Marienbad: the Dissimulation of Memory and Identity

Austerlitz's obsessive professional interest in train stations continually drives us away from the repressed railway journeys that underscore the text: his own

---

[202] Alain Resnais (dir.), *Toute La Memoire du Monde* (1956) (http://www.youtube.com/watch?v=KKvhp6kL4N4).
[203] Ibid., p.401.   [204] Sebald, *Austerlitz*, p.341.
[205] Christopher Gregory-Guilder, *Autobiogeography and the Art of Peripatetic Memorialization in Works by W.G. Sebald, Patrick Modiano, Iain Sinclair, Jonathan Raban and William Least Heat-Moon* (unpublished PhD thesis) (University of Sussex, 2005), p.217.

journey from Prague to London; and those of his mother and father in their final journeys east, from Prague and Paris respectively, to meet their deaths at the hands of the Nazis. This pattern is paralleled by Austerlitz's name, which, as James Wood has pointed out, bears 'historical resonance [that] continually pulls us away from his Jewishness (from his individuality), and towards a world-historical reference that has nothing much to do with him'.[206]

It is interesting, in this respect, that the narrator's and Austerlitz's first meeting in Paris occurs at a bistro called Le Havane on Boulevard Auguste-Blanqui. Both street and bistro exist, situated just around the corner from where Austerlitz is supposed to be staying at 6, Rue des cinq Diamants. These locations are in the same part of the thirteenth *arrondissement* that Austerlitz finds the last trace of his father. Yet the Boulevard Auguste-Blanqui is significant in another sense: in a powerful example of Sebald's overdetermination of space and place, the setting here seems to allude subtly to his reading of Walter Benjamin, since Blanqui's 1872 text *L'Éternité par les astres* (*Eternity Through the Stars*) provided an arresting image used by Benjamin in his second, 1939 'Exposé' of the *Arcades Project*.

In the lines quoted by Benjamin, Blanqui observes that, since the universe is infinitely large, 'nature' must infinitely repeat itself in every possible variation in order to fill it:

> Every human being is thus eternal at every second of his or her existence. What I write at this moment in a cell of the Fort du Taureau I have written and shall write throughout all eternity—at a table, with a pen, clothed as I am now, in circumstances like these. And thus it is for everyone [...] The number of our doubles is infinite in time and space. One cannot in good conscience demand anything more. These doubles exist in flesh and bone—indeed, in trousers and jacket, in crinoline and chignon. They are by no means phantoms; they are the present eternalized.[207]

Benjamin's quotation of these lines was darkly prescient of his work with the *Arcades*, doomed to endless proliferation and unfinishedness: as Susan Buck-Morss has commented in her 1989 reconstruction, *The Dialectics of Seeing*, the project 'was originally conceived as an essay of fifty pages [but] ultimately all of Paris was drawn in'.[208] The submerged reference to it in *Austerlitz*'s Paris sections was surely deliberate, suggestive of the way in which places and people connect together prismatically in the text.

---

[206] Ibid., p. xxiii.   [207] Quoted in Benjamin, *The Arcades Project*, pp.25–6.
[208] Susan Buck-Morss, *The Dialectics of Seeing: Walter Benjamin and the Arcades Project* (London: MIT Press, 1989), p.5.

Blanqui's idea of endless repetition, recalling the *mise-en-abyme* effect of the 'abyss after abyss' in *The Emigrants* (and Benjamin's 'The Task of the Translator'), has an analogue in Austerlitz's description of his problems with time:

> I feel more and more as if time did not exist at all, only various spaces interlocking according to the rules of a higher form of stereometry, between which the living and the dead can move back and forth as they like.[209]

'Stereometry' here invokes the idea of the double, indeed of repeated doubling, which recurs throughout the text. It is notable, for instance, that Blanqui made his speculation from a fortress—a form whose endless proliferation formed a focal point of Austerlitz's ruminations in Antwerp. Austerlitz's uncanny memory of a 'a twin brother who had been with me on that long journey' and who 'towards the end of that journey... had died of consumption' is one alternately articulated example. On a formal level, the idea of doubling is closely linked to Sebald's interest in photography and film as an authenticating process that nevertheless problematizes the 'research into the past' that forms Austerlitz's story.

As Clive Scott notes, Sebald 'double-sidelined' the passage in *Camera Lucida* where Barthes writes that 'photography is [...] intimately linked with the presence of the double'.[210] As Barthes put it in his study *Camera Lucida*, 'the photograph's essence is to ratify what it represents'—'what I see is not a memory, an imagination, a reconstruction, [...] but reality in a past state: at once the past and the real'.[211] The tension here is explored closely in Austerlitz's discovery of a film made in the ghetto at Theresienstadt, which he copies and slows down in the hope of finding an image of his mother. Austerlitz's description of the slowed-down film is followed by a double-page, highly pixelated image and, after this, a frame which features the fleeting, ghostly appearance of the woman who turns out not to be her. When he is provided with a real photograph, the sensation is one of deflation—what difference does it make, if he has no 'real' recollection of her? Ironically, given the case made by Walter Benjamin in 'The Work of Art in the Age of its Technical Reproducibility' (1936), photography here seems to have been re-inscribed with a sense of 'aura' that Benjamin associates with artworks *before* photography's advent—a sense that he characterizes as 'the unique phenomenon of a distance, however close'.[212]

This sequence can hardly fail to remind us of the tension developed in 'Max Ferber' between Ferber's (and Frank Auerbach's) distinctive technique of agonized

---

[209] Sebald, *Austerlitz*, p.261.
[210] Clive Scott, 'Sebald's Photographic Annotations', in Catling and Hibbitt, *Saturn's Moons*, pp.239–40.
[211] Roland Barthes, *Camera Lucida: Reflections on Photography*, trans. Richard Howard (London: Vintage, 1993), p.82.
[212] Benjamin, in *Illuminations*, p.222.

re-inscription of drawn and painted imagery and the fraudulent photograph of a Nazi book-burning, with which Ferber's uncle becomes preoccupied. But, in this connection, it is interesting to note that scholars have sometimes overreacted to Sebald's prompt towards 'suspicion' of the photographic material in his texts. Deane Blackler, for instance, claims that in a photograph that purports to be of a group of people at Andromeda Lodge, one of them bearing an African Grey Parrot,

> Careful scrutiny reveals that the face on the male figure in the left of the photograph has been removed and replaced. The hairlines are different: a penumbra of blonde or white curls appears above the face of a man with short dark hair.[213]

Yet as Mererid Puw Davies points out, noting the strange 'reverse telescope' experience sometimes produced 'when reading *Austerlitz* with detailed awareness of Welsh context', 'in Welsh history, the man with the parrot is Evan Frederic Morgan, 2nd Viscount Tredegar' (the question of whether Sebald was aware of Tredegar's connection with East London, as one of the area's most significant landowners, remains tantalizing). Even the parrot itself, known as 'Blue Boy', has been described separately as being among 'the most notorious parrots of the 20th century'.[214]

The point here is not to condemn Blackler's scholarship—such misreadings are an almost unavoidable symptom of Sebald's devious approach to the idea of photography straightforwardly 'ratify[ing] what it represents', and perhaps of his anticipatory interaction with future scholars of his work. Close examination of the Viscount's hairline *does* make the image look faked. What is important here is rather Sebald's critical interest in how photography, as a medium, orders and structures the world, but the individual photographic image can itself escape control, becoming an agent of the misreadings and unexpected encounters to which both Sebald and his characters are extremely sensitive. This, in turn, is always rooted in particular locations. In the essay 'Moments Musicaux' (2001), for instance, Sebald describes the vertiginous experience of discovering a postcard in a junk shop in London's East End, depicting 'a painted panorama of the Allgäu mountains in snow and in front of it the Oberstdorf folk dancers in their traditional costumes'—an image that seemed to be lifted directly from his own childhood.[215]

---

[213] Blackler, *On Reading W.G. Sebald*, p.178.
[214] Mererid Puw Davies, 'On (Not) Reading Wales in W. G. Sebald's *Austerlitz* (2001)', p.87; p.96; p.98.
[215] 'On finding this card, which had no message written on the back and which must certainly have gone on a long journey, I really felt as if the ten costumed men and women of Oberstdorf had been lying in wait for me here in their dusty English exile, just to remind me that I would never be able to escape the early history of my native land, where costumes and tradition played a not insignificant part' (Sebald, *Campo Santo*, pp.190–1).

188   LANDSCAPE AND SUBJECTIVITY

In light of this discussion, one location that becomes particularly important in *Austerlitz* is that of the spa: Austerlitz explains to the narrator how Theresienstadt was fraudulently presented to emigrant Jewish people as 'Theresienbad', a 'most salubrious' resort.[216] A small stamp, depicting a bucolic scene, is included as evidence. This dissimulation links it closely to another place in *Austerlitz*: the Bohemian spa town of Marienbad, less than 100 miles away, which also takes on huge importance in relation to Sebald's use of photographic imagery in his texts. It is from the Brasserie Le Havane that Austerlitz describes having visited Marienbad with his then-partner Marie de Verneuil in 1972 and recounts the severe nervous breakdown that he suffered there.

One of the reasons that this sequence is interesting is the strange absence of women in Sebald's work. Just as each of *The Emigrants* is male, along with the vast majority of the characters in *The Rings of Saturn*, *Austerlitz* is fundamentally rooted in the empathic relationship between its two male figures. Women rarely appear (Marie herself is not mentioned at all until halfway through the text), and when they do—as in the case of the 'Goddess of time past' in Antwerp Station—they are often reduced to mere unapproachable symbols, this condition strangely paralleling the 'aura' of the photograph. Indeed, though it is not the subject of his argument, one thing that is interesting about Martin Modlinger's discussion of the weight of similarity between Austerlitz's biography and that of the real-life *Kindertransport* refugee Susi Bechhöfer is the light it throws on how Sebald adapted a woman's story into a man's—even transforming (or *translating*) Bechhöfer's twin sister Lotte into Austerlitz's uncanny memory of a vanished twin brother.[217]

In the course of his argument, Modlinger mentions 'the many parallels between his story and her history'. Yet the overall effect is not so much one of 'parallel' as an unsettling process of elision by which 'her history' becomes 'his story', correlating with the more widespread elision of the feminine as an active presence in Sebald's work. Self-conscious or not, Austerlitz's inability to sustain his relationship with Marie de Verneuil could well be seen as synecdochizing Sebald's failure to include women as empathic subjects. It is in this sense, first of all, that the Marienbad sequence in *Austerlitz* stands out, since it takes the form of what seems like a fairly improbable romantic getaway. Yet the significance of the location soon puts paid to any frivolousness for other reasons, too. Austerlitz's horror, he later discovers, has a basis. As he later finds out from his former nanny in Prague, this was the destination of his last family holiday in 1934. The revelation makes it clear that Austerlitz's experience of immobilization upon (re)visiting the resort with

---

[216] Sebald, *Austerlitz*, p.335.
[217] Modlinger, '"You can't change names and feel the same": The Kindertransport Experience of Susi Bechhöfer in W.G. Sebald's *Austerlitz*', p.227.

Marie years later was bound up with an unwelcome disturbance of a traumatic memory.

By setting the sequence at Marienbad, however, Sebald is also engaging in a meta-textual game. From the very first description of the dilapidated 'Palace Hotel', whose foyer is lined, disorientatingly, with mirrors, it is clear that Sebald is writing in conscious interaction with yet another of Alain Resnais's films—his 1961 version of Alain Robbe-Grillet's 'Ciné-Roman' *Last Year at Marienbad*.[218] This notoriously ponderous work, populated by a group of characters named 'A', 'M', and 'X', is centred on the impossibility of being certain whether or not 'A' and 'X' met the previous year. In fact, even Resnais and the script-writer, Robbe-Grillet, disagreed about this—as Jean-Louis Leutrat relates, 'probably not, according to the novelist, the film-maker's response being the opposite'.[219] In the film, a drawer full of copies of a photograph which 'proves' the meeting lampoons the capacity of the image to provide certainty. And just as Resnais's moving camera 'discovers' the space of the hotel in the same manner as it did the library in *Toute la Mémoire du Monde*, so its chequerboard floors, sometimes perpetuated in the pictures displayed on the walls, recall those of the Masonic temple at Liverpool Street while pointing to a certain high-brow, highly demoralizing sense of gameplay that is present in both *Marienbad* and *Austerlitz*.

Remarkably, Robbe-Grillet is absent from Judith Ryan's otherwise perceptive essay 'Sebald's Encounters with French Narrative', despite his connection with Michel Butor as a *nouveau romancier*. Perhaps this is because the connecting filament is not so much the *nouveau roman* itself as the place. After all, Ryan's judgement that 'Sebald does not plumb the depths of his characters' subconscious' but merely 'remains on the surface of things' because his form 'virtually forbids interior monologue' overlooks the fact that Sebald's project centres on the *exteriorization* of psychology onto the landscape and built environment, a turning inside-out that forms the very basis of his mythologization of place *and* his enquiry into its interrelation with subjectivity.[220]

In the Marienbad sequence of *Austerlitz*, the overlaps with Robbe-Grillet are clear: just as 'A' and 'M' almost match up with 'Austerlitz' and 'Marie' (in fact, A is the woman and M her husband), Sebald has Marie comment on how everything in the hotel bedroom is immaculately clean except 'the writing desk', which 'had not been dusted for years'. It is in the writing desk that the stack of photographic 'evidence' is discovered in the film.[221] Yet Sebald's superimposition of narratives performs this sense of the uncanny by referencing Resnais's film without any specific mention of it: 'I kept feeling as if someone else were walking beside me', Austerlitz remarks, observing how he and Marie 'stood [...] a couple of paces

---

[218] Alain Resnais (dir.), *Last Year at Marienbad* (Argos, 1961).
[219] Jean-Louis Leutrat, *Last Year at Marienbad*, trans. Paul Hammond (London: BFI, 2000), p.19.
[220] Ryan, in Zisselsberger, *The Undiscover'd Country*, 135.   [221] Sebald, *Austerlitz*, p.294.

apart, like two actors on stage'.[222] The episode dramatizes the way that memories in different media converge with one another in Sebald's work, while all the time reminding us of the crucial significance of *place* to this conjunction.

Martin Klebes discusses this in his essay 'If You Come to a Spa', explaining the environment of Marienbad as a 'fundamentally theatrical space' where people went not just to recuperate but to shake off their regular social coats, and where

> political deal-making, social and sexual adventure afforded through anonymity, gambling, and exotic shopping opportunities all became defining parts of the spa experience, bearing little direct relation to any notion of restoring or maintaining bodily health.[223]

In this sequence we also rediscover the distinctive thread of urbane, cultivated 'Mitteleuropa' that runs through Sebald's narratives—in *The Emigrants*, Max Ferber's mother is described reading the 'Spa news', a kind of society column, in the newspaper; *The Rings of Saturn* includes a brief rumination on the East Anglian coast as a region of highly salubrious nineteenth-century spas. But what is most interesting about Marienbad is that it does explicitly what almost every other significant location in *Austerlitz* does implicitly: if the spa is a self-consciously theatrical space, then it is no more so than the *Salle des pas perdus*, at Antwerp Station, or the Ladies' Waiting Room at Liverpool Street.

The sense of infinite mnemonic regression that is explicit in *Last Year at Marienbad* clearly reverberates through *Austerlitz*, where a precise 'constatation of places' is offset by a constant, vertiginous sense of slippage into other places and significances by means of an ever-increasing network of associations, spiralling into one another. The narrative's circular return to Breendonk—and Dan Jacobson's *Heshel's Kingdom*, another tale of loss and suffering—is precisely part of this. The effect is to render space and place prismatic; to complicate them with layers of traumatic experience. In this way, by constantly revisiting, rereading and rewriting particular sites, placing them into unexpected constellations, Sebald's distinctive *oeuvre* offers a unique emulsion of space and subjectivity that is always both singular and multiple.

---

[222] Ibid., p.298; p.303.   [223] Klebes, in Zisselsberger, *The Undiscover'd Country*, pp.123–5.

5

Iain Sinclair's Early Writing

The Arcane Scholarship of Place

On the acknowledgements page of his 1987 novel *White Chappell, Scarlet Tracings*, Iain Sinclair split his early writing into two groups. *White Chappell*, he averred, 'closes a triad begun with *Lud Heat* (1975) and *Suicide Bridge* (1979): it opens, hopefully, a second triad'.[1] This would be completed by *Downriver* and *Radon Daughters*, published in 1991 and 1994 respectively. As the intersection of these 'triads' suggests, Sinclair's early work is best considered as one ever-expanding project, circulating perpetually around the same or overlapping themes and territories. In fact, probably its most characteristic feature is the way that it insists on the inseparability of these two things: its territory—principally that of East London and the Thames Estuary—*is* its theme, and the perceived 'energies' and mythologies of space and place are inseparable from the affective experience of the narrating subject. To speak of a *topos*, then—with its suggestion of both theme and location—makes particular sense here.

The continuity of the Sinclair *topos* has often been noted. Robert Sheppard, for example, has described the sense of an overall 'intratext' connecting his various works.[2] If something does shift across Sinclair's output, considered in the round, then it is the narrative mood: the way that a playful interest in ley lines, occult symbolism, and elaborate conspiracy theories in his earlier work is increasingly folded into a paranoiac atmosphere of 'madness' that consumes landscape, culture, and the narrating subject. Increasingly trapped 'within a charmed circle impossible to break out of, mesmerised by the charm of his own designs', as Rod Mengham has put it, Sinclair's narrative persona becomes increasingly ill at ease, venomous, and embittered. In the process, the 'relational network' of the space he depicts becomes an ever more tightly closed circuit, cut off from outside interference.[3]

In exploring this shift, this chapter demonstrates how Sinclair's move from poetry and fiction to a highly idiosyncratic brand of non-fiction writing in the 1990s was all but inevitable. Across the period connecting *Lud Heat* to *Radon*

---

[1] Iain Sinclair, *White Chappell, Scarlet Tracings* (London: Penguin, 2004), p.194.
[2] Robert Sheppard, *Iain Sinclair* (Tavistock: Northcote House, 2007), p.19.
[3] Rod Mengham, 'The Writing of Iain Sinclair', in Richard Lane Mengham and Philip Tew (eds.), *Contemporary British Fiction* (Cambridge: Polity, 2002), p.58.

Landscape and Subjectivity in the Work of Patrick Keiller, W.G. Sebald, and Iain Sinclair. David Anderson, Oxford University Press (2020). © David Anderson.
DOI: 10.1093/oso/9780198847199.001.0001

Daughters, it suggests, his verve for the arcane and the disorientating, his tendency towards grotesquery and caricature, lapsed into stagnation; the ever-increasing weight of the 'intratext' became too heavy a burden to be supported by a framework that was always only ambivalently fictional, in part producing the lurch towards the documentary texts examined in the subsequent chapter.

'The Spiral We Are Pacing Out': Low Experience and Occult Speculation

In his designation of Sinclair as a 'neo-modernist'—a term that ties him to an American tradition running through Ezra Pound, William Carlos Williams, and Charles Olson and that asserts his commonality with writers of the 'British Poetry Revival' of the 1960s and 1970s, such as J.H. Prynne and Lee Harwood—the critic Robert Bond has emphasized this school's tendency to 'draw on a range of specialist knowledges'. In Sinclair's case, this is often combined with an attraction to 'sub-literary prose': ghostwritten gangster memoirs like John Pearson's bestselling 1972 memoir *The Profession of Violence: The Rise and Fall of the Kray Twins* and 'neglected London writing' like Alexander Baron's 1963 novel *The Lowlife*, which Sinclair praised in a 1992 article for the *London Review of Books* for its 'scrupulous accuracy' and 'wonderfully precise physical movement'.[4] Such writings are not connected by genre or style but rather by shared territory, so that place, and in particular East London, is the determinant of Sinclair's eclecticism.

In working with such texts, Sinclair both discovers and creates an alternative, local canon and is alert to the complicity of fiction in shaping perceptions of place: as he wrote in the poem 'Labrys: Eve of Beltaine' (1977), 'the red map folds into his pocket/easy as a paperback'.[5] Part of the point of his work, in fact, is surely to confound the very distinction between these two things: Sinclair's instruction to his reader is that, if one wishes to really know a place, paperbacks might actually *be* the most useful maps. His focus on East London means that the result is not only the matching up of spatial peripherality with a correspondingly peripheral, offbeat literary canon (in his essays written for the *London Review of Books* in the 1980s and 1990s, Sinclair is often found bemoaning the supposed blinkeredness and stagnancy of established tastes) but also—as in the manner of Keiller and Sebald—the incorporation of eccentric, autodidactic, frequently arcane scholarship into the work itself, detailing the excavation and examination of this alternative canon.

---

[4] Robert Bond, *Iain Sinclair* (Cambridge: Salt, 2005), p.2; p.9; Iain Sinclair, 'Lady Thatcher's Bastards', *London Review of Books* 27 February 1992 (https://www.lrb.co.uk/v14/n04/iain-sinclair/lady-thatchers-bastards).

[5] In *Brown Clouds: In the Tin Zone, Pendeen, Cornwall, April–May 1977* (Newcastle upon Tyne: Pig Press, 1977), unpaginated.

Lud Heat (1975), for example, is structured around Sinclair's own experiences as a casual worker in the Tower Hamlets parks department. The first edition of this text—self-published by his own Albion Village Press, named after the street in which he still lives in Hackney, East London—is peppered with photographs of Sinclair at work mowing the grass (see Figure 5.1). As is common with his work, this visual material is inexplicably left out of later editions, yet its interplay with the text emphasizes how the narrating persona, moving around and through different locations in this capacity, comes upon the idea of networks of relation based primarily on *immediate* experience of space and environment: the 'autoptic'

Figure 5.1 Photograph of Sinclair with his lawnmower, standing in front of Hawksmoor's church of St George-in-the-East in *Lud Heat* (1975). Courtesy of Iain Sinclair.

approach elaboratively developed in an inset discussion of Stan Brakhage's experimental 1971 film *The Act of Seeing With One's Own Eyes* (a literal translation of the Greek 'autopsy').

Fittingly, Sinclair in *Lud Heat* cultivates what Patrick Wright has called a 'scavenging poetic': rumbling around Tower Hamlets on his lawnmower, he becomes an ironic double of Christiana in Bunyan's *Pilgrim's Progress* (1678), who—with her 'muck rake'—appears in a long epigraph.[6] Wielding his own figurative and actual rakes, Sinclair becomes what Michael Moorcock called in a later introduction to the poem 'an archivist of the marginal': just as prose and verse fragments are brought together into one baggily autobiographical assemblage, material observations and discoveries are blended with arcane scholarship.[7] Sinclair's sources include, among others, Thomas De Quincey, Kerry Downes (author of the Thames and Hudson guide to Nicholas Hawksmoor), Herodotus, M.R. James, J.G. Frazer, Thomas Browne, William Maitland (author of a 1739 *History of London*), and Elias Ashmole.

Lud Heat's composite form and variegated allusiveness find it incorporating themes as disparate as the apparently ominous arrangement of Hawksmoor's eighteenth-century baroque churches across the map of London and presences like the 1960s gangsters and pop-culture celebrities Reggie and Ronnie Kray (later, in *Suicide Bridge*, transfigured into 'Hand and Hyle' after Blake's *Jerusalem*). Sucking these sources into a multifarious, polysemous figuration of the space of East London, *Lud Heat* digs up overlooked texts just as it 'digs' into the supposed mythical significance of place, piling up resonances upon each another in an accretive manner. The finished artefact thus comes to resemble a teetering stack of sometimes discordant elements whose determining factor is their association with both locality and Sinclair's own experience—attesting to a poetic sensibility in tune with David Jones's idea, expressed in connection with his 1952 poem *The Anathemata*, that 'the arts abhor any loppings off of meanings or emptyings out, any loosening of the totality of connotations, any loss of recession and thickness'.[8]

If the tone here is one of serious inquiry, the bathos of the 'muck rake' coyly ironizes this process as an activity born of boredom and tedious manual labour, foregrounding the narrative persona as a wayward, alienated figure. The more diaristic accounts of tending to the parks' greenery include the tale of one of Sinclair's colleagues losing a toe to his lawnmower and the pathetic story of the accidental destruction of a nest of goldfinches. It is this blend of the high and low, the reflective and the immediate, that suggests an adaptation of Wright's diagnosis: Sinclair is here *both* 'abracadabra man' *and* 'laureate of the welfare state'.[9] The

---

[6] Iain Sinclair, *Lud Heat* (London: Albion Village Press, 1975), p.3.
[7] Michael Moorcock, in Iain Sinclair, *Lud Heat and Suicide Bridge* (London: Granta, 1998), p.5.
[8] David Jones, *The Anathemata: Fragments of an Attempted Writing* (London: Faber, 1952), p.24.
[9] Patrick Wright, *A Journey Through Ruins: The Last Days of London* (Oxford: Oxford University Press, 2009), p.220.

effect is that not only are the mythologies of place explored: the very activity of place's mythologization is smudged into its depiction. In the process, Sinclair's diverse sources are factored into a model of territorial 'heat' or 'energies' where, following Frazer—whose *The Golden Bough* (1890) was cited by T.S. Eliot as a key source for *The Waste Land* (1922)—'things which have once been in physical contact continue to act on each other at a distance after contact has been broken'.[10]

It is interesting to note that although Sinclair's 'triads' figure *Lud Heat* as a beginning, he had been self-publishing poetry in London since the 1970s, when the collection *Back Garden Poems* was assembled. A set of dated diary entries in verse and prose, paralleling the 8mm 'Diary Films' he was shooting at the same time, these run (for no clear reason) chronologically backwards. In them, a somewhat meek narrative persona recounts a motley, often humorous selection of anecdotes immersed in the prosaic stuff of petit-bourgeois dwelling (falling over in the shower, for instance) and included with the published text is a hand-drawn map of the local 'Albion Village' area, with Sinclair's friends' and collaborators' addresses marked on (see Figure 5.2).

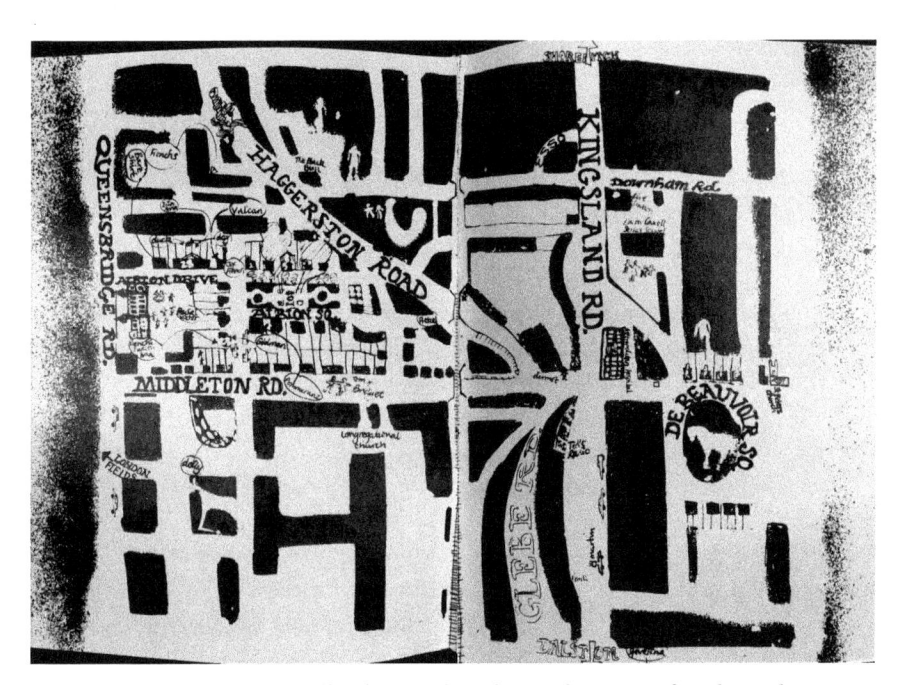

Figure 5.2 Map of 'Albion Village' printed on the inside covers of *Back Garden Poems* (1970), drawn by Renchi Bicknell. Courtesy of Iain Sinclair and UCL Special Collections.

---

[10] Frazer, quoted in Sinclair, *Lud Heat and Suicide Bridge*, p.20.

The wryly humorous tone of this collection is largely in keeping with the mood of 1971's *The Kodak Mantra Diaries*, an account both of Allen Ginsberg's visit to London for the 1967 'International Congress of the Dialectics of Liberation for the Demystification of Violence' and of Sinclair's hapless attempts, with the Dutch film-maker Robert Klinkert, to film him for the German television channel ZDF. Yet the context of this event also helps explain how a playful map of urban bohemia should morph into a landscape of arcane, competing 'energies'. *The Kodak Mantra Diaries* includes an interview with one of the Congress's organizers, R.D. Laing. Explaining to Sinclair how Manhattan, emblematic of the modern metropolis in general, is 'Hell', Laing remarks that pollution and noise mean that 'I can't imagine a more horrible environment has ever been devised by human beings for human beings to live in'. He goes on, nevertheless, to observe that

> the kids are looking at their environment in a very clear-sighted way. They are attempting to discover the original layout of the land under the cities. What were the sacred spots. They are trying to devise a new tribalism.[11]

Both the rancour and hopefulness of Laing's position can be traced as forces that increasingly infect Sinclair's work, with the former tending ever more to smother the latter. By the time of his 1972 collection *Muscat's Würm*, the congenial warmth of the *Diaries* has ceded place to something more severe: wounds oozing 'yellow green pus' ('Household God, Bitten By Rats'), and visions of 'the boneyards of the earth' ('Water is Your Hinge').[12] *The Birth Rug* (1973) shows this new style having taken root. Though the form is still diaristic, such events as the birth of Sinclair's daughter are now found alongside more sinister imagery, like 'the corpse of my grandfather' being 'devoured'.[13] The whole is loomed over by the presence of a 'black / mantic labyrinth' and the spectre of 'THE OLD ENERGIES / RE-CONNECTED', the abrupt capitalization of which is of a piece with a burgeoning sense of the incantatory, spiritualistic, or occult.[14]

The influence of this type of thinking on Sinclair's work is certainly pronounced. In the initial proposals for a 1974 exhibition at the Whitechapel Gallery, *Albion Island Vortex*, Sinclair was already pre-empting the charge of being 'too "mystical"'—even at the same time as he declared to the Gallery's Jenny Stein that the exhibition had 'no absolute importance in itself', comprising merely 'a stage in the spiral we are pacing out'.[15] Certainly by the time of 1977's

---

[11] Sinclair, *The Kodak Mantra Diaries* (London: Albion Village Press, 1971), Book 2 Ch.3 (unpaginated).
[12] Sinclair, *Muscat's Würm* (London: Albion Village Press, 1972), unpaginated.
[13] Sinclair, *The Birth Rug* (London: Albion Village Press, 1973), unpaginated.   [14] Ibid.
[15] Sinclair, letter to Jenny Stein dated 26 November 1973. Echoed by Stein herself in her response of 7 December 1973. Whitechapel Gallery Archive.

Brown Clouds, pregnant references to such phenomena as the only '*seemingly* casual/alignments of fallen stones' (my emphasis) had become commonplace.[16] The 1989 collection *Flesh Eggs and Scalp Metal* cemented the shift, 'editing' his work in an interestingly selective way: only three poems are included from *Back Garden Poems*, compared with most of *Muscat's Würm* and *The Birth Rug*. The effect is to assert Sinclair's self-fashioning in a 'shamanistic' mode and push his earlier, more hapless persona to one side. So it was that, with *Lud Heat*, Sinclair had settled into the kind of literary sensibility or persona that might employ a word like 'triad' in the first place.

Semiological Enthusiasm in *Prehistoric London* and *Lud Heat*

Sinclair's use of the term 'triad' might also have been prompted by perhaps the most significant influence on *Lud Heat*: Elizabeth Oke Gordon's 1914 text *Prehistoric London: Its Mounds and Circles*. This study, which frequently refers to the ancient Welsh texts by that name (and which perhaps resonated with Sinclair at least partly because of his own Welsh background) is certainly the most arcane—but possibly the most decisive—of Sinclair's sources. As Patrick Wright would confirm of Gordon's work, while discussing Sinclair's early writings in his 1991 collection of articles written for the *Guardian* about London, *A Journey Through Ruins*, 'it was from the pages of this obscure tome that King Ludd stepped out onto the post-war scene'.[17] Part of an esoteric tradition of seeking and revealing mystical significance in landscape, it stands in oblique relation to Alfred Watkins's 1925 *The Old Straight Track*, which popularized the idea of 'ley lines' and also bore an indirect influence: as Robert Sheppard writes of Watkins (echoing Sinclair's own comment on J.G. Frazer), his

> description of the invention of ley lines is crucial to understanding Sinclair's psychogeographical and literary politics. His 'original revelation' is that 'everything connects and, in making those connections, streams of energy are activated'.[18]

Elizabeth Gordon is a curious figure, whose other writings include a life of St George and a biography of her father, the eccentric palaeontologist and Dean of Westminster William Buckland, a polymath known for having discovered megalosaurus remains in Oxfordshire. According to his daughter's testimony, Buckland was also once able to recognize that he was in Uxbridge when lost one

---

[16] Sinclair, *Brown Clouds*.   [17] Wright, *A Journey Through Ruins*, p.218.
[18] Sheppard, *Iain Sinclair*, p.17.

night, purely by 'taking up a handful of earth' and smelling it.[19] This combination of the eccentric and the practical seems to have been a family trait: *Prehistoric London*, which Sinclair was apparently handed by chance in a bookshop in Buckingham Palace Road, restates Geoffrey of Monmouth's legend that the pre-Roman King Ludd ('Llud' in her rendition) 'was buried in a vault' underneath the eponymous gate of the City of London; it includes as its frontispiece a scale map showing the triangulation of Parliament Hill, 'Penton' (now the Angel), 'Bryn Gwyn' (where the Tower of London is sited) and 'Tothill' (where the playing fields of Westminster School are now located) (see Figure 5.3).[20] These diagrams demonstrate the clearest way in which *Prehistoric London* informs *Lud Heat*: Sinclair's map of Hawksmoor's churches borrows and develops Gordon's 'triangulation' of mounds (see Figures 5.4 and 5.5). Yet in its elaboration of the mythic, prehistoric significance of London's territory, *Prehistoric London* bears a similar relation to *Lud Heat* as Frazer's *The Golden Bough* or Jessie Weston's *From Ritual To Romance* does to Eliot's *The Waste Land*.

Patrick Wright's gloss of the connection between Gordon, Watkins, and Sinclair is convincing: the wider discussion within which his comments are nested is about the architect Theo Crosby's abortive idea for an extravagant memorial to the Battle of Britain in London's Docklands (later satirized in *Downriver*, Crosby's idea took the form of a pyramid). Wright compares the perceived contemporary need for memorials and monuments, following the era of practical and often destructive redevelopment projects after the Second World War, with the rebuilding of a sense of nationhood and territorial significance following the First. In this light, he avers that 'the original visionaries of the leyline were benevolent Christian enquirers, bent on redeeming and, if at all possible, re-enchanting the face of a nation that was still only emerging from the ruinous trauma of the Great War'.[21]

The only problem with Wright's assessment is that, as Robert Bond has pointed out, he misdates Gordon's work to 1925.[22] In fact, it was first published in 1914. Yet this is a problem that, observed obliquely, becomes instructive: indeed, it seems likely that the very irrationality of Gordon's text was precisely what appealed to Sinclair. Dedicated to one Lady Beachcroft, apparently 'the lineal descendant of Beli Mawr, King of All Britain and Wales, B.C. 132', the volume ripples with inconsistencies and wild assumptions while nevertheless maintaining an ostensibly scientific poise: its full title is *Prehistoric London: Its Mounds And*

---

[19] '"Uxbridge," he exclaimed, his geological nose telling him the precise locality.' Elizabeth Oke Gordon, *The Life and Correspondence of William Buckland* (London: John Murray, 1894), p.30; Megalousaurus incident, p.203.
[20] 'I remember being with somebody in a bookshop in Buckingham Palace Road, some strange little outlet, and the woman in there said "You should read this", and gave me *Prehistoric London: Its Mounds and Circles* by Elizabeth Gordon.' In Kevin Jackson, *The Verbals: Iain Sinclair in Conversation with Kevin Jackson* (Kent: Worple, 2003), p.69; Gordon, *Prehistoric London* (London: Elliott Stock, 1914), p.148.
[21] Wright, *A Journey Through Ruins*, p.218.   [22] Bond, *Iain Sinclair*, p.61.

IAIN SINCLAIR'S EARLY WRITING   199

```
                    ● The Llandin
                      (Parliament Hill)

    Barrows ●●
    (Primrose Hill)


                    ● Penton
                      (Site of the New River Reservoir)


    ● Tothill
      (Westminster)


                    ● Bryn Gwyn
                      (The White Mound of the
                       Tower of London)
```

PLAN OF THE LONDON MOUNDS
(By Stanford)

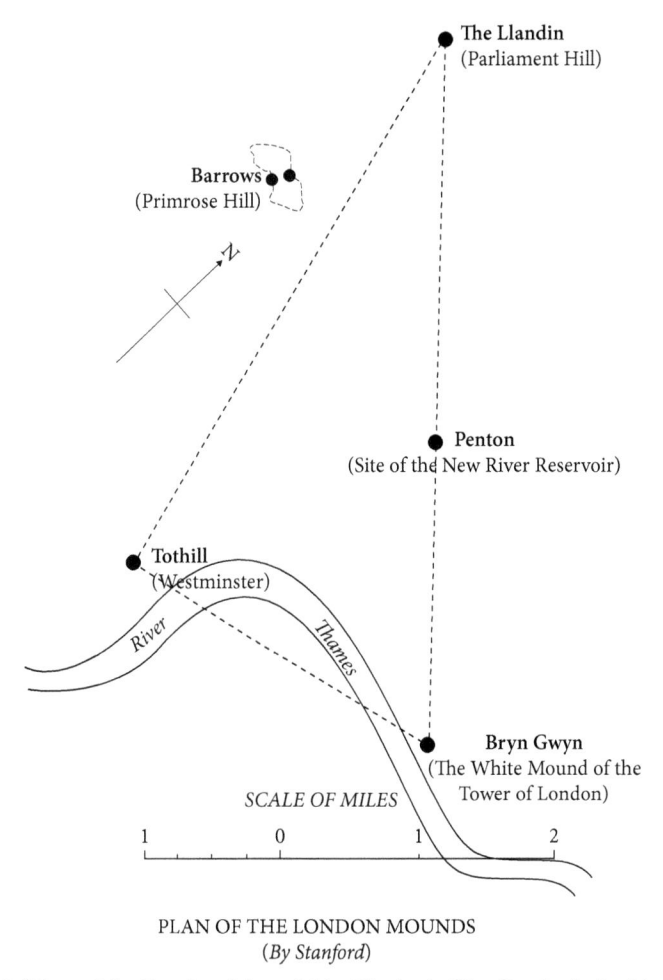

Figure 5.3 'Plan of the London Mounds' in Elizabeth Oke Gordon's *Prehistoric London: Its Mounds and Circles* (1914). Courtesy of British Library (redrawn).

Circles, Religion and Civilization; With Notes On Their Scientific Application From Comparative Antiquity. As the text goes on, it is clear that Gordon's methodology—combining an ostensibly transparent, scientific approach with a deeply opaque, subjective intuition—bore heavy influence on Sinclair's occult-inflected structuring of space and place. Her eagerness to see interconnected patterns of significance everywhere informs Sinclair's own deductions and his ability to entertain diverse and seemingly discordant connections as complementary rather than inconsistent: the obelisks and pyramids within Hawksmoor's baroque designs are linked with the Egyptian deities Isis, Nephythys, Neith, and Selkis, as well as to 'the lost pyramids of Glastonbury that banked the burial place

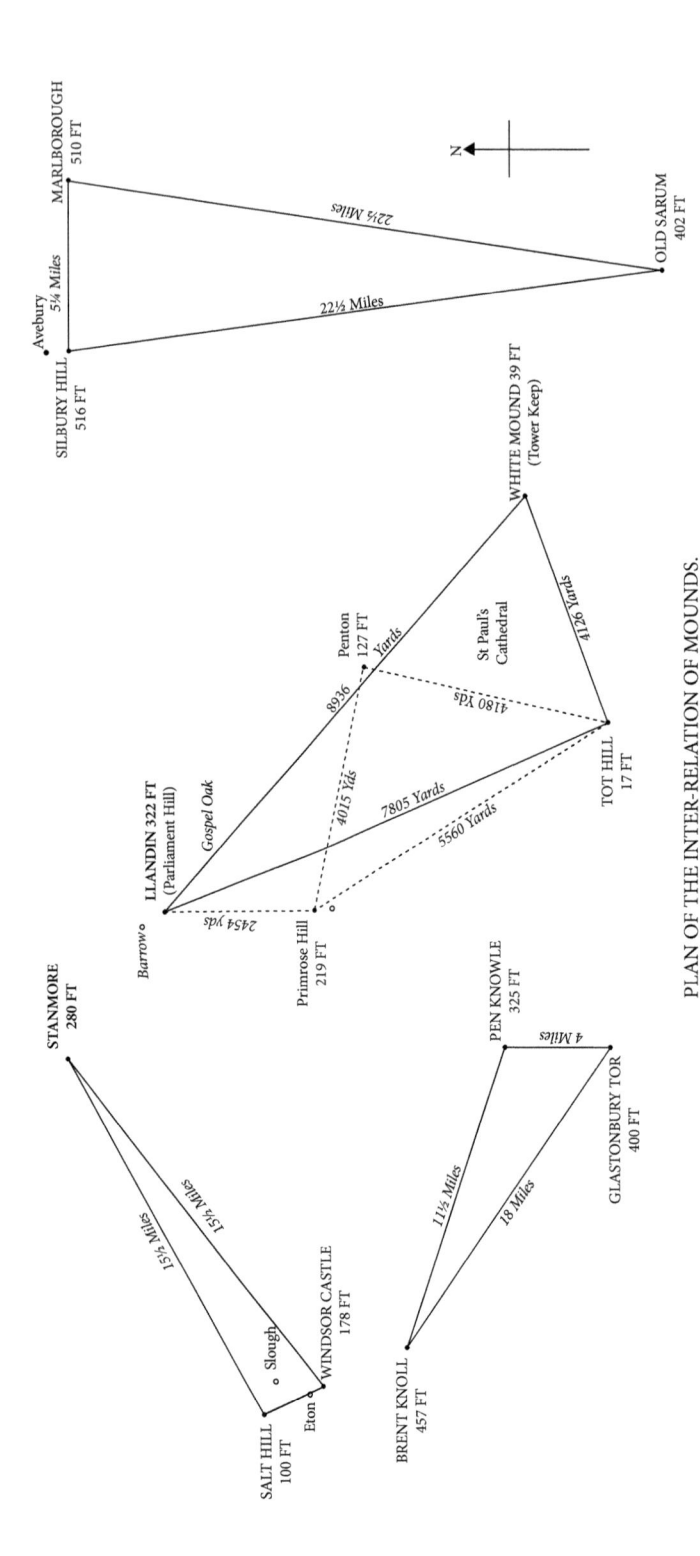

Figure 5.4 'Plan of the Inter-relation of Mounds' as depicted in Gordon's *Prehistoric London: Its Mounds and Circles*. Courtesy of British Library (redrawn).

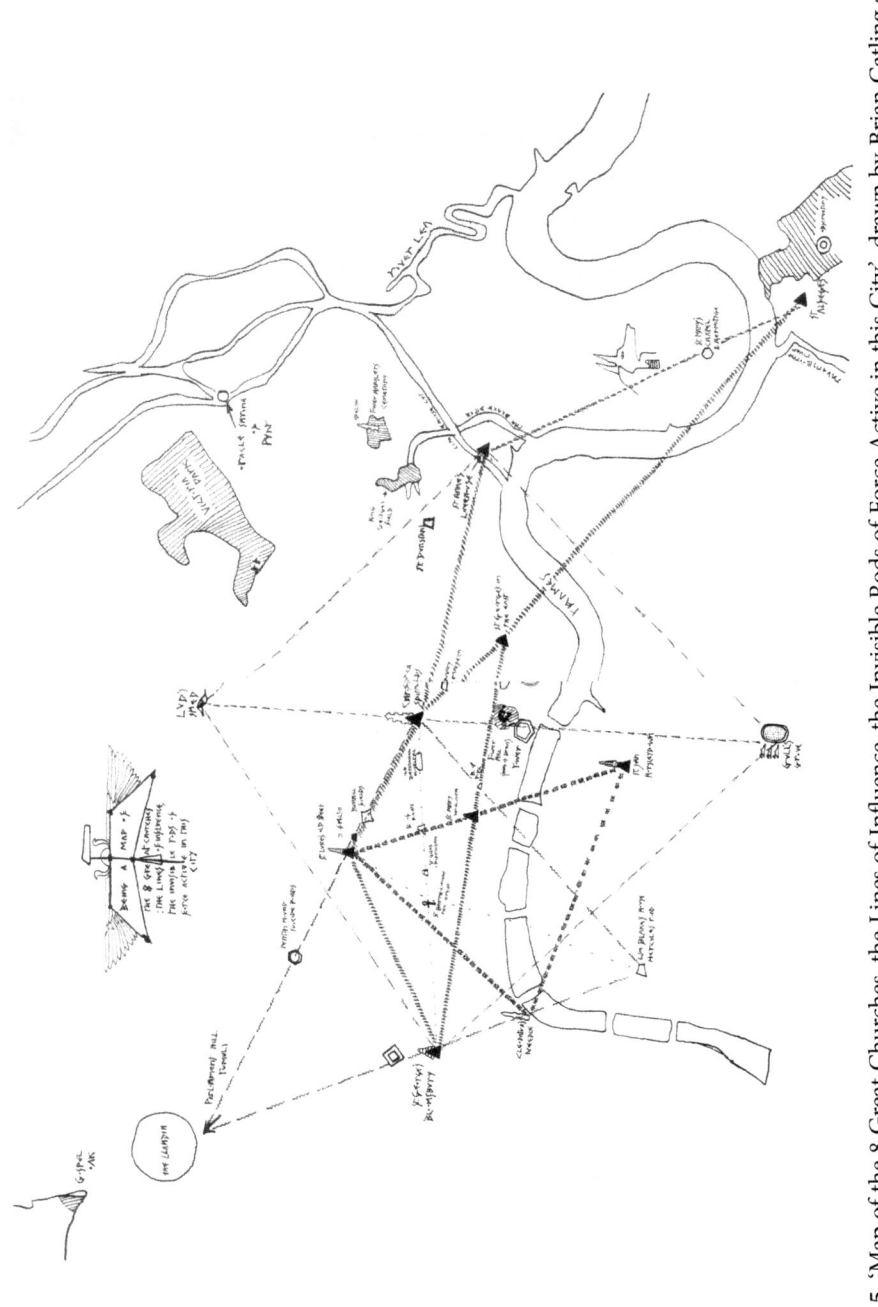

Figure 5.5 'Map of the 8 Great Churches, the Lines of Influence, the Invisible Rods of Force Active in this City', drawn by Brian Catling and included with Iain Sinclair's *Lud Heat* (1975). Courtesy of Iain Sinclair.

of Arthur'.[23] A link is also made between Hawksmoor's obelisks and Cleopatra's Needle, 'the obelisk set up by Thothmes III in front of the Temple of the Sun at Heliopolis' and removed in 1878 from Alexandria to London, where it now stands overlooking the Thames between Waterloo and Blackfriars bridges.[24] The effect is to tie London into an apparently ancient and highly inclusive symbolic heritage, merging proximity and distance as a means of investing place with mystic profundity.

Gordon's methodology is built largely around what might be described as topographical philology, foregrounding the role of language in the deciphering of landscape: yet place here is not so much a 'book to be read', as W.G. Hoskins saw it, as an esoteric cryptogram to be pored over. Bizarre conclusions are frequently drawn on the basis of wild speculations about place names, often attributed with dubious Welsh or 'Keltic' origins. Contrary evidence is dismissed or simply excluded. Thus Geoffrey of Monmouth's theory of the Trojan refugee Brutus being the founder of Britain is roundly endorsed ('Chaucer, Caxton, Denham, Milton', Spenser, and more are all invoked as supporters), but the fact that London has never been known as 'Troynovant' or 'Caer Troia' is explained away by the idea that this simply never caught on over the 'older prehistoric name of Llandin'—all without any particular evidence.[25] Similarly, Cricklade in Wiltshire is designated as the original college of the Greek philosophers brought to Britain by Brutus—a version of Plato's 'academy'—on the basis that its name might be a corruption of 'Greek-lade': a tantalizing insight that sadly has no historical justification, since the town was founded in the 9th century AD.[26]

Prehistoric London teems with speculation like this. Modifiers like 'probably', 'possibly', 'might', and 'may have' become increasingly conspicuous motifs as the text goes on. Gordon is never found pausing to consider hypotheses that might reject her thesis, clearly arrived at in advance, that there is some kind of deep prehistoric significance—preferably exotic or arcane—to be found, reversing Keiller's judgement that 'there was nothing here before the Romans came'. In regard to the triangulation of London's mounds, for instance, Gordon conjectures:

> It *may* have been the sight of the mounds round about the ancient Caer of London and the tumuli at one point to be seen in the neighbourhood of the Llandin (Parliament Hill) and Primrose Hill, that reminded the exiled Prince of what *he must have been told* of the ancient glory and commercial importance (as

---

[23] Sinclair, *Lud Heat and Suicide Bridge*, p.34.   [24] Gordon, *Prehistoric London*, p.111.
[25] Ibid., p.126; p.113.
[26] Ibid., p.34. n.b. In his 1946 *A Short History of Cricklade*, T.R. Thomson in fact notes specifically: 'It should be noted in passing that the word Cricklade has nothing to do with "Greek" or "Creek." The first element probably means hill and the second is the common old English (ge)lād which means crossing or passage. Cricklade means "the (river) crossing by the (little) hill.' T.R. Thomson, *A Short History of Cricklade* (Minety, Wilts.: Taylor and Sons, 1946), p.3.

we learn from Leaf) of the famous city of his ancestors, Troy, and suggested to Brutus the name, together with the possibility of founding a New Troy which should rival in brilliance and supremacy the city of his fathers [my emphasis].[27]

Later, the origins of 'Maiden Lane'—which now gives its name to a housing estate north of Kings Cross, not far from the 'Penton'—is explained as a corruption of the Arabic for 'open square' (in the sense of 'agora'):

> In this name we have an interesting link with the first wave of Aryan settlers, "Maiden" being a corruption of the Sanskrit and Arabic word *Maidan*, signifying, Professor Margoliouth informs us, *an open place of public meeting*, like the "Maidan" of Calcutta and the "Maidan" of Cairo.[28]

Whilst this is not necessarily impossible, Gordon does not once attempt to refute or even mention the more obvious similarity with the modern English word 'maiden'.

Gordon's associative method seems to have profoundly influenced Sinclair. The closing moments of her text form a bizarre, charismatic sequence where her system, still outwardly rational, slides into an almost ecstatic enthusiasm. Her thinking becomes almost impossible to follow and lapses into a discussion of Welsh stone circles. Three stones together, she claims, represent 'the ancient Kymric symbol of the Awen, or Holy Wings, the three rays or rods of light signifying the Eye of Light, or the radiating light of the Divine Intelligence shed upon the Druidic Circle'.[29] These are directly mirrored by the final section of *Lud Heat*, tracing the Lea Valley to a supposed 'point of force, of maximum push'

> sited on the Northern Sewage Outflow, raised Ridgeway, slanting south-east, Crows Road, East London Cemetery, Saxon Road, running into the Thames at Barking Creek. But the shrine is at the precise spot where this secret route passes above the River Lea—the ancient English/Danish border, as ratified by the Treaty of Wedmore (878).[30]

At this intersecting point we find the 'oracle bunker', an old machine gun emplacement, newly endowed with profound spiritual significance, one of many 'high energy structures' like 'the fence that traps the Cerne Abbas Hercules giant'.[31] Sinclair here relocates a site of more generally acknowledged 'heritage' interest onto a wasteland in East London; the energy of his depiction is punctured by the bathetic unceremoniousness of the site, on an artificial ridge formed by a sewage pipe. This is elaborated in the clumsiness of the narrating subject, who

---

[27] Gordon, *Prehistoric London*, p.7.   [28] Ibid., p.140.   [29] Ibid., p.172.
[30] Sinclair, *Lud Heat and Suicide Bridge*, p.137.   [31] Ibid., pp.140–1.

senses the energy, 'feels for it, understands that it has meaning: does not know what that meaning is'.[32]

The bathos here recalls the sensibility of *Back Garden Poems* and is of a piece with the incongruous image of the civic gardener musing on the arcane significance of Hawksmoor's obelisks while simultaneously using one to lean upon while eating his lunch.[33] It could also be read as an oblique commentary on the elaborately irrational methods of Gordon. Indeed, Sinclair's decipherment of Hawksmoor's 'pattern' includes a similar, subtly self-defeating feature: the churches' arrangement across London, which in actual fact hardly seems to form any discernible pattern at all, is explained as forming the shape of a 'set', an Egyptian tool for both castration and 'for making cuneiform signs'.[34] Ostensibly there is little clear explanation for this, apart from a sheer verve for arcane speculation. Yet the idea of the sign being itself a tool for making signs forms a subtly ironic send-up of the topographical-philological method, endlessly producing and reproducing patterns of signification without any ultimate resolution. In this way, the comparison with *Prehistoric London* reveals a subtle humour to *Lud Heat*'s apparently serious, even menacing constatation of space and place.

Suicide Bridge, Buried History, and the Mythology of Jack the Ripper in *White Chappell, Scarlet Tracings*

Appropriately, given the theme of semiological discordance and disorientation, one specific motif that drifts from Gordon's work into Sinclair's is that of the maze. Gordon describes the presence of hedge mazes in Britain as a 'memory of Trojan colonization', observing that they are often referred to colloquially as 'Troy Towns' and attempting to show that the shapes of certain mazes are directly linked with particular examples in Asia Minor.[35] Of London, Gordon remarks that the 'the names of Maze Pond, Maze Street, and Maze Lane, near the site of the old Ferry on Bankside, Southwark (Wark, fortification), preserve the memory of yet another of these places of amusement'—which overlap with the pleasure gardens described by Keiller in his 'Poetic Experience' essay.[36] None of these three mazes appears in *Lud Heat*, but 'Maze Hill', which runs alongside Greenwich Park, the other side from Hawksmoor's church of St Alfege, is mentioned as 'the bank of light that faces the Isle of Dogs'—which, following Blake's scheme in *Jerusalem* (1805-20) is designated as an unhappy place, radiating negative energy.[37] Figures of the 'labyrinth' and the 'labyrinthine', meanwhile, abound: Greenwich

---

[32] Ibid., p.141.   [33] Ibid., p.107.   [34] Ibid., p.16; p.137.
[35] Gordon, *Prehistoric London*, p.117.   [36] Ibid., p.119.
[37] Sinclair, *Lud Heat and Suicide Bridge*, p.15.

observatory is described as 'the labyrinth of all recorded knowledge'; Sinclair's friend the artist Brian Catling's narrative of 'his expedition to St Anne, Limehouse' is entitled *'The Labyrinth of the Jackal'*. The British Museum is also figured as a labyrinth, guarded by Hawksmoor's church of St George in Bloomsbury.[38]

Despite the spuriously explanatory, guidebook style of many of the prose passages in *Lud Heat*, Sinclair's clipped, chaotic language—notable for its lacing together of arcane terminology ('vatic', 'mantic', 'hierophant'), bookish allusiveness, and a slangy, imitative 'skaz'—attempting a direct transcription of local dialect—is often itself labyrinthine and disorientating. In like manner, *Suicide Bridge*, whose subtitle runs *A Book of the Furies: a Mythology of the South & East, Autumn 1973–Spring 1978* and which again adapts figures from Blake's *Jerusalem* into contemporary London, begins with a confusing section of intersected text where two passages seem to compete with one another for precedence. Although the first-person 'I' does crop up occasionally, Sinclair with his muck rake has gone. But the idea of a 'vortex' of energy, centred around place and dragging in competing, confusing narratives, is insisted upon.

In circulating around the same localities as *Lud Heat*, *Suicide Bridge* builds into the metonymic 'intratext', operating along the lines of the principle of accretion mentioned earlier: each text establishes familiarities and 'resonances' which, in subsequent works, are taken as given. This process is legible in the case of the 'suicide bridge' itself. Located at the point where Queensbridge Road crosses the Regent's Canal in Hackney, not far from Sinclair's house, the significance of this site is explained not in *Suicide Bridge* itself but rather in *Lud Heat*, as the place 'where the Krays offered their weapons to the water after the mutilation and death of Jack the Hat'.[39] Likewise, Hawksmoor's churches are frequently alluded to in various of Sinclair's later works, their significance to the 'energies' of place taken as given.

These examples concretely illustrate the way that ideas developed in Sinclair's earlier works are often found 'buried' in subsequent ones—continuity of *topos* again contributing to the sense of an overall 'intratext' identified by Sheppard. And burial is not only a formal principle of Sinclair's work but also an increasingly preoccupying theme. Indeed, Sinclair's early descriptions of East London are notable for a surfeit of death, contributing to a resolutely morbid timbre and taking up Gordon's comment on the City of London that 'probably no mile in the world covers more buried history'.[40] *Lud Heat* discusses the burial pits of the Black Death (beginning with Bunhill Fields, burial place of Blake and Bunyan) and the interment of George Williams, the supposed 'Ratcliffe Highway Murderer' of the early nineteenth century, at the 'quadrivium' of Cannon Street Road and the street now known simply as 'The Highway': an act, we are told, influenced by 'the

---

[38] Ibid., p.15.   [39] Ibid., p.138.   [40] Gordon, *Prehistoric London*, p.10.

imprecise itch of ritual observance'.[41] Hawksmoor's churches, meanwhile, are incorporated into the sinister geography of the 'Jack the Ripper' murders two centuries later, with Sinclair claiming that 'the whole karmic programme of Whitechapel in 1888 moves around the fixed point of Christ Church' in Spitalfields.[42]

In *Suicide Bridge*, Sinclair is interested in the graves of Kings Arthur and Harold—which in their 'alignment', we read, 'mark the limits, pin down a force-field: Glastonbury to Waltham Abbey, where the light is born, where the light dies'.[43] Allusions like this key Sinclair's ideas into a conventional imaginary of 'deep England' associated with places like Stonehenge or Cerne Abbas. Yet in both a metaphorical and actual sense East London increasingly comes to form an entire burial ground unto itself, in a way that bears parallels with the approach of W. G. Sebald: Sinclair not only quotes from Thomas Browne's *Hydriotaphia* but also arrives at the idea that 'the Hawksmoor churches have a close connection with burial sites, Roman and pre-Roman. The Romans regarded east London not as a place for the living but as a necropolis for the dead'.[44] Later, he avers that 'place, finally, can only be one thing: where you die'.[45]

Death and burial echo through Sinclair's work: the presence of the Kray twins, for instance, achieves closure in the June 1995 'Diary' article for the *LRB*, later adapted into a chapter of *Lights Out for the Territory*. Documenting Ronnie Kray's elaborate funeral procession from Bethnal Green to Chingford, this piece forms a kind of coda to *Suicide Bridge*'s preoccupations.[46] Yet Sinclair's move to prose fiction in 1987's *White Chappell, Scarlet Tracings* was presaged by another writer's development of the themes of death and burial as found in *Lud Heat*. Peter Ackroyd's 1985 novel *Hawksmoor* fitted into a pattern of historical London fictions—preceded by 1982's *The Great Fire of London* and 1983's *The Last Testament of Oscar Wilde*, and followed in 1987 by *Chatterton*—but arrived at its subject matter by way of Sinclair's ideas about Hawksmoor's churches, elaborating the sense of their occult significance into a trans-historical murder-mystery.

In Ackroyd's novel, a seventeenth-century architect named Nicholas Dyer is orphaned as a result of the Great Fire in 1666 and subsequently raised by an obscure society led by the mysterious 'Mirabilis'. Under the influence of Mirabilis's doctrines, Dyer—an analogue of the historical Hawksmoor—conducts sacrifices under the churches he is building. Ackroyd exploits the absence of information about the real Hawksmoor, repurposing what his biographer Kerry Downes called a 'self-effacing humility' so that he becomes an inscrutable,

---

[41] Sinclair, *Lud Heat and Suicide Bridge*, p.24. [42] Ibid., pp.21–2. [43] Ibid., p.200.
[44] Ibid., p.27. [45] Ibid., p.153.
[46] Sinclair, 'Diary', *London Review of Books* 8 June 1995 (https://www.lrb.co.uk/v17/n11/iain-sinclair/diary).

enigmatic agent of the arcane and irrational.[47] In the narrative's present day, intercut in alternating chapters, a detective named Nicholas Hawksmoor is tasked with solving an uncannily parallel set of murders at the sites of the various churches. A disorientating array of correspondences emerge between Dyer and Hawksmoor and the people and places that surround them, but the detective arrives at no concrete explanation as such, certainly no rational one: only an implicit suggestion of the inevitable repetitiousness of history.

Ackroyd was open about the germinal influence of Sinclair's text on his own: 'I would like to express my obligation', he wrote in *Hawksmoor*'s acknowledgements, 'to Iain Sinclair's poem, *Lud Heat*, which first directed my attention to the stranger characteristics of the London churches.'[48] But if Sinclair's own shift to prose was itself partly motivated by Ackroyd's example, then *White Chappell, Scarlet Tracings* submerged the Hawksmoor theme within a much wider set of local resonances and histories. Built around Sinclair's experiences working in the 'ullage' cellars of the Truman Brewery, Brick Lane, as well as his time spent as second-hand book-dealer, it develops and clarifies Sinclair's investigations into the mythologies and mythologization of space principally by means of an obsessive interest in the Jack the Ripper murders of 1888–91.

Already a background presence in *Lud Heat*, the narrative potential of the Ripper mythology—perhaps the most famous set of unsolved crimes in London's history—is explored in *White Chappell* as an archetypally unfinished text. The basic Ripper narrative is built around an elaborate conspiracy theory substantially the same as that outlined in Stephen Knight's 1976 book *Jack The Ripper: The Final Solution*, which also fuelled Alan Moore's graphic novel *From Hell*, published serially from 1989 to 1998. Knight's outlandish 'solution', touched upon briefly in *Suicide Bridge*, hinges on the supposed nefarious activity of the historical figures of Queen Victoria's doctor, William Gull, and his associate James Hinton (granted greater prominence here than that afforded him by Knight). This theory is succinctly glossed in another context by the critic Harvey O'Brien: '[T]he Ripper is ultimately revealed to be a two-man team: a fanatical royalist abetted by the royal surgeon, both of them trying to cover up the fact that the Prince of Wales has fathered a Catholic child with a woman of the lower orders.'[49]

Sinclair's use of this Ripper narrative follows the pattern of drawing on highly dubious scholarship, here lent extra fuel by the fusion of mysticism and science found in James Hinton's writings (Hinton's actual letters are included in the text, variously cut up and elaborated upon). As in *Lud Heat*, the point of its use is not the provision of a 'final solution' but quite the reverse. It is precisely the immense

---

[47] Kerry Downes, *Hawksmoor* (London: Thames & Hudson, 1969), p.12.
[48] Peter Ackroyd, *Hawksmoor* (London: Penguin, 1985), p.218.
[49] Harvey O'Brien, 'The Curious Case of the Kingdom of Shadows: The Transmogrification of Sherlock Holmes in the Cinematic Imagination', in *Sherlock Holmes and Conan Doyle: Multi-Media Afterlives*, ed. Sabine Vanacker and Catherine Wynne (London: Palgrave, 2013), p.72.

profusion of conspiracy surrounding the Jack the Ripper case—its unresolved and probably unresolvable state—which attracts Sinclair. As Bond points out, 'it is clear that Sinclair is far more interested in the *process* of investigation and then decipherment of narratives and traces of the city's history, than in any potential uncovering of fixed facts'. It is precisely the unsolved condition of the Ripper case which means that 'the novel has no option but to foreground the procedure of detection *per se*'.[50]

The aforementioned laying to rest of Ronnie Kray in 1995 is the exception that seems to prove this rule. Sinclair is clearly interested in bringing narratives into motion (the alternating chapters of *White Chappell* emphasizes their interplay) but has no such interest in calling them to a halt. As Christopher Gregory-Guilder has put it, his 'ceaseless search for variety and undiscovered intersections between past, present and future is driven not by a desire to master the city's narratives, but to contribute to their endless proliferation'.[51] The felicity of *White Chappell* is that he settled upon a theme that, unlike his theory of the alignment of the Hawksmoor churches, is popularly regarded in this way: as an unfinished and unfinishable set of theories and ideas, fated to be perpetually excavated and turned over while remaining ultimately irresolvable. Put another way, in the case of Jack the Ripper Sinclair is far from the only one wielding the 'muck rake'. Instead, he lights on a theme that is emphatically discursively constituted, emblematically 'postmodern' in the sense that it seems to forever elicit narratives that are partial, flawed, and subject to constant revision.

It is this process of endlessly deferred signification that Roger Luckhurst had in mind when coining his description of the 'contemporary London Gothic' in a 2010 essay, remarking on 'a structure of melancholic entrapment' in works like *Hawksmoor* and *White Chappell*, where to 'actually lay a ghost to rest would be the height of bad manners'.[52] This activity aptly captures Sinclair's method of perpetually unfurling the complex significances and 'energies' of place while keeping the resolution of this mythic significance perpetually at arm's length: a vast elaboration of that phrase at the close of *Lud Heat*, at the site of maximum 'energy', when the narrator 'feels for it, understands that it has meaning: does not know what that meaning is'.

As in that instance, a shade of ironic humour is not absent from this field. Richard Whittington-Egan, author of several Ripper books, wrote in his 1984 foreword to a re-issue of *Jack the Ripper: The Final Solution*: 'It may be that [...] I don't *want* the answer to be found. [...] For what is deader than a puzzle solved, a crossword completed?'[53] Later, punning on the terms given to those who

---

[50] Bond, *Iain Sinclair*, p.91.   [51] Gregory-Guilder, *Autobiogeography*, p.36.

[52] Roger Luckhurst, 'The Contemporary London Gothic and the Limits of the "Spectral Turn"', *Textual Practice* Vol.16, No.3, (January 2002), p.535.

[53] Richard Whittington-Egan, in Stephen Knight, *Jack The Ripper: The Final Solution* (London: Chambers Harrap, 1984), p.6.

endorse different prime suspects in the case, he remarks dryly: 'After following Mr Knight's strongly supported indictment of those he considers to be the guilty parties, it is difficult to resist becoming a converted "'Gullible"'.'[54]

In a 2003 interview, Sinclair emphasized that he first encountered the Gull and Hinton Ripper theory from hearsay at the now non-existent Farringdon Road book market, which brought him into contact with Joseph Sickert, putative illegitimate son of the painter Walter Sickert—who is supposed to have put the Prince of Wales in contact with the woman from the 'lower orders'.[55] This origin is not mentioned in *White Chappell*, though the Farringdon Road market, which sits (or sat) above the submerged River Fleet, is the subject of an elegant physiognomy as the site towards which 'everything in the end floats...deaths and libraries, sacks and tea-chests, confessions, testaments'.[56] The text of *White Chappell* reports instead that Sinclair and his friend Joblard discovering this theory via a television programme called *The Ripper File* and Stephen Knight's book, but it is through their positions at the Truman Brewery, at the 'labyrinth' that extends imaginatively onto the wider area around Brick Lane, that they are able to gain special access to other kinds of localized, orally transmitted knowledge and to observe the way that such knowledge is obsessively dwelt on and worked over by figures like their older colleagues Brandon and Eves. As Sinclair and Joblard (a fictionalized version of Brian Catling) become *amateurs* of the Ripper mystery, their interactions with these figures inflect their perception of the area as a space open to speculation, so that *White Chappell* opens up considerable space to inquire into fiction's role in the perception of environment. The role of hearsay or amateur conspiracy theories passed around verbally at locations like the book market and the brewery also acts as a street-level counterpoint to the scholarliness, or mock-scholarliness, of the 'investigations' undertaken by Sinclair and Joblard.

The book trade is implicit in the 'scarlet tracings' of *White Chappell*'s title, which refer to an interwoven plot—centred within Sinclair's real-life book-dealing milieu—about tracking down a valuable first edition of Conan Doyle's *A Study in Scarlet*, the first appearance of Sherlock Holmes, in the 1887 edition of *Beeton's Christmas Annual*. This part of the text stages Sinclair's enthusiasm for the perpetual working-over of space as an array of competing narratives. While the obsessive desire of the book collector 'J. Leper-Klamm' to possess this edition mirrors the obsessiveness with which the Ripper story has been constantly rewritten and revisited by its enthusiasts, Leper-Klamm's wish to possess and seal away the volume represents a kind of stagnation quite opposed to Sinclair's taste for the 'endless proliferation' of narratives. The collector's deathly personification is a product of this contradiction, presaging later characters like Todd Sileen in *Downriver* (of whose collection of Joseph Conrad it is observed that 'he

---

[54] Ibid., p.6.   [55] Jackson, *The Verbals*, p.13; p.104.   [56] Sinclair, *White Chappell*, p.93.

did not read these things, or even handle them') or the policeman in *Radon Daughters* who observes, in a parody of Tory attitudes towards the arts, that 'reading is a social misfortune; collecting is a vocation'.[57]

It is at such moments that Sinclair's ironic distance from the idea of narrative as such becomes clear—as in the Ripper case, any particular narrative is just one story, or version of events, open to interpretation and subversion in the 'crime scene' of literature, whose production is always represented as something of an eccentric transgression. Sinclair's own self-fashioning as first-person narrator in *White Chappell*, as a hard-boiled book dealer interested in narratives purely for what monetary value can be extracted from them, dramatizes the same dynamic. 'Stories' are just grist for the mill. Yet the fact that the lusted-after text in *White Chappell* is *A Study in Scarlet* marks a sly subversion of Leper-Klamm's own desire, since Sherlock Holmes might well be seen as the pre-eminent fictional creation to have escaped his author's grasp and taken on a life of his own as part of the mythology of nineteenth-century London. As Sinclair wrote in a 2001 introduction to *A Study in Scarlet*, 'the public understood [...] that Arthur Conan Doyle was a smokescreen, a front, the facilitator of these extraordinary adventures'.[58] In his own introduction to the second Holmes novel *The Sign of Four* (1890), reissued in the same series at the same time, Peter Ackroyd largely agreed when he observed of Jack the Ripper that

> the real murderer has assumed the mantle of fiction and of fable just as Sherlock Holmes has been lent the carapace of reality, since in truth both are equal combatants in the strange somnambulistic and phantasmagorical world of the late Victorian city.[59]

The 'real' Holmes almost never visited East London—a tale like 1904's 'The Adventure of the Six Napoleons', in which he travels to a workshop in Stepney, is a notable exception. Yet in *White Chappell* he and the Ripper are specifically associated with the 'labyrinth' of the area where, as Joblard puts it, 'certain fictions laid out a template that was more powerful than any documentary account', creating 'presences' too strong 'to be contained within the conventional limits of fiction'.[60] The presence of Holmes in *White Chappell* might also mark the influence of Ackroyd, who in the sacrificial themes of *Hawksmoor* developed the idea of place gaining significance 'when you die' (as in *Suicide Bridge*) into the motif of site-as-crime-scene. Yet *White Chappell*, responding to Sinclair's view of the

---

[57] Sinclair, *Downriver (Or, The Vessels of Wrath): A Narrative in Twelve Tales* (London: Penguin, 2004), p.50; *Radon Daughters* (London: Granta, 1994) p.95.
[58] Sinclair, in Arthur Conan Doyle, *A Study in Scarlet*, ed. Ed Glinert (London: Penguin, 2001), p.ix.
[59] Ackroyd, in Arthur Conan Doyle, *The Sign of Four*, ed. Ed Glinert (London: Penguin, 2001), p.ii.
[60] Sinclair, *White Chappell, Scarlet Tracings*, p.117.

pre-eminence of place in the construction and circulation of narratives, also upends the conventional procedural form of detective fiction. 'Our narrative', he writes, 'starts everywhere. We want to assemble all the incomplete movements, like cubists, until the point is reached where the crime can commit itself.'[61] As this confusing expression suggests, the effect on the depiction of space is, again, labyrinthine: just as the precepts of the 'London Gothic', in Luckhurst's formulation, preclude ultimate resolution, the suggestion is that this method forces the crime to continually commit itself in the imagination, as if stuck on repeat.

Sinclair's text is certainly conscious of this. Joblard, for instance, remarks that

> there's something inherently seedy and salacious in continually picking the scabs off these crimes, peering at mutilated bodies, listing the undergarments, trekking over the tainted ground in quest of some long-delayed occult frisson. I abhor these hacks with their carrier bags of old cuttings.[62]

This view is echoed by the figure of Inspector Abberline in Alan Moore's *From Hell*, who remarks of a man selling kitschy walking sticks at Mitre Square that 'in 'undred years there'll still be cunts like 'im, wrapping these killings up in supernatural twaddle'.[63] In each case, the writers' consciousness of their complicity in the mythologization and subsequent touristic commodification of place is clear. Yet Moore's text also shows on a more local level how ideas can echo through creative responses to place. In the appendix of *From Hell*, he observes of Hawksmoor's Christ Church that its looming *trompe l'oeil* impression of two-dimensionality might suffer as a result of the development of the area before deciding that this is probably unlikely: '[I]t is interesting to note the way in which certain shapes and symbols seem to propagate themselves in certain places, if only by seizing the imagination of the next generation of architects to work upon the site.'[64]

In fact, Moore's own example shows that this observation should be extended to all creative artists working 'upon' a site, collectively reinforcing a particular mythology of place while also contributing to a certain coterie-like atmosphere centred on locality. This is marked subversively in *From Hell* itself, when William Gull takes his driver and assistant Netley on a tour of occult sites in London. Taking in, among other things, the pattern of Hawksmoor's churches, the pair also travel past Sinclair's address in Albion Drive, Hackney—a diversion for which there is otherwise no clear basis, particularly since the view of the 'dismal patch of grass' and the 'slums' that surround it is not borne out by Charles Booth's

---

[61] Ibid., p.51.   [62] Ibid., p.47.
[63] Alan Moore, *From Hell: Being a Melodrama in Sixteen Parts* (London: Knockabout, 2000), Ch.9 p.2 (no overall pagination).
[64] Ibid., Appendix 1 p.17.

contemporaneous poverty maps, which show this area to be largely 'Fairly comfortable. Good ordinary earnings.'[65] Remarking that '[t]his very street, Albion Drive, resounds with poetry, with Blake's mad prophecies and visions', Gull emits a sudden burst of laughter. Although Steven Knight does refer to Gull being 'possessed of a bizarre sense of humour', this moment is explicable only as a response to Moore's own metatextual joke about what the 'MYSTERY here [...] A RESONANCE' really is—both the anachronistic presence of Sinclair in the vicinity and Moore's stated failure to find the spot marked 'Lud's Shed' on Brian Catling's map in *Lud Heat* (see Figure 5.5).[66]

Like *Hawksmoor*, *From Hell* demonstrates how themes and motifs, unearthed and turned over by Sinclair, have been seen to 'propagate themselves' in writing on East London in the 1980s and 1990s by other wielders of the figurative 'muck rake'. What it shares with *White Chappell* is an anxiety about the potential for meaninglessness and a need to search out 'resonances' or echoic structures reverberating through history. The project is not to resolve them but merely to establish them and, in turn, to establish some sort of rootedness to place, however morbid this might be (Moore is especially interested by the peculiar repetitiousness of dates and names in the history of violent crime). The reason seems to be an anxiety about the lapse of 'meaning' or sense of place in the modern city, in tune with ideas about the rise of the 'non-place' outlined by theorists like Marc Augé but also extending back—in the case of Holmes and Jack the Ripper—to the city's huge increase in size during the nineteenth century and the doubling of its population. Ackroyd, for example, was able to write of Holmes that 'in truth, such a detective—such an intellect—ought to exist, if only to bring order to apparent chaos and introduce meaning to the otherwise inchoate and meaningless'.[67] A parallel anxiety emerges in *From Hell*, as in *White Chappell*, that the modern city is pervaded by jejune indifference to locality: in Moore's text the nineteenth-century coroner repeats of the Ripper's crimes that 'they were no meaningless acts', yet in one of Gull's flashes forward to the present, the words 'indifferent', 'disaffection', and 'lustless' appear in quick succession. Gull cries to modern office workers to 'think not to be inured to history. Its black root succours you. It is INSIDE you.'[68]

Works like *White Chappell* and *From Hell*, then, should be read as both a symptom of and an attempted salve for this anxiety. Yet they are also open to arbitrariness, signalling that same combination of a sensitivity to the 'deep'

---

[65] Ibid., Ch.4 p.10.
[66] Knight, *The Final Solution*, p.28; as Moore writes in his Appendix to *From Hell*, 'After weeks of research and a day-long trip around key points of the diagram [...] I could locate no reference to any such place as Lud's Shed. Finally, in despair, I contacted Mr Sinclair himself, who informed me that the inclusion of Lud's Shed at that point on the diagram had been a personal reference shared between himself and Mr Catling.' Moore, *From Hell*, Appendix I, p.11.
[67] Ackroyd, in Conan Doyle, *The Sign of the Four*, p.ii.
[68] Moore, *From Hell*, Ch.8 p.14; Ch.10 p.21.

Figure 5.6 William Gull looking up at Tower 42 (formerly known as the NatWest Tower) in Alan Moore and Eddie Campbell's *From Hell* (1989–98). Copyright Alan Moore and Eddie Campbell. *From Hell* is published by Knockabout.

resonances of place with a mood of playfulness shared by Keiller, Sebald, and Sinclair. The inclusion of Sinclair's house in Gull's occult 'tour' attests to this, as does Moore's slight adaptation of geography which, during the Ripper's brutal disembowelment of his fourth victim, Catherine Eddowes, has Gull flashing forward not to present-day Mitre Square (where Moore claims the crime took place) but to Tower 42 on Old Broad Street, at that time the tallest and most conspicuous new building in the City and known as the 'NatWest tower' (see Figure 5.6). This not only reflects back onto the slippery imprecision of texts like Elizabeth Gordon's and Stephen Knight's; it also tells us something about Sinclair's taste for the 'proliferation of narratives': the sensibility behind these lucubrations is one that is more agonized by the potential for a lack of meaning than by its presence; the real anxiety about laying ghosts to rest is not that this might constitute 'bad manners' but that it would leave an empty space, robbed of any significance at all.

Downriver and Sinclair's Representation of the Thames Estuary

One curiosity relating to Sherlock Holmes's presence in *White Chappell* is Conan Doyle's own widely acknowledged indifference to the actual topography of London: in spite of Holmes's claim that 'it is a hobby of mine to have an exact knowledge of London', Conan Doyle mostly relied on memory and outdated maps. The result is often a sense of discord between imagined and actual space. Conan Doyle's ignorance of East London is especially notable: his descriptions of 'maritime London' in 'The Adventure of the Six Napoleons', for instance, are markedly hazy.[69] As Franco Moretti has shown in his *Atlas of the European Novel* (1998), emphasizing the discord, the fact that very few of the crimes happen there is also in marked contrast with actual crime statistics and the findings of inquiries like that of Charles Booth, whose 'poverty maps' show by far the greatest density of 'vicious, semi-criminal' streets in the East End.[70]

The east—both East London and the Thames estuary—is ambivalently depicted in Sinclair's work. In part it is equated with authenticity: '[I]f you need to understand nineteenth-century Southwark', Sinclair remarks in *Downriver*, 'you must float downstream to Deptford. The old qualities migrate, drift like continental plates, move out from the centre: rings on a pond.'[71] At the same time, this is emphasized by a consistent 'othering', transforming the region into a mysterious, exotic, even antique space. Perhaps in echo of Gordon's work, the figure of the 'labyrinth' is repeatedly used as part of this characterization.[72] First employed in the initial proposal for the *Albion Island Vortex* exhibition—in which Sinclair wrote that 'the press [Albion Village Press] and Whitechapel exist in the same geographical vortex: the labyrinth that runs from, say, London Fields south to the London Hospital'—the term becomes increasingly frequent. In *White Chappell* it is metonymically extended from the vaults and passageways of the Truman Brewery to the wider area of Whitechapel and Spitalfields, and, following the principle of the 'intratext', it is repeatedly deployed with the same association in both *Downriver* and *Radon Daughters*.

In her writing on Sinclair's depiction of East London and the Thames Estuary, Rachel Potter has accused Sinclair of being a 'voyeur', declaring his project to be one of 'slum-tourism'.[73] *Downriver* and *Radon Daughters* certainly perpetrate a

---

[69] Conan Doyle, 'The Adventure of the Red-Headed League', in Richard Lancelyn Green (ed.), *The Adventures of Sherlock Holmes* (Oxford: Oxford University Press, 2008), p.64; 'The Adventure of the Six Napoleons', in Lancelyn Green (ed.) *The Return of Sherlock Holmes* (Oxford: Oxford University Press, 1993).

[70] Franco Moretti, 'City of Clues', in *Atlas of the European Novel* (London: Verso, 1998), pp.134–40.

[71] Sinclair, *Downriver*, p.446.

[72] Examples of 'labyrinth' used in this way in White Chappell: p.6, p.27, p.40, p.98, p.136, p.187.

[73] Rachel Potter, 'Culture Vulture: the testimony of Iain Sinclair's *Downriver*', in *Parataxis: Modernism and Modern Writing* No.5 (1993), p.43.

voyeuristic estrangement of East London and the downstream stretches of the Thames: *Downriver*'s allusions to Conrad's *Heart of Darkness* implicitly draw on his narrator Marlow's suggestion that 'this, too, was once one of the dark places of the earth', with Sinclair's narrator conspicuously citing this statement at the text's opening in Tilbury, across the river from Conrad's Gravesend. Later, when Sinclair and Joblard travel in a boat from the Isle of Dogs to the Isle of Sheppey, 'the engine fired at the first touch of the rope. The *Reunion*, with previously suppressed reserves of oomph, surged gratefully off the chart. There were no maps for where we were going.'[74] A performance-art piece devised by Joblard for the unveiling of Theo Crosby's aforementioned Battle of Britain memorial—freezing the dock and re-enacting Captain Scott's expedition—amplifies this: '[W]e had been marching for at least three hours by any real estimate;' writes Sinclair, 'therefore, we should be out on the Thames itself, and heading for the North Sea, Spitzbergen, the Arctic Ocean.'[75]

Angela Carter's 1991 review of *Downriver* gives a sense of the currency of this perception of East London and the Thames estuary in the 1990s as uncharted precincts. Though characterizing herself as a Londoner who 'doesn't scare easily', Carter remarked that 'I never went to Whitechapel until I was thirty, when I needed to go to the Freedom Bookshop (it was closed)'. '[E]verything was different' in the East End, she continued:

> People spoke differently, an accent with clatter and spokes to it. They focused their sharp, bright eyes directly on you [...] The streets were different — wide, handsome boulevards, juxtaposed against bleak, mean, treacherous lanes and alleys. Cobblestones. It was an older London, by far, than mine. I smelled danger.[76]

Carter's reticence alludes implicitly to the way in which this depiction, in Sinclair's work, renders East London as a tough, rugged, and overtly male and macho space. This is consistent from *Lud Heat*, which speculates on the windows of Christ Church, Spitalfields, as representations of ejaculating phalluses, through to *Downriver*, whose most prominent female character Edith Cadiz supplements her income as a stripper. Only in *Radon Daughters* do any significant female characters appear, and this centres on a luridly depicted boxing match that takes place on the Isle of Grain: Sinclair has Helen (a television weather girl who works under the pseudonym Isobel) and another character named Andi brawl in front of a baying, betting crowd whose only real desire is that they undress.[77]

---

[74] Ibid., p.472. [75] Ibid., p.336.
[76] Angela Carter, 'Adventures at the End of Time', *London Review of Books* 7 March 1991 (https://www.lrb.co.uk/v13/n05/angela-carter/adventures-at-the-end-of-time), reprinted in *Shaking a Leg: Collected Journalism and Writings* (London: Vintage, 2013), pp.242-3.
[77] Sinclair, *Radon Daughters*, p.407.

When Helen and the novel's protagonist Todd Sileen subsequently elope, they board a ship at Tilbury where the policeman Drage-Bell is giving a lecture about 'the shamanism of intent', a term borrowed from a 1991 exhibition overseen by Sinclair at the gallery owned by *White Chappell*'s original publisher, Mike Goldmark. Drage-Bell is busy defining 'the phallocentric way male novelists, such as [William Hope] Hodgson, develop their own force-fields, pressing innocent civilians and adopting the characteristics of their fictional prototypes', in a way that certainly reflects back onto Sinclair's own work.[78] Even the caustic characterization of Margaret Thatcher as 'the Widow' in *Downriver* specifically figures her in relation to an absent masculinity (possibly an allusion to her famously aloof husband, Denis). And Edith Cadiz, whose name is taken from the list of victims of a wreckage in the Thames Estuary in 1865, never really makes the transition from object to subject of Sinclair's narrative.

Sinclair's renditions of East London as a lurid and titillating site of the unfamiliar, the uncanny, and the potentially threatening or dangerous are processed in the same way. If Sinclair himself is the maverick explorer, his othering of East London is built on a perception of danger and hostility that extends at least as far back as Jack London's turn-of-the-century 'abyss'. The idea of Wapping, for instance, as a nest of IRA conspirators recalls the area's appearance in films like Alfred Hitchcock's version of *The Man Who Knew Too Much* (1934) in which an anarchist syndicate operates out of a sun-worshipping church. In this rendition, as if in parallel with London's inability to convince Thomas Cook to arrange a trip to the East End, the area is made to seem further away from comfortable, bourgeois London than the Swiss mountain resort of San Moritz, where the film opens.

Sinclair's work is timely in that its depiction of East London as an area open to predatory speculation juxtaposes the imaginative, literary variety of this with a financial and political one based around property development. This is certainly a counterpoint to which he is consistently alert. As he wrote in a 1994 review of a novel by P.D. James (whose 1971 book *The Maul and the Pear Tree* reconstructed the Ratcliffe Highway Murders), '*Original Sin* does for Wapping what the Docklands Development Board did for the Isle of Dogs.'[79] The opening of *Suicide Bridge* advances a similar sentiment: '[W]here there is unclaimed space, unwritten land', Sinclair writes, 'there is the quest, & there is mining, a sickly clawing, not only for minerals, crops, dead artefacts, but also for mythologies. What tales the land holds buried.'[80] For Sinclair, East London provides the prime setting where mysteries, like that of Jack the Ripper, can be 'cultivated'.[81] *White*

---

[78] Ibid., p.422.
[79] Sinclair, 'The Cadaver Club', *London Review of Books* 22 December 1994 (https://www.lrb.co.uk/v16/n24/iain-sinclair/the-cadaver-club).
[80] Sinclair, *Lud Heat and Suicide Bridge*, p.150.   [81] e.g. Sinclair, *White Chapell*, p.153.

Chappell, for instance, alludes to the 'the ghost of some old sin, some concealed disgrace' in reference to Robert Louis Stevenson's *Strange Case of Dr Jekyll and Mr Hyde* (1886), while Sinclair's attraction to a text like Pearson's *Profession of Violence* surely owed something to the establishment cover-up, then still unexposed, of Ronnie Kray's involvement in a sexual relationship with the Conservative politician Lord Robert Boothby.[82]

At the same time, the mode of satire is one in which Sinclair sees what is happening around him and amplifies it to grotesque proportions, producing a depiction that bears unexpected commonalities with Margaret Thatcher's famous 'no such thing as society' remark, made in October 1987. Although there is a strong hint of the Thatcherite free market's complicity in perpetuating the 'abyss' (the Rabelaisian motif 'do what you will', also featured in Keiller's *Robinson in Space*, is recurrent in the Gull and Hinton sections of *White Chappell*), Sinclair responds to the idea of a place that is 'not society' rather by elaborating it than opposing it.[83] If his own topographical preoccupations shadow Thatcher's apparent interest in moving 'the axis downstream', he also chooses to meet the perceived venality and cynicism of British society with one of his own, presenting himself as 'asset-stripping' narrative from place.[84] It is when observing 'the only surviving towerblock' on the Isle of Dogs, for instance, 'the last refuge of society's lepers', that Thatcher's remark is quoted: '"There is no such thing as society," stated the Widow. And, observing this rat pack, it was difficult not to agree with her.'[85] Moore's Inspector Abberline makes a parallel allusion in *From Hell* when he observes that 'Whitechapel's not society at all. It's something else.'[86]

Several years later, reporting on a meeting with W.G. Sebald's friend Stephen Watts, Sinclair explicitly reversed his 'asset stripping' formulation. 'You can be in a place and of a place, Stephen implied, and you can even visit, a day at a time like Professor Sebald, but you cannot asset-strip location.'[87] His earlier use of the term may well have been ironic; nevertheless, his writings cultivate their own sense of extraordinary disorientation and alienation, depicting a hopeless world whose profusion of narratives fends off any attempt to successfully wade through them. Docklands, then being comprehensively redeveloped under the aegis of the London Docklands Development Corporation (LDDC), is rendered in *Downriver* as 'VAT City', aping the formulation 'UK plc'. In Sinclair's version, having been purchased by the Vatican State, the rechristened 'Isle of Doges' is overseen by monks who, adding a compressed allusion to the association of nearby Cable Street with Oswald Mosley's 1930s fascist 'blackshirts', are referred to as 'blackskirts'.[88]

---

[82] Ibid., p.152.   [83] 'Do what you will'—Sinclair, *White Chappell*, p.8.
[84] Sinclair, *Downriver*, p.288.   [85] Ibid., p.424.   [86] Moore, *From Hell*, Ch.11 p.37.
[87] Sinclair, *Austerlitz & After: Tracking Sebald* (London: Test Centre, 2013), pp.12–13.
[88] Sinclair, *Downriver*, p.365.

As Patrick Wright has shown, the absurdity of this 'Isle of Doges' was at least partly paralleled in reality—the rapidity with which streets changed names and layouts meant that lifetime residents often found themselves disorientated.[89] Yet the sense of Sinclair's own aesthetic complicity—rather than competition—with what the writer and translator Gilbert Adair called the 'debased and debasing culture' of the 1990s, where 'virtually anything is permitted, virtually anything goes', is frequently legible in his work. Adair was referring to both the 'prejudice and corruption' of British politics and 'the endless subjection of London's pavements and roads to gruesome open-heart surgery'.[90] Sinclair's mode of expression isn't so restrained. In his works, and increasingly in *Downriver* and *Radon Daughters*, the Thames from Tower Bridge to the Isle of Sheppey is depicted with ever more gusto as a depleted, even toxic landscape. His narrative mode becomes in turn increasingly venomous and cynical. Just as in his writings for the *LRB*, where housing estates in East London are figured as 'botched Utopias', the landscape is depicted in close mirror of the view of the Estuary as simply a series of 'Riverside Opportunities'.[91] Although *Radon Daughters* has a postscript set—after William Hope Hodgson's fantastical 1908 horror novel *The House on the Borderland*—in the west of Ireland, both it and *Downriver* follow a geographical trajectory running east from London to the north Kent coast. In each case these areas—the Isle of Grain, the Isle of Sheppey, Allhallows-On-Sea—are presented as the resorts of criminals and an assortment of society's unwanted. Sheppey, for instance, in the voice of Joblard (himself parodying Sinclair's mode), is home to a 'scrofulous gathering of subhuman shacks' inhabited by 'humanoid life forms'.[92]

In *White Chappell*, Sinclair's self-fashioning as an astute market pragmatist picks up on his idea in a 1973 pamphlet that Groucho Marx 'is the perfect anarchic projection of the writer's idea of himself as a man of affairs (in every sense): conman, hustler, shuffler of inspired insults, master of the monologue'.[93] After all, he is quite happy to sell the *Beeton's Annual* containing *A Study in Scarlet* to Leper-Klamm, in spite of his misgivings. And just as Sinclair's position as a businessman well-versed in street and business argot ('dog', for a book that won't sell, appears in *White Chappell* and becomes a running motif in *Downriver*), his most striking expressions increasingly become put-downs and insults. The imagined unveiling of Crosby's monument, for example, is attended

---

[89] Of one resident, a Mr Woodard, Wright observes that recent developments are 'certainly confusing: as a local who has lived here all his life, it is with some reluctance that he admits, "I get lost sometimes".' Wright, *A Journey Through Ruins*, p.227.

[90] Gilbert Adair, 'A letter to the times', in *The Postmodernist Always Rings Twice* (London: Fourth Estate, 1992), pp.89–90.

[91] Sinclair, 'Diary', *London Review of Books* 6 November 2014 (https://www.lrb.co.uk/v36/n21/iain-sinclair/diary).

[92] Sinclair, *Downriver*, p.517; p.519.

[93] Sinclair, *Groucho Positive/Groucho Negative* (London: Albion Village Press, 1973), unpaginated.

by 'a sad knot of anorak-draped proles [...] bussed in from outlying geriatric hospitals and day centres'.[94]

This is partnered with a sustained mockery of the supposed tastelessness exhibited by these 'proles': at the luridly depicted all-female boxing match that forms the culmination of *Radon Daughters*, the narrative voice remarks on the 'challenge' presented by 'the glycerene mouth of the Medway, for the crocodile-skin slip-ons, the heels that had you tripping like Nureyev.'[95] The tone is the same one that appears in Sinclair's writings for the *LRB*, declaring the gangsters Reggie and Ronnie Kray as 'disadvantaged precursors of the Goldsmith Brothers' and 'premature Thatcherites' and marvelling at the crass showmanship of their over-blown floral tribute to the criminal Albert Dimes: '"To a Fine Gentleman From Reg And Ron." At £25 a letter.'[96]

These examples show Sinclair's increasing attachment to what he perceives to be tasteless or sordid. The boxing match in *Radon Daughters* is of a piece with Helen's fantasy of a full-body cut-throat shave at a Turkish barber's shop on Cambridge Heath Road, as it is of Sinclair's always gruesomely described fried breakfasts. Sometimes these merge: as Helen and Sileen have sex, Sinclair serves up a description of 'her labial trim, thick as gristle'.[97] Increasingly, women, food, and place are all objects that are consumed by Sinclair's 'scavenging poetic', and it is germane to this point that 'dog' can mean both a male chauvinist as well as an unattractive woman. It is also clear that Sinclair is increasingly preoccupied by not only by aestheticizing dross and waste but by aestheticizing his chosen territory *as* dross and waste. The East is a land where things wash up, just as the brewery was associated with 'ullage' in *White Chappell*, and the market on Cheshire Street was the home to 'the legendary backs of lorries that things fall off of'.[98]

Exclusivity, Negativity, and the Narrator's Fantasy of Self-Effacement

Sinclair's texts have often been attributed with left-wing commitment. Bond, for instance, sees Sinclair's originality as deriving 'from his emphasis on the irrational quality of the city's capitalist activity', a view arrived at with reference to Theodor Adorno's thesis that interest in the occult results from 'our forced adaptation to the irrationality of capitalist rationality' (Bond's words) and supposedly 'rational mensurational approach to place'.[99] Working in a similar vein, Alex Murray has read Sinclair through a lens of Benjamin and Adorno's cultural criticism: suggesting that

---

[94] Sinclair, *Downriver*, p.333.   [95] Sinclair, *Radon Daughters*, p.398.
[96] Sinclair, 'Diary', *London Review of Books* 8 June 1995; 'Monster Doss House', 24 November 1988 (https://www.lrb.co.uk/v10/n21/iain-sinclair/monster-doss-house).
[97] Sinclair, *Radon Daughters*, p.396.   [98] Sinclair, *White Chappell*, p.29.
[99] Bond, *Iain Sinclair*, p.17; p.62.

his writing is responsive to the idea that 'art uses irrationality to critique the irrational rationality of capitalist society', Murray argues that 'Sinclair's irrational aesthetic may function as a means of complex criticism'.[100]

In fact, Sinclair's very attraction to perceived morbidity, decay, and grotesquery—*Downriver* is described within its own pages as a 'grimoire'—undermine this view, even if Sinclair himself seemed to endorse it. As he has argued in interview, 'Thatcher introduced occultism into British political life' because

> she wanted to physically remake, she wanted to destroy the power of London, the mob, all of those things, which finally through the Poll Tax riots brought her down. I can't look at in in any other way but as actual demonic possession.[101]

Exploring the idea of a rejection of the capitalist exchange system with the burgeoning of small presses like Sinclair's own 'Albion Village Press', Bond notes the comment on the final page of 1985's *Autistic Poses* that 'any person found selling this item will be congratulated on his audacity'.[102] Certainly, this reads on the surface like an affront to 'market forces'. Yet it is also suggestive of a recurrent blend of attitudes in Sinclair's writing. On the one hand, the atmosphere of his early work has to be taken into account: as he has himself remarked, the ability to read books like Gordon's was

> a privilege of that era. Everything felt very comfortable, there was no fright about getting employment. No one I knew had any ambition to be this or that, or to have any kind of career, or even to get Jonathan Cape to publish them.[103]

On the other, the 'audacity' remark reads like a subtle joke at the expense of those who are unlucky enough to fall outside of Sinclair's knowledgeable fold or coterie. 'No one I knew' would be so gauche as to try to sell something *for money*, but the precise class relations undergirding the 'privilege' to adopt this position are quietly elided. There is a certain sense here in which the idea of a clued-up cognoscenti sharing around these volumes presupposes the existence of dim-witted, 'anorak-draped' outsiders for whom such opaque writing will literally be thought of as worthless: those like his character Todd Sileen, who wastes time attempting to track down the actual 'House on the Borderland'—'difficult to accept', as Sinclair remarks pompously, 'but William Hope Hodgson practised a form known as fiction'.[104]

---

[100] Alex Murray, 'Literary Genealogy and the Aesthetics of Critique in the Work of Iain Sinclair' in Robert Bond and Jenny Bavidge (eds.), *City Visions: The Work of Iain Sinclair* (Newcastle upon Tyne: Cambridge Scholars, 2007), p.75.
[101] Jackson, *The Verbals*, p.135.   [102] Bond, *Iain Sinclair*, p.14.
[103] Jackson, *The Verbals*, p.70.   [104] Sinclair, *Radon Daughters*, p.442.

This *sprezzatura* is often funny: the scene in *Downriver* where a corrupt focus-group meets to give support to Theo Crosby's already-validated plans presents 'the architect' (whose 'Roman brow' suggests the real-life model of Richard Rogers) in a manner humorously pastiching Ayn Rand's depiction of the heroic, arrogant architect Howard Roark in *The Fountainhead* (1943).[105] Yet the humour is less frequently ironic or self-effacing; more often it radiates a cynical self-satisfaction. This works in parallel with Sinclair's posture of authenticity: the idea that what we are reading can't be clarified into digestible prose because its very essence is its indigestibility, and that it therefore belongs to a separate, rarefied clique of writer-readers. As Sinclair himself has said of *Radon Daughters*: '[I]t's strange, it's the most fictional of all my books in its form and it's the favourite of people like William Gibson and Michael Moorcock and so on, but it's absolutely unreadable to the general reader.'[106]

This sense of coterie should be registered as an implicit component of what Bond himself admires as the 'neo-modernist ambition for an audience of collaborators': the 'social character' that this inscribes in the work is misleading, since it is not open and redemptive but exclusive and oppositional.[107] Likewise, if Sheppard, in characterizing Sinclair's *oeuvre* as an 'intratext', writes that 'the intratext is not just a body of work; it is a model for culture that, as soon as it is proposed, disestablishes itself', then he also gives a sense of the writing's feinting, its oppositional positioning, its *negativity*; its refusal to form solid ground.[108] Sheppard writes that 'to borrow from a title of Peter Ackroyd, Sinclair's works approximate "notes for a new culture"'—yet this is not true: they do not present a positive example so much as supply variations on a theme of failure and collapse; not notes but crossings-out.

This process is also visible in one of Sinclair's favourite formal principles: that of the cut-up. This appears frequently in his work. After *Ah! Sunflower*—the film whose making *The Kodak Mantra Diaries* describes—Sinclair planned a documentary featuring William Burroughs entitled *The Face on the Fork*. While this did not happen, Burroughs's cut-up technique became central to Sinclair's texts. An early, late-1970s draft of *White Chappell*, without the book-dealing sections, contained sections about fluctuations in the world silver market which 'seemed to double up in a kind of alchemical way with what was going on in Whitechapel' and was given at a reading after Sinclair had 'literally, in a Burroughs way, cut it up, and chucked it in a hat, and read really the whole novel in these fragments'.[109] One of the text's running motifs, the cryptic cipher 'MANAC ES CEM JK' attempts to draw some significance from the initials of Jack the Ripper's victims, while cut-ups of the opening of *A Study in Scarlet* and Rimbaud's *Illuminations*

---

[105] 'Unashamed, she met his arrogant gaze.' Sinclair, *Radon Daughters*, p.320.
[106] Jackson, *The Verbals*, p.128.   [107] Bond, *Iain Sinclair*, p.14.
[108] Sheppard, *Iain Sinclair*, p.19.   [109] Jackson, *The Verbals*, p.102.

form attempts to explain the murders. Hinton's theory of the 'fluxion' ('a thing we need to have, but are not intended to hold') matches up with this too.[110] In *Downriver*, the arrangement of Joblard's twelve 'Heart of Darkness postcards' (included on the flyleaf of the first edition), which he shuffles around on the table of the *World's End* pub as if they were tarot cards, implicitly maps onto the twelve speculative tales of which the narrative is composed.

Yet the idea and formal principle of rearrangement is increasingly displaced by deletion, so that negativity becomes the presiding link between place and text in Sinclair's early works. In *Lud Heat*, Sinclair writes of the Ratcliffe Highway Murders that 'the transcripts of the witnesses are full of cancelled stories, lies, wrong dates, infinitely adjustable times'.[111] Later, in *White Chappell*, the character Dryfeld's room is a 'cancelled space'; the bell inside the obelisk of a church (presumably Hawksmoor's St George in the East, left as a hollow shell after a Second World War bomb) is a 'cancelled bell'.[112] Hinton's martyr-complex centres on the belief that 'In erasing myself I should truly become'—the verb left mystically intransitive—and Gull's justification of himself is that 'I acted out the description of an act that was always there. And in doing this I erased it. I freed that space.'[113] Later, in *Downriver*, the narrator describes 'the cancelled village of Hackney Wick'; on the boat trip to Sheppey 'this pulsing yellow trawl [...] bounced across the estuary towards the cancelled land', and all of this is underpinned by a running theme of the 'cancelled' plans of Fredrik Hanbury (Sinclair's fictionalization of Patrick Wright) for BBC television programmes.[114]

These negations are often applied to the cityscape itself, rendering its space highly disorientating. 'Long-deleted stations' of the Underground are a feature of the space where the characters 'crossed and recrossed deleted railway bridges, trying to find our way to City Airport'.[115] On the Isle of Dogs 'the deleted catalogue of housing solutions' are described as 'vertical graveyards', while after the trip to 'VAT City' Sinclair's narrator declares that 'the Isle of Doges had nothing more to say'[116] and later: 'It had served its purpose. It was deleted.'[117] Particularly notable is the reference in the chapter entitled 'The Case of the Premature Mourners' to 'a deleted icon of St Christopher': in the midst of Sinclair's disorientatingly dense prose, the patron saint of travel is himself conspicuously erased.[118] At the same time, Sinclair's narrator himself begins to entertain a fantasy of self-deletion. With the failure of his typewriter, he hands over the job of finishing his typescript to Joblard, along with a handwritten request that he help facilitate 'a magical getout. The one that lets the narrator melt from the narration.'[119] If Sinclair's early work made frequent references to the idea of a

---

[110] Sinclair, *White Chappell*, p.161. [111] Sinclair, *Lud Heat and Suicide Bridge*, pp.24–5.
[112] Sinclair, *White Chappell*, p.132; p.127. [113] Ibid., p.159; p.177.
[114] Sinclair, *Downriver*, p.88; p.530. [115] Sinclair, *Downriver*, p.58; p.328.
[116] Ibid., p.349. [117] Ibid., p.382. [118] Ibid., p.475. [119] Ibid., pp.490–1; p.489.

'vortex', echoing Ezra Pound's association with 'Vorticism' in the 1920s, then it is apt that his struggles here should seem to echo Pound's own grappling with the unfinishable *Cantos* in his later years.

At this point in *Downriver*, the prospect of Sinclair's own cancellation moves to the centre. As 'he tries to relate everything to everything' he becomes 'a man possessed' and a 'headcase'.[120] This last section is telling because its narration by Joblard allows Sinclair's own 'madness' to be observed, turning his subjectivity itself into an object of examination and placing him within the landscape, his association with which has become the 'sickness vocation' that he referred to in the 'Shamanism of Intent' exhibition in 1991, quoting Mircea Eliade's 1964 book *Shamanism, Archaic Techniques of Ecstasy*.[121]

As a correspondent in the *LRB* pointed out in 1994, referring to a review of *Radon Daughters*, radon 'is a naturally occurring radioactive gas' and its 'breakdown particles, called "daughters", are a serious cause of lung cancer'.[122] This idea of sickness lines up with Sinclair's comments when asked about 'psychogeography', a term he only retrospectively applied to his early works. His response pointed, on the one hand, to a businesslike approach aping the Thatcherite veneration of the marketplace: 'I thought psychogeography could be adapted quite conveniently to forge a franchise—which is what happened, more than I could have imagined!' On the other, it adapted 'psychogeography' in a significant way, playing with the words to supply a variant meaning: 'I think of it, I suppose,' Sinclair observed, 'as a *psychotic* geography—stalking the city.'[123]

The emergence of this perspective can be tracked through Sinclair's early work. In *Lud Heat* we find, for instance, Sinclair's elaboration of Stan Brakhage's film-making technique:

Open the shutter, like a vein, to all possibilities, without calculation, but with the deftness of long familiarity. First hand. Live. Raw. The uncooked moment. Document, not documentary. Direct, not directed.[124]

Later, in *White Chappell*, the bookish and the bodily elide when the Ripper-obsessive Mr Eves's skin is described as 'waxy and fibrous, unset parchment'.[125] In *Downriver*, this develops again—on the boat trip from the Isle of Dogs to Tilbury, 'the river outpaced my fear of it: a tightening roll of mad calligraphy, scribbled wavelets, periods of gold. I was buffeted through a book that had turned to water.'[126] Likewise, Sinclair is shocked to discover that the Ripper theorist John Millom's crazed manuscript 'was in my own hand'.[127] By the time of

---

[120] Ibid., p.500; p.515.   [121] Ibid., p.521.
[122] Stuart Silverman, *London Review of Books* 8 December 1994 (https://www.lrb.co.uk/v16/n23/letters) (in response to Jenny Turner's review of the novel in *LRB* 19 June 1994).
[123] Jackson, *The Verbals*, p.75.   [124] Sinclair, *Lud Heat and Suicide Bridge*, p.5.
[125] Sinclair, *White Chappell*, p.39.   [126] Sinclair, *Downriver*, p.440.   [127] Ibid., p.274.

Radon Daughters, it is as if the burden of the 'intratext' itself generates this psychosis: just as Hope Hodgson's *The House on the Borderland* is finally characterized as 'a condition [...] a pathology, *not* a specific location'.[128] The entire area of Whitechapel has become a 'psychosis', 'a rootless pestilence, a state of self-renewing bile'.[129]

The increasing venom of Sinclair's writing—a mode where, for instance, 'spastics' will be used as a verb—bears the mark of his reading not only of American writers like Burroughs but also figures like Louis Ferdinand Céline. Again, the connection is overlapping locality: Céline's *Guignol's Band* (1944), like *Radon Daughters*, is topographically preoccupied with the Royal London Hospital and the area around it, sharing in its hyperactive rhythms and tone of rancorous cynicism. In *Downriver* and especially in *Radon Daughters*, a vast accumulation of pithy, staccato sentences produces a 'dolly zoom' or 'reverse telescope' effect familiar from Hitchcock's *Vertigo* (1958). Like Céline's writing, the text threatens constantly to become crowded in terms of form, while spare in terms of content, turning away from any signified and towards its own chaotic act of signification, thereby shifting focus inwards onto the narrating subject's psychic breakdown. By this point, Sinclair's humorous, ironic approach to the depiction of space and place seems to have yielded to a negative, caustic vision, soaked in cynicism and increasingly inseparable from the thing it ostensibly seeks to critique. If *Radon Daughters* was in some ways his most straightforwardly fictional work, it also showed his enthusiasm for fiction to be at a low ebb. Although he has occasionally returned to it, the move to a straighter form of travel-writing with 1997's *Lights Out for the Territory* released him from any duty towards coherent narrative; at the same time, it allowed him to draw on the heterogeneous themes explored in his earlier writings—the whole of the 'intratext' thus far—as fuel for his continuing explorations at the end of the 1990s and the commencement of the new millennium.

---

[128] Sinclair, *Radon Daughters*, p.442. [129] Ibid., p.131; p.269.

6

Crosses, Circles, and Madness

Iain Sinclair's *Lights Out for the Territory*, *London Orbital*, and *Edge of the Orison*

In the late 1990s and early 2000s, Iain Sinclair's writing slid away from fiction towards a more straightforwardly documentary mode, producing texts like 1997's *Lights Out for the Territory*, 2002's *London Orbital*, and 2007's *Edge of the Orison* and helping him achieve, as Phil Baker has put it, 'the height of his celebrity'.[1] Pivoting on these three works in particular, this final chapter explores Sinclair's idiosyncratic appropriation of the Situationist coinage 'psychogeography'—with which he became increasingly associated—as 'psychotic geography', examining how his depictions of space and place were increasingly shaped by an agonized egocentricity built around his creative misreading of the term. In the process, it shows how Sinclair's work met the millennium's turn with an appropriately millenarian narrative sensibility, flip-flopping between the utopian and the apocalyptic and ultimately describing its own 'microclimate of entropy and nostalgia' to match that which it discovered in the landscape itself.[2] The chapter closes with Sinclair tending to his own archive in *Ghost Milk: Calling Time on the Grand Project* (2011), before looking briefly at his writing on W.G. Sebald in 2018's *The Last London: True Fictions from an Unreal City*.

Walking as Chaos and Curation in Sinclair's Later Work

One of the keynotes of Sinclair's first fictional outing, *White Chappell, Scarlet Tracings* (1987), was the caffeine-fuelled, wide-eyed scouring of England for second-hand books—specifically a first edition of Arthur Conan Doyle's *A Study in Scarlet*—on four wheels. The tenor and rhythm of his later works, however—which reprise the non-fictional, diaristic form of *The Kodak Mantra Diaries*, *Back Garden Poems*, and the 8mm 'Diary Films'—is determined not so

---

[1] Phil Baker, 'Psychogeography and the End of London', in Joe Kerr and Andrew Gibson (eds.), *London from Punk to Blair* (London: Reaktion, 2012), p.284.
[2] Iain Sinclair, *Edge of the Orison: In the Traces of John Clare's 'Journey out of Essex'* (London: Penguin, 2006), p.181.

much by the carriageway as the footpath. In *Lights Out, London Orbital*, and *Edge of the Orison*, pedestrianism is the thread that ties together places, people, and things, conceived as a skein of competing narratives that the walker negotiates and orchestrates into narrative form. In this sense, walking facilitates subjectivity: an individual and necessarily unique response to the memories and thoughts lying dormant within the landscape and the mind before some particular conjunction brings them to the surface. Even in the case of the film of *London Orbital*, for which Sinclair and Chris Petit drove the complete loop of the M25, it might well be argued that this exercise is intended primarily to set the walking tour conducted in the book into relief.

In this later work, walking becomes increasingly central to Sinclair's frequently damning responses to sanctioned 'heritage' or official monuments of any kind. As he puts it in *Edge of the Orison*, 'being allowed, even encouraged, to move in a particular direction kills the desire'.[3] Although in this instance he might be in the process of travelling to the relatively established tourist destination of John Clare's home village of Helpston, Northamptonshire, in word if not in deed Sinclair resents sanctioned prompts to walk, think, and remember. And it is this resistance that is fundamental to Sinclair's ever more prominent self-fashioning less as a creator than as a *curator*, first and foremost, of an extensive array of non-mainstream British culture (it is notable, for example, that Keiller's writings on the 'Nine Elms Coal Hopper' appear in a 2006 volume edited by Sinclair, *London: City of Disappearances*). If Patrick Wright described the Sinclair of the 1970s and 1980s as an 'abracadabra man', then from *Lights Out For The Territory* onwards he positioned himself less as a magician, more as the ringmaster of a vast circus whose performers include figures like J.G. Ballard, Chris Petit, and Marc Atkins. Even in the case of comparatively well-established artists like Samuel Palmer and John Clare, Sinclair's interest seems partly to be driven by some 'outsider' quality these figures share. Walking provides the framework for marshalling them into a wider history, establishing their place in the cultural geography of London and the south-east of England. In the process, Sinclair's work becomes a curatorial-archaeological project, excavating and reinstating marginal or damaged histories at the same time that it structures narratives of loss, displacement, and decay. Sinclair himself—accompanied by and discussing the work almost exclusively of other men—is often situated as a correspondingly marginalized but nevertheless perceptive figure, transgressive and, often, self-consciously absurd.

Walking, then, from *Lights Out for the Territory* onwards, becomes not simply a theme for Sinclair but the key to his creative-critical practice. Yet in the three works principally under discussion in this chapter, it does undergo some

---

[3] Ibid., p.12.

important modulations, shifting from an ebullient, heroic phase into a voided, husk-like state where the form of the walk remains as a compulsion that precedes and exceeds any particular purpose to which it might be put, and the idea of 'psychosis' re-asserts itself. The early stages of this transition are discernible between *Lights Out* and *London Orbital*: where the earlier text consists of nine intersecting 'excursions in' the city, the second explodes these into a circumambulation that follows the M25 motorway and hangs from the inner fulcrum (and Sinclair's *bête noire*) of the Millennium Dome. In the process, *London Orbital* increasingly associates the figure of the walker with madness and the self-stated absurdity of treating the circular M25 'as your destination'.[4] The act of walking is rendered as a conspicuously temporary palliative to psychic unrest, an addictive practice which only precipitates the need for more of the same and which—even if Sinclair is not regularly thought of as a melancholic writer—maps closely onto the outline of Freud's idea of melancholia as 'unfinished mourning'. The second part of the transition comes with *Edge of the Orison*, where Sinclair and his assorted cohorts follow in the 'shadow' of the English Romantic poet John Clare. Here, the walk takes a final lurch into the status of an utterly mad pilgrimage, tracing Clare's 1841 journey on foot from High Beach Asylum in Essex to his home in Northamptonshire and the corresponding course of his mental decay.

Where, in *Lights Out*, the act of walking forms a means of tying together the tangled web of memorials and monuments of which the landscape is composed, by the time of *Orison* it functions as an epitaph in motion—increasingly forming a *topos* of its own, in the sense that the subject *is* Clare's walk, rather than any of the sites he passes in particular, and the act of re-walking the route is presented as the means by which the subject can achieve some kind of being, however temporary this might be. As Sinclair himself puts it, 'a walk is a floating autobiography'.[5] And if this is true, it records a life of disorder, divergence, and burgeoning dissolution, structured around an idea of movement as neurotic compulsion: following Clare, Sinclair renders himself as 'homeless at home', and his meditations on the idea of a constant return, combined with musings on T.S. Eliot's *Four Quartets* and James Joyce's writing, play up the idea of a looping and unfinishable structure. In this way the narrating subject remains haunted by the anti-narrative circularity of the M25. This anticipates the way in which, in *Ghost Milk*, Sinclair's work also becomes haunted most of all by itself: his journeys through a landscape described in ever more venomous terms producing a feedback loop of personal reflection wherein his own 'grand project' collapses the twin archives of self and place.

---

[4] Sinclair, *London Orbital: A Walk Around the M25* (London: Penguin, 2003), p.46.
[5] Sinclair, *Edge of the Orison*, p.160.

Essayistic Alchemy: The Paranoiac Curation of London in *Lights Out for the Territory*

Rachel Whiteread's 1993 sculpture *House*, which won the Turner Prize that year, appears in the sixth walk of Sinclair's *Lights Out for the Territory*. Filling a 'conventional' residential house in Grove Road, Mile End—the last in a condemned Victorian terrace—with concrete, Whiteread's project offered itself as a tombstone to a version of everyday, working class life that had been deemed outmoded by civic planners. Its background was formed by concrete tower blocks and Victoria Park, described by the artist as the work's 'plinth' and itself the unplanned outcome of Second World War bombing. The project—a rare instance of Sinclair engaging with the work of a female artist—forms a neat counterpoint to *Lights Out* as a whole, which explodes *House*'s spatial density: Sinclair more than once refers to the nine walks of which *Lights Out for the Territory* is composed as 'essays', offering a sense of experiment, trial, and Wordsworthian composition in motion. 'I can't let this opportunity pass', he declares at one point: 'It rounds off my essay so neatly.'[6]

If the essay form is a 'trial', then what these journeys 'in' the city seem to test is the observant walker's dedication to the task of recording and transcribing experience in a landscape characterized by oppression of the subject and 'an increasingly deranged populace'.[7] They are 'attempts to navigate', whose provisional quality transfers to the form of the finished work as a kind of 'speculative literature'.[8] Initially, following the manner of *Lud Heat*, language and inscription take centre stage: the first walk is conducted by following the shape of the letter 'V' drawn on the map of London over the Lea Valley, with its bottom point in Greenwich and its upper ends at Abney Park Cemetery in Stoke Newington and Chingford Mount Cemetery (site of the Kray twins' burial plot). Increasingly, however, Sinclair's affective topography of London involves carving the city into territories ascribed to particular writers, film-makers and artists—a troupe that includes, among others, Alan Moore, Stewart Home, Laurence 'Renchi' Bicknell, Chris Petit, Patrick Keiller (alongside whom Sinclair worked at the North-East London Polytechnic in the 1970s), and the photographer Marc Atkins, whose images grace the centre pages of the book and whose hand-drawn maps appeared in its first edition (see Figure 6.1).

Lights Out meditates on the kind of patronage that it affords these figures. In doing so, it connects Sinclair's long-standing interest in the occult with the movement and emplacement of economic capital in contemporary London. The fifth walk, entitled 'Lord Archer's Prospects', centres on a visit to the disgraced

---

[6] Sinclair, *Lights Out for the Territory: 9 Excursions in the Secret History of London* (London: Penguin, 2003), p.54; p.203.
[7] Ibid., p.1.   [8] Ibid., p.161.

CROSSES, CIRCLES, AND MADNESS 229

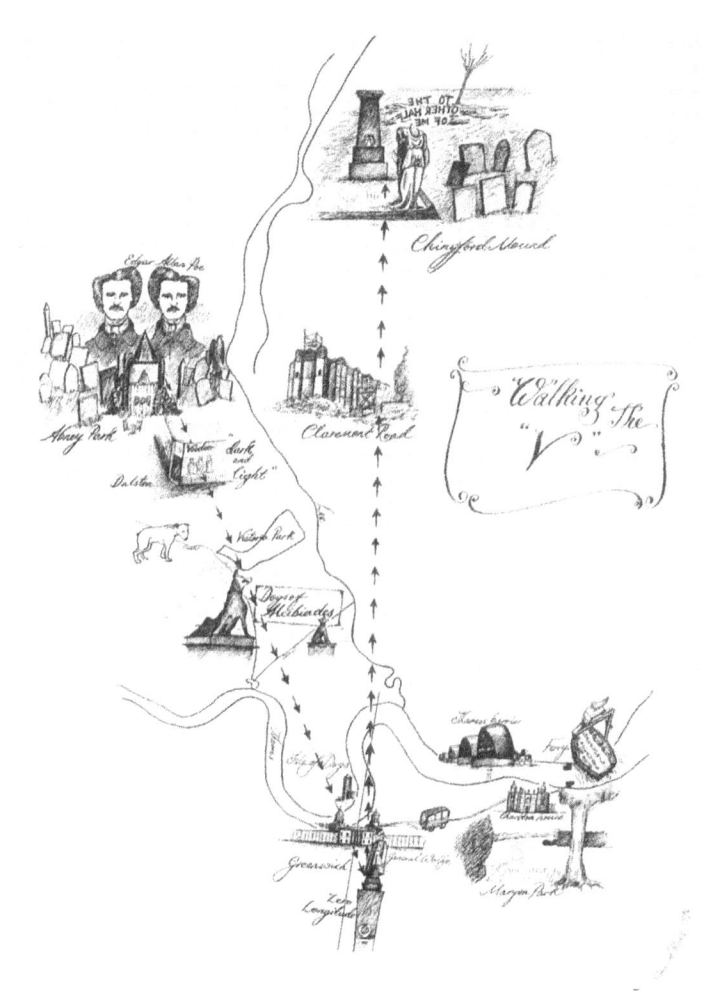

Figure 6.1 The route of the 'V' in *Lights Out for the Territory* (1997), as drawn by Marc Atkins. Courtesy of Marc Atkins.

Conservative politician and novelist Jeffrey Archer's penthouse apartment in Alembic House, on the south bank of the Thames in Lambeth—a residence that is home to one of the city's largest privately owned art collections and, we are told, immediately 'hit you with a sense of its separateness. The qualitative difference that Scott Fitzgerald saw as dividing the rest of us from the seriously rich'.[9]

As a low-budget curator of space and culture, Sinclair situates himself as an oblique reflection of Archer: a profane overseer of a vast horde of 'cultural capital' that is scattered across the city rather than gathered up on one site. The visit to Alembic House also occasions thoughts on the possibility of some arcane, cryptic

[9] Ibid., p.170.

motive behind the activities of collecting, collating, and curating culture and implicitly on the idea of a similarly occult logic governing the movement of large amounts of money. This emerges first of all in response to the name of Archer's building. As Sinclair points out, 'Archer's Alembic House is named after a standard item of alchemical equipment, a vessel used in distilling.'[10] The idea is reasserted by way of geographical association: deflated and somewhat patronized by Archer's failure to receive him personally, Sinclair elaborates on the alchemical theme by situating himself in line with the Elizabethan occultist John Dee and the naturalists, astrologers, and alchemists Elias Ashmole and John Tradescant—both of whom were buried in nearby St Mary's Churchyard, where Tradescant's 'Ark' was also located in the seventeenth century.

The arrangement or cataloguing of curiosities—'the pursuit of the rare and strange' in which these figures engaged—offers a model for Sinclair's practice, and he observes that 'the gardener, like the poet, the architect and the musician, served at the court of some great temporal lord, helping him to express political power in a visible form'.[11] Now figuring himself not only as a parallel to Archer but also in deference to him as a 'temporal Lord', Sinclair also suggests that there is some sense in which, like Dee, Ashmole, and Tradescant, he himself occupies a supernatural, extra-temporal space—both in a strange, 'shamanic' sense and by the very act of committing his collection or curation (that is, the text of *Lights Out*) to posterity.

These elective affinities are complicated and developed by means of geographical connections. Sites like Alembic House, Tate Britain gallery just over the river, and Tradescant's 'Ark' become nodes in a network of significant sites in this locality, their resonance permeating through time. Punning on his own theme of the arcane, mystic energies emitted by place while he is discussing Tate Modern, Sinclair describes the 'deplanting' of Bankside as 'an assault on the energy field'.[12] The motif of 'degaussing' the area—removing unwanted magnetism—both alludes to the quasi-scientific activity of alchemy and imagines the 'improvement' of the area in terms appropriate to Sinclair's vision of intersecting lines and fields of energy. Later, he observes that the price of entry to Tradescant's Ark— sixpence—was 'a privatised culture-for-cash transaction that showed the way to future riverrine enterprises'.[13] These include the Tate Modern gallery further downriver, described by Sinclair as 'the latest mutation of the Salomon's House paradigm' in an obscure reference to the ideal museum mooted in Francis Bacon's 1627 utopian proposal, *New Atlantis*.

Other contemporary 'riverrine enterprises' in the vicinity include Terry Farrell's MI6 building, described as an 'Aztec jukebox', a 'marzipan sandcastle', a 'daffy ziggurat', and a 'phoney temple' in an apt illustration of what Peter Barry

---

[10] Ibid., p.189. [11] Ibid., p.185; p.183. [12] Ibid., p.182. [13] Ibid., p.184.

has described as Sinclair's 'disjunctive, pronomialised, "kennistic" and registerially fluid' prose style.[14] 'Aztec' is particularly significant, connecting Farrell's structure with a panel on Tradescant's Ark and thereby becoming another ligament in Sinclair's chain of free association in space. In the image of it included in a volume entitled *The Thames and its Views* in the Pepys Library at Magdalen College, Cambridge, we are told, the side facing west 'features a monastic ruin'. In reality, as Sinclair remarks, emphasizing the special insight afforded by his authentic, first-hand experience,

> [t]he eastern panel (inaccurately represented in the Pepys Library sketch) is the most remarkable of all: an urban apocalypse.... Vegetable life exposing the pretensions of stone, reducing the city's temples to an Aztec desolation... Floods and inundation...the Tradescant tomb is a monolith revealed by a retreating tide. It is both a retrieval and a warning.[15]

It is this apocalyptic scene against which the 'temporal Lord' Archer seems to have fortified himself. On the other hand, it is the extra-temporal lord—the pedestrian-explorer-shaman Sinclair—who is privileged with unique, if paranoiac, foresight of it.

The double bind of Sinclair's narrative persona is to be afforded special insights like this while not necessarily being able to do anything practical with them. There is also a persistent sense in which spatial organization aligns with psychological condition, the differences between Archer and Sinclair's approach to the production and cataloguing of culture—tidy, private collection or messy, public network—lining up with the tension between their approaches to writing. Archer is a part-time novelist who is able to draw a neat line between the 'bad manners' of fiction and his political career.[16] By contrast, the associative practice of Sinclair means that the 'easy congress between fictional and historical ontologies', as Niall Martin has put it, and his essayistic openness to new connections, energies, and networks of relationship, comes to form a kind of disability.[17] Unable to tease apart the filaments of imagination and truth, Sinclair's narrative persona is implicitly against the privatization of culture (and superb river prospects); yet if he discovers in Archer a negative image of himself, then it is one that is seemingly better adjusted to the spirit of the age.

---

[14] Ibid., pp.191–2; Peter Barry, '"You Can Get It From The Street": The Prose Style of Iain Sinclair', in Robert Bond and Jenny Bavidge (eds.), *City Visions: The Work of Iain Sinclair* (Newcastle upon Tyne: Cambridge Scholars, 2007), p.53.
[15] Sinclair, *Lights Out for the Territory*, p.187.   [16] Ibid., p.162.
[17] Niall Martin, *Iain Sinclair: Noise, Neoliberalism and the Matter of London* (London: Bloomsbury, 2017), p.136.

'Spraying', the Appropriation of Urban Space, and the City as a Frontier

Geographically and tonally, the Alembic House sequence maps onto the uneasy 'atmosphere of conspiracy' to which Keiller drew attention in *London* and which is reinforced by Sinclair's chance encounter with the notorious drug smuggler and memoirist Howard Marks immediately after leaving Archer's penthouse. The developments that Sinclair points to among his 'riverrine enterprises', meanwhile—including structures like the 'hollow boast' of Canary Wharf, the sold-off County Hall building by Westminster Bridge, and Farrell's MI6—form an ensemble reminiscent of Keiller's postcards and offering 'a new definition of shame'.[18] Appropriately enough, the visit to Alembic House is soon followed by an accidental encounter with a location from Keiller's *London*: Vauxhall Park. This moment is registered as another fundamentally disorientating experience, bound up with a sense of having trespassed or transgressed. 'Walking, unprepared, into another man's film', Sinclair avers, 'is an hallucinatory experience. We didn't know where we were and we didn't know how to proceed.'[19] Implicitly echoing *London*, Sinclair's account of the Ark is shortly followed by the 'miserable farce' of the Conservative leadership election.[20]

In her account of *Lights Out*, the Canadian critic Kim Duff has argued that Sinclair 'revises Benedict Anderson's "imagined community" by writing an intensely inclusive history of London's urban space'.[21] Although Sinclair's vision is certainly more 'inclusive' than Archer's fortress-like apartment complex, the tone of this sequence, 'walking into another man's film' is in its own way strikingly proprietorial. As Sinclair insists, offering perhaps more insight to his own practice than that of the film-maker, 'Keiller's London is not your London.' Not only does this observation reflect Sinclair's own foregrounding of subjectivity in the experience of urban space; it also gives away a subtle cynicism that has little in common with the tone of Keiller's film. The space is *not* yours, and Sinclair's addressee—the reader—is dismissed as 'the commuter, the person who knows where s/he is going'.[22] 'You', in Sinclair's version, is implicitly this detached and indifferent figure, the real opposite of Sinclair himself, and is consequently dealt with in a slightly defensive, disdainful manner.

Lights Out for the Territory was published two years before *Rodinsky's Room*, a text and *topos* with which it can be usefully compared in order to explore certain proprietorial issues. First brought to light in Patrick Wright's 1987 review of *White Chappell, Scarlet Tracings*, the mystery of the 'disappearing caretaker'

---

[18] Sinclair, *Lights Out for the Territory*, p.163.   [19] Ibid. p.194.   [20] Ibid., p.197.
[21] Kim Duff, *Contemporary British Literature and Urban Space* (New York: Palgrave Macmillan, 2014), p.15.
[22] Sinclair, *Lights Out for the Territory*, p.301.

David Rodinsky and his room above a disused synagogue in Princelet Street, off Brick Lane in East London, became the basis for a volume co-authored by Sinclair and the artist Rachel Lichtenstein, whose interest in the subject emerges from and folds back into a rediscovery of her family's Jewish Ashkenazy background and led to other volumes such as 2007's *On Brick Lane*.

Sinclair's own interest in Rodinsky seems to have been piqued by, on the one hand, his interest in the trope of the narrator's self-effacement (as in *Downriver*): even if it turns out to be an erroneous perception, Rodinsky's supposed disappearance in the 1960s is repeatedly made out as 'the Great Work'.[23] On the other hand, Sinclair is clearly attracted by the rich discursive space—both actual and figurative—opened up by Rodinsky's room concerning the way that the narrativization of place is bound up with its creation in the public consciousness and ultimately its sale in the form of real estate (at which time it is 'lights out' for the place, as Duff notes of Sinclair's punning titular citation of *The Adventures of Huckleberry Finn*).[24] As Christopher Gregory-Guilder points out,

> while Sinclair continues to refer respectfully (even reverentially) to Lichtenstein's establishing of the exact details of Rodinsky's life, it becomes increasingly clear that Lichtenstein's privileging of facts and explanatory narrative conflicts with Sinclair's preference for the mythic potentialities of the unresolved; it is this elusive otherness that he celebrates most about Rodinsky's life and, indeed, about London more generally.[25]

In keeping with the tension Gregory-Guilder identifies between Lichtenstein's 'protective and deeply personal' approach and Sinclair's 'exploratory and discursive' desire to 'multiply the interpretative possibilities of Rodinsky's life', which is paralleled by the tension between 'withdrawing objects from circulation and re-introducing them back into circulation', the discovery of Rodinsky's crudely annotated *A to Z* map fed into a series of explorations published as *Dark Lanthorns* in 1999.[26] In this text, Sinclair reads the *A to Z* as 'an act of displaced biography' which leads to little else than the powerful sense, at sites like Claybury Mental Hospital in Essex, that 'he was *here*'.[27]

Yet it is precisely this ambiguity, the openness of the Rodinsky text, that appeals to him and contrasts with, for instance, the nearby museum known as Denis Severs's house, constructed with the intention, at least, of being an immaculate and timeless replica of a Huguenot dwelling. Sinclair's contrasting insistence on the Rodinsky *topos* as a radically unfinished text—an accidental (and hence authentic) museum—deliberately rubs up against the profusion of inauthentic

---

[23] Iain Sinclair and Rachel Lichtenstein, *Rodinsky's Room* (London: Granta, 2000), p.34; p.93.
[24] Duff, p.15.   [25] Christopher Gregory-Guilder, *Autobiogeography*, p.127.
[26] Ibid., p.146; p.151.   [27] Sinclair, *Dark Lanthorns* (Uppingham: Goldmark, 1999), p.21.

rebranding and regeneration exercises that he sees—not least the creation of 'Spitalfields' as a distinct *topos* in itself, separated from the less seemly 'Whitechapel' in a move certain to have financially advantageous effects for local property owners and developers, particularly as it came in unison with the area's colonization by artists of the 'YBA' generation. The tension here parallels that which Svetlana Boym sketched between 'restorative' and 'reflective' nostalgia and the tendency of 'urban renewal' projects towards the former. 'Any project of exact renovation', she writes, echoing a formulation often used by Sinclair, 'arouses dissatisfaction and suspicion, it flattens history and reduces the past to a façade, to *quotations* of historic styles' (my emphasis).

In her discussion of *Lights Out* and the idea of 'heritage', Duff remarks the way that it counterpoints the 'official' heritage spectacle of St Paul's Cathedral with the radically open mnemonic text of East London. *Lights Out*, she writes, 'is a locally focused (East End) heritage-like project that looks to the edges of society, the identities, and spaces that had been cast off by Thatcherism as dirty and uneconomically viable'.[28] Such an interpretation risks downplaying the fact that the City itself—London's financial district, the epicentre of the deregulated Thatcherite free market and where St Paul's is situated—is crucial to Sinclair's text. Developing an implicit connection with Eliot's rendition of London in *The Waste Land* (1922), Sinclair figures the City as a 'Dantesque module' subject to intensive surveillance and associates it with William Burroughs's 'interzone', declaring that it 'aspires to the condition of virtual reality'. Within this setting, the brutalist housing and cultural centre known as the Barbican—in fact the City's most populous housing development and specifically designed to attract a residential population back into the centre of London after the Blitz—is made culpable for a sense of marginalization: 'It's how they want you to feel,' Sinclair asserts, 'uncomfortable: the stranger in town.'[29]

In Sinclair's City, the marginal individual is emblematized by the figure of the smoker. Expelled from non-smoking office buildings onto the street, this outdoor figure is depicted as subject to an attenuated mode of experience and a hemmed-in perspective. The passing pedestrian suffers the same problem: as Sinclair observes, in this space, 'there is no encouragement to look up at the sky'.[30] In a lineage consistent with Eliot's 'unreal city' and 'Robert Frank's bankers, photographed in 1951, uniform drudges purposefully scuttling under the lee of tall grey buildings', natural phenomena such as the weather seem to be absent. Pausing to acknowledge the place as a natural one is proscribed: 'it's forbidden to stop, to admit changes in atmospheric pressure'.[31] Soon, the suggestion that 'an unfocused stare into the middle-distance has been cultivated' modulates into the idea that the landscape itself has actually been effaced, and Sinclair announces that 'there's no

---

[28] Duff, p.33.   [29] Sinclair, *Lights Out*, p.99.   [30] Ibid., p.88.   [31] Ibid., p.88.

landscape outside the train window'.[32] The workers here don't see daylight, and it is notable that instead of coming 'over London Bridge' as in Eliot's poem (and Keiller's film), which would imply homes in Kent or Surrey, they are depicted as having poured in from Essex, a county 'parasitical upon this mess' and sharing in the qualities ascribed to its blinkered denizens.[33]

The supposed transgressiveness of Sinclair's observant narrative persona is cultivated in direct contrast to the perceived indifference of this abstract commuter. Pre-occupied with the 'perversity' of his desire to explore, he becomes a subversive figure; if the commuters and city workers are sealed off, blind to landscape and to experience more generally, Sinclair imagines his own work as 'a visionary exploration'.[34] Here, too, the idea that 'walking, moving across a retreating townscape, stitches it all together' joins with Sinclair's professed predisposition to be 'congenitally incapable of accepting the notion of "accident"'.[35] And if this alludes to his interest in the possible occult or arcane significance of the apparently trivial or coincidental, then it also draws him into the realm of Baudelairean 'correspondences' and a nineteenth-century version of urban modernity. Developing this notion, Sinclair describes himself as a 'born-again *flâneur*' but one that is rather less a languid dandy than a neurotic compulsive, 'noticing everything' obsessively.[36]

Indeed, Sinclair differentiates himself as privileged narrative subject largely by means of the professed madness of his undertaking ('spoken aloud, put into words, our journey sounds insane. It *is* insane'), and the effect of his own kaleidoscopic vision is to render the 'territory' he covers as strange, uncharted, and ominous.[37] His themes of alchemy, mysticism, and 'the occult configuration of the borough of Hackney' see the 'numinous' begin to equate with the 'unchartered', necessitating the construction and embellishment of place as a threatening frontier. As part of this, people, places, and things are painted thickly with the arcane, mythologizing brush of Sinclair's prose. Patrick Wright's 1991 *A Journey Through Ruins* (in which 'Rodinsky's Place' was anthologized), for instance, is described as being steeped in 'numismatic force'—a slightly odd malapropism that nevertheless seems to convey a sense of the mystical.[38] Dalston Junction, where Wright then lived and where his text begins, is called by Sinclair a 'quadrivium'; Dalston itself 'a ghost'.[39] The conveniently named 'Kingsland Waste', connecting Dalston and the City, is rendered as wild and bizarre. A 'voodoo boutique' is stocked with 'unhoused definitions of the weird'.[40] In such descriptions, orientalizing the near-at-hand, the tawdry and run-down become exotic and titillating.

Sinclair finds that the graffiti scrawled around this area constitute precisely the 'authentic urban experience' from which the suburbanized City workers are sealed

---

[32] Ibid., p.90. [33] Ibid., p.90. [34] Ibid., p.102; p.5. [35] Ibid., p.103.
[36] Ibid., p.4. [37] Ibid., p.46. [38] Ibid., p.15. [39] Ibid., p.15; p.12.
[40] Ibid., p.16.

off. Typographically registered in his text in bold or upper case, these play to the idea of reportage as a denotative, photographic task. They also reflect Sinclair's own conflicted entanglement with the machinery of capital and a low-budget mode of experience, as both the 'marginalia of corporate tribalism' and the effluvium of an artist who, like the writer himself, is figured as a 'wandering philosopher'.[41] Yet the crucial role played by graffiti in Sinclair's text is as a symbol of his own practice of territorial marking and appropriation as a masculine, acquisitive act of 'spraying'. 'Hackney', he is moved to avow, 'has been mercilessly colonised by competing voices from elsewhere'—one of them being his own.[42]

Sinclair's text abounds with descriptions suggesting an area ripe for colonization by this conventionalized male explorer figure. In Woolwich, for instance, he remarks that 'we're so far off the map that nobody has found it worthwhile to close down the free ferry'.[43] Here Sinclair's practice parallels that of Artangel—the arts organization that commissioned Whiteread's *House* and whose projects often 'involve journeys to unfamiliar locations, from underground hangars to abandoned libraries'.[44] Sinclair's walking is bound up with precisely the aesthetic of frontiersmanship suggested here, framing his journeys through London as Conrad-esque incursions 'into the interior'.[45] 'The belching treacle factory at Silvertown', he writes, while discussing Tate's art patronage, makes 'the Congo as relevant as the Thames' in Sinclair's characterization of London, just as it was for Conrad's narrator Marlow in *Heart of Darkness* (1899).[46]

Yet if Sebald's discussion of the connection between sugar, slavery, and art in *The Rings of Saturn*, framed by the topographical connection between East Anglia and the Netherlands, was bound up with an empathic response to the violence inflicted on the body of Aris Kindt in Rembrandt's *Anatomy Lesson*, then Sinclair's own response to the relationship between sugar, slavery, and art is simply to stage a lurid parody of colonialist excess and depict himself in the guise of a ruthless imperialist speculator in a scarred and shattered landscape. A discussion in the eighth 'essay', 'Cinema Purgatorio', of the figure of 'Robinson' in both Patrick Keiller's films and Chris Petit's 1993 novel of the same name ties Conrad's Congo to the fiercely individualist, cynical rendition of it in Louis-Ferdinand Céline's *Journey to the End of the Night* (1932), where a character named Robinson makes an appearance as a ruthless and pessimistic colonist. If Sinclair invokes Conrad, his narrative 'I' nevertheless has more in common with Céline's narrator Ferdinand Bardamu than Conrad's pensive, horrified Marlow: the landscapes of *Lights Out*, if figured as themselves untamed or wild, are met by a pioneer subject, actively seeking out the unwritten and 'unfamiliar' so that he might project himself into it.

---

[41] Ibid., p.1.   [42] Ibid., p.3.   [43] Ibid., p.47.
[44] Artangel Press Release, available at http://www.culture24.org.uk/am49890.
[45] Sinclair, *Lights Out for the Territory*, pp.43–4.   [46] Ibid., p.175.

The London Psychogeographical Association

Sinclair's depiction of a violently untamed or inhospitable space, and of himself as its deranged explorer and chronicler, is frequently tempered by a subtle but knowing air of self-mockery from which much of the humour in his work derives, cultivated in part by means of a semi-ironic obsession with ley-lines, mysticism, alchemy, Freemasonry, and conspiracy theories that often lapses from the serious to the absurd. This humour follows the manner of a series of pamphlets produced in 1993 by a group calling itself the 'London Psychogeographical Association' and thereby identifying itself with a spurious organization originally concocted by Guy Debord and his friend Ralph Rumney in 1957 to lend an air of internationalism to their 'Situationist' project. The LPA's newsletters are supposedly the work of its 'East London Section'—a militaristic designation intended both to inflate the alleged scale of the organization and as an ironical mock-avant-garde gesture—which had its address on Kingsland High Street (not far from Sinclair's 'Voodoo boutique'). They garner specific attention in *Lights Out*, where Sinclair refers to them as 'fictional documentary'.[47]

Dated 'Imbolc', 'Beltaine', 'Lughnassadh', and 'Samhain' after Celtic festivals, these reports combine pranksterism and political radicalism with outlandish conspiracy theory. An obituary for the psychedelic jazz musician Sun Ra, for instance, shares column space with a 'Bus Stop of the Year' competition, while a report on an expedition to Oxford centres on the search for an early-morning hot drink that leads, anticlimactically, to a McDonald's restaurant.[48] Elsewhere, in a discussion of the approaching 'perihelion' and the lunar eclipse which will precede it, the anonymous author remarks drily: 'Truly the Moon is having an exceptionally exciting time this month.'[49] Couched in terms of alternate enthusiasm and anorakishness, the pamphlets' writers share Sinclair's own 'constitutional inability to countenance coincidence'. So it is on 'The Winchester Trip':

> At 7.49 a firework rocket was set off in the valley below from the vicinity of the Water Meadows near the college. We do not know who did this, nor exactly why. But we considered it connected with our own exploits.[50]

Elsewhere, the reading of obscure books like P.J. Rich's 1991 *Chains of Empire: English Public Schools, Masonic Cabalism, Historical Causality, and Imperial Clubdom* lends an eccentric, mock-scholarly flavour to things.

In a separately published pamphlet entitled 'The Great Conjunction', which outlines the same expedition and claims to be 'a report by the London

---

[47] Ibid., p.25.   [48] Anon., *London Psychogeographical Association Newsletter* No.2 (1993).
[49] *LPA Newsletter* No.1, p.5.   [50] Ibid., p.2.

Psychogeographical Association and the Archaeogeodetic Association', the maze at Winchester College is figured as a classical labyrinth. A place on the 'Rufus Line' connecting St Catherine's Hill with the location of a tree which deflected an arrow that killed William Rufus, son of William the Conqueror, in 1100, is located in connection with a theory of ritualistic king-sacrifice.[51] This oddball mixture of occultism and the mundane often lurches into a politics that acts as if its preconditions might be taken for granted: the idea that Christianity seized on sacrificial folk mythologies in order to make Christ into 'the slaughtered King for all time' is followed by the observation that '[t]his whole transition took many centuries, only really being completed in the seventeenth century, unlike the transition from real to formal domination of capital which has taken place this century'.[52] Later, in passing, the writer mentions that 'the notion that anyone can own land is simply a justification for robbery'.[53]

For all its subversiveness, however, the LPA's rendition of psychogeography is really about reorganizing landscape and reorientating the subject within it. The article entitled 'What is an Omphalos?', for instance, referring to the Greek word for a centre or hub, such as Delphi—or simply one's navel—is presented as a response to the fact that 'in modern Britain [...] we are embedded in a web of interleaved cultures and competing value systems'. If an Omphalos is 'the psychogeographical centre of any culture, myth or system of dominance' then there is, it seems, 'no clear omphalos' at present. A correspondent who suggests that 'the most vital omphalos is the television studio where they make Cilla Black's *Blind Date*!' aptly sums up this brand of playfulness, adding that 'this is really an ancient ritual with mystical primitive communist power that has been recuperated and turned into a dating agency reducing human beings to the level of commodities in the form of Kevins and Sharons'. The correspondent claims to be a member of 'The Central Berkshire Psychogeographical Association (External Fraction)'—a name ironically blending the discordant images of avant-garde militancy and home-counties tranquillity.[54]

The LPA's second pamphlet features an article on the NatWest Tower (now known as Tower 42) 'recentering spectacular development back into the City itself' after years of focus on the Docklands development project. 'Spectacular' here is clearly freighted with the significance of Guy Debord's 1967 polemic *The Society of the Spectacle*, but there are very few references to the Situationist inheritance in the LPA material. Only in the third number of the newsletter is there a definition of psychogeography as 'the study of the specific effects of the geographical environment, consciously organised or not, on the emotions and behaviour of individuals', echoing Debord's 1955 'Introduction to a Critique of

---

[51] Anon., *The Great Conjunction: A Report by the London Psychogeographical Association and the Archaeogeodetic Association* (London: Unpopular Books, 1993), p.6.
[52] *LPA Newsletter* No.2, p.19.   [53] *LPA Newsletter* No.1, p.4.
[54] *LPA Newsletter* No.4, p.20.

Urban Geography'.[55] This is accompanied by a scruffily reproduced photograph of the SI outside the 'Empire Hostel of the British Sailors Society' in Poplar, East London (now redeveloped into luxury apartments), after their conference there in September 1960. The fourth and final number carries a neat exemplification of the merger of Situationist ideas with a wonky English mock-parochialism in its brief article on the 'Society of the Spectacle Makers', an ancient City livery company set up in the seventeenth century whose actual name—The Worshipful Company of Spectacle Makers—is quietly adjusted to form a sly pun on Debord's text.

Sinclair's own approach to psychogeography in *Lights Out* tallies with this playful approach to perceived cultural decay. His intimation that maps are a 'convenient fiction', for instance, is plainly connected with the system of measuring space not by any objective schema but rather in terms of its effects on 'the emotions and behaviour of individuals', as demonstrated in the Alembic House sequence. Sinclair is also happy to subvert the strictures of Debordian rhetoric, so that there is even, as he puts it, a 'psychogeography of retail'.[56] Yet as with the punning and acerbic light-heartedness of the LPA pamphlets, it seems that his interest is more in disrupting the 'spectacle' than offering any consistent programme for an alternative, enlightened understanding. The seductiveness of conspiracy theories and absurd conjunctions always outweighs any desire to debunk them.

The Contentious Spaces of Image-Making

One particular area of overlap between the LPA and Sinclair's work comes through the issue of taking photographs: moments when eccentric rambling suddenly shifts into an act of transgression. On 'The Winchester Trip', the anonymous LPA reporter notes:

> As we walked into the town we tried to take a photograph of the rose which adorned the centre of a square outside the magistrates court. A policeman promptly came out and informed us that it fell within an area in which photography is banned.[57]

In *Lights Out*, Sinclair is stopped while trying to take a photograph of a CCTV camera, and he increasingly associates the logics of observation with those of crime.[58] The fact that Tate Britain (which he discusses) is built on the site of Millbank Prison, constructed after the model of Jeremy Bentham's panopticon, is one meeting point of these ideas. Another can be found in the frequent references

---

[55] *LPA Newsletter* No.2, p.4; Guy Debord, 'Introduction to a Critique of Urban Geography', in Ken Knabb (ed.), *Situationist International Anthology* (Berkeley: Bureau of Public Secrets, 1981).
[56] Ibid., p.21.   [57] *LPA Newsletter* No.1, p.2.
[58] Sinclair, *Lights Out for the Territory*, pp.105–7.

to Michelangelo Antonioni's 1966 film *Blow-Up* and Maryon Park in Charlton, South East London, where Antonioni's photographer-protagonist, loosely modelled on David Bailey, inadvertently records a crime. Referring Sinclair to the 'utopianism of the Sixties' and the era's 'enlightened boredom', the link with criminality connects with his enthusiasm for the Kray twins, famously photographed by Bailey, who also counted property speculation among their business interests.[59]

Lights Out does contain a modest insert of photographs, taken by Sinclair's collaborator Marc Atkins—whom he met during the making of Chris Petit's 1992 film *The Cardinal and the Corpse*, much of which is set in one of the Krays' pubs, The Carpenters Arms, on Cheshire Street, East London. In the text, Atkins is registered alongside the artist Brian Catling as illuminating a 'torpid darkness' in the landscape. In Sinclair's reading, 'every image was an elegy'.[60] More of his photography appears in *Liquid City*, published in 1999 by Reaktion as part of their *Topographics* series (alongside the printed version of Keiller's *Robinson in Space*).[61] Some of the photos from *Lights Out* reappear here, along with others that interact with the other book's themes, such as a photograph of Sinclair playfully 'doubled' in the reflective glass of Jeffrey Archer's penthouse (see Figure 6.2). Thinking of *Lights Out* and *Liquid City* in concert provides a strong sense of the vagrant disposition of Sinclair's output and his enthusiasm for collaborative enterprise. The latter also casts light on the former. Sinclair writes of his own compulsion to record: 'I suffered (exposure to Jack Kerouac at an impressionable age) from the impulse to sketch, note, improvise, revise, double back, bifurcate, split like an amoeba.'[62] The busy punctuation and brackets here typify a sense of urgent and crowded thoughts and the non-linear process of editing and revisiting that is, in effect, central to his creative method.

Sinclair's description of the Atkins of *Lights Out* as 'a fictional construct' follows suit, designating him 'an analogue of what he ought to be if I were a small mad God laying out my own multiverse'.[63] Yet the volume mostly shares in this fictionalizing, or mythologizing, proclivity. The book's photographs, which plot a dichotomy between ghostly, analogue, darkroom-enabled multiple exposures (produced by Atkins's 'old Leica cameras held together with sticking plaster') and grainy CCTV imagery, radiate the productive tension between analogue and digital technologies in Sinclair's narrative 'multiverse'.[64] The ruined church in Abney Park cemetery, one of the earliest destinations in *Lights Out*, sits alongside the so-called 'Hardy Tree' in St Pancras Churchyard. Described in *Lights Out* as 'an island shaded with torpor, heavy with melancholy, the drowned dead', this territory overlaps with that of Aidan Dun's 1995 poem *Vale Royal*, praised by

---

[59] Ibid., p.5.   [60] Ibid., p.270.   [61] Marc Atkins, *Liquid City* (London: Reaktion, 1999).
[62] Sinclair, in *Liquid City*, p.8.   [63] Ibid. p.7.   [64] Ibid., p.15.

Figure 6.2 Sinclair 'doubled' in the reflective glass of Jeffrey Archer's penthouse in *Liquid City* (1999), by Marc Atkins. Courtesy of Marc Atkins.

Sinclair in the *London Review of Books*, which is named after a street that runs through the former industrial area behind Kings Cross Station.[65]

The recent corporate redevelopment of this area echoes the theme of *Lights Out* as a whole, indulging in ruins and arcane suggestiveness, figuring the writer as both visionary subject and cynical land speculator. The poem 'A serious of photographs', included in *Liquid City*, provides evidence of Sinclair's preoccupation with such themes—he hymns the prospect of 'underexploited air' and offers the idea that 'we've trafficked too much in obscenery' (coining a term that he uses again in *Edge of the Orison*) as a reason for the poem's disorientated atmosphere.[66] Sinclair's elegiac reading of Atkins's photographs helps to explain his own melancholic vision here. Twin double-page images of the Houses of Parliament also play out the argument between established viewpoints and those which run counter to them: one is a formal, full-colour downstream panorama, crisp as a guardsman's tunic, the other a foggy monochrome rendition recalling Monet's Savoy paintings.[67]

---

[65] Sinclair, *Lights Out*, p.143; Aidan Dun, *Vale Royal* (Uppingham: Goldmark, 1995); Sinclair, 'Mysteries of Kings Cross', *London Review of Books* 5 October 1995 (https://www.lrb.co.uk/v17/n19/iain-sinclair/mysteries-of-kings-cross).
[66] Sinclair, *Edge of the Orison*, p.135.   [67] Atkins, *Liquid City*, p.32.

Surrounded by portraits of some of the cast of *Lights Out*—Eric Mottram, Harold Pinter, Alan Moore, Martin Stone, Derek Raymond, David Gascoyne, Kathy Acker, Peter Ackroyd, Michael Moorcock, and John Healy—Atkins's images of pylons, streetscapes, and industrial ruins also include subjects that suggest a self-referential nudge from Sinclair, such as a view from the Hawksmoor Church of St Anne's in Limehouse. The volume features an epigram from James Thomson's poem *City of Dreadful Night* (1874), a masterpiece of the urban Gothic, which charts its speaker's insomniac wandering through a symbolic city based on London. It is likely that this speaker is a thinly veiled rendition of Thomson himself, a depressive and heavy drinker whose wayward life, littered with failure (collapsed business enterprises, travels in America and Europe, court-martial, homelessness), is worthy of Céline's Robinson.

The lines chosen by Sinclair as the epigraph to *Liquid City* are from *City of Dreadful Night*'s second part, describing the speaker's pursuit of a man 'who, shadowlike and frail / Unswervingly though slowly onward went'. The way that this figure moves along '[r]egardless, wrapt in thoughts as in a veil' is particularly important, bringing a sense of pushing on without a care for conditions and of a gaze as hemmed-in as that of Robert Frank's bankers or Eliot's 'unreal' city workers in Sinclair's rendition of the City.[68] The trope of the pursuit also suggests the need for an artist or inspired thinker to have a fellow 'explainer' figure to do the obsessive 'noticing everything', like Holmes and Watson, or Poe's Dupin and his anonymous associate: someone to take on the job of narrativizing events and thoughts into a coherent sequence. In *Liquid City*, Atkins takes up the role of Holmes or Dupin, an artist figure, questing after an idealized 'unimplicated image'; Sinclair's relation to this is as a hack, as someone who compulsively 'pours out' words.[69] Again, this is significant in terms of the light it casts on Sinclair's later work, in which the gradual confounding of these two figures into one—himself—might be seen as central to the collapse of his narrative project into a self-haunting closed circuit.

Sinclair's patronage of Atkins parallels the relationship developed with 'unwritten' or 'unexploited' territories, claimed at the very same moment that they are either photographed or written about. Writers, says Sinclair, are 'predators who exploit the photographer's skill, to come up with the fictions, essays, improvisations that will grant darkness a history and draw it, tentatively, towards the light'.[70] Dramatizing Atkins's activities in Gothic terms, he declares that 'whatever he notices shall live'.[71] The theme of subjective memorialisation is in keeping with the contention of *Lights Out* that 'the past is an optional landscape', but it also means that Atkins's 'dreadful library' constitutes an alternative city in itself.[72] Combined with the danger that their journeys might cause them to 'lose it completely', this is,

---

[68] Ibid., p.5. [69] Sinclair, in Atkins, *Liquid City*, p.7. [70] Ibid., p.11. [71] Ibid., p.59.
[72] Sinclair, *Lights Out*, p.208.

claims Sinclair, 'a millennium philosophy'.[73] In this way, it anticipates the perimeter explorations of *London Orbital* and Sinclair's account of the new millennium's arrival.

The Unofficial Countryside and *London Orbital*: Absence, Fecundity, and Madness

In his 2010 introduction to the naturalist Richard Mabey's *The Unofficial Countryside* (first published in 1973), Sinclair expanded on the theme of 'the transitional quality of unwritten places' and the idea that writing about unexploited territories is bound up with the imminence of their cultivation and consequent disappearance. 'Without a proper accounting for their loss, these acts are final: not a scratch on our consciousness when the listed building is replaced by a loud nothing, protected by a corrugated fence and a battery of surveillance cameras.'[74] His point is clear: transitional spaces are mute and need to be given voice by the concerned writer—even if this means that he too must don the guise of ruthless prospector or speculator in order to carry out this 'accounting'.

Sinclair's introduction was written at the same time as his response to the preparations for the London 2012 Olympics, *Ghost Milk*, which itself provides evidence of Mabey's significance for his own practice and his reaction against what he perceived as the clinical 'non-places' produced by contemporary modernity. One of *Ghost Milk*'s themes is the contrast between London's 'buried history' and the '*tabula rasa*' of the Harry Ransom Center in Texas, to which Sinclair's archive was about to be transferred. Contrasting the two, Sinclair intones that 'writing in London is about archaeology: trawling, classifying, presenting'.[75] It is clear from his introduction to *The Unofficial Countryside* that Mabey's work offered early guidance on where this was best carried out, alert to the potential in 'spurned and disregarded places' and 'the tough fecundity of the margin'.[76]

Mabey's work is indeed strewn with emotive responses to vacant lots, canal towpaths, and waste ground. The prologue to his book stages the author's temporarily bleak state of mind against the zest for life found among plants and wildlife in unexpected places. At an early scene by a canal, this duality is explicitly counterpointed:

> I think it was my black frame of mind that made the unexpected late fruitfulness of this place strike me with such intensity. I had never noticed before that the canal here was as clear as a chalk stream.[77]

---

[73] Atkins, *Liquid City*, p.59.
[74] Sinclair, in Richard Mabey, *The Unofficial Countryside* (Wimborne Minster: Dovecote, 2010), p.7.
[75] Sinclair, *Ghost Milk: Calling Time on the Grand Project* (London: Hamish Hamilton, 2011), p.392.
[76] Mabey, *The Unofficial Countryside*, pp.9–10.   [77] Ibid., p.18.

244 LANDSCAPE AND SUBJECTIVITY

Later, after 'seeing a blackcap in a borough council park' and a cuckoo free itself from a barbed-wire fence, Mabey finds himself 'morbidly elated by the slight wrangle between the natural and the man-made'.[78] His text is full of such figurations, ample evidence for Sinclair's analysis of a circular, mutually constitutive relationship between writing and physical movement: 'writing by walking, and walking again to gather up the will to write'.[79]

Yet as much as Sinclair elects Mabey as a 'prophet' and model for his own practice, there are clear distinctions between the two. These are partly manifested though Sinclair's obsession with the mystical and the occult and partly through his appropriation of the language of speculation and finance. Phrases like 'accounting for their loss' and the observation that he has 'trafficked in too much obscenery' are a case in point, marking how this discourse seeps into his language in a manner that would seem ironic were it not so pervasive. His reading of *The Unofficial Countryside* itself as a 'proper reckoning, the Domesday Book of a topography too fascinating to be left alone' is another example, referring to the first and most famous survey or account of the territory of Britain.[80]

The contrast between Sinclair and Mabey's narrative personae is also illustrative. Sinclair is very much the hero of his own work. Mabey, by contrast, adopts an endearingly familiar, everyman persona. His diffident, tender, and composed manner sets Sinclair's into sharp relief: 'lighting out' for the territory as a colonist or explorer, dramatizing his progress through forgotten spaces. Where Sinclair's narrative is built around excursions, Mabey rejects such a system, structuring his text around the seasons and merging various trips together in his exposition of marginal landscapes. The idea of planned expeditions is, to him, 'a ludicrously inappropriate formula'; mere 'frontiersman daydreaming'. It is, he claims, the result of the English winter, which 'strands you at home with nothing more than maps and checklists to pore over'.[81] As much as Sinclair puts himself at the mercy of coincidence and contingency, planned expeditions are precisely what his works are, and his style invites us into the drama of that whole enterprise: the greasy-spoon breakfasts; the gruesomely blistered feet.

If Mabey's practice can be seen as 'a mediated response to a dim period of failing industries, social unrest, power cuts: suppression of the imagination after the unbridled utopianism of the Sixties', then Sinclair's own activities, working in that same shadow, increasingly form the appropriate parallel for an age defined by the lapse of that utopianism.[82] The sense of post-political glaciation under the aegis of the Thatcher, Major, and Blair governments, with New Labour's shift to the centre ground seeming to consolidate the displacement of conventional political discourse by the imperatives of the global marketplace, is increasingly clear in Sinclair's later work. In light of this, the dissimulation of politics as

---

[78] Ibid., pp.28–9.   [79] Sinclair, in Mabey, *The Unofficial Countryside*, p.7.   [80] Ibid., p.10.
[81] Ibid., p.26.   [82] Ibid., p.9.

apolitical pragmatism—the 'Nude Labour' that Sinclair is ever more preoccupied by—becomes an increasingly prominent analogue for a duplicitous and 'fraudulent' landscape in his work.[83]

As Niall Martin has written in his 2017 monograph *Noise, Neoliberalism and the Matter of London*, the M25—Sinclair's theme and map in *London Orbital*—is entirely apt here, being, 'in effect, the public space of neoliberalism'.[84] And this choice of *topos* is doubly appropriate in that, as Roy Phippen noted in a 2005 book about the road, the M25's bridge over the Thames at Dartford was the first major public engineering project in Britain to be financed entirely by private capital.[85] Along this most emphatically motorized of structures, the apparently subversive practice of the walk becomes perversely apt to the new structure of feeling, wherein—as Phil Baker neatly puts it, referring to Thatcher—psychogeography's 'recent fetishization has accompanied a post-consensus, post-societal sense that society as a whole (famously declared not to exist in 1987) offers no salvation, only one's own routes and places'.[86]

Accordingly, expeditions on foot—described as a 'discipline' in *Lights Out*—are refigured in *London Orbital* as a nervous obsession, moving towards what Martin calls 'a compulsive stenography of place'.[87] Re-articulating '*flânerie*' as '*fugueurie*', Sinclair newly renders the journey on foot as a mechanism of escape, even if the motifs of exploration and the frontier are still employed in the description of this 'unresolved landscape'. ('Like America to the Norsemen', remarks Sinclair on his way to the orbital motorway, 'it's still a rumour.')[88] In a context where the pedestrian is necessarily marginalized, Sinclair plays up the notion of transgression by emphasizing his anti-clockwise movement—a doomed anti-temporal gesture designed to undo the encroaching millennium and its material manifestation, the Millennium Dome. This building is central to the text: its construction was simultaneous with the composition of the book (the celebrations, observed from across the river, form its finale), and its twelve-pointed structure, aping a clock face, is reflected in Sinclair's decision to divide his circuit into twelve discrete expeditions.

This breaking up of the walk points to an increasingly central element of Sinclair's practice—the drama of trying to piece together his text into a coherent whole. 'Here it begins, the walk proper', he declares, a quarter of the way into his text, once the walk from his home in Hackney to the motorway itself has been completed. The declaration 'no detours, no digressions' seems oddly placed here after what amounts to an enormously digressive introductory sequence, where the territory covered overlaps with the Lea Valley walk of *Lights Out*.[89] Sinclair's

---

[83] Sinclair, *London Orbital*, p.403.
[84] Martin, *Noise, Neoliberalism and the Matter of London*, p.150.
[85] Phippen, Roy, *M25: Travelling Clockwise* (London: Pallas Athene, 2005).
[86] Baker, in *London from Punk to Blair*, p.281. [87] Sinclair, *London Orbital*, pp.5–6.
[88] Ibid., p.69. [89] Ibid., p.125.

Figure 6.3 A motorist gestures at Sinclair and Petit in the film of *London Orbital* (2002). Courtesy of Iain Sinclair. *London Orbital* directed by Chris Petit and Iain Sinclair, produced by Illuminations.

declarative, monologic statement performs the increasing prominence of a tension within the consciousness of the narrating subject, who already seems to exhibit a neurotically ambivalent relation to the inevitable repetitiousness of his projects.

Sinclair's 2002 film of *London Orbital*, made with Chris Petit, stages the walks of the book by providing their negative image—the smooth gaze of the automotive passenger, a timely equivalent to the 'blinkered' commuters of *Lights Out* (see Figure 6.3).[90] One important fact in both the book and the film is that the disintegration or failure of the enterprise is a foregone conclusion. The notion of one continuous walk is, anyway, impossible, and likewise the idea of a *fugue* conducted in a circle—an escape that closes back in on itself—means that the project of unwinding the millennium countdown is acknowledged in advance as an impossible task. In this respect, the form of *London Orbital* sets out the basis of a method that is sustained in Sinclair's later work—in *Ghost Milk*, for instance, he claims that 'I wanted to walk away and keep on walking', ascribing this compulsion to the traumatic sense of unfinishedness generated by *Orbital*—'I had not recovered from my orbital circuit, my tramp around the M25 motorway loop, that perfect icon of endlessness.'[91] Even the form of 2015's *London Overground*, repeating the same circular journey on the more restrained circumference of the newly refurbished inner-orbital rail link, seems to evince the continued shadow of the motorway's circuit on Sinclair's work.

The road becomes emblematic of madness in another way, too, being so far out from the centre of London that it forms a parallel universe quite separate from the inner city. This alternate realm is not only inscribed with the tensions of corporate exclusivity (patches like the Wentworth golf club and housing estate), embattled greenbelt land, and fecund margins: it is also peppered with the insane asylums

---

[90] See Chris Petit and Sinclair (dirs.), *London Orbital* (Illuminations, 2004).
[91] Sinclair, *Ghost Milk*, p.104.

that have at various points removed from inner-city locations to the suburbs—Colney Hatch, the Bethlem Royal Hospital (formerly Bedlam), and many more. In this respect the idea of *fugueurie* or 'flight' is doubly appropriate. The man who declares 'sir, I can frequently fly' in Dickens's 1861 'Night Walks' is a patient of Bedlam, then at its Lambeth site.[92] Tracing the asylum where David Rodinsky was incarcerated, along with many others, motifs of 'consciousness misplaced in long corridors' and 'hysterical' imagery summon the disorientating institutional atmosphere of Resnais and Robbe-Grillet's *Last Year at Marienbad* (1961) and in turn Sebald's treatment of the same theme in *Austerlitz*.[93] The descriptions also lean proleptically on the subject matter of *Edge of the Orison* and John Clare's 1841 'escape' from the High Beach Asylum in Essex.

The Millennium Dome as a Sublime Object

Charing Cross has conventionally been used as the centre of London for mapping and planning purposes. The green belt, for instance, was 'conceived in desperation' by G.L. Pepler, who 'proposed a parkway encircling London at a ten-mile radius from Charing Cross' in 1911. In like manner, Sinclair chooses to nominate this site as the specific fulcrum of his own walk in *London Orbital*.[94] Yet his project has as its second, figurative hub or 'omphalos' the Millennium Dome, a project conceived under John Major's conservative administration and taken up by Tony Blair's New Labour government after it swept to power in 1997. In this reading, the hollow centre of the Dome reflects the margin; both, typical of Augé's 'non-places' of circulation, consumption and communication, are defined by absence. At the same time, the language used in the context of the Dome's promotion is also satirized by Sinclair as itself disorientating and confusing.

The idea of a self-defeating, ritualistic journey to nowhere around the motorway is acted out in knowing reference to the profoundly arbitrary social ritual of the millennium celebration. Countering the event with his own vagrant sense of narrative chronology, Sinclair embeds a section from a year after the Dome's opening (the book wasn't published until 2002), when entry prices have been slashed and the extent of the haemorrhage of public funds has become clearer. Specifically, the Dome itself becomes the battleground over which Sinclair mounts his attack on New Labour's supposed reduction of political language to banality—an extension of Thatcherite 'doublespeak' and the phenomenon noted in *Lights Out* where Jeffrey Archer speaks in 'soundbites'.[95] In this respect, the Dome sets the precedent that the 2012 Olympiad is seen to follow in *Ghost Milk* (as 'a theme

---

[92] Charles Dickens, 'Night Walks', in *The Uncommercial Traveller* (New York: Hurd & Haughton, 1873), p.180.
[93] Sinclair, *London Orbital*, p.289.   [94] Ibid., p.85.   [95] Sinclair, *Lights Out*, p.203.

park without a theme') and of which Sinclair would later write that 'it was the betrayal of language that caused the most pain. Every pronouncement meant its opposite: *Improving the image of construction. Constructing a place where people want to live.*'[96]

Sinclair's idea of New Labour's 'destruction' of language in *London Orbital* should not be dismissed as mere vitriol. A look at Elizabeth Wilhide's *The Millennium Dome*, published as a guide for visitors (and featuring a foreword by Tony Blair) bears this out almost instantly, with its bizarre opening declaration that 'the Dome is not a building'. Wilhide goes further when she adds that it 'is not even a dome. It has the profile of a shallow dome, but none of its structural properties. It looks something like a tent, but it is not a tent either.' The Dome is marketed here as a singularity that evades description: 'it is soft and hard, rounded and spiky, it hugs the ground and reaches for the sky'; it is 'a simple idea achieved in a complex way'; it is 'a knotted web, a network, an envelope'; its 'structural tensions' even 'make explicit the turning point of time it has been destined to mark'.[97] Other contributors follow suit: Alex Madina of the 'New Millennium Experience Company' declares that 'people think they've got a handle on it. But I don't think the Dome is a graspable structure.' Mike Davis of the architects in charge, Richard Rogers, says simply that 'the Dome is a conundrum'.[98]

Rogers's later revelations that he had been 'gagged from talking about the budget' might suggest that the 'conundrum' Davis was referring to wasn't only the one presented by the Dome's physical shape. As he revealed in a 2007 interview, ultimately only 7 per cent of the total £789 million cost was actually spent on the building itself, so that this icon of humanity's entry into the new millennium 'was a super-cheap structure, the same price per square metre as a supermarket shed'.[99] But if his peers' struggles with language bear a strange echo of the Kantian sublime, then the point that they can agree on—its sheer size—states this in the most simplified terms. 'The Dome is so big', writes Wilhide, 'that quantity becomes a different quality.'[100] It is in this respect that the Dome comes to represent the world of 'name artists' and hollow celebrity that Sinclair deals with so scornfully—underscoring his connection between the motorway, the Dome, and contemporary celebrities like the former Spice Girl Victoria Beckham.

In Sinclair's rendition, the effect of the Dome's sheer scale is inverted from one of wonder to one of repulsion. Appearing to be perversely divine, this transcendent object is revealed as having no care for actual human existence, seeming to

---

[96] Sinclair, *Ghost Milk*, p.11; p.167.
[97] Elizabeth Wilhide, *The Millennium Dome* (London: HarperCollins, 1999), p.9.
[98] Ibid., p.25.
[99] Richard Rogers, in Oliver Wainwright, 'How We Made the Millennium Dome', *Guardian* 7 March 2015 (https://www.theguardian.com/culture/2015/mar/17/how-we-made-the-millennium-dome-richard-rogers).
[100] Wilhide, *The Millennium Dome*, p.10.

operate of its own accord in spite of the various individual agencies that must have contributed to its construction—quite literally following the mechanism of Marxian alienation. Like the M25, it is an ostensibly corporate body that renders the individuals that inhabit it obscure and apparently meaningless, trivializing them. As a site of genuine commonality, where society confronts itself, it is clearly flawed, and, like Peer Gynt's onion, the emptiness of the Dome gestures towards the perceived hollowness of modernity—akin to London's 'civic void' in Keiller's rendition.

The Dome's hollowness connects with a sense of the total breakdown of conventional politics. As Martin points out, the transition of the Dome from a Tory project to a New Labour one is 'sinister' because

> it comes to symbolize Labour's endorsement of the neoliberal premise that the market represents the ultimate horizon of politics. It becomes, in effect, the symbol of the post-political condition: an emblem of the general loss of faith in politics and democracy.[101]

As the 'omphalos' of *London Orbital*, this bears out for the project as a whole. It is paralleled by Anthony Gormley's sculpture on the North Woolwich peninsula, *Quantum Cloud*, unveiled in 1999 and itself figured by Sinclair as an adequate rendition of 'the reality of this site' expressly because 'it gives form to inherited melancholy'.[102] Sinclair's point is that if language is one means by which humanity orients itself, a kind of gut response allowed to 'pour through', as he put it in *Liquid City*, then the disruption of it is a fundamentally disorientating and alienating activity—the Dome forming an obscene echo of this in actual space.[103]

In a parodic replay of Wilhide's linguistic wrangling that recalls his description of the MI6 building in *Lights Out*, *London Orbital* is strewn with scathing terms for the Dome: at one point a 'Teflon marquee'; elsewhere 'Mandelson's tent'—a reference to Peter Mandelson, Tony Blair's 'spin doctor' and a key proponent of the scheme.[104] Sinclair's 1999 pamphlet *Sorry Meniscus*, an advance salvo against the project, displayed the same proclivity. Initially observing the Dome from the carefully chosen vantage point of 'Folly Wall' on the Isle of Dogs, he variously calls it 'a pale intruder on the downriver mud', 'a poached egg designed by a committee of vegans', and 'a skin with no pudding'.[105] All of this entertaining material is bound up with the idea of time itself as 'the final privatisation'.[106] *London Orbital* reprises this terminology and refracts it onto the motorway, which becomes a

---

[101] Martin, *Noise, Neoliberalism and the Matter of London*, p.144.
[102] Sinclair, *London Orbital*, p.549.   [103] Atkins, *Liquid City*, p.8.
[104] Sinclair, *London Orbital*, p.550; p.34.
[105] Sinclair, *Sorry Meniscus: Excursions to the Millennium Dome* (London: Profile, 1999), p.11; p.14; p.87.
[106] Ibid., p.41.

'thoroughfare to nowhere'; 'an asteroid belt for London's Rubble'.[107] Dome and motorway also come together in the idea of the 'non-place'. Sinclair mostly uses the term 'non-space', but his focus is the same as Marc Augé's: the voided, depersonalized arenas of logistics and leisure generated by the demands of capital, balancing the free movement of cash and commodities with the associated preponderance of a permanently detached, touristic gaze.

Sorry Meniscus also reveals something intriguing about Sinclair's apparently obsessive recording of experience. Shortly after his comment on the 'post-political condition' emblematized by the Dome, Niall Martin notes the moment when Sinclair attempts to travel to the site from his home in Hackney and takes a shuttle bus on the Isle of Dogs, only to find some 'old ladies huddled against the cruel zephyrs and down drafts that swept through this Blade Runner architecture' waiting more than half an hour for their own local bus connection.[108] Martin's entirely convincing gloss of this scene is that it demonstrates the way that 'global cities', even as the coefficient of their 'global' character, confront their actual (poor) inhabitants with 'political disenfranchisement' and the 'fragmentation of urban space'.[109] Yet it is also striking that this 'Blade Runner' passage bears an uncanny similarity to the geographer Doreen Massey's comment in her *Space, Place and Gender* (cited by the narrator of Keiller's *Robinson in Space*) that 'amid the Ridley Scott vision of world cities' much of many people's lives still 'consists of waiting in a bus shelter with your shopping for a bus that never comes'.[110]

The suggestion here is not only that Sinclair was aware of Keiller and Massey's work but that the scene may in fact be invented: not a result of his 'compulsive stenography' of place and his insistence on first-hand encounter but rather of the 'easy congress between fictional and historical ontologies'. In this way, Sinclair's own imaginative 'speculation' on and in place is sustained in both of its senses. Even in the context of overt commitment to the protection of spaces as they actually exist against the ways in which they are re-imagined for investment purposes by the ruthless forces of capital, Sinclair's East London remains a place that he also feels at liberty to create and invent. Once more, the author's role is not so much steward or archaeologist as pioneer explorer, expropriating space from its occupants' voices just as blithely as any property developer.

Spaces of Consumption and Crime: Bluewater and Carfax

Sinclair's depiction of space and place in *London Orbital* draws heavily on the culture of the 1990s—the boom in 'reality television' and its accompanying

---

[107] Sinclair, *London Orbital*, p.35; p.72.
[108] Sinclair, quoted in Martin, *Noise, Neoliberalism and the Matter of London*, p.145.
[109] Ibid., p.145.
[110] Doreen Massey, *Space, Place and Gender* (Cambridge: Polity, 1994), p.163.

celebrity culture and associations between the motorway and Essex nightclubs, criminality, and the era's most emblematic recreational drug, Ecstasy. Cultures of consumption, and specifically of retail, are highly significant to his affective topography of the ring road. Apart from the Dome, the key sites in *London Orbital* are Heathrow and the Thames estuary, twin poles of London's logistical might and home to competing retail 'non-places'. The former is closely associated with J.G. Ballard (the book includes a pilgrimage to his home in Shepperton), charting the supposed dissipation of modern life into a miasma of competing urges towards sex and carnage. Ballard's 1973 novel *Crash*, in particular, with its protagonist's noirish persona and single-minded pursuit of an automotive collision with the actress Elizabeth Taylor, informs the idea of the M25 as a realm of madness and perverse 'drives'. The latter is home to the Bluewater shopping centre.

For Sinclair, the ring-road landscape is one in which television supplies the fictions within which people live and where the real spaces of home and garden bleed into the virtual ones of the television and the home computer. For him, the eastern edge of the motorway is also fed by Ballard's conception of modernity as 'a world ruled by fictions of every kind' where 'the writer's task is to invent reality'.[111] The Bluewater shopping centre first opened in 1997, and with its pseudo-vernacular oast-house architecture sunken into a vast former chalk quarry, it is for Sinclair 'a Ballardian resort' akin to 'Estrella del Mar' in *Cocaine Nights* (1996) or 'Eden-Olympia' in *Super-Cannes* (2000). It also seems to anticipate the 'Brooklands Metro Centre' of his late novel *Kingdom Come* (2006), which— under the charge of a dashing television personality—attempts to secede from the United Kingdom and has to be retaken by force. 'Bluewater is aspirational. Profoundly conservative', writes Sinclair. It is, he continues—spoofing that very aspirationalism—'the measure that separates those who belong, who know the rules and the language, from the sweaty, unshaven mob who rush the Channel Tunnel.'[112]

Like the motorway (and unlike the Lakeside shopping centre in Essex, which it thrust into a state of sudden outmodedness), Bluewater is constructed as a loop. It is presented as the inverse of the insane asylums that pepper the city's periphery:

> Bluewater is the contrary of the sanatorium in Thomas Mann's *The Magic Mountain*. Instead of a high place in which interestingly tubercular eccentrics rehash the great European themes, here is a hole in the ground in which ordinary, unsuspecting citizens crack up, develop the downmarket equivalent of yuppie flu.

---

[111] Ballard, quoted in Zadie Smith, 'On *Crash*', *New York Review of Books*, 10 July 2014 (http://www.nybooks.com/articles/2014/07/10/on-jg-ballard-crash/).
[112] Sinclair, *London Orbital*, p.467.

They wander the levels, under the soft cosh of muzak, feeling the lifeforce drain. These are the Retail Undead. De-blooded victims of the Purfleet kiss.[113]

Sinclair's reference here is to the association made with Bram Stoker's *Dracula* (1897), via the location of Dracula's castle at Carfax Abbey in Purfleet, on the northern shore of the estuary, close to the Lakeside shopping centre.

Dracula's presence on the orbital motorway is crucial to Sinclair, connecting the theme of logistics with the resonance of the Gothic in his work. In Stoker's novel, the Carfax estate is effectively used as a storage facility, holding the coffins by means of which Count Dracula orchestrates his attack on London. The idea of the motorway as a circulatory system, its vehicles so many blood vessels rushing around, makes the fortuitous connection seem almost ready-made, whilst implicitly dislocating the axiomatic 'heart' of the city to its fringe. The impression of the 'Retail Undead', meanwhile, leans heavily on both this Gothic inheritance and the notion of 'supermodernity' central to Augé's theorization of the non-place. The suggestion of contemporary crime and criminality also sits tidily alongside the theme of the M25 as a gangster's ideal getaway, explored through the involvement of the 1995 'Essex Boys' gangland murders (latterly adapted into several films) in the film of *London Orbital*. As Sinclair remarks in the film, 'bad news, like landfill, travels east. In the direction of Rainham Marshes, Rettendon—locations whose only ambition is to appear in "scene of the crime" photographs'.[114]

The balance between Bluewater and Carfax Abbey is highly characteristic of Sinclair's method, which cultivates a lurid front line between gloss and grime. The stubborn materiality of the walker's experience is always set against the motorist's detached, touristic gaze. The blend between this point of view and that of CCTV cameras in the film version of *London Orbital* (see Figure 6.4) asserts this, as does the increased prominence granted to Samuel Palmer's now incongruously sited 'Valley of Vision' around the Darent river in Shoreham, Kent. The tension here—the clash of low-resolution imagery and the smooth gaze of the automotive passenger, intercut with handheld-camera shots of monitors and postcards—also recalls the clash of technologies in *Dracula*, where an epistolary form is lent added pace by the overlapping speeds of letters and telegrams.

The tension between media also speaks to Petit's description of the M25, in the film of *London Orbital*, as both 'anti-cinema' and 'anti-image'—a subject on which Esther Leslie elaborated in her 2007 essay 'Image Refusal in Iain Sinclair's Refuse Aesthetics'.[115] In this essay, Leslie explores the 'circuit of seeing' in which surveillance footage is embroiled—endless unwatched imagery that will lie dormant until the event of a crime, at which point it is finally reviewed and reused in an attempt to retrospectively ascertain a narrative. Describing the analysis of CCTV footage

---

[113] Ibid., p.468.   [114] Sinclair and Petit, *London Orbital*.   [115] Ibid.

Figure 6.4 CCTV footage in the film of *London Orbital* (2002). Courtesy of Iain Sinclair. *London Orbital* directed by Chris Petit and Iain Sinclair, produced by Illuminations.

of a local criminal, in the supermarket, in the street, and in hospital, she finds this process played out:

> All this surveillance film of him turned up in a TV documentary later. Degraded but evidential images passed through commerce and the state to the police and then on to the TV company, in a circuit of seeing, in which re-consumption of images amounts to a type of recycling.[116]

Leslie's idea of the motorway as a source of endless visual detritus sits neatly with Sinclair's own introduction to the film, with the intimation that 'my London had been trashed, Balkanised. I'd stayed too long in one place. I'd seen Sixties towerblocks rise, and I'd seen them tumble.'[117] Footage of Margaret Thatcher about to cut the ribbon and open the road in October 1986, which appears near the film's opening, ironically sends up this moment as a 'crime' by revisiting the imagery later on: Sinclair and Petit scrutinize it, as if it were CCTV, attempting to ascertain the scene's precise location. And CCTV is in itself an appropriate metaphor for the road, too. In *Lights Out*, Sinclair had apocalyptically described it as a form of 'post-human cinema'—that is, a form of documentation that surveys the subject in the twin sense of both recording their actions for the purposes of security and literally *over*-looking them, as indifferent to the individual human subject as the vast structures of the M25 and the Dome.[118]

As the vehicles loop past in Sinclair and Petit's film, like the 'tin hulks' passing under the footbridge in Keiller's *Stonebridge Park*, their drivers become a dazed and glazed analogue of Dante's lustful in the *Inferno*, itself constructed in

---

[116] Esther Leslie, 'Image Refusal in Iain Sinclair's Refuse Aesthetics', in Bond and Bavidge (eds.), *City Visions*, p.91.
[117] Sinclair and Petit, *London Orbital*.   [118] Sinclair, *Lights Out*, p.320.

concentric circles. The film plays on the unsatisfying narrative produced by this endless closed circuit, playing on the theme of the 'road movie' motif with which Petit found his only modest measure of commercial success in 1979's *Radio On*, where the linearity of the M4 motorway supplies a narrative that is otherwise rather lacking.[119] Cutting together scenes of the endless motorway movement and archival footage from, among other sources, Sinclair's Albion Square 'Diary Films' of 1969–75, *London Orbital* turns all watching into a process of revisiting, eliding memory and experience into one narrative-resistant emulsion.

The film of *London Orbital* includes an additional segment on the A13— running from Aldgate in London, where it is known as Commercial Road, to the Essex seaside town of Shoeburyness. This road runs past the former 'Beckton Alp' dry ski slope and the vast Ford motor works at Dagenham, whose presence reinforced the peculiar sense of Americana that fed back into aesthetic representations like the Barking-born singer Billy Bragg's 1983 song 'A13, Trunk Road to the Sea'. It is designated by Sinclair as his 'favourite road', and in the text of *London Orbital* he remarks that it

> drains East London's wound, carrying you up into the sky; before throwing you back among boarded-up shops and squatted terraces. All urban life aspires to this condition; flux, pastiche. A conveyor belt of discontinued industries. A peripatetic museum, horizon to horizon, available to anyone; self-curated.[120]

Sinclair reads the A13 as an essay in the industrial sublime and as an English 'Highway 51'. The structure becomes a foil to the infinite circularity of the M25 and the principle of *London Orbital* as a whole: with its ability to 'drain the wound', it achieves precisely what the M25, read through Sinclair's narrative persona, cannot manage. 'A failed bypass', as Petit puts it, the orbital motorway's 'wound' is not so much Dracula's 'Purfleet kiss' as the 'open' one of Freud's melancholia, perpetually kept open in a cycle of unfinished mourning.[121]

The Eleanor Crosses and Freud's 'Unpractical Londoners'

Figurations of the M25 as a Jungian 'mandala' are recurrent in *London Orbital*. In the film, the colonies of insane asylums on the city's edge are in turn described as 'black mandalas of madness'. Yet it is through Freudian, rather than Jungian, themes that the elision of landscape and psychology is really made manifest. In his study of Sinclair, Niall Martin discusses the idea of 'noise' in relation to the 'return of the unselected' in *The Psychopathology of Everyday Life* (1901) and the concept

---

[119] See Chris Petit (dir.), *Radio On* (BFI, 2008). [120] Sinclair, *London Orbital*, pp.45–6.
[121] Sinclair and Petit, *London Orbital*.

of *Nachträglichkeit* in *Beyond the Pleasure Principle* (1920).[122] This forms part of his argument that Sinclair's writing is centred on the tension between 'neoliberalism's avowed commitment to the promotion of the free and frictionless circulation of information'—of which the M25 is, in intention at least, emblematic—'and the neoliberal subject's increasing sense of surveillance and restraint'.[123] The 'noise' of the local creates blockages in the circulatory system. The actual topography of London offers another compelling way of reading *London Orbital* and others of Sinclair's texts in relation to Freud's work, centring on the ability of the landscape to either reveal or conceal historical data, and even to do the one while intending the other.

If the ersatz epitaphs of graffiti in *Lights Out* stood for 'authentic' urban experience, then the clumsy detritus of memorialization to be found scattered on the capital's periphery in *London Orbital* redounds with the potential to mislead, always threatening to disorientate the subject—an experience figured prominently in Sinclair's difficulties locating the precise point where Margaret Thatcher cut the ribbon that officially opened the road, even though this moment was broadcast live on television. This sets the tone for a disorientated culture, where placelessness elides with political fraudulence and 'doublespeak'. The particularity of walking, the narrowing of scale, operates in futile opposition.

Rod Mengham has observed that in Sinclair's work 'civic memory is derided, official monuments regarded as symptoms of a collective amnesia'.[124] This mood is illustrated early in *Lights Out*, where Sinclair is found contrasting graffiti with publically sanctioned memorials, merely

> a way of forgetting, reducing generational guilt to a grid of albino chess pieces, bloodless stalagmites. Shapes that are easy to ignore stand in for the trauma of remembrance. [...] These funerary spikes, unnoticed by the locals as they go about their business, operate a system of pain erasure; acupuncture needles channelling, through their random alignment, the flow of the energy field.[125]

Although they are not named specifically, his words seem to refer uncannily to the so-called 'Eleanor Crosses', which come to feature prominently in *London Orbital*. Indeed, alongside the Dome, Sinclair specifically chooses to nominate the Eleanor Cross at Charing Cross as the fulcrum of his own walk.[126] Recording the progress of Eleanor of Castile's funeral cortège from Lincoln to London in the thirteenth century, these crosses were built by the widowed King Edward I at the sites where the procession paused overnight on its journey south. Hence they inscribe the landscape with elegiac sentiment. Yet, perhaps more importantly than this, the

---

[122] Martin, *Noise, Neoliberalism and the Matter of London*, p.15.   [123] Ibid., p.9.
[124] Rod Mengham, Richard Lane, and Philip Tew (eds.), *Contemporary British Fiction* (Cambridge: Polity, 2002), p.62.
[125] Sinclair, *Lights Out for the Territory*, p.9.   [126] Sinclair, *London Orbital*, p.85.

crosses' meaning is all but forgotten today—a fact in tune with Sinclair's aforementioned contention that 'the past is an optional landscape'. In two cases (Waltham Cross and Charing Cross), the word 'cross' has been seamlessly incorporated into the places' names, habitualized into insignificance.

In the first of his *Five Lectures on Psycho-Analysis*, delivered in 1909, Freud specifically discussed the Eleanor Crosses (along with the Monument to the Great Fire of London) as a material analogue for the successful repression of trauma. As he put it, '*hysterical patients suffer from reminiscences*. Their symptoms are residues and mnemic symbols of particular (traumatic) experiences':

> These monuments, then, resemble hysterical patients in being mnemic symbols; up to that point the comparison seems justifiable. But what should we think of a Londoner who paused today in deep melancholy before the memorial of Queen Eleanor's funeral instead of going about his business in the hurry that modern working conditions demand or instead of feeling joy over the youthful queen of his own heart? Or again what should we think of a Londoner who shed tears before the Monument that commemorates the reduction of his beloved metropolis to ashes although it has long since risen again in far greater brilliance? Yet every single hysteric and neurotic behaves like these two unpractical Londoners. Not only do they remember painful experiences of the remote past, but they still cling to them emotionally; they cannot get free of the past and for its sake they neglect what is real and immediate. This fixation of mental life to pathogenic traumas is one of the most significant and practically important characteristics of neurosis.[127]

On its surface, this episode from the *Five Lectures* renders the mechanism of Sinclair's work in a manner that complements the ideas of *Nachträglichkeit* or 'the return of the unselected': Sinclair's literary excavation of mnemonic sites reinstates a traumatic heritage that is relayed back onto the psyche of the walker himself, who is unable to successfully repress traumatic memories. His performance of neurosis, walking the motorway for an inherently impossible purpose, renders the landscape as a vastly 'unpractical' environment through which to pass. It fuels his cynical rendition of sites like Waltham Cross, where the memorial is figured as 'a nibbled Gaudí pillar':

> webbed in with protective nets, restored, cleaned to an ivory sheen, the Eleanor Cross is more like a radio mast than an item of funerary sculpture. It's the focal point of this prolapsed market town.[128]

---

[127] Sigmund Freud, *Two Short Accounts of Psychoanalysis*, ed. and trans. James Strachey (London: Penguin, 1970), pp.39–40.
[128] Sinclair, *London Orbital*, pp.130–1.

Sinclair's 'unpractical' inability to simply ignore the cross, as everybody else seems to, energises his impatience with the town and its inhabitants.Designating the local resident Victoria Beckham as 'the future Eleanor Cross' emblematizes his distaste for contemporary culture: she 'is famous for shopping'.[129]

But what makes Freud's text—with its subject 'going about his business' in anticipation of Sinclair's imagined 'locals'—doubly germane to the concerns of *London Orbital* is the specific history of the Eleanor Cross he describes: the 'richly carved Gothic column' outside 'one of the great railway termini'—that is, Charing Cross Station. What Freud didn't note is that this monument is itself a replica. As James Strachey pointed out in a 1959 footnote to Freud's text, this particular column is nothing but 'a modern copy of these monuments'. His further information, apparently drawn from a conversation with Freud's disciple and biographer Ernest Jones, that '"Charing" is believed to be derived from the words "*chère reine*"' feels as though it might have been included by way of atonement for this mistake—in fact, the etymology of 'Charing' is still debated.[130]

Either way, Strachey needn't have been concerned: Freud's oversight only increases the validity of his case, by proving that the monumental repression of regnal sorrow had been so effectively achieved that, 500 years later, Eleanor had been so completely forgotten that the disappearance and subsequent reconstruction of the column caused no significant resurgence of trauma. The original cross was located at the top of Whitehall, where the equestrian statue of Charles I now stands (included in Keiller's *London* as a site of pilgrimage for 'groups of Anglo-Catholics and other ultra-monarchists'). The Monument, meanwhile, which was constructed not only as a memorial but also as a watchtower to help guard against further conflagration, would hardly serve this purpose today: it is dwarfed by the monolithic skyscrapers constructed after regulations restricting buildings to the height of a fireman's ladder were lifted in 1956.

The notion that this anecdote points us towards, of London and its environs as a jigsaw of competing and potentially *inauthentic* monuments, is clearly significant for Sinclair's own practice. At the time of his writing *London Orbital*, the drama of the Eleanor Cross, comfortably repressed, was being replayed in parallel by the case of Temple Bar. This is now situated in Paternoster Square, outside the London Stock Exchange, but in *London Orbital* Sinclair visits it in Theobald's Park, Hertfordshire, where 'removed from its location, [it] is also removed from time. Its energies are released.'[131] In its exile it becomes, like the Eleanor Crosses, one of 'the beacons of our walk'.[132] Temple Bar functions as a key locus, too, in *Edge of the Orison*—but by this time it has been moved back to the City. For Sinclair, this retrieval is profoundly unsettling. It transforms the structure into merely

---

[129] Ibid., p.132. [130] Freud, *Two Short Accounts*, p.40.
[131] Sinclair, *London Orbital*, p.110. [132] Ibid., p.161.

[a] heritage trophy. A lifeless version of itself: no gate, no psychic marker, not even a folly in a rich brewer's path. A naked and all too pristine freak. London, once again, reduced to an exhibition of fraudulent symbols.[133]

In typically agitated staccato rhythms, Sinclair offers ample evidence for Mengham's claim that he regards 'official monuments [...] as symptoms of a collective amnesia'. Even if the structure itself is original, precisely the *conscious* recuperation of Temple Bar into the regime of 'heritage' spectacle is what renders it an inauthentic and 'fraudulent symbol'. This may seem counterintuitive, but even if his anger seems an uneasy fit with the gentler reflectiveness of Keiller and Sebald, Sinclair's frustration here marks a similar tendency towards Svetlana Boym's idea of 'reflective' rather than 'restorative' nostalgia, his interest more in the act of memory itself than in the 'total reconstruction of monuments of the past'.

The 'Idea of Landscape' and John Clare's Journey Out of Essex in *Edge of the Orison*

Its history occluded as it becomes part of the 'official' heritage spectacle, Temple Bar reveals how essential the 'unofficial' remains to Sinclair's affective mapping of space. In his own exposition of the 'unofficial', Richard Mabey specifically referred to 'John Clare's Helpston' as part of his denunciation of travel narratives that use planned journeys and pre-ordained situations 'to hang the story round'. 'I did not want to travel in the same spirit as them', he writes:

> more and more they seemed to follow in each others' tracks, lured to Selbourne and John Clare's Helpston, as if it were difficult to confront the modernised countryside face to face without an earlier impression to compensate for the hedgeless gaps in your own.[134]

Yet in 2007's *Edge of the Orison*, Sinclair did exactly that, replicating Clare's flight from High Beach asylum in Epping Forest, Essex, to his home in Northamptonshire, conducted 20–24 July 1841. The trip sought to replicate, too, Clare's 'anxiety', madness, and gradually increasing 'state of hallucinatory exhaustion': 'Hungry, hobbled, deluded. An expedition to recover a self he had no use for, a wife he didn't recognise, a cottage he loathed.'[135]

Sinclair first undertook this walk in July 2000, meaning that it overlapped with those of *London Orbital*; he variously revisited it over the following years.[136] His record of it opens with a restatement of the earlier text's conclusions, an insistence

[133] Ibid., pp.102–3.   [134] Mabey, p.26.   [135] Sinclair, *Edge of the Orison*, p.152; p.123.
[136] See ibid., p.124.

on the validity of that journey and the supposed need to reassert it with another one.

> You might think that a circuit of London, twelve walks, inside and outside the orbital motorway, would have cured me of this neurosis: the compulsion to be on the hoof, burdened with packs, sketchbooks, cameras. Future memories. The gravity of London had to be escaped by a final, unwritten chapter, a shaky attempt to place my boots in John Clare's hobbled footsteps.[137]

This time he acknowledges, however, that closure is not to be expected:

> I imagined that stretching the length of the orbital circuit of the M25 into the English countryside, into somewhere as obscure (to me) as the territory between Peterborough, Market Deeping, Stamford and the A1, would complete the episode, bury it. But that's never how it works. My attempted divorce only confirmed another ring, another shackle. London, better known, less understood, was more London than it had ever been; a monster greedy for expansion, eager to swallow underexploited ground and to bury it in satellite development.[138]

If the insistence here is on the impossibility of finality, then the new figuration of the Lea Valley as a 'commonplace' scene characterized by 'the absence of the tragic, suspended melancholia' suggests the way that this journey ultimately comes to replicate the problem presented by *London Orbital*, in the sense of being an unfinishable project, trapping the narrating subject in a cycle of reminiscences that replicates Freud's 'unfinished mourning'.[139] When Sinclair finally 'breaks free' from this setting, traversed in both *Lights Out* and *London Orbital*, his journey takes the new form of a straight line, a linear movement from one place to another. Yet digressions tug constantly at the straight-line narrative, threatening to unpick its threads.

In *Edge of the Orison*, Clare's journey from Essex to Helpston is not merely a walk but a 'frantic pilgrimage', underpinned by anxiety and physical and psychological decay.[140] Although Clare lived at a time when pedestrianism, particularly within England, was experiencing a new vogue—partly a response to the perceived dangers of continental Europe after the French Revolution and the consequent decline of the 'Grand Tour'—his own flight from Essex was hardly a touristic, aesthetic choice. Clare was no aristocratic *voyageur* but rather, as W.G. Hoskins has observed, 'the great exception, an articulate peasant', and his decision to walk was neither whimsical frippery nor the 'radical assertion of autonomy' that Robin Jarvis discusses in *Romantic Writing and Pedestrian Travel*, which offered other

---

[137] Ibid., pp.5–6. [138] Ibid., p.8. [139] Ibid., p.142. [140] Ibid., p.122.

writers freedom 'from a culturally defined and circumscribed self'.[141] As a victim of parliamentary enclosure, displacement, and ultimately institutional confinement, Clare was not dallying with the dangers of 'social deviance or class non-conformism' but was subject to the powerful and repressive pressures generated by capital and state power.[142]

Writing in *The Country and the City*, Raymond Williams saw in Clare 'the culmination, in broken genius, of the movement which we can trace from a century before him: the separation of Nature from the facts of the labour that is creating it, and then the breaking of nature, in altered and now intolerable relations between men'.[143] It is clear that the elective affinity Sinclair establishes with Clare—in spite of the privilege inherent in its being only elective—responds to this sense of separateness, isolation, and disorientation. He notes that their names share a common root: 'John Clare' forming an anglicization of the Welsh 'Iain Sinclair'. And the characterization of Clare as 'self-appointed laureate of a corner of disputed land' might just as well be directed at himself in East London.[144] Sinclair chooses to see himself in Clare's shadow, just as Clare figured himself to be 'swimming' in his own shadow, establishing a chain of mental unrest that elides with the reorganisation of land and property instituted by enclosure.

Marshalling Clare's work as a prompt to his own, Sinclair's subjective free association now mirrors Clare's own unpunctuated, stream-of-consciousness account of his flight from High Beach to Northamptonshire: its denotative, documentary style and its 'chilling' mid-sentence end, which finds Clare writing:

> July 24th 1841 Returned home out of Essex and found no Mary – her family are as nothing to me now though she herself was once dearest of all – 'and how can I forget'[145]

'Obliged to clerk the specifics of place', Sinclair continues, here applying his familiar language of accountancy and obsessive compulsion to Clare, 'at whatever cost he must transcribe the natural history of nowhere'.[146] Clare's psychological deterioration also allows Sinclair to pick up on the themes of hollowness rehearsed earlier in relation to the M25 and the Millennium Dome—'the portraits and life masks of John Clare', he remarks, 'confirm an absence. They reflect a person who is no longer there.'[147]

---

[141] W.G. Hoskins, *The Making of the English Landscape* (Toller Fratrum: Little Toller, 2013), p.178; Robin Jarvis, *Romantic Writing and Pedestrian Travel* (Basingstoke: Macmillan, 1997), p.28.
[142] Ibid., p.36.   [143] Williams, *The Country and the City*, p.141.
[144] Sinclair, *Edge of the Orison*, p.90.
[145] John Clare, in Eric Robinson (ed.) *John Clare's Autobiographical Writings* (Oxford: Oxford University Press, 1983), p.160.
[146] Sinclair, *Edge of the Orison*, p.90.   [147] Ibid., p.122.

'Orison' in itself suggests a development of the idea of margins and an endpoint that is constantly receding. This is a perverse parallel to the politics Sinclair later described in *Ghost Milk*, where 'the New Labour era was about a remorseless push towards a horizon that must, of necessity, remain out of reach: the next big idea'.[148] In a solitary quotation from John Barrell's 1972 study *The Idea of Landscape and the Sense of Place*, he notes that 'the horizon, according to Barrell, is "at once the climax and the starting point of the composition"'—an idea that Barrell in fact credits to the art historian T.J. Clark.[149] For Sinclair, this idea of the horizon, which Barrell characterizes as the sense of a dynamic, simultaneous multiplicity of overlapping impressions, is key to the poetic that he sees as being shared between Clare and the Olsonian school that he subscribes to:

> Contemporary poets reiterate Clare's experience: and in doing so discover themselves. Myth becomes truth. Modernist 'open field poetics', as proposed by Charles Olson, defy the system of enclosures placed on language by formalist reactionaries. Rip out hedges, prohibitions, for a method of reading the world from horizon to horizon. No ceilings in time. No knowledge that may not be accessed and inserted.[150]

As Sinclair observes elsewhere, forging a similar connection between Clare and twentieth-century American writers, Clare's prose is continually 'racing ahead of itself in accordance with the (future) Kerouacian recipe for composition: first thought, best thought.'[151]

The view here aligns with that of Eric Robinson, editor of the 1983 edition of *John Clare's Autobiographical Writings*, that 'the skies of the fens always overshadowed' Clare and that 'there is no other writer from whom one gets a better sense of an unbroken horizon or of the scarlet flames of sunrise and sunset'.[152] On the other hand, the abstract notion of the 'open field' is at marked and deliberate odds with the actual woe caused by enclosure, which saw Clare's native Northamptonshire riven and rearranged, restructured for economic gain as part of the agricultural 'improvements in the management and use of land' of his age—a process described in detail by John Barrell. For Sinclair, 159 years later, this activity finds its parallel in the vortex of property speculation that he discovers on the trip from Essex to Northampton and which institutes a similar violence on language's ability to signify: 'civic signs are traduced by the pseudo destinations of developers, locations become locations only when they have been rechristened'.[153]

---

[148] Sinclair, *Ghost Milk*, p.148.
[149] John Barrell, *The Idea of Landscape and the Sense of Place, 1730–1840: An Approach to the Poetry of John Clare* (Cambridge: Cambridge University Press, 1980), p.18.
[150] Sinclair, *Edge of the Orison*, p.278.   [151] Ibid., p.79.
[152] Robinson, *John Clare's Autobiographical Writings*, p.x.
[153] Sinclair, *Edge of the Orison*, p.137.

The sense of the horizon here is actually at odds with Barrell's, who, in spite of the lines quoted by Sinclair, in fact goes on to characterize Clare's poetic method as a kind of short-sightedness, a resilient and obstinate localism, and an almost obsessive particularity. The poet's method was wrapped up in 'the concreteness of Clare's experience and its incapacity for being abstracted'.[154] To leave Helpston was, for Clare, to go 'out of his knowledge', and his eye for detail was such that he struggled to effectively render distance in his poetry. Clare was so trained to the local that, Barrell points out, it is as though he

> is happy to look into the distance only if it is empty, if there is nothing there, and if there is a thing there, it destroys for Clare the illusion of space and depth, because it makes him want to examine it, in its particularity and detail, and thus he focuses on it too sharply.[155]

This technique means that Clare's style frustrates the conventions of the picturesque, the 'orderly, Claudian composition'.[156] It is as if, in photographic terms, he suffered from an inability to manipulate depth of field, producing a compulsive requirement for detail that mirrors Sinclair's inescapable need to always complete one more walk. For Barrell, Clare's comparative lack of mobility was integral to this limitation, and he contrasts Clare with the 'more mobile writers, James Tyley and James Thomson' (the 1700-born author of *The Seasons* rather than his nineteenth-century namesake) in this respect. The rise in mobility—both of people and artworks—and the growth of an agricultural middle class fuelled the development of the picturesque, which itself hinged on 'a comparison of scene with scene' (as Wordsworth put it in *The Prelude*), but it was precisely Clare's *immobility* that set his 'sense of place' against the prevailing 'idea of landscape' in the late eighteenth and early nineteenth centuries.[157]

Sinclair's Elective Affinities: A Landscape of Duplicates

These issues of mobility meant that, for Clare, the trip from Essex to Northamptonshire was conducted beyond the frontiers of knowledge. This lines up conveniently with Sinclair's own well-practised cultivation of a frontier aesthetic where 'off the map' territory is met with 'psychosis' in the experiencing subject. And, in turn, it parallels the aesthetic cultivation of the uncultivated that Clare and contemporary enthusiasts of the picturesque inherited from earlier

---

[154] Barrell, *The Idea of Landscape*, p.184. [155] Ibid., pp.145–6. [156] Ibid., p.136.
[157] Ibid., p.63; Wordsworth, *The Prelude* (1805), XI.158, in *The Prelude: 1799, 1805, 1850*, eds. Jonathan Wordsworth, M.H. Abrams, and Stephen Gill (New York: Norton, 1979).

theorists of the sublime like Kant and Burke.[158] Yet in light of Clare's attachment to such a slim 'corner' of England, it is curious that Sinclair should determine mobility itself as his epitaph—'the ghost walk', he declares, is 'his true memorial'.[159] Though this echoes the 'floating autobiography' of David Rodinsky, there is also a burgeoning sense that the real epitaph is Sinclair's own.

This is elaborated when Sinclair begins to elide Clare's physicality with the landscape itself, declaring of the Great North Road (running roughly from Sinclair's home in Hackney through Clare's Helpston and on to York and Edinburgh) that 'the road was his spine'.[160] Here place and personality are both territories to be colonized by the speculative writer-explorer, occupying the space of others. The activity also provides more evidence of the way that Sinclair's subjectivity washes other artists' work with the colour of his own concerns. The blood metaphor of *London Orbital* recurs—Sinclair's sight of a man 'dressed in ragged but respectable clothes' is read as one of 'the robotic, disenfranchised walkers who keep the arteries of the city open'.[161] The association of walking with despair is refracted through the scenery, here called 'obscenery', picking up on the term deployed in *Liquid City* in order to describe a landscape swamped by the bland architecture of Travelodge and Ibis hotels.[162]

In Clare's own movements, the idea of the 'fugue' is developed and turned inwards—in his attempt at 'escape from Essex', Clare '*lost himself*'. His landscape, for Sinclair, radiates this sense: Northborough, where the Clare family moved after leaving Helpston in 1832,

> is heavy with absence; of all the cemetery villages encountered on our walk out of Essex, this is the paradigm. Internal exile as a prelude to the Big Sleep.[163]

Steeped in melancholy, these lines allude to the problem suffered by Clare on his own move to Northborough and the enclosure of his native village of Helpston: his state of being 'homeless at home'. As Barrell contends, the enclosure generated not only a real, psychic disorientation in Clare but also a literary and formal one: he was 'so thoroughly dependent in these poems on that tradition of the poetry of melancholy which opposes the permanence of nature to the transience of youth' that the shifting arrangement of his native village left him peculiarly unmoored.[164] His gradual drift away from punctuation and metre paves the way for the stream-of-consciousness text of the fragmentary 'Journey out of Essex' that fuels Sinclair's own expedition.

Recreating Clare's walk, Sinclair refers to the approach to Helpston as 'the meeting with Clare that we have been soliciting for three days, but which we have

---

[158] Ibid., p.62.　[159] Sinclair, *Edge of the Orison*, p.27.　[160] Ibid., p.213.
[161] Ibid., p.105.　[162] Ibid., p.135.　[163] Ibid., p.70.　[164] Ibid., p.112.

done everything in our power to postpone'.[165] Arriving there, having seen the portrait of Clare's cottage in Bill Brandt's 1951 book *Literary Britain* (where it is printed alongside a stanza of his long poem *The Village Minstrel*), he discovers in the real thing merely 'a whitewashed replica'—simple 'real estate'.[166] His frustration is clearly pitched around an unsatisfied desire for authenticity. Referring to the biographer Richard Holmes's writings on Shelley, Sinclair intones that 'what we want is a way of hiding the poetry, that difficulty, so we trade in the fiction of biography; selective quotation dresses a dramatic life'.[167] Yet his response is bound up with the desire for difference, just as the 'picturesque' absorbed the uncultivated and uncivilized into itself: as Jarvis points out, 'the term designates with a certain semiotic knowingness the discovery of essential otherness'.[168]

For Sinclair, the touristic exploitation of Helpston as a holiday destination misses the flipside of Clare's 'indigenous eye'—the way in which place was also a prison.[169] Sinclair writes of the Northampton library where Clare's papers are stored that

> The municipal shrine is a secondary imprisonment, keeping the poet in Northampton, along with his papers, his much-prized library. Patty cleared the shelves. The books travelled, as he did, into definitive exile.[170]

As Barrell confirms:

> It seems that the more he came to know of what lay outside the parish, the more he understood that his existence as a writer depended on his remaining within the area that he knew, and writing about that only [...] the desire to write 'locally', to make the individuality of Helpston the content of his poems, was not the product of an unambiguous love which Clare felt for the place.[171]

These themes, of an intense and even morbid or psychotic attachment to place, lapse into the idea of a dangerous immersion in one's chosen medium—crucial to the supposed authenticity of Clare's own prose account of his flight. Revisiting one of the subjects of *Lud Heat*, Sinclair refers to the avant-garde 1960s film-maker Stan Brakhage, who 'developed cancer from the dye in film; from painting directly on to emulsion, years of intimate handling: scratching, smearing, licking'.[172] This image of sickness is crucial: just as London's periphery is 'infected by nightmares in asylums and hospitals', Sinclair writes of Clare that 'his melancholy was a potent infection'.[173]

---

[165] Ibid., p.23. [166] Ibid., p.42. [167] Ibid., p.208. [168] Ibid., p.51.
[169] Ibid., p.27. [170] Ibid., p.219. [171] Barrell, *The Idea of Landscape*, p.123.
[172] Sinclair, *Edge of the Orison*, p.167. [173] Ibid., p.5; p.211.

The Torpid Landscape of the Fens: Walt Disney and Walter Benjamin

Dragged further into the Cambridgeshire fens in the search for his wife's ancestors, Sinclair's journey exceeds Clare's and launches into 'this melancholy land'.[174] 'Melancholia', he writes, 'drifts through the Fens like clammy autumn mists.'[175] The region, which also provides the rainswept closing location of Chris Petit's 1993 novel *Robinson*, is on the one hand his wife's family's 'own turf'; on the other, Sinclair's established practice requires that it be estranged and demonized as an unnerving frontier—hence the unconventional approach to Peterborough made by hired narrowboat along the 'vitreous carpet' of the River Nene.[176] On this journey, depicted in a forlorn light, Fotheringay, a village caught up in Peterborough's despondent solar system, is declared by Sinclair's wife as the 'saddest place in England', 'a landscape in mourning'; an earth mound there is described as 'incubated melancholy'.[177] Stilton, Werringham, Whittlesey are all brushed with the same saddened glaze.

Sinclair reserves much of what Patrick Wright has called the 'acid negativity' of his prose for Peterborough itself, discovering in it a miniature of the London from which he has flown.[178] Even its outline on the map suggests to him a version of Hackney 'cut loose, transported into a planners' wilderness, with no proximate boroughs, no Islington or Bethnal Green, to temper its supernatural malignancy'.[179] At one point, a hill is compared with the Beckton Alp, and, as Sinclair points out, Peterborough has its own orbital motorway, having 'spun from its entrails a network of ring roads, roundabouts, underpasses, and retail parks designed to confuse motorists'.[180] The city's Queensgate Centre, 'a retail labyrinth' of chain-stores and fast-food buffets, anaesthetizes an idiot public with 'remorseless good times'.[181] Discounted copies of J.G. Ballard's *Millennium People* lie unsold outside one of its shops like some wantonly ignored gospel, eliciting an embittered assertion that the locals, fed up on all-you-can-eat Chinese buffets, 'are not agile enough to bend down and check the price ticket'.[182] In the context of Sinclair's lionization of Ballard, the criticism is biting. Cutting through the shopping centre's promotional material describing 'a relaxed environment', Sinclair declares it 'an arcade project owing more to Walt Disney than Walter Benjamin'—a description that clearly pleased him, since he used it again in *Ghost Milk* to describe Berlin's Sony Centre (characterized as 'a collaboration between the two Walts, Disney and Benjamin').[183]

---

[174] Ibid., p.330. [175] Ibid., p.270. [176] Ibid., p.328; p.309. [177] Ibid., p.350; p.352.
[178] Patrick Wright, 'Downriver: From the Far Side of the Thames Estuary', Literary London Society Seminar 14 April 2015.
[179] Sinclair, *Edge of the Orison*, p.14. [180] Ibid., p.13. [181] Ibid., p.279. [182] Ibid.
[183] Ibid, p. 278; Sinclair, *Ghost Milk*, p.347.

In one sense, as he compares Peterborough to London and the Queensgate Centre to anaesthetic shopping centres in general, Sinclair's narrative technique here sees him become a perverse parallel of the picturesque tourist, for whom (as Barrell claims) '*a* landscape was fitted into *the* established set of landscape patterns, and so became part of the *universal* landscape, which included any tract of land the connoisseur chose to examine'.[184] That is, he has slipped into a habituated way of seeing. Yet for Barrell, the traveller's application of 'picturesque rules' to a landscape was bound up with the aesthetic cultivation of the uncultivated, a kind of colonizing, demystifying process; Sinclair's contrasting desire to see Peterborough in terms of other places' negative rather than positive qualities makes his activities a profane mirror of the picturesque traveller's implicitly civilizing mission.

At the same time, the architectural and atmospheric homogeneity of structures like the Queensgate Centre, the result of mass consumer culture, is precisely the point—that they foster in the tourist-shopper something parallel to Clare's disorientation. Acting with the same rationalizing vigour as the practice of enclosure itself, they shatter and frustrate the local and the particular so that everywhere seems merely to be a duplicate of everywhere else. The Ibis hotel chain is a case in point: these are first characterized as 'forty-four hotels in places you'd rather not be', occupied by 'bemused transients' reminiscent of the glazed commuters of *Lights Out* or the motorists of *London Orbital*.[185] Later, Sinclair observes that 'an hotel Ibis is singular and universal, somewhere and everywhere, customised oddity, generic virtue'.[186] It is apt to this description that Sinclair's repetition of the Walt Disney/Walter Benjamin pun in *Ghost Milk* comes alongside a comment that in the Sony Centre's 'shuffling tourist mob you do not experience reality, you experience a facsimile of experience'.[187] In the landscapes of contemporary commerce, 'Sony' and 'Queensgate' are just the empty markers required to distinguish between fundamentally indistinctive spaces.

Later, drawing on his taste for coincidences as well as the way that Peterborough, his wife's hometown, is rendered as a strange double of Hackney, Sinclair makes the odd remark that 'if Anna was lost and I had to search for a duplicate, I'd launch my search in Peterborough'.[188] Taking up this theme of duplication and simulacra, which seems to have unmoored itself from its original emergence in the repetition of chain shops and amenities and drifted into the space of human identities, he later misinterprets a memorial to 'James Stewart' as being meant for the actor and star of Hitchcock's *Vertigo*. The sequence then lurches from this accidental, creative misreading into a contention of the subjectivity of all readings of place: 'we remember what we want to and forge our own autobiographies. The Clare I found will not be your John Clare, not the poet

---

[184] Barrell, *The Idea of Landscape*, p.7. [185] Sinclair, *Edge of the Orison*, p.153.
[186] Ibid., p.217.   [187] Sinclair, *Ghost Milk*, p.350.   [188] Ibid., p.65.

Geoffrey Hadman [an ancestor of his wife] claimed as relative.'[189] If these comments reveal that 'the abiding note of the contemporary pastoral [...] is melancholic'—as Martin puts it—they also reveal it to be highly involuted, echoing Sinclair's insistent remark that 'Patrick Keiller's London is not *your* London' in *Lights Out*.[190]

Sinclair's insistence on the incommensurability of individual memory and experience forms a reaction against the banal, depersonalized quality of spaces such as the Queensgate Centre. At the same time, Sinclair's work increasingly seems to be haunted by nothing so much as itself (as the Walt Disney/Walter Benjamin repetition implies), with *Edge of the Orison* looping back to resonances developed in earlier writings. The presence of nearby Bedford precipitates a discussion of John Bunyan's 'pedestrian parable' *The Pilgrim's Progress* (1678), a text not mentioned since the epigraph to *Lud Heat* in 1975.[191] Elsewhere, noting the bookshop in Stamford that featured in the opening scenes of *White Chappell, Scarlet Tracings*, he elides his own journeys with that of Clare by imagining the latter in a coach that 'overtakes a stalled Volvo in which reprints of his books are so much ballast, among sacks of provincial trufflings that will be traded in London markets'.[192] Here Sinclair's journeys through landscape fold back on themselves in imaginative palimpsest.

As the text goes on, Sinclair's thoughts on Clare, landscape, and his own project modulate into a meditation on the inadequacy of all grand schemes: insisting on this text's situation as a 'final' chapter in Sinclair's oeuvre even if it has since been followed by several other works. *Edge of the Orison* processes this by taking up the modernist trope of formal circularity, recalling texts like James Joyce's *Finnegans Wake*. Joyce is certainly present in the text: the chapter title 'Salt Green Death', for example, is an allusion to *Ulysses*, and the phrase 'forge our own autobiographies' could also be a subtle reference to the final lines of Joyce's *Portrait of the Artist as a Young Man* and Stephen Dedalus's resolution 'to forge in the smithy of my soul the uncreated conscience of my race'.[193] Such a connection makes sense within this topographical focus, given that Lucia Joyce (James's daughter) features regularly in *Edge of the Orison*, having been consigned to the same hospital—the Northamptonshire General Lunatic Asylum—that John Clare was removed to after his return home and where he spent the last two decades of his life. Samuel Beckett, himself a distant relative of Sinclair, would visit her there.

The emphasis on individual subjectivity accounts for the shift to Sinclair's much more modest proposal that 'forging' conscience or biography can only be valid for a single person, much less a 'race'. But the trope of closing a work with the keynote of its own conception is crucial. As the final chapter begins, Sinclair

---

[189] Ibid, p.362. [190] Martin, *Noise, Neoliberalism and the Matter of London*, p.177.
[191] Sinclair, *Edge of the Orison*, p.294. [192] Ibid., p.96.
[193] James Joyce, *A Portrait of the Artist as a Young Man* (London: Penguin, 2000), p.276.

remarks that 'now, crossing the main street at Stilton, we felt a pressure lifted. The materials for the Clare book were in place, I could start a primitive assembly.'[194] As he writes later:

> James Joyce (always) and Beckett (at the beginning) constructed their works by a process of grafting, editing: quotations, submerged whispers. Correspondences.[195]

If it is true, as Martin writes, that the 'problem confronting every reader of Sinclair' is 'the sense of their own belatedness' and that his methodology owes something to the Freudian concept of *Nachträglichkeit*, then the appearance of Joyce's circular text here points us back to the problematic irresolution of the narrative issues provoked by the M25. The theme recurs through a visit to Little Gidding, which gave its name to one of Eliot's *Four Quartets* and the notion that 'In my end is my beginning'. In Sinclair's rendition, these ideas feed into his grander scheme, where the re-enactment of losing the plot becomes a means to dramatize the rediscovery of narrative, this time via the distinctive modernist trope of the work that is about the process of its own creation.

Richard Mabey might have disparaged those who cannot travel to Helpston without Clare as a model, but, by accommodating the Northamptonshire peasant-poet into his own system, Sinclair effectively uses *Edge of the Orison* to perform the dissolution of psychology and personality and its entanglement with the destruction, or re-arrangement, of landscape. The quest for 'authenticity' creates its own dilemmas, but it is nevertheless a fitting closure for the arc of pedestrian disorientation described by Sinclair's documentary rambles. Negotiating the competing 'energy fields' of place, the always incomplete map of memory, the attractions and antagonisms of space and psychology, Sinclair's work continually regenerates itself as an unfinishable project, a fact attested by the scale of his work since *Edge of the Orison* and its constant revolutions around the same localities and themes. As it does so, narrative and identity are caught in the vortex, perpetually dissolved and reconstructed.

Opening and Closing the Loop: Sinclair's Later Work

Pedestrianism does not modulate so profoundly in Sinclair's later work. By 2015's *London Overground*, walking is rendered 'merely a device on which to hang anecdotes and observations'—a reversal of Mabey's injunction.[196] *Ghost Milk* alone is notable for some useful statements and clarifications on the theme of

---

[194] Sinclair, *Edge of the Orison*, p.350.   [195] Ibid., p.234.
[196] Sinclair, *London Overground: A Day's Walk Around the Ginger Line* (London: Hamish Hamilton, 2015), p.47.

CROSSES, CIRCLES, AND MADNESS   269

pedestrian locomotion. Here Sinclair lauds the 'energies' of walking—contrasting the original philanthropic development of the Hackney Marshes with their ruthless subordination to the whims of the London 2012 Olympic project. 'The vertical thrust of a single structure, dominating place by overlooking it' here represents a cynical exploitation of place that is countered by the 'horizontal energies' of the pedestrian, 'which are always democratic, free-flowing, uncontained'.[197] However pre-emptive, this text also offers some kind of closure on Sinclair's own career. Just as Sinclair uses the Olympics to see London through the prism of other notable Olympic cities (1936 Berlin, 2008 Beijing, and Athens in perpetuity) the writer figures himself as closing the book on 'my own grand project', charting the sale of his own papers to the Harry Ransom Center in Texas—from 'a tin box in Whitechapel' to the 'tabula rasa' of this pristine archive facility, 'bereft of ghosts'.[198]

The close of *Ghost Milk*, amid endless shelving stacked in 'avenues that slide open at the touch of a sensor', hones in on a speck of dirt that falls out of an old notebook.[199] It might be 'processed, made safe', but it remains potentially disruptive, a force for accident and chance within this perfectly ordered system: 'a residue of the Lower Lea Valley. Of the Stratford railway sheds.'[200] Yet with the Stratford landscape about to be smothered by the Westfield shopping centre complex and the Olympic Park, the original too is on the cusp of effacement. Reality has caught up with Sinclair's simulation: 'I longed to rub the grains into my skin, to snort the essence of Chobham. The incident was such a neat conclusion, it framed a narrative.'[201]

In Niall Martin's argument that the introduction of the 'noise' of the local into the circuit of interchangeable non-places is essential to Sinclair's own project, the goal is the production of the 'disagreement' necessary for political thought to take place—a case influenced by the philosopher and historian Jacques Rancière's study *Disagreement: Politics as Philosophy* (1999). This is a convincing argument, but the scene in *Ghost Milk* re-enacts a more subtle element in Sinclair's depiction of the interactions between landscape and subjectivity. The transfer of his papers to the Harry Ransom Center is not the *achievement* of any 'grand project' but the meeting of an ever-expanding, unfinishable project with the Rodinsky-esque 'Great Work' of self-effacement; the abracadabra man's disappearing act. The laureate of place does not offer a solution, but simply vanishes.

Linking the storage of his own papers with his discovery of Ballard's archive, Sinclair calls the Texan facility a 'word hoard for future scholars'.[202] Rejuvenating a kenning from the Old English poem *Beowulf* in a tacit performance of his panoramic literariness, this sequence illustrates how the significant energies of Sinclair's own language are ultimately powerless against the forces determining

---

[197] Sinclair, *Ghost Milk*, p.103.   [198] Ibid., p.392.   [199] Ibid., p.394.   [200] Ibid., p.397.
[201] Ibid., p.397.   [202] Ibid., p.393.

270 LANDSCAPE AND SUBJECTIVITY

contemporary space and place. The downbeat sense of closure at the Harry Ransom Center replicates an earlier scene where, forced to take a position on what a writer can do in the face of savage changes to his environment, Sinclair retreats to the idea that *recording* is the only thing possible:

> People came up to me afterwards, none of them British, exiles living in Hackney, Tottenham, Walthamstow, with versions of the same question. 'What can we do?' 'How can we stop it?'
>
> 'Nothing', I said. 'The fix is in and it goes all the way. Bear witness. Record and remember.'[203]

In these ways, *Ghost Milk* plays out the idea in *Edge of the Orison* that 'writers begin with discovery, discovering their subject matter, marking out their own turf. And finish with dissolution. Learning to suppress conditioned reflexes. Learning to forget. Arranging for their own disappearance.'[204] The disruptive potential of the walk as an intervention into social space, set against a quieter urge to simply bear witness and record, is here inscribed by the physical and psychological frailty of the experiencing and narrating subject. Lapsing again into a correspondence between the effacement of place and the effacement of the self, Sinclair's own 'grand project' ultimately grinds to a halt. At this pre-eminent site of memory, the twin archives of self and place are swallowed up as a single unit.

Since this moment of closure, Sinclair's output has nevertheless continued apace. His more recent interventions have included a text on W.G. Sebald that has taken various forms: beginning as a limited edition pamphlet excised from 2014's *American Smoke: Journeys to the End of the Light* due to its having been thematically at odds with the rest of the volume, 'Austerlitz and After: Tracking Sebald' appeared in 2013 (shortly before publication of *American Smoke* itself). An adapted version went to press in a more widely available form within 2017's *The Last London: True Fictions from an Unreal City*.

Anticipated by a chance discovery of a copy of *Austerlitz* floating in the Regent's Canal, Sinclair's chapter on Sebald begins with an apparently unconnected set of observations; as the scene resolves into a view from the mezzanine level of Liverpool Street Station, familiar tropes soon resurface. 'Take care to avoid the bronzed Kindertransport models', Sinclair warns of the 'official' commemorative statues,

> dwarfish aliens with empty suitcases. Sentiment betrays memory. Contemplate the scuttling dance of inky figures on a ballroom floor: the retail concourse of Liverpool Street Station.[205]

Here we find the distaste for mnemonic 'prompts' of any sanctioned kind; here too the outline of the 'inky figures' of shopper-commuters that reprise the

---

[203] Ibid., p.144.   [204] Ibid., p.8.
[205] Sinclair, *The Last London: True Fictions from an Unreal City*, pp.47–48.

'retail undead' of Bluewater shopping centre in *London Orbital*—now with the addition of mobile technologies so that they move about 'Heads down, eyes in their hands [...] a lowly manifestation of the human soup'.[206] Contemporary Liverpool Street in Sinclair's depiction is a surveilled, corporatized space far from its 'carbon-coated' former self, where the writer remembers having done casual work during the time that he also held his bookstall in Camden Passage, Islington (thus drawing us back to the period depicted in *White Chappell, Scarlet Tracings*). Drawing on his reservoir of first-hand experience of the former station, he is able to praise Sebald's description of its earlier incarnation. Though the description of the 'Ladies' Waiting Room' where Austerlitz had his epiphanic moment 'may have been embroidered', Sinclair continues,

> it caught the atmosphere of the pre-development Liverpool Street with preternatural accuracy: a Bluebeard's castle of locked doors, ramps without function, cancelled corridors; spaces in which the lost souls of the city took up residence on hard benches.[207]

The counterweight to his estrangement from the contemporary space, his enthusiasm for this pre-development environment is clear: a playground of speculation for a young writer ready to add imagined rooms behind the 'locked doors'; to supply functions to the ramps and chart the forgotten corridors.

As it goes on, Sinclair's text centres on a meeting and walk with Sebald's friend and 'priest of place', the poet Stephen Watts.[208] As if feeling a need to set out the differences between his own and Sebald's work—as writers 'laying down different maps of the same space'—it includes various reflections back onto Sinclair's own practice.[209] In a discussion of Watts's rucksack—the one whose image appears in *Austerlitz* and which is presented as belonging to the titular character—Sinclair mentions how the photograph sits 'cropped tight' within 'Sebald's generously spaced text'.[210] Here he points to the difference between the German writer's long, meditative sentences and his own crowded, urgent prose style. Walking eastwards with Watts through Spitalfields, across Brick Lane, along Greatorex Street and out towards Austerlitz's house on Alderney Road, Sinclair reflects on near-encounters with Sebald: having been in the same audience as Watts and Sebald for a reading of *The Waste Land* at Wilton's Music Hall, for example, not long before the latter's death. Describing a later memorial event to Sebald held at the same venue, Sinclair pulls on a phrase from the local area to characterize the readers' relation to the deceased author. '"One Well-Known, Yet Unknown": as it says above a waterless drinking fountain on Whitechapel Road.'[211] This is a highly typical moment in Sinclair's recent work, in that it 'quotes' not only from the vicinity but from Sinclair's own writings: this is a phrase that appears gnomic,

---

[206] Ibid., p.48. [207] Ibid., p.49. [208] Ibid., p.56. [209] Ibid., p.54.
[210] Ibid., p.51. [211] Ibid., p.57.

incantatory, in *White Chappell, Scarlet Tracings*. It is typical, too, in the fact that it does not state this connection: instead, the allusion is 'seeded' into his text (to use the term Sinclair deploys to describe Sebald's use of photographs) like a clue or knowing wink.[212]

Further descriptions of St Clements Hospital and Tower Hamlets Cemetery point to even earlier experiences, from the time of Sinclair's days as a gardener, as depicted in *Lud Heat*. Referring to the Tower Hamlets Local History Library on Bancroft Road, Sinclair remembers having 'been given the freedom to rummage through file boxes of pamphlets and cuttings, when I was a gardener looking for information on Hawksmoor's churches.'[213] As it edges forward across well-written territories and sites, this new text is constantly preoccupied with filling in spaces in what Sheppard called the 'intratext' of Sinclair's work. In alluding to *Lud Heat*, this moment points us back to the heroic period of Sinclair's interaction with space and place, a territory of eclectic, arcane enthusiasms and literary verve, richly embroidering the affective experience of writing and reading London: one less preoccupied by 'cancelled' spaces and more interested in the wild accretion of narratives and ideas.

Later, after rubbing quietly against what he sees as 'the cult of managed English melancholy and weekend breaks in moody winter resorts' that indicates a burgeoning 'cultural industry' of Sebald events in Suffolk, Sinclair is found examining a photograph of Sebald in which he holds a copy of Rachel Lichtenstein's *Rodinsky's Whitechapel*.[214] He is brought to reflect on Sebald's home in 'the commuter village of Poringland',

> the inspiration for John Crome's painting *The Poringland Oak* (1818–20); a work which is now to be found in the Tate Britain collection. Crome is frequently credited as the founder of the Norwich School, a group of nineteenth-century artists notable for the elevation of landscape painting as a serious concern: a primary subject of the craftsman's attention, rather than a strategic backdrop against which to show off clothes, property, possessions, dogs and wives.[215]

It is fitting that this comment on the idea of aesthetic representation of landscape 'as a serious concern' should occur here, as if to certify what Sinclair clearly sees as the crucial family resemblance between his own work and that of 'Professor Sebald': the investment in an 'authentic' representation of space and place. Yet his interest in Sebald's biography emphasizes too, almost indirectly, in what this authenticity consists: not merely landscape as the 'subject *of* the craftsman's attention' (my emphasis), but the 'craftsman's attention' *as* the subject in itself. For it is precisely this 'attention'—one that is often obsessive, neurotic, producing a disorientating and provocative 'psychotic geography'—that motivates and energizes Sinclair's practice, fuelling a body of work that bristles with vital energy and in which, finally, 'place is burnished and confirmed'.[216]

---

[212] Ibid., p.60.   [213] Ibid., p.63.   [214] Ibid., p.59.   [215] Ibid., p.61.
[216] Ibid., p.54.

Conclusion

In 1955's *The Making of the English Landscape*, W.G. Hoskins more than once echoed Keats's 'Grecian Urn' in his description of 'the gentle unravished English landscape' visible from the window where he sat, perhaps consciously also echoing the position of Christopher Hussey when he first noticed Uvedale Price's writings on his uncle's bookshelf—the image with which this book began.[1] Hoskins, however, writing a world war and almost three decades after Hussey, went on to note that even wastelands like the 'almost lunar landscape' of sterile industrial ground at St Austell, Cornwall, offered up spectacles 'possessing a profound melancholy beauty'.[2] From the earliest stages of industrialization in the late eighteenth century, he remarked, there was not only a 'discord between the natural beauty of the landscape and what man had done to it' but also a growing recognition 'that an unrestrained industrial landscape has a considerable element of sublimity about it'.[3]

As this book has shown, it is often in places like this that the work of Keiller, Sebald, and Sinclair discovers its most significant moments: not 'natural' beauty spots but rather run-down, peripheral, sometimes seemingly conspiratorial landscapes and townscapes bearing the scars of human enterprise, often located in overlooked parts of cities, 'at the ends of roads', at sites of large-scale redevelopment, or even at extraterrestrial-seeming former military facilities like Orford Ness. In this respect, the spectacle of ruination and decline is central to each of these figures' meditations, bound up with a general tendency towards Svetlana Boym's 'reflective' over 'restorative' nostalgia (a greater interest in the activity of 'longing' itself than in the actual retrieval of any particular lost or forgotten home) and often literally exploring what she characterizes as the 'sideshadows and back alleys...of progress' or at least of the neoliberal consensus.[4]

Connected with this tendency is the way that Keiller, Sebald, and Sinclair's work rubs up against the expectations associated with a 'touristic' approach to space and place. Perhaps inevitably, their work could itself be taken as simply suggesting an alternative set of waypoints for a different kind of tourism. Yet it certainly seems possible to argue that by virtue of its constant suggestion of new networks of significance and memory—subjective networks that interfere and

---

[1] W.G. Hoskins, *The Making of the English Landscape* (Toller Fratrum: Little Toller, 2013), p.272.
[2] Ibid., pp.210–11.   [3] Ibid., p.198.
[4] Svetlana Boym, *The Future of Nostalgia* (NewYork: Basic Books, 2001), p.xvii.

entangle with one another, always shifting and recalibrating—it makes some attempt at resisting this. It is in this way, by positing landscape as a rich texture of significances while also seeking to disrupt the creation (or curation) of a straightforward 'heritage' agenda, that their work can indeed be seen as offering us a *critical* theory of contemporary space and place. It can, at least, be seen as a highly distinctive mode particular to the close of the twentieth century in England, problematizing the 'network' society by constantly creating new networks that are not necessarily rational, ordered, or efficient, but often quite the reverse, and frustrating the idea of the 'non-place' by reasserting *placeness* to a degree that actually threatens to become disorientating, even overwhelming, in itself.

The commonalities between Keiller, Sebald, and Sinclair's work are certainly manifold. They include the foregrounding of contingency and subjective experience, frequently culminating in acute disorientation; the depiction of space as a rich archive of variously obscured and sometimes damaged histories; the problematization of fiction and documentary forms by means of a transgressive 'essayistic' mode, merging visual imagery with written or spoken text by way of 'bricolage' or 'raking' things together; and the telescoping of near and far (or the 'exotic' and the 'homemade') by bringing a circumspect, ironically touristic eye to the humdrum and near-at-hand.

These trends may certainly be read as symptoms of and responses to the uneven experience of globalization and modernity, even what Marc Augé calls 'supermodernity', in England. At the same time, they are variously pointed critiques of that experience: of social and political disaffection under the conditions of neoliberalism and the problems that this brings with it—not least the uneasy sense of 'history' threatening to congeal into an uncritical 'heritage' that was undoubtedly exacerbated by debates surrounding, for instance, the National Trust in the 1980s. The unorthodox curation of space undertaken by Keiller, Sebald, and Sinclair—digging up peripheral figures and texts and making them into central reference points—reacts against stagnation by insisting on the way that canonicity is always a matter of contingency, variability, subjectivity, and even whimsy, evidencing a melancholic attachment to objects, people, and places that nevertheless refuses to objectify the landscape itself.

Situated between the smooth 'flows' and 'circulations' of contemporary logistics and the rough surfaces of first-hand, often pedestrian travel, the work of Keiller, Sebald, and Sinclair occupies an ambivalent, transgressive space somewhere in between these two modes of experience, It celebrates, criticizes, and condemns, often in the same breath, while always insisting on the reading of space as a thickly determined and open-ended texture or archive. The result is the production of the 'loose ends and missing links' hymned by Doreen Massey and, by virtue of constantly tending towards a surfeit or oversupply of information, of a kind of formal roughness that rubs up against the demands of smooth information (and capital) exchange—the 'economy' of form required for the 'economy' of money to run smoothly.[5] At the same time, the balancing of a familiar and a touristic eye discovers in the relationship between landscape and subjectivity a Wordsworthian 'renovating virtue' appropriate to its moment. If, in these three figures' work, such a thing as 'English psychogeography' exists, then this is perhaps its most distinctive feature and achievement.

Other commonalities in these three figures' work are more problematic. Theirs can, for instance, seem like an exclusive field of enquiry, dominated by comparatively privileged white men. The significance of all the 'buried' history of East London in Sinclair and Sebald's work, for example, is not matched by any particular interest in the area's contemporary ethnic and cultural diversity. The trope of the male 'explorer' figure is one that constantly recurs, even if it is problematized in various ways—such as, for instance, the homosexuality of Keiller's characters or the homosocial experiences and horror of the feminine sometimes detectable in Sebald's work. Sinclair's writing, as has been shown here, is perhaps the most notable in its failure to engage critically with the issue of gender. Sinclair's stylized cosmos of ring roads and inner city wheeler-dealers is one that seems to preclude the possibility of convincing female characters. Then again, the stylized character of these depictions is probably the point.

In any case, it seems that these works probably fail to reverse the regressive gender politics of Surrealism's attitude to space and place described in the introduction, or to do anything to combat the idea cited by Yi-Fu Tuan of ruins as 'exclusively male constructions'.[6] Ultimately, these are all texts written from positions of comparative privilege. But if they can sometimes seem elitist, they nevertheless posit space and place as radically open, forming a lively territory within which to engage in cultural enquiry and critique and chipping away at the perceived glaciation of culture and politics. In these ways, they mark a highly significant moment in the representation of English culture to itself at the end of the twentieth century, channeling cultural criticism through the prism of landscape and subjectivity and forcing open new windows on space, place and identity.

---

[5] Doreen Massey, *For Space* (London: Sage, 2005), p.11.
[6] Yi-Fu Tuan, *Topophilia: A Study of Environmental Perceptions, Attitudes and Values* (Englewood Cliffs, NJ: Prentice-Hall, 1974), p.54.

List of Works Cited

Ackroyd, Peter, *Hawksmoor* (London: Penguin, 1985).
Adair, Gilbert, *The Postmodernist Always Rings Twice* (London: Fourth Estate, 1992).
Adorno, Theodor, 'Cultural Criticism and Society', in *Prisms*, trans. Samuel and Sherry Weber (Cambridge, MA: MIT Press, 1967).
Adorno, Theodor, *Minima Moralia: Reflections from Damaged Life*, trans. E.F.N. Jephcott (London: Verso, 2005).
Adorno, Theodor, and Max Horkheimer, *Dialectic of Enlightenment*, ed. Gunzelin Schmid Noerr and trans. Edmund Jephcott (Stanford, CA: Stanford University Press, 2002).
Agamben, Giorgio, *Nudities*, trans. David Kishik and Stefan Pedatella (Stanford, CA: Stanford University Press, 2010).
Anon., *London Psychogeographical Association Newsletter* Nos.1–4 (1993).
Anon., *The Great Conjunction: A Report by the London Psychogeographical Association and the Archaeogeodetic Association* (London: Unpopular Books, 1993).
Anz, Thomas, 'Feuer, Wasser, Steine, Licht', in *Porträt 7: Sebald*, ed. Franz Loquai (Eggingen: Edition Isele, 1997).
Apollinaire, Guillaume, 'L'amphion faux messie', in *L'hérésiarque et Cie* (Paris: Stock, 2003).
Aragon, Louis, *Paris Peasant*, trans. Simon Watson Taylor (London: Cape, 1971).
Aragon, Louis, 'On Décor', in Paul Hammond (ed.), *The Shadow and its Shadow: Surrealist Writings on the Cinema* (San Francisco, CA: City Lights, 2000).
Atkins, Marc, *Liquid City* (London: Reaktion, 1999).
Atlas, James, 'W.G. Sebald: a Profile', *Paris Review* No.151 (Summer 1999).
Atze, Marcel, and Franz Loquai, *Sebald: Lektüren* (Eggingen: Edition Isele, 2005).
Augé, Marc, *Non-Places: An Introduction to Supermodernity*, trans. John Howe (London: Verso, 1995).
Bacon, Jean, and Stuart Bacon, *Dunwich Suffolk* (Marks Tey, Essex: Segment, 1988).
Baker, Phil, 'Psychogeography and the End of London', in Joe Kerr and Andrew Gibson (eds.), *London From Punk to Blair* (London: Reaktion, 2012).
Barrell, John, *The Idea of Landscape and the Sense of Place, 1730–1840: An Approach to the Poetry of John Clare* (Cambridge: Cambridge University Press, 1980).
Barthes, Roland, *Mythologies*, ed. and trans. Annette Lavers (London: Granada, 1973).
Barthes, Roland, 'An Introduction to the Structural Analysis of Narratives', in Susan Sontag (ed.), *A Barthes Reader* (London: Cape, 1982).
Barthes, Roland, *Camera Lucida: Reflections on Photography*, trans. Richard Howard (London: Vintage, 1993).
Barwell, Claire, '*Flanêur* of London', in Ilona Halberstadt (ed.), *Pix* No.2 (London: British Film Institute, 1997).
Baudelaire, Charles, *The Painter of Modern Life and Other Essays*, ed. and trans. Jonathan Maybe (London: Phaidon, 1964).
Baudelaire, Charles, *The Parisian Prowler*, trans. Edward Kaplan (Athens: University of Georgia Press, 1997).

Baudrillard, Jean, 'Simulacra and Simulations', trans. Paul Foss, in Mark Poster (ed.), *Selected Writings* (Cambridge: Polity, 1988).
Baudrillard, Jean, *The Perfect Crime*, trans. Chris Turner (London: Verso, 1996).
Bazin, André, 'Ontology of the Photographic Image', in *What is Cinema? Vol. 1*, trans. Hugh Gray (Berkeley: University of California Press, 1967).
Becher, Bernd, and Hilla Becher, *Tipologie, Typologien, Typologies* (Munich: Schirmer/Mosel, 1990).
Benjamin, Walter, *One-Way Street*, in *Reflections*, ed. Peter Demetz and trans. Edmund Jephcott (New York: Schocken, 1986).
Benjamin, Walter, 'Surrealism: The Last Snapshot of the European Intelligentsia', *Reflections: Essays, Aphorisms, Autobiographical Writings*, ed. Peter Demetz and trans. Edmund Jephcott (New York: Schocken, 1986).
Benjamin, Walter, 'A Little History of Photography', in *Selected Writings Vol. 2: 1927-1934*, ed. Michael Jennings, Howard Eiland, Gary Smith, and Rodney Livingstone, trans. Livingstone (Cambridge, MA: Belknap, 1999).
Benjamin, Walter, *The Arcades Project*, trans. Howard Eiland and Kevin McLaughlin (Cambridge, MA: Belknap, 2002).
Benjamin, Walter, *Illuminations*, ed. Hannah Arendt and trans. Harry Zohn (New York: Schocken, 2007).
Benjamin, Walter, *The Origin of German Tragic Drama*, trans. John Osborne (London: Verso, 2009).
Berger, John, *Selected Essays*, ed. Geoff Dyer (London: Bloomsbury, 2014).
Bigsby, Christopher, *Writers in Conversation* (Norwich: Arthur Miller Centre, 2000).
Blackler, Deane, *Reading W.G. Sebald: Adventure and Disobedience* (Rochester, NY: Camden House, 2007).
Blythe, Ronald, *Akenfield: Portrait of an English Village* (London: Penguin, 2005).
Bohrer, Karl-Heinz, *Ein Bißchen Lust Am Untergang* (Munich: Hanser, 1979).
Bond, Robert, *Iain Sinclair* (Cambridge: Salt, 2005).
Bond, Robert, and Jenny Bavidge (eds.), *City Visions: The Work of Iain Sinclair* (Newcastle upon Tyne: Cambridge Scholars, 2007).
Borges, Jorge Luis, *Labyrinths*, ed. Donald Yates and James Irby (Harmondsworth: Penguin, 1970).
Bowring, Jackie, *A Field Guide to Melancholy* (Harpenden: Oldcastle, 2008).
Boym, Svetlana, *The Future of Nostalgia* (New York: Basic Books, 2001).
Breton, André, *Manifestoes of Surrealism*, trans. Richard Seaver and Helen Lane (Ann Arbor: University of Michigan, 1974).
Breton, André, *Nadja*, trans. Richard Howard (New York: Grove Press, 1994).
Brown, Wendy, 'Resisting Left Melancholy', in *boundary 2* Vol.26, No.3 (Autumn, 1999).
Browne, Thomas, *Major Works*, ed. C.A. Patrides (Harmondsworth: Penguin, 1977).
Bruno, Giuliana, *Atlas of Emotion: Journeys in Art, Architecture and Film* (New York: Verso, 2002).
Buck-Morss, Susan, *The Dialectics of Seeing: Walter Benjamin and the Arcades Project* (Cambridge, MA: MIT Press, 1989).
Burgin, Victor, 'The City in Pieces', in *The Actuality of Walter Benjamin*, eds. Marcus, Laura and Lynda Nead (London: Lawrence and Wishart, 1998).
Burgin, Victor, 'Situational Aesthetics', in Alexander Streitberger (ed.), *Situational Aesthetics: Selected Writings by Victor Burgin* (Leuven: Leuven University Press, 2009).
Burke, Andrew, 'Nation, Landscape and Nostalgia in Patrick Keiller's *Robinson in Space*, in *Historical Materialism* Vol.14, No.1 (2006).

Burton, Robert, *The Anatomy of Melancholy* (New York: New York Review Books, 2001).
Butor, Michel, *Passing Time*, trans. Jean Stewart (London: John Calder, 1965).
Carter, Angela, 'Adventures at the End of Time', *London Review of Books* 7 March 1991 (https://www.lrb.co.uk/v13/n05/angela-carter/adventures-at-the-end-of-time).
Castells, Manuel, *The Rise of the Network Society* (Oxford: Wiley-Blackwell, 2010).
Catling, Joe, and Richard Hibbitt (eds.), *Saturn's Moons: W.G. Sebald: A Handbook* (London: Legenda, 2001).
Celan, Paul, *Paul Celan: Poems*, ed. and trans. Michael Hamburger (Manchester: Carcanet, 1980).
Celan, Paul, *Paul Celan: Die Gedichte*, ed. Barbara Weidemann (Frankfurt: Suhrkamp, 2003).
De Certeau, Michel, *The Practice of Everyday Life*, trans. Stephen Rendall (Berkeley: University of California Press, 1988).
Charles, Prince of Wales, *A Vision of Britain* (London: Doubleday, 1989).
Chtcheglov, Ivan, 'Formulary for a New Urbanism' (1956), trans. Ken Knabb (http://www.bopsecrets.org/SI/Chtcheglov.htm).
Clare, John, *John Clare's Autobiographical Writings*, ed. Eric Robinson (Oxford: Oxford University Press, 1983).
Clark, Kenneth, *Civilisation* (London: John Murray, 2005).
Cohen, Nick, 'Dumping the Poor', *Independent*, 16 January 1994 (http://www.independent.co.uk/news/uk/dumping-the-poor-nick-cohen-unravels-the-homes-for-votes-scandal-engulfing-dame-shirley-porter-and-1407226.html).
Comber, Philippa, *Ariadne's Thread: In Memory of W.G. Sebald* (Norwich: Propolis, 2014).
Conan Doyle, Arthur, 'The Adventure of the Six Napoleons', in *The Return of Sherlock Holmes*, ed. Richard Lancelyn Green (Oxford: Oxford University Press, 1993).
Conan Doyle, Arthur, 'The Adventure of the Norwood Builder', in *The Return of Sherlock Holmes*, ed. Richard Lancelyn Green (Oxford: Oxford University Press, 1993).
Conan Doyle, Arthur, *A Study in Scarlet*, ed. Ed Glinert (London: Penguin, 2001).
Conan Doyle, Arthur, *The Sign of Four*, ed. Ed Glinert (London: Penguin, 2001).
Conan Doyle, Arthur, 'The Adventure of the Red-Headed League', in *The Adventures of Sherlock Holmes*, ed. Richard Lancelyn Green (Oxford: Oxford University Press, 2008).
Cook, Jon (ed.), *After Sebald: Essays and Illuminations* (Full Circle, 2014).
Corrigan, Timothy, *The Essay Film: From Montaigne, After Marker* (Oxford: Oxford University Press, 2011).
Coverley, Merlin, *Psychogeography* (Harpenden: Pocket Essentials, 2006).
Cowley, Jason, 'The New Nature Writing', *Granta* No.102 (Summer 2008).
Cowper, William, *The Task* (London: John Sharpe, 1817).
Curtis, David (ed.), *The Elusive Sign: British Avant-Garde Film & Video 1977–1987* (London: Arts Council, 1987).
Curtis, David, *A History of Artists' Film and Video in Britain* (London: BFI, 2007).
Daniels, Stephen, *Fields of Vision: Landscape Imagery and National Identity in England and the United States* (Cambridge: Polity, 1992).
Daniels, Stephen, 'Paris Envy: Patrick Keiller's *London*.' *History Workshop Journal* No.40 (Autumn 1995).
Danino, Nina, and Michael Mazière (eds.), *The Undercut Reader: Critical Writings on Artists' Film and Video* (London: Wallflower, 2003).
Dante, *Purgatorio*, ed. and trans. John D. Sinclair (London: Oxford University Press, 1971).
Darke, Chris, and Hadba Rashid (eds.), *Chris Marker: A Grin Without A Cat* (London: Whitechapel Gallery, 2014).

Dart, Gregory, 'Daydreaming', in Matthew Beaumont and Gregory Dart (eds.), *Restless Cities* (London: Verso, 2010).
Dave, Paul, 'The Bourgeois Paradigm and Heritage Cinema', *New Left Review* Vol.1, No.224 (July–August 1997).
Dave, Paul, '*Robinson in Ruins*: New Materialism and the Archaeological Imagination', *Radical Philosophy*, No.169 (September/October 2011).
Davies, Mererid Puw, 'On (Not) Reading Wales in W. G. Sebald's *Austerlitz* (2001)', *Oxford German Studies* Vol.47, No.1 (February 2018).
Debord, Guy, 'Theory of the Dérive' (1958), trans. Ken Knabb (http://www.bopsecrets.org/SI/2.derive.htm).
Debord, Guy, *The Society of the Spectacle* (1967), trans. Ken Knabb (http://www.bopsecrets.org/SI/debord/1.htm).
Dickens, Charles, 'Night Walks', in *The Uncommercial Traveller* (New York: Hurd & Haughton, 1873).
Dillon, Brian, *Essayism* (London: Fitzcarraldo Editions, 2017).
Dimendberg, Edward, *Film Noir and the Spaces of Modernity* (Cambridge, MA: Harvard University Press, 2004).
Doré, Gustave, *Doré's London: All 180 Illustrations from London: A Pilgrimage* (Mineola, NY: Dover, 2004).
Downes, Kerry, *Hawksmoor* (London: Thames & Hudson, 1969).
Duff, Kim, *Contemporary British Literature and Urban Space* (New York: Palgrave Macmillan, 2014).
Dun, Aidan, *Vale Royal* (Uppingham: Goldmark, 1995).
Dyer, Geoff, *Working The Room* (Edinburgh: Canongate, 2010).
Evans, T.H., *Llanwddyn and Lake Vyrnwy: Centenary Edition* (DLA Archive).
Farley, Paul, and Michael Symmons Roberts, *Edgelands: Journeys Into England's True Wilderness* (London: Vintage, 2012).
Fest, Joachim, *Inside Hitler's Bunker* (London: Pan Macmillan, 2004).
Fletcher, Geoffrey, *The London Nobody Knows* (London: Penguin, 1962).
Foucault, Michel, 'Fantasia of the Library', in Donald Bouchard (ed.) and Bouchard and Sherry Simon (trans.) *Language, Counter-Memory, Practice: Selected Essays and Interviews* (Ithaca, NY: Cornell University Press, 1977).
Foucault, Michel, 'Of Other Spaces, Heterotopias', in *Architecture, Mouvement, Continuité* No.5 (1984) (https://foucault.info/doc/documents/heterotopia/foucault-heterotopia-en-html).
Freud, Sigmund, *Two Short Accounts of Psychoanalysis*, ed. and trans. James Strachey (London: Penguin, 1970).
Freud, Sigmund, *On Murder, Mourning and Melancholia*, trans. Shaun Whiteside (London: Penguin, 2005).
Fukuyama, Francis, *The End of History and the Last Man* (London: Penguin, 1992).
Gandy, Matthew, 'Marginalia: Aesthetics, Ecology, and Urban Wastelands', *Annals of the Association of American Geographers* Vol.103, No.6 (2013).
Gee, Grant (dir.), *Patience: After Sebald* (SODA: 2012).
Gidal, Peter (ed.), *Structural Film Anthology* (London: BFI, 1976).
Gilmour, Ian, 'Napoleon Was Wrong', *London Review of Books* Vol.15, No.12, 24 June 1993 (https://www.lrb.co.uk/v15/n12/ian-gilmour/napoleon-was-wrong).
Gilpin, William, *Observations on the River Wye and Several Parts of South Wales* (London: R. Blamire, 1792).
Gilroy, Paul, 'A Land of Tea Drinking, Hokey Cokey and Rivers of Blood', *Guardian* 18 April 2008 (https://www.theguardian.com/commentisfree/2008/apr/18/britishidentity.race).

Glass, Ruth, with UCL Centre for Urban Studies, *Aspects of Change* (London: Macgibbon & Kee, 1964).
Gordon, Elizabeth Oke, *The Life and Correspondence of William Buckland* (London: John Murray, 1894).
Gordon, Elizabeth Oke, *Prehistoric London: Its Mounds and Circles* (London: Elliott Stock, 1914).
Görner, Rüdiger, *The Anatomist of Melancholy: Essays in Memory of W.G. Sebald* (Munich: Iudicium, 2003).
Gray, Christopher (ed.), *Leaving the 20th Century: The Incomplete Work of the Situationist International* (London: Rebel Press, 1974).
Gregory-Guilder, Christopher, *Autobiogeography and the Art of Peripatetic Memorialization in Works by W.G. Sebald, Patrick Modiano, Iain Sinclair, Jonathan Raban and William Least Heat-Moon* (unpublished PhD thesis) (University of Sussex, 2005).
Griffiths, Keith, 'Anxious Visions.' *Vertigo* Vol.1, No.4 (1994).
Gropius, Walter, *The Bauhaus Manifesto* (1919) (http://michaellaiskonis.typepad.com/files/bauhaus-manifesto-and-program-walter-gropius-1919.pdf).
Harris, John, *No Voice from the Hall: Early Memories of a Country House Snooper* (London: John Murray, 1998).
Heidegger, Martin, 'Building Dwelling Thinking', in *Poetry, Language, Thought*, trans. Albert Hofstadter (New York: HarperCollins, 1971).
Home, Stewart, *69 Things To Do with a Dead Princess* (Edinburgh: Canongate, 2003).
Hoskins, W.G., *The Making of the English Landscape* (Toller Fratrum: Little Toller, 2013).
Hunting, Penelope, *Broadgate and Liverpool Street Station* (London: Rosehaugh Stanhope Developments, 1991).
Hussey, Christopher, *The Picturesque: Studies in a Point of View* (London: Cass, 1967).
Jackson, Kevin, *The Verbals: Iain Sinclair in Conversation with Kevin Jackson* (Kent: Worple, 2003).
Jacobs, Jane, *The Economy of Cities* (New York: Random House, 1970).
Jarvis, Robin, *Romantic Writing and Pedestrian Travel* (Basingstoke: Macmillan, 1997).
Jones, David, *The Anathemata: Fragments of an Attempted Writing* (London: Faber, 1952).
Joyce, James, *A Portrait of the Artist as a Young Man* (London: Penguin, 2000).
Kardia, Peter (ed.), *Cross Currents: Ten Years of Mixed Media* (London: Royal College of Art, 1984).
Keay, Douglas, Interview with Margaret Thatcher, *Women's Own*, 31 October 1987.
Keiller, Patrick (dir.), *Stonebridge Park* (1981).
Keiller, Patrick, *Drawings, Tape-Slide and Sound* (London: Tate, 1982).
Keiller, Patrick, 'In der Dämmerstunde, Berlin', *Undercut* No.5 (Summer 1982).
Keiller, Patrick (dir.), *Norwood* (1983).
Keiller, Patrick (dir.), *The End* (1986).
Keiller, Patrick (dir.), *Valtos* (1987).
Keiller, Patrick (dir.), *London* (British Film Institute, 1994).
Keiller, Patrick, 'Filming London Obliquely' (1995).
Keiller, Patrick, interview with Anna Price, *Artifice* No.3 (1995).
Keiller, Patrick, 'Photogenie', *Scroope: The Cambridge Architectural Journal* No.8 (1996/7).
Keiller, Patrick, 'Longshots Special: Interview with Robinson', *Time Out*, 8 January 1997.
Keiller, Patrick (dir.), *Robinson in Space* (British Film Institute, 1997).
Keiller, Patrick, interview with John Wrathall, *Blueprint*, February 1999.
Keiller, Patrick, *Robinson in Space, and a Conversation with Patrick Wright* (London: Reaktion, 1999).

Keiller, Patrick, 'Popular Science', in *Landscape*, ed. Anne Gallagher (London: British Council, 2000).
Keiller, Patrick, interview with David Martin-Jones, *Journal of Popular British Cinema* No.5 (2002).
Keiller, Patrick, 'Imaging', in Matthew Beaumont and Gregory Dart (eds.), *Restless Cities* (London: Verso, 2010).
Keiller, Patrick, (dir.), *Robinson in Ruins* (British Film Institute, 2011).
Keiller, Patrick, *The Possibility of Life's Survival on the Planet* (London: Tate, 2012).
Keiller, Patrick, 'On Chris Marker', *Artforum*, January 2013.
Keiller, Patrick, *The View From The Train* (London: Verso, 2013).
Keiller, Patrick, interview with David Anderson in *The White Review*, January 2014 (http://www.thewhitereview.org/feature/interview-with-patrick-keiller/).
Keiller, Patrick, 'Atmosphere, Palimpsest and Other Interpretations of Landscape', in Danino and Mazière (eds.), *The Undercut Reader*.
Keiller, Patrick, 'The Poetic Experience of Townscape and Landscape, and Some Ways of Depicting It', in Danino and Mazière (eds.), *The Undercut Reader*.
Kermode, Frank, *The Sense of an Ending: Studies in the Theory of Fiction* (Oxford: Oxford University Press, 2000).
Kerr, Joe, and Andrew Gibson (eds.), *London from Punk to Blair* (London: Reaktion, 2012).
Kinik, Anthony, 'A Bridge Between Imagination and Reality Must Be Built: Film and Spatial Critique in the Work of Patrick Keiller', *Intermediality: History and Theory of the Arts, Literature and Technologies* No.14 (2009).
Knabb, Ken (ed.), *Situationist International Anthology* (Berkeley, CA: Bureau of Public Secrets, 1981).
Knight, Stephen, *Jack The Ripper: The Final Solution* (London: Chambers Harrap, 1984).
Lefebvre, Henri, *The Production of Space*, trans. Donald Nicholson Smith (Oxford: Blackwell, 1991).
Leroy, Annik, 'In der Dämmerstunde, Berlin', *Le Soir* (Belgium), 25 April 1987.
Leutrat, Jean-Louis, *Last Year at Marienbad*, trans. Paul Hammond (London: BFI, 2000).
Löffler, Sigrid, '"Wildes Denken" Gespräch mit W.G. Sebald', in *Porträt 7: W.G. Sebald*, ed. Franz Loquai (Eggingen: Edition Isele, 1997).
Long, J.J., *W.G. Sebald: Image, Archive, Modernity* (Edinburgh: Edinburgh University Press, 2007).
Luckhurst, Roger, 'The Contemporary London Gothic and the Limits of the "Spectral Turn"', *Textual Practice* Vol.16, No.3 (January 2002).
Mabey, Richard, *The Unofficial Countryside* (Wimborne Minster: Dovecote, 2010).
Macfarlane, Robert, '4x4s Are Killing My Planet', *Guardian*, 4 June 2005 (https://www.theguardian.com/books/2005/jun/04/featuresreviews.guardianreview32).
Martin, Niall, *Iain Sinclair: Noise, Neoliberalism and the Matter of London* (London: Bloomsbury, 2017).
Marx, Karl, *Capital*, trans. Ben Fowkes (London: Penguin, 1990).
Marx, Karl, and Friedrich Engels, *Manifesto of the Communist Party*, trans. Samuel Moore (https://www.marxists.org/archive/marx/works/1848/communist-manifesto/ch01.htm).
Massey, Doreen, *Space, Place and Gender* (Cambridge: Polity, 1994).
Massey, Doreen, *For Space* (London: Sage, 2005).
Massey, Doreen, 'Landscape/Space/Politics: An Essay' (with Keiller, *Robinson in Ruins*).
Mawson, T.H., *The Life and Work of an English Landscape Architect* (London: Batsford, 1927).

Mayer, Robert, 'Not Adaptation but "Drifting": Patrick Keiller, Daniel Defoe, and the Relationship Between Film and Literature', in *Eighteenth-Century Fiction* Vol.16, No.4 (2004).
Mayer, Susanne, 'I Am a Kind', *Die Zeit* 28 July 1989 (http://www.zeit.de/1989/31/i-am-a-kind).
McSmith, Andy, *No Such Thing as Society* (London: Constable, 2010).
Melly, George, *Paris and the Surrealists* (London: Thames and Hudson, 1991).
Mengham, Rob, Richard Lane, and Philip Tew (eds.), *Contemporary British Fiction* (Cambridge: Polity, 2002).
De Montaigne, Michel, *Essays*, trans. J.M. Cohen (London: Penguin, 1993).
Moore, Alan, *From Hell: Being a Melodrama in Sixteen Parts* (London: Knockabout, 2000).
Moretti, Franco, *Atlas of the European Novel* (London: Verso, 1998).
Mulvey, Laura, *Death 24x a Second* (London: Reaktion, 2005).
O'Brien, Harvey, 'The Curious Case of the Kingdom of Shadows: The Transmogrification of Sherlock Holmes in the Cinematic Imagination', in *Sherlock Holmes and Conan Doyle: Multi-Media Afterlives*, ed. Sabine Vanacker and Catherine Wynne (London: Palgrave, 2013).
O'Pray, Michael, Review of *Norwood*, *Monthly Film Bulletin* No.51 (October 1984).
O'Pray, Michael (ed.), *The British Avant-Garde Film, 1926 to 1995: An Anthology of Writings* (Luton: University of Luton Press, 1996).
Osborne, Dora, *Traces of Trauma in W.G. Sebald and Cristoph Ransmayr* (London: Legenda, 2013).
Petit, Chris, *Robinson* (London: Cape, 1993).
Petit, Chris (dir.), *Radio On* (BFI, 2008).
Petit, Chris, and Iain Sinclair (dirs.), *London Orbital* (Illuminations, 2004).
Phippen, Roy, *M25: Travelling Clockwise* (London: Pallas Athene, 2005).
Pichler, Barbara, *Landscapes of the Mind* (Birkbeck, University of London: unpublished MA thesis, 1998).
Plant, Sadie, *The Most Radical Gesture: The Situationist International in a Postmodern Age* (London: Routledge, 1992).
Platt, Lise (ed.), *Searching for Sebald: Photography After W.G. Sebald* (Los Angeles: Institute of Cultural Enquiry, 2006).
Poe, Edgar Allan, *Selected Tales*, ed. David Van Leer (Oxford: Oxford University Press, 2008).
Porter, Roy, *London: A Social History* (London: Penguin, 2000).
Potter, Rachel, 'Culture Vulture: The Testimony of Iain Sinclair's *Downriver*', in *Parataxis: Modernism and Modern Writing* No.5 (1993).
Powell, Emeric, and Michael Pressburger (dirs.), *A Matter of Life and Death* (Rank: 1946).
Priestley, J.B., *An English Journey* (London: Penguin, 1997).
Raban, William (dir.), *Thames Film* (BFI: 1986).
Radden, Jennifer (ed.), *The Nature of Melancholy: From Aristotle to Kristeva* (Oxford: Oxford University Press, 2000).
Rascaroli, Laura, and Ewa Mazierska, *Crossing New Europe: Postmodern Travel and the European Road Movie* (London: Wallflower, 2006).
Rasmussen, Steen Eiler, *London: The Unique City* (London: Jonathan Cape, 1937).
Rees, A.L., *A History of Experimental Film and Video: From the Canonical Avant-Garde to Contemporary British Practice* (Basingstoke: Palgrave Macmillan, 2011).
Resnais, Alain (dir.), *Toute La Memoire du Monde* (1956) (http://www.youtube.com/watch?v=KKvhp6kL4N4).

Resnais, Alain (dir.), *Last Year at Marienbad* (Argos: 1961).
Robbe-Grillet, Alain, *Last Year at Marienbad: A Ciné Novel*, trans. Richard Howard (London: Calder, 1962).
Ross, Kristin, *The Emergence of Social Space: Rimbaud and the Paris Commune* (London: Verso, 2008).
Royle, Nicholas, *The Uncanny* (Manchester: Manchester University Press, 2003).
Rubinstein, W.D., *Capitalism, Culture and Decline in Britain* (London: Routledge, 2002).
Rushdie, Salman, *Imaginary Homelands: Essays and Criticism 1981-1991* (London: Granta, 1992).
Said, Edward, *Orientalism* (London: Penguin, 2003).
Schenk, Hans Georg, *The Mind of the European Romantics* (Oxford: Oxford University Press, 1979).
Schivelbusch, Wolfgang, *Disenchanted Night: The Industrialisation of Light in the Nineteenth Century*, trans. Angela Davies (Oxford: Berg, 1988).
Schütte, Uwe, *W.G. Sebald* (Liverpool: Liverpool University Press, 2018).
Sebald, W.G., *Austerlitz*, trans. Anthea Bell (London: Penguin, 2011).
Sebald, W.G., *The Revival of Myth: A Study of Alfred Döblin's Novels* (unpublished PhD thesis) (Norwich: University of East Anglia, 1973).
Sebald, W.G., *Nach der Natur* (Nördlingen: Franz Greno, 1988).
Sebald, W.G., *Die Ringe des Saturn* (Frankfurt: Fischer,1998).
Sebald, W.G., *The Rings of Saturn*, trans. Michael Hulse (London: Harvill, 1998).
Sebald, W.G., *Die Beschreibung des Unglücks* (Frankfurt: Fischer, 2001).
Sebald, W.G., interview with Maya Jaggi, 'The Last Word', *Guardian* 21 December 2001 (https://www.theguardian.com/education/2001/dec/21/artsandhumanities.highereducation).
Sebald, W.G., interview with Michael Silverblatt, *Bookworm*, KCRW Radio, 6 December 2001 (https://www.youtube.com/watch?v=pSFcTWIg-Pg).
Sebald, W.G., *After Nature*, trans. Michael Hamburger (London: Hamish Hamilton, 2002).
Sebald, W.G., *The Emigrants*, trans. Michael Hulse (London: Random House, 2002).
Sebald, W.G., *Vertigo*, trans. Michael Hulse (London: Random House, 2002).
Sebald, W.G., *On the Natural History of Destruction*, trans. Anthea Bell (London: Penguin, 2004).
Sebald, W.G., *Campo Santo*, trans. Anthea Bell (London: Penguin, 2005).
Sebald, W.G., *Über das Land und das Wasser*, ed. Sven Meyer (Munich: Hanser, 2008).
Sebald, W.G., *Across the Land and the Water: Selected Poems 1964-2001*, ed. and trans. Iain Galbraith (London: Hamish Hamilton, 2011).
Sebald, W.G., *A Place in the Country*, trans. Jo Catling (London: Penguin, 2014).
Sekula, Alan, and Noel Burch (dirs.), *The Forgotten Space* (Doc.Eye Film: 2010).
Sheppard, Robert, *Iain Sinclair* (Tavistock: Northcote House, 2007).
Simmel, Georg, *Simmel On Culture*, ed. David Frisby and Mike Featherstone (London: SAGE, 1997).
Sinclair, Iain, *Back Garden Poems* (London: Albion Village Press, 1970).
Sinclair, Iain, *The Kodak Mantra Diaries* (London: Albion Village Press, 1971).
Sinclair, Iain, *Muscat's Würm* (London: Albion Village Press, 1972).
Sinclair, Iain, *Groucho Positive/Groucho Negative* (London: Albion Village Press, 1973).
Sinclair, Iain, *The Birth Rug* (London: Albion Village Press, 1973).
Sinclair, Iain, *Lud Heat* (London: Albion Village Press, 1975).
Sinclair, Iain, *Brown Clouds: In the Tin Zone, Pendeen, Cornwall, April-May 1977* (Newcastle upon Tyne: Pig Press, 1977).

Sinclair, Iain, 'Monster Doss House', *London Review of Books*, 24 November 1988 (https://www.lrb.co.uk/v10/n21/iain-sinclair/monster-doss-house).
Sinclair, Iain, 'Lady Thatcher's Bastards', *London Review of Books*, 27 February 1992 (https://www.lrb.co.uk/v14/n04/iain-sinclair/lady-thatchers-bastards).
Sinclair, Iain, *Radon Daughters* (London: Granta, 1994).
Sinclair, Iain, 'The Cadaver Club', *London Review of Books* 22 December 1994 (https://www.lrb.co.uk/v16/n24/iain-sinclair/the-cadaver-club).
Sinclair, Iain, 'Diary', *London Review of Books*, 8 June 1995 (https://www.lrb.co.uk/v17/n11/iain-sinclair/diary).
Sinclair, Iain, 'Mysteries of Kings Cross', *London Review of Books*, 5 October 1995 (https://www.lrb.co.uk/v17/n19/iain-sinclair/mysteries-of-kings-cross).
Sinclair, Iain, *Lud Heat and Suicide Bridge* (London: Granta, 1998).
Sinclair, Iain, *Dark Lanthorns* (Uppingham: Goldmark, 1999).
Sinclair, Iain, *Sorry Meniscus: Excursions to the Millennium Dome* (London: Profile, 1999).
Sinclair, Iain, *Lights Out for the Territory: 9 Excursions in the Secret History of London* (London: Penguin, 2003).
Sinclair, Iain, *London Orbital: A Walk around the M25* (London: Penguin, 2003).
Sinclair, Iain, *Downriver (or, The Vessels of Wrath): A Narrative in Twelve Tales* (London: Penguin, 2004).
Sinclair, Iain, *White Chappell, Scarlet Tracings* (London: Penguin, 2004).
Sinclair, Iain, *Edge of the Orison: In the Traces of John Clare's 'Journey out of Essex'* (London: Penguin, 2006).
Sinclair, Iain (ed.), *London: City of Disappearances* (London: Hamish Hamilton, 2006).
Sinclair, Iain, *Ghost Milk: Calling Time on the Grand Project* (London: Hamish Hamilton, 2011).
Sinclair, Iain, *Austerlitz & After: Tracking Sebald* (London: Test Centre, 2013).
Sinclair, Iain, 'Diary', *London Review of Books*, 6 November 2014 (https://www.lrb.co.uk/v36/n21/iain-sinclair/diary).
Sinclair, Iain, *London Overground: A Day's Walk Around the Ginger Line* (London: Hamish Hamilton, 2015).
Sinclair, *The Last London: True Fictions from an Unreal City* (London: Oneworld, 2018).
Sinclair, Iain, and Rachel Lichtenstein, *Rodinsky's Room* (London: Granta, 2000).
Smith, Phil, *On Walking...and Stalking Sebald: A Guide To Going beyond Wandering around Looking At Stuff* (Axminster: Triarchy, 2014).
Smith, Zadie, 'On *Crash*', *New York Review of Books*, 10 July 2014 (http://www.nybooks.com/articles/2014/07/10/on-jg-ballard-crash/).
Solnit, Rebecca, *Wanderlust: A History of Walking* (London: Verso, 2001).
Sontag, Susan, *Under the Sign of Saturn* (New York: Random House, 1981).
Sontag, Susan, 'A Mind in Mourning', *Times Literary Supplement*, 25 February 2000.
Sontag, Susan, *On Photography* (London: Penguin, 2008).
Stallabrass, Julian, *Documentary* (Cambridge, MA: MIT Press, 2013).
Sterne, Laurence, *Tristram Shandy*, ed. Melvin New (London: Penguin, 1985).
Swift, Graham, *Waterland* (London: Picador, 1984).
Taylor, Craig, *Return to Akenfield: Portrait of an English Village in the Twenty-First Century* (London: Granta, 2006).
Thatcher, Margaret 'Speech to the Institute of Socioeconomic Studies', 15 September 1975 (http://www.margaretthatcher.org/document/102769).
Thompson, E.P., 'Time, Work-Discipline and Industrial Capitalism', *Past and Present* No.38 (December 1967).

Thomson, T.R., *A Short History of Cricklade* (Minety, Wilts.: Taylor and Sons, 1946).
Thornley, Andy, *The Crisis of London* (London: Routledge, 1992).
Traverso, Enzo, *Left-Wing Melancholia* (New York: Columbia University Press, 2016).
Tuan, Yi-Fu, *Topophilia: A Study of Environmental Perceptions, Attitudes and Values* (Englewood Cliffs, NJ: Prentice-Hall, 1974).
Uerlings, Herbert (ed.), *Theorie der Romantik* (Stuttgart: Reclam, 2013).
Virilio, Paul, *Bunker Archaeology* (New York: Princeton Architectural Press, 1994).
Wainwright, Oliver, 'How We Made the Millennium Dome', *Guardian*, 7 March 2015 (https://www.theguardian.com/culture/2015/mar/17/how-we-made-the-millennium-dome-richard-rogers).
Walker, Ian, *City Gorged With Dreams: Surrealism and Photography in Interwar Paris* (Manchester: Manchester University Press, 2002).
Walker, Ian, *So Exotic, So Homemade: Surrealism, Englishness and Documentary Photography* (Manchester: Manchester University Press, 2007).
Wallace, Anne, *Walking, Literature, and English Culture: The Origin and Uses of Peripatetic in the Nineteenth Century* (Oxford: Clarendon, 1993).
Warf, Barney, and Santa Arias (eds.), *The Spatial Turn: Interdisciplinary Perspectives* (London: Routledge, 2009).
Webber, Mark (ed.) *Shoot Shoot Shoot: British Avant-Garde Film of the 1960s and 1970s* (London: Lux, 2006).
Whiteread, Rachel, *House* (London: Phaidon, 2000).
Wilhide, Elizabeth, *The Millennium Dome* (London: HarperCollins, 1999).
Williams, Raymond, *Culture and Society 1780–1950* (New York: Columbia University Press, 1959).
Williams, Raymond, *The Country and the City* (Oxford: Oxford University Press, 1975).
Wittkower, Margot and Rudolf Wittkower, *Born Under Saturn: The Character and Conduct of Artists* (New York: New York Review Books, 2007).
Wolfreys, Julian, 'Undoing London or, Urban Haunts: The Fracturing of Representation in the 1990s', in Pamela Gilbert (ed.), *Imagined Londons* (Albany, NY: SUNY Press, 2002).
Woodward, Christopher, *In Ruins* (London: Random House, 2002).
Wordsworth, William, *The Prelude* (1805), in *The Prelude: 1799, 1805, 1850*, eds. Jonathan Wordsworth, M.H. Abrams, and Stephen Gill (New York: Norton, 1979).
Wright, *On Living in an Old Country: The National Past in Contemporary Britain* (Oxford: Oxford University Press, 2009).
Wright, Patrick, 'Wrapped in the Tatters of the Flag', in the *Guardian*, 31 December 1994 (http://www.patrickwright.net/wp-content/uploads/pwright-wrapped-in-the-tatters-of-the-flag-final.pdf).
Wright, Patrick, *A Journey Through Ruins: The Last Days of London* (Oxford: Oxford University Press, 2009).
Zisselsberger, Marcus, *The Undiscover'd Country: W.G. Sebald and the Poetics of Travel* (Rochester, NY: Camden House, 2007).
Zweite, Armin (ed.), *Typologies: Bernd and Hilla Becher* (Cambridge, MA: MIT Press, 2004).

Index

Note: Figures are indicated by an italic "*f*", respectively, following the page number.

For the benefit of digital users, indexed terms that span two pages (e.g., 52–53) may, on occasion, appear on only one of those pages.

Ackroyd, Peter 206–7, 210, 221, 242
Adair, Gilbert 218
Adorno, T.W. 133–4, 219–20
 'Commitment' 132–3
 'Cultural Criticism and Society' 132–3
 Dialectic of Enlightenment 157
 Minima Moralia 101–2, 107, 132–3, 139
Agamben, Giorgio 68–9
Alison, Archibald 104
Allgäu 118–19, 122
Amateurism 6–8, 14–15
Antwerp 166–70, 177
Apollinaire, Guillaume 20, 56
 L'hérésiarque et Cie 21, 52
Aragon, Louis 25, 92
 'On Décor' 47–8
 Paris Peasant 19, 21, 48–9, 109–10, 139, 158–9, 168, 177
Archer, Jeffrey 228–32, 240, 247–8
Artangel 236
Ashmole, Elias 7–8, 194, 228–30
Atget, Eugène 21
Atkins, Marc 226, 228, 228*f*, 240–3, 240*f*
Auerbach, Frank 124–8, 186–7
Augé, Marc 3–4, 17–18, 115, 124–5, 212, 247, 249–50, 274
Austen, Jane 84–5

Bacon, Francis 230
Bacon, Jean and Stuart 148
Baker, Phil 225
Ballard, J.G. 148, 226, 250–1, 265
Baron, Alexander 192
Barrell, John 2–3, 261–4, 266
Barry, Peter 230–1
Barthes, Roland 36–7, 73, 145–6, 186
Bartlett School of Architecture 20
Battersea Power Station 25–6
Baudelaire, Charles 20, 45, 56–7, 59–62, 64, 80
 'Salon of 1846' 63–4
 'Sea Ports' 89
Baudrillard, Jean 9

Bazin, André 47–8
Becher, Bernd and Hilla 23–5
Bechhöfer, Susi 176–7, 188
Beckett, Samuel 177
Beer, Gillian 161–2
Belgium 141–2, 158, 166–70
Benjamin, Walter 51, 57–60, 75, 78–9, 120, 133–4, 137–8, 163, 219–20, 265–6
 Arcades Project 57, 68–9, 90–1, 166, 181–2, 185
 'A Little History of Photography' 47
 One-Way Street 163
 'On Some Motifs in Baudelaire' 45
 Origin of German Tragic Drama 102–3, 148
 'The Storyteller' 11–12
 'Surrealism: The Last Snapshot of the European Intelligentsia' 48–9, 51, 69, 176
 'The Task of the Translator' 135–6, 186
 'Theses on the Philosophy of History' 17–18, 120–3, 157–8
 'The Work of Art in the Age of its Technological Reproducibility' 37, 186
Bergen Belsen 161
Berger, John
 'The Changing View of Man in the Portrait' 99–100, 104–5
 'Mathias Grünewald' 117
Bibliothèque Nationale 32
Bicknell, Laurence 195*f*, 228
Blackpool 88–9, 88*f*
Blackler, Deane 110, 114–15, 148–9, 161–2, 164, 177, 186–7
Blanqui, Auguste 185–6
Blair, Tony 92–3, 248
Bluewater Shopping Centre 250–4
Blythe, Ronald 15–17, 153–7, 164
Bohrer, Karl-Heinz 130
Bombing 56, 112, 119–20, 126–7, 143–4, 172–3, 222, 228
Bond, Robert 192, 198–202, 207, 219–21
Booth, Charles 211–12, 214

Borges, Jorge Luis
  'On Exactitude in Science' 4
  Tlön, Uqbar, Orbis Tertius 144–5
Boym, Svetlana 9, 11, 17, 68, 70–1, 233–4, 258, 273
Brandt, Bill 263–4
Brakhage, Stan 193–4, 223, 264
Breendonk 169–71, 190
Breton, André
  Les Pas Perdus 168
  Manifesto of Surrealism 139, 157
  Nadja 21, 48–9, 96–7, 139, 168, 172
Bricolage 7n.22, 52–3, 134, 274
Brown, Wendy 75
Browne, Thomas 7–8, 141, 144–7, 155, 162–3, 194
  The Garden of Cyrus 145–6
  Hydriotaphia 144–6, 179, 206
  Religo Medici 145
Bruno, Giuliana 7, 42–4, 114
Brussels 166–8
Buck-Morss, Susan 185
Buckminster-Fuller, Richard 86
Buckminsterfullerenes 86, 97, 146
Burch, Noël 80–1
Burgin, Victor 21–2, 36, 183
Burroughs, William 221–2, 224
Burton, Robert 39, 77–8, 147–8
Burwell (Lincolnshire) 172–3
Butor, Michel 113–14, 124, 130–2, 158–9

Cabinet of curiosities 7–8, 58, 146, 173
Campbell, Eddie 212–13*f*
Cardinal, Roger 20–1
Carter, Angela 215
Casanova, Giacomo 163–4
Castells, Manuel 4
Catling, Brian 197–8*f*, 204–5, 209, 240
Celan, Paul 133–4
Céline, Louis-Ferdinand 224, 236
Certeau, Michel de 39, 72, 162–3
Charles, Prince of Wales 65, 68–9, 103, 183–4
Chateaubriand, François-René de 141–3
Chirico, Giorgio de 20, 39, 171
Chtcheglov, Ivan 39, 171
'City Symphony' 52
Clare, John 226–7, 258–65
Clark, Kenneth 10–11
Cliveden 83–5
Comber, Philippa 145, 152
Coetzee, J.M. 149
Conan Doyle, Arthur 40, 57, 75, 83–4, 209–11, 214, 221–2

Conrad, Joseph 137–8, 141–2, 166, 209–10, 214–15, 236
Conservatism 29–30, 44–5, 53–5, 64–7, 74–5, 79–80, 83, 155, 209–10, 219, 228–9
Containerization 80–1
Country houses, *see* Stately homes
Cowper, William 106–7
Cricklade 202
Curtis, David 29–30, 36–7

Daniels, Stephen 15–17, 68–9, 151–2
Dante 163–4
Davies, Mererid Puw 174, 187
Debach 153–4
Debord, Guy 5–6, 26, 237
  'Introduction to a Critique of Urban Geography' 58, 238–9
  'Theory of the Dérive' 22
  Society of the Spectacle 23, 238–9
Dee, John 228–30
Defoe, Daniel
  Journal of the Plague Year 57
  Robinson Crusoe 57, 60–1, 96
  Tour Through the Whole Island of Great Britain 5–6, 70, 74–6, 89–90
Deregulation 9, 74–7, 95
Die Zeit 150, 177
Dillon, Brian 7
Dimendberg, Edward 47
Disraeli, Benjamin 121–3
Döblin, Alfred 109–10
Documentary film 50, 52–3, 68–9
Doré, Gustave 17–18, 66, 121
Downes, Kerry 194, 206–7
Dresden 120
Duff, Kim 232–4
Dürer, Albrecht 117–18, 141, 148
Dun, Aidan 240–1
Dunwich 140–1, 147–8, 163–4
'Dwelling' 8–9, 11–12
Dyer, Geoff 145–6

Eliot, T.S. 63
  Four Quartets 227, 268
  The Waste Land 63, 194–5, 197–8, 234
Elwes, Anneke 81–2
Engels, Friedrich 128–9
'English journey' 71
'Englishness' 11–12, 15–17, 60–1, 70, 79, 81–3, 112–13, 151–7, 164, 174
'Essayism' 6–7, 36–7, 60, 107, 114–16, 137–9, 228
'Essay film' 52
Evelyn, John 7–8, 58, 146, 152

Farley, Paul 9
Fletcher, Geoffrey 68
Fortifications 169–71, 186
Foucault, Michel
 'Fantasia of the Library' 7–8
 'Of Other Spaces' 39
Fragmentation 55–6, 74, 81
Freud, Sigmund 10–11, 48–9, 226–7, 254–8

Galbraith, Iain 132–3
Gee, Grant 110, 110f, 141, 161
Geodesic domes 86
Gibson, William 86, 221
Gilpin, William 2–3
Ginsberg, Allen 196
Gilroy, Paul 112
Glass, Ruth 55
Gordon, Elizabeth Oke 197–204, 209, 220
Gormley, Anthony 249
Görner, Rüdiger 115–16, 124
Gray, Christopher 22, 27
Greater London Council (GLC) 54–5
Greenham Common 104–5, 104–5f
Gregory-Guilder, Christopher 7–8, 183–4, 208, 233
Grierson, John 52–3
Griffiths, Keith 52–3
Gropius, Walter 183
Grünewald, Mathias 117–18, 120–1, 135–6

Hague, the 157–8
Halle 118
Hamburg 119
Hamburger, Michael 140
Handel, George Frederick 41–2
Harris, Arthur ('Bomber Harris') 52–3, 56, 112
Harris, John 172
Hawksmoor, Nicholas 194, 197–202, 204, 206–7, 211, 222, 242
Hebel, Johan Peter 168–9
Heidegger, Martin
 'Being Dwelling Thinking' 8–9, 11–12, 51, 93, 99–103
 Black Notebooks 101
Helpston 226, 258–62
Heritage 81–5, 113, 173, 234, 273–4
 Heritage Act 1980 83, 274
 'Heritage film' 84
Herzen, Alexander 57
Hitchcock, Alfred 216, 224
Hodgson, William Hope 216, 218, 220
Home, Stewart 155–6, 228
Horkheimer, Max 157
Hoskins, W.G. 5–8, 202, 259–60, 273

Hui, Barbara 141
Hussey, Andrew 1, 103–4, 106–7, 273

Inefficiency 8
Ireland 158–9
Isenheim 117–18, 121, 135

Jacobs, Jane 128–9
Jacobson, Dan 170–1, 190
James, P.D. 216–17
Jameson, Fredric 95–6
Jarvis, Robin 259–60
Jefferies, Richard 75–6, 98–9, 174
Jennings, Humphrey 52–3
Jerrold, Blanchold 17–18
Jones, David 194
Jordan, Peter 125, 127
Joyce, James 163, 168, 227, 267–8

Kafka, Franz 58, 94, 166–7
Kardia, Peter 27, 30–1, 64
Keiller, Patrick 112–13, 202, 228
 'Architectural Cinematography' 76
 The City of the Future 87–8, 103
 The Clouds 24–5
 'The Dilapidated Dwelling' (essay) 91–2, 100–1
 The Dilapidated Dwelling (film) 51, 91–3
 Drawings, Tape-Slide and Sound 31–2
 The End 32–3
 'Imaging' 34
 'In Der Dämmerstunde, Berlin' (review) 46
 London 5, 10–11, 24–5, 50–70, 100, 107–9, 137, 157, 176, 232, 257
 'London in the Early 1990s' 70
 'Londres, Bombay' 87–8
 'Nine Elms Coal Hopper' 23–4f, 23, 27, 68, 226
 Norwood 21, 40–5, 57
 'The Poetic Experience of Landscape and Townscape, and Some Ways of Depicting It' 19–20, 26–8, 32, 38–9, 45–7, 72, 75
 'Popular Science' 25–6, 64, 94–5, 107
 'Port Statistics' 81, 91–2
 The Possibility of Life's Survival on the Planet 91, 94
 Robinson in Space 19–20, 24–5, 70–91, 94, 107–8, 137, 217, 250
 Robinson in Ruins 19–20, 91–108
 'The Robinson Institute' (essay) 88
 The Robinson Institute (exhibition) 94
 Stonebridge Park 33–40, 57
 'Tram Rides and Other Virtual Landscapes' 87–8

Keiller, Patrick (*cont.*)
  Valtos 24–5, 32–3, 67
  The View from the Train 20–1
Kiefer, Anselm 126
Kinik, Anthony 45–6
Klebes, Martin 190
Klee, Paul 120
Kluge, Alexander 144
Knight, Stephen 207–9
Kray, Ronnie and Reggie 192, 194, 205–6, 208, 216–17, 219, 239–40
Kufstein 123

Laing, R.D. 196
'Landscape film' 46, 63–4
Lanzmann, Claude 161
Le Corbusier (Charles Jeanneret) 86
Lefebvre, Henri 26, 28, 66–7, 72
Leroy, Annik 46–7
Leslie, Esther 252–3
Lichtenstein, Rachel 232–4, 272
Liverpool 81, 81*f*, 86–7
Locke, John 56
London
  A13 road 254
  Albion Drive 211–12
  'Albion Village' 195
  Battersea 25–6
  Bloomsbury 204–5
  Brent Cross 55–7
  Brick Lane 207, 209, 232–3
  British Library 183–4
  Bunhill Fields 205–6
  Cannon Street 58–9, 58–9*f*
  City of London 53–4, 175–80, 197–206, 234–5, 238–9, 270–1
  Charing Cross 247, 255–7
  Chingford 206, 228
  Dalston 67, 235, 237
  Deptford 214
  Docklands (inc. Isle of Dogs) 55–6, 63–7, 214–18, 222–3, 238–9, 249–50
  East London 178–81, 187, 191
  Farringdon Road 209
  Greenwich 204–5, 228
  Kennington 67
  Kings Cross 203
  Lambeth 228–30
  Lea Valley 203–4, 228
  Leicester Square 56, 58
  Lincoln's Inn Fields 53–4*f*, 55–6
  Liverpool Street Station 175–80, 270–1
  London Bridge 63
  London Fields 214
  M25 motorway 10–11, 226–7, 245–7
  Mile End 228
  Mitre Square 211
  Nine Elms Lane 23
  Norwood 40–5
  Old Broad Street 212–13
  Piccadilly Circus 60–1
  Regent's Canal 205
  Savoy Hotel 61–2, 61–2*f*
  Spitalfields 205–6, 211, 233–4
  Stepney 210–11
  Stoke Newington 59–60, 228, 240–1
  Stonebridge Park 33–40
  Temple Bar 257–8
  Tilbury 214–15
  Tower Bridge 52–3, 63
  Tower Hamlets Cemetery 180–1
  Vauxhall 56–7, 60–1, 232
  Victoria Park 228
  Wapping 216–17
  Whitechapel 214–15, 223–4, 233–4
London Film-Maker's Co-operative (LFMC) 28–30, 33, 37, 46, 102
London, Jack 216
London Psychogeographical Association 237–9
London Review of Books 192, 206, 223, 240–1
Long, J.J. 115, 141, 146, 151, 167–8*n*, 168, 176
Los Angeles 85
Lowestoft 155–6, 159
Luckhurst, Roger 208, 210–11
Lüneburg 143–4

Mabey, Richard
  Food for Free 10
  The Unofficial Countryside 5–6, 10, 97–8, 243–5, 258
Macfarlane, Robert 11, 151–2
Maidenhead 77–8, 77–8*f*
Major, John 51–2, 64, 74–5
Manchester 24–5, 117–19, 121–36
Manuskripte 117
Marías, Javier 152
Marienbad 188–90
Marker, Chris 7n.22, 52
  La Jetée 32, 52–3
Martin, Niall 231, 245, 254–5, 268–9
Marx, Karl 60, 79, 95–6
Massey, Doreen 92–4, 274
  For Space 4, 144
  'Landscape/Space/Politics: An Essay' 94, 102
  Space, Place and Gender 85, 250
Mawson, T.H. 88–9
Mazes 140–1, 204–5, 209–10, 214
Mazierska, Ewa 67–9

McAlpine, Alistair 83
Melancholy/melancholia 9–11, 39, 51, 56–8, 65–7, 70, 76–7, 80, 90–1, 102–3, 109, 137, 141–3, 147–8, 150–1, 163, 226–7, 258–60, 262–5
 'Left melancholy' 74–5
Melly, George 14
Mengham, Rod 191, 255, 258
Millar, Jeremy 110, 110f
Millennium Dome 10–11, 226–7, 247–50
'Mise-en-abyme' 117, 170–1, 186
Modlinger, Martin 176–7, 188–9
Monet, Claude 52–3, 61–2, 241
 'Charing Cross Bridge' 61–2f
Montaigne, Michel de 36–7, 52, 60, 115
Moorcock, Michael 194, 221, 242
Moore, Alan 207, 211–13, 212–13f, 217, 228, 242
More, Thomas 166
Moretti, Franco 214
Morrisson, Arthur 58–9
Mulvey, Laura 38
Murray, Alex 219–20

National Trust 83–4, 148–9, 151, 274
'Nature writing' 10
Nazism 117–18, 128, 143–4
Neoliberalism 9, 24–5, 53–4, 64–7, 74–7, 79, 95, 102, 217, 223, 244–5, 254–5, 273
'Neo-modernism' 192
Newbury 97–8, 97f
New Labour 156, 244–5, 247–50
'New nature writing' 6–7
Nieuwenhuys, Constant 22–4
Norris, Julie 27
Norwich 139–40, 144–6
Nuremberg 119–20

'Off-modern' 11
Orford Ness 148–9, 151, 153–4
Osborne, Dora 115
Oxford 77–8, 94, 100

Palmer, Samuel 226
Paris 21, 32, 160, 181–4
Pearson, John 192, 216–17
Pedestrianism 8–9
Peterborough 265–8
Petit, Chris 57, 99, 225–6, 228, 236, 240, 252–4, 265
Picturesque 1–3, 103–8, 156–7, 266
Pilgrimages 137–8, 140–1, 152
Pissarro, Camille and Lucien 40–1, 44
Plant, Sadie 22–3
Platt, Lise 116, 124, 161

Poe, Edgar Allan 20, 32–3, 36–7, 40, 59–60, 130, 145
Polanyi, Karl 97
Porter, Roy 15–17
Porter, Shirley 54–5
Portsmouth 78–9
Potter, Rachel 214–15
Pound, Ezra 192, 222–3
Powell, Michael 86–7
Pressburger, Emeric 86–7
Price, Uvedale 1–2, 103, 273
Priestley, J.B. 5–6, 112–13, 121–2, 129, 144, 156
Promio, Alexander 34, 86–7
Psychogeography 5–6, 58, 197, 223, 225, 237–9, 245, 274–5

Raban, William 46–7
 Thames Film: London 1984–86 52, 62–4, 68–9
Rand, Ayn 221
Rascaroli, Laura 67–9
Rasmussen, Steen Eiler 93
Ray-Jones, Tony 61, 89
Redgrave, Vanessa 94
Reading 70, 72–3, 75–7
Rembrandt van Rijn 119–20, 157–8, 236
Resnais, Alain
 Last Year at Marienbad 189–90, 246–7
 Toute la Mémoire du Monde 32, 183–4
Riegl, Alois 17–18
Rimbaud, Arthur 50–1, 56, 59–62, 65, 73–4, 221–2
Robbe-Grillet, Alain 189, 246–7
Rock art 90–1, 90–1f
Rogers, Richard 93, 248
Romanticism 50, 63–4
Ross, Kristin 73
Rousseau, Jean-Jacques 141–2
Royal College of Art 20–1, 26–7, 30–1, 33, 46
Rubinstein, W.D. 79–81, 92–3
Runcie, Robert (Archbishop) 54–5
Ruttmann, Walter 46, 52
Ryan, Judith 131–2, 189–90

Said, Edward 166–7
Schenk, Hans Georg 128–9
Schivelbusch, Wolfgang 160
Scofield, Paul 52, 57–8, 63, 94, 112–13
Scott, Ridley 85, 250
Sebald, W.G. 76, 116, 206, 217
 'A Comet in the Heavens' 163, 168
 After Nature 113–14, 116–28, 133–8, 158–9
 'An Attempt at Restitution' 123, 143
 'The Alps in the Sea' 158
 Austerlitz 165–90, 270–2

Sebald, W.G. (*cont.*)
   'Bleston. A Mancunian Cantical' 113–14, 124–36
   Campo Santo 112, 169
   'Corsica Project' 147, 158
   Die Beschreibung des Unglücks 113–14, 157
   'Die hölzernen Engel von East Anglia' 150–1
   'Erinnertes Triptychon einer Reise aus Brüssel' 117
   The Emigrants 109, 112–13, 124–38, 141, 170–1, 174, 180, 186–7, 190
   'Le promeneur solitaire: A remembrance of Robert Walser' 124
   Leben Ws 180
   'Moments Musicaux' 187
   On The Natural History of Destruction 111–12, 119, 143–4, 162
   The Revival of Myth: A Study of Alfred Döblin's Novels 110
   The Rings of Saturn 5, 10–11, 109–10, 113, 119–20, 137–64, 178–9, 190, 236
   Vertigo 50, 111–12, 119
Second World War 52–3, 56, 75, 86–7, 111–12, 119–20, 143–4, 169–70, 172–3, 198, 222, 228
Sekula, Alan 80–1
Self, Will 153
Sennett, Richard 101
Sheppard, Richard 130–1
Sheppard, Robert 191, 197, 205–6, 221
Shingle Street 148
Shklovsky, Viktor 104
Simmel, Georg 56–7
Sinclair, Iain
   Albion Island Vortex (exhibition) 196–7, 214
   Albion Village Press 193–4, 220
   'Austerlitz and After' 217, 270
   Autistic Poses 220
   Back Garden Poems 195–7, 204, 225–6
   Brown Clouds 196–7
   The Birth Rug 196–7
   Dark Lanthorns 233
   'Diary Films' 195, 253–4
   Downriver 65, 191, 209–10, 214–24
   Edge of the Orison 225–8, 241, 258–68
   Flesh Eggs and Scalp Metal 196–7
   Ghost Milk 227, 243, 246, 268–72
   The Kodak Mantra Diaries 196, 221–2, 225–6
   'Labrys: Eve of Beltaine' 192
   The Last London 270–2
   Lights Out for the Territory 5, 52, 61, 206, 224–43
   Liquid City 240–3

   London: City of Disappearances 226
   London Orbital (book) 99, 225–8, 243–58
   London Orbital (film) 225–6
   London Overground 268–9
   Lud Heat 191–5, 197–205, 215, 222–3, 228
   Muscat's Würm 196–7
   Radon Daughters 191–2, 209–10, 214–16, 218–20, 223–4
   Rodinsky's Room 232–4
   Sorry Meniscus 249–50
   Suicide Bridge 191, 204–6, 216–17
   White Chappell, Scarlet Tracings 191, 204–14, 216–18, 221–6
Situationists, the 5–6, 20–6, 39, 46–8, 58–60, 72, 225, 237–9
Smith, Phil 151–2, 156
Smithson, Robert 65
Solnit, Rebecca 1, 7–8, 137–8, 140–1
Somerleyton 140–1, 143, 156–7
Sontag, Susan 21–2, 109–10, 114, 120, 181
Southampton 80
Spatial turn 3
Spectacle, the 22–3, 26
Stallabrass, Julian 69
Stately homes 83–5, 140–1, 156–7, 171–4
Steller, Georg Wilhelm 117–18, 121–2
Sterne, Laurence 56, 58, 151–2
   Tristram Shandy 56, 77
Stoker, Bram 75–6, 250–4
Stowe 84
'Subjective camera' 30–3, 36–7, 43–4, 183–4
Suffolk 137–64, 272
Surrealism 5–6, 14, 20–6, 36, 46–9, 51, 61, 68–9, 72, 84–7, 89, 96–7, 117–18, 139, 176
Swales, Martin 114–15
Swift, Graham 159
Symmons Roberts, Michael 9

Tape-slide assembly 31
Tate galleries 23–4, 26, 31, 157–8, 230, 239–40
Taylor, Craig 155
Terezín / Theresienstadt 171, 184–90
Territory covered by Keiller, Sebald, and Sinclair 16*f*
Thatcher, Margaret 25–6, 29–30, 53–5, 64–5, 74–5, 79–80, 83, 154–5, 216–17, 220, 223, 234, 247–8, 253
Thomson, James 242
Thompson, E.P. 8, 14–15
Thornley, Andy 54–5, 64–5
Tradescant, John 229–31
Traverso, Enzo 10, 17
Tuan, Yi-Fu 14, 274
Turner, J.M.W. 77–8*f*, 103

Undercut 28, 46
Uxbridge 197–8

Vaneigem, Raoul 27–8, 40, 48–9, 72, 89
Vertov, Dziga 46, 52
Virilio, Paul 170, 182

Wales 23–4, 174–5
Walker, Iain
    City Gorged With Dreams 6, 49
    So Exotic, So Homemade 61, 89–91
Watkins, Alfred 197
Watts, Stephen 175–6, 217, 271–2
Wells, H.G. 75–6
Welles, Orson 75–6
Welsby, Chris 46–7, 63–4
Wertach 119, 169

Whitby 75–6
Whitechapel Gallery 196–7
Whiteread, Rachel 228, 236
Whittington-Egan, Richard 208–9
Wilde, Oscar 78–9
Wilhide, Elizabeth 248–50
Williams, Raymond 85, 173, 260
Wittkower, Margot and Rudolf 9
Woking 75–6
Wordsworth, William
    'Composted upon Westminster Bridge' 63
    The Prelude 2, 262, 274
Wright, Patrick 65, 81–5, 89, 93–4, 173, 194–5, 197–202, 218, 222, 226, 232–3, 235, 265
Wyndham, John 98–9

Zisselsberger, Marcus 116, 118–19, 124